Literary Imagination, Ancient and Modern

(*Chicago Tribune* photo by Anne Cusack.)

Literary Imagination, Ancient and Modern

Essays in Honor of David Grene

EDITED BY TODD BREYFOGLE

The University of Chicago Press
Chicago and London

TODD BREYFOGLE is a fellow at the Liberty Fund. He is a contributor to the *Oxford Classical Dictionary, Ancient Magic and Ritual Power,* and *Augustine through the Ages: An Encyclopedia.*

The University of Chicago Press, Chicago 60637
The University of Chicago Press, Ltd., London
© 1999 by The University of Chicago
All rights reserved. Published 1999

08 07 06 05 04 03 02 01 00 99   1 2 3 4 5
ISBN: 0-226-07424-2 (CLOTH)
ISBN: 0-226-07425-0 (PAPER)

Library of Congress Cataloging-in-Publication Data

Literary imagination, ancient and modern : essays in honor of David
    Grene / edited by Todd Breyfogle.
          p.   cm.
      Includes bibliographical references and index.
      ISBN 0-226-07424-2 (cloth : alk. paper). — ISBN 0-226-07425-0
    (pbk. : alk. paper)
        1. Literature—History and criticism. 2. Classical literature—
    History and criticism. I. Breyfogle, Todd   II. Grene, David.
    PN36.G741.58   1999
    809—dc21   98-50892
                                                             CIP

Contents

Postlude

Acknowledgments

What novel thanks could be given to someone who, over the span of more than four score years, has given more than can ever be repaid? This book was conceived one day over lunch in Hyde Park with David Tracy, as we contemplated a fitting offering to our dear friend David Grene. I am grateful for the encouragement and patience of this volume's contributors in bringing this offering to fruition. Many people made generous suggestions for improvement of the introduction and other aspects of the manuscript. Among those, special thanks are due to John Alvis, A. P. David, Wendy Doniger, Robert McMahon, and Stephanie Nelson, who also helped prepare the bibliography. The comments of the two anonymous readers for the University of Chicago Press greatly improved the shape of the book in its parts and as a whole. Julie Wakley cheerfully assisted in the preparation of the manuscript and the index. Pamela Bruton copyedited the manuscript. A special debt of gratitude is owed to Penelope Kaiserlian, Associate Director of the Press, for her guidance and goodwill. Of course, my most profound debt is to the inspiration and imagination of David Grene.

Introduction: Texts and the Rendering of Imaginative Reality

TODD BREYFOGLE

The most important things, Plato's Socrates tells us, are learned and not taught. All of the contributors to this volume have had the pleasure and privilege of learning with David Grene and offer these essays in tribute to his extraordinary intellect and humanity. Each essay in its own way carries on an existing conversation with David while addressing common themes which have long been a subject of David's reflection: the phenomenon of human pride, the wisdom which yields self-knowledge, and the insight into these questions reflected in texts and the rendering of imaginative reality, or what we might call, more broadly, the literary imagination.

The literary imagination in these essays includes but is not limited to what we today call fiction, nor is it explicitly an aspect of methodology in the field of literary criticism.[1] Rather, the literary imagination is that realm of poetic truth about the human condition expressed through the recounting of myths, stories, and historical events, as well as in the philosophical or theological accounting of those remarkable political animals called human beings. These essays in their different ways illuminate diverse imaginative renderings of the human predicament and the drama which invariably emerges whenever one enters into the activity of conversation with friends past and present.

David once remarked that it was in the Abbey Theatre, on the doorstep of his youth, that "My reading world, till then shared with so very few people, was coming alive and totally realizable."[2] This was, in part, because of the presence in the audience of figures like Sean O'Casey and W. B. Yeats, but also in part because on the stage imaginative reality took physical form. Briefly at Harvard, and since 1937, when he was hired by Robert Maynard Hutchins at the University of Chicago, David has, through a disposition which is at once serious and exuberant, made the reading worlds of countless students and colleagues come alive and totally realizable. The force of the literary imagination in rendering human verities—however obscure—has animated much of David Grene's teaching, writing, and translation. Few could fail to be infected by this animation, and the essays collected here all bear some aspect of its mark.

From an old friend from undergraduate days at Trinity Dublin to recent students from the University of Chicago's Committee on Social Thought, contributors to this volume represent the chronological and intellectual span of David's university calling. This span is ever increasing. Although emeritus for many years, David continues to offer as full a course load as anyone at the university. Limiting the field of those who might have contributed to this volume has not been easy. It is a melancholy fact, moreover, that David has outlasted other distinguished friends and colleagues who might have contributed to an earlier volume in his honor, or who might have contributed to this one had it not been for their untimely passing—Hannah Arendt, Allan Bloom, Friedrich Hayek, Shirley Letwin, A. K. Ramanujan, Leo Strauss, and Otto von Simson were among David's many distinguished friends, colleagues, and students over the years in and around the Committee on Social Thought. The late Arthur Adkins from Chicago's Department of Classics wished very much to contribute to the volume; alas, his health did not permit him to do so. To note these omissions, however, is simply to underscore the breadth and power of David Grene as an intellectual companion and friend.

I

For several generations, now, David Grene has been synonymous with Greek literature. To those of us who first encountered the Greeks through his translations, David Grene himself emerged enfolded in the haunting glow of fifth-century Athens—a name, with that of Sophocles or Euripides, to be marveled at and revered. Such were my impressions, anyway, upon reading his Sophocles as a high school junior. David Grene has brought the Greeks to us. His Complete Greek Tragedies series, edited with Richmond Lattimore, has become our century's definitive rendering into English of Greek drama. Equally definitive are his translation, with introduction, of Herodotus and his edition of Hobbes's Thucydides.

The very success of his translations is a sign of David's uncanny ability to bridge the gap between ancient and modern literary imaginations. Any translation is, of course, an interpretive act requiring an imaginative sensitivity to the worlds and languages of both the author and the translator. "It is true," David noted, "that most translations must be made anew in each generation. As the words of the translator's language live on and change, those he has employed in his translation express less adequately, or misleadingly, the ideas of the original." A few translations, however, have leaped across the boundaries of time and have "rendered in a new language the movement and truth of the original in the same way in which the translated author created both." Thucydides' original and Hobbes's English translation, for example, possess "the same feeling of independence and freedom." Nonetheless, if one knows both the original and a great translation, "one is conscious of them as two independent creations."[3]

The translation is an independent creation in part because a literal correspondence between two languages simply does not exist. The richness of English, especially, expands the possibilities of the translator while expanding also the possibilities for mistakes. David eschews the idea of a "literal" translation, which "can never be more than a kind of approximation, in those terms." Nor should a translator seek to render "hidden" meanings explicit.[4] Yet, the translator must strive for a rendering that captures the tenor of the original, that reproduces the author's world of thought and feeling. David's attempts are based upon "perhaps a rather dubious principle I have, which is, that if the original only had one word, it is a weakness if you have to use two in the translation."[5] This principle carries with it an element of drama—those who have had the astonishing and heartwarming experience of translating with him in class know that very often a Greek particle can be rendered (and rendered it must be) simply by a shrug or raised eyebrow, or that only an appropriately ironic inflection in English will reproduce the color of the Greek phrase.

The range and subtlety of his knowledge of Greek are legendary. A colleague once disputed David's interpretation of the meaning of a word with an appeal to the Liddell and Scott *Greek-English Lexicon*. David, it is said, shrugged and simply replied, "the lexicon is wrong"—incredulous at the thought that a lexicographer's entry could somehow preemptorily contain the full weight expressed by the text itself. Yet for all his erudition and linguistic sensitivity, David remains remarkably circumspect about the possibilities of living within the Greek language the way one lives within one's native tongue. "One has no way of gaining any fresh insight into the Greek, except from what blossoms inside yourself as you grow older and see different meanings emerge from the words you have grown familiar with." The literary and linguistic transaction flows both ways, for one may also gain insight into Greek "through the occurrences of new literature in your own language which throw a light on the classics."[6] David's mastery is one of respectful intimacy—a care and attention to detail the way a groom might curry a fine thoroughbred he can coax but never wholly dominate.

David brings to his translations not only the keenest understanding of meaning in Greek and a rich English vocabulary but also an intimate knowledge of the dramatic power of the stage and an ear for the rhythms of the spoken word. David's rendering of Herodotus captures both the oddness of his Ionic dialect and the clarity of the Greek, a literary directness which retains Herodotus's own mask and reads with surprise and enjoyment. It is not easy for a modern reader to imagine the Greek world—or any distant world—from the inside. "Translations of great works from the past appear when there is a demand for them. This demand seems to spring from some sort of understanding between the two ages, however distant." Hobbes recognized a connection between Periclean Athens and seventeenth-century English history and thus renders Thucydides as "a seventeenth-century Englishman, but he does not falsify him in doing so."[7] The power of David's own rendering of Greek authors comes from an exquisite ear for the English language and his profound understanding of the pathos of the world of the Greek mind. But it stems further from a recognition that the Greeks' pathos is in some way our own.

II

It is unfortunate that the sheer brilliance of David's translations has tended to overshadow his equally perceptive work as a commentator upon history and literature. His introductory essay to the translation of Herodotus is one of the finest essays on the *History* and its literary presentation. The brief essays introducing the plays in The Complete Greek Tragedies series are frequently departures from traditional interpretations and, with David's characteristic brevity and precision, at the very least help to move the reader into a more receptive state of mind. These qualities are also present in three books that have spanned his career as a teacher and translator: *Man in His Pride* (1950), *Reality and the Heroic Pattern* (1967), and *The Actor in History* (1988), each of which encapsulates both the style and the substance of David's teaching and reading.[8] David's suggestive prose ushers us down the path of the imagination and illuminates a world that is both recognizable and different from our own.

Fifth-century Athens fascinates David, as it has so many for so long, because of its moral crisis and doubt, its experiment with democratic government and attendant public pressures, and its experience of total war. In his early treatment of Plato and Thucydides, David remarked upon the similarities between their world and ours:

It is, rather, the total humanity of political life that brings fifth-century Athens so close to us; not, certainly, humanity in the sense of humaneness—for both they and we have had to face, in our different circumstances, the extremes of human cruelty—but humanity in the sense that it is man and man alone, without cosmic or supernatural sanction, who is both the source and the resolution of conflict.[9]

Man is a problem to himself, and to the Greek mind pride lay at the root of the problem. Man cast back upon his own moral and intellectual resources becomes both "the source and the resolution of conflict," a conflict which becomes intelligible in the Greek insight into the depths of human pride, and the recognition that wisdom comes through suffering. Pride, then, is an obscurer of self-knowledge and of the knowledge of others. Experience is a stern teacher, yet literature and imagination permit both the record and the articulation of the wisdom of humility.

Wisdom is far the chief element in happiness
and, secondly, no irreverence towards the gods.
But great worlds of haughty men exact
in retribution blows as great
and in old age teach wisdom. (*Antigone*, trans. Grene, lines 1420–24)

The folly of men, their strengths and frailties, the complexities of character and humanity—these are the data of the historian, philosopher, and literary artist alike. The Oedipus myth, for example, was for Sophocles "the treatment of the generic aspect of human dilemmas."[10] The myth itself was well known to Sophocles' audience, but the playwright's genius is his ability to distill the myth as somehow a unity of event and timelessness. Ultimately, it is the evaluation of the character in human, not theoretical, terms that counts.

The unity of thought and action—of concept and experience—in the person is the final arbiter of art and imagination for David. Thus, he can write of the Oedipus of the *Oedipus at Colonus:* "The light plays

fitfully on the humanity of the man he still is, and will soon cease to be,"
though his mysterious end is ultimately humanly inexplicable. Oedipus
does not evoke Aristotelian pity and fear. The sense of tragedy is something different. "[H]e goes, not to a fitting disaster, but to a dubiously
fitting triumph. But pity and fear in a more general sense, for the human
condition, is perhaps evoked by the somber majesty of the last scenes."[11]
These judgments strike to the core of humanity. Mere scholarly dispute
gives way to observation of taut humanity and dramatic mood; secondary
material takes second place to the illumination of the texts and characters themselves.

In literature, as in life, David does not suffer gladly either fools or the
self-absorbed. The shrewdness with which he judges literary characters
mirrors the penetrating gaze he casts upon people. Such shrewdness is
foremost a directness that is not malicious save in turning malice back
upon itself. David is a master of observation, a penetrating eye that captures the essence of a character, dramatic setting, or play—from the inside.
The human weight of a matter always qualifies the temptation to articulate
too sharp an analytical valuation. An education in the classics used to be
(and in some places still is) called *literae humaniores*—humane letters. A
conversation with David is first and foremost a conversation, full of humanity, humor, common sense, intolerance of silliness or pompous argumentation—the criterion is always what is true to the thing itself. One
must get at what the author or play or character is truly saying and then
weigh the truth of the author or character or play's articulation and illumination of the human condition.

So, too, David feels the full force with which the poet's language itself
discloses dramatic truth. Thus, he writes of Ariel as "the spirit of lyric
poetry touching tragedy and changing it. He has just enough humanity
for the task and not too much." By the end of the *Tempest,* Prospero exhibits the "weariness of an old man" with no more "passionate concern"
and his poetry expresses this. "The doubleness of life in beauty and ugliness, the imperfection of consummation, the frailty of humanity, the terror of death's meaninglessness, are too much for him—as a person. . . .
and as he grows weary and ready for death, we enter into his mood."[12]

Those who know David know that for him, a life without passions is
not a fully lived life, nor is it a particularly interesting one. True, the
passionate may find themselves bereft and unhappy, but they are deserving
of condolence, forgiveness, and perhaps pity wrapped in friendship for
having ventured forth in exploration of humanity. Those who did not so
venture receive uninterested contempt, for fullness of soul (if not greatness
of soul), however tragic, far outshines in humanity the soul that does not

live and love life broadly. Pound wrote of David's countryman Yeats: "He knows life . . . he learns by emotion" and is one of the few people "who see[s] from the centre of it—instead of trying to look in from the rim."[13] This is true of David. What moves him are characters—fictional and real—who neither live nor look in from the rim but live solidly and always in the center.

One of David's consuming passions, and one which he has seen from the center, is farming. To mix the life of a classics professor with the cultivation of crops and milking of cows is not an obvious choice. Both vocations are out of place in these modern days. In David, however, the two fit closely and effortlessly in the wide cast of experience in and out of books. With equal energy David discusses hog prices with a farmer in County Cavan or the finest point of Greek grammar with a colleague in classics. David's experience of this aspect of the natural world—of animals in particular—contributes greatly to his understanding of literary and especially classical texts. At home with rural details that escape most others, he feels with special clarity the natural world of Herodotus or Vergil, for example, details that for ancients would have been essential and that as late as early this century would have been at least within reach. David has remarked on the wisdom of understanding the balance that inheres in farming and, analogously, in human justice.[14] One can discern a great deal of a person's character by observing how he deals with animals. David's love of the natural world is anything but sentimental. It is animated by a real wonder and often shock at the particularities and the oddness of animals—their grace and awkwardness, their stubbornness, at once independent and threatening and equally vulnerable and dependent upon our care. Man's taming of nature, as the "Ode on Man" from Sophocles' *Antigone* makes clear, reminds us that nature tames man too: "Only against death / can he call on no means of escape."[15] The subjection of the farmer to scarcity, to hard work, and to death reminds one—like the example of literature or the experience of history—of the wonder and danger of forces beyond human control.

To wrestle with these forces and form some accommodation with them animates heroic characters. The hero in history and in literature captures the imagination precisely because he embodies most acutely the confrontation with these forces and in so doing becomes a dynamic force of his own. "The power of the hero is a kind of natural force and as such is never adequately judged or expressed by men's notion of moral excellence." The hero is human, all too human, and yet transcends humanity. The strength of Sophocles' plays "lies in their rendering of what it feels like to be this hero, caught between the gods and men." The hero of course casts shadows upon ordinary men. "There is an expression here histrionically of moral values which are not entirely translatable into human moral values, because there is for Sophocles a split between those that man rationally accepts for society . . . and . . . those values that belong to the dynamic of the spiritual universe."[16]

III

The dynamic of the spiritual universe is not amenable to theoretical comprehension. What distinguishes literature (and especially ancient literature, which would include Thucydides and Plato as well as Homer and the tragedians) is that the sharp theoretical edges are always moderated, rendered more subtle and true to life, by human characters. Thus, literature is the imaginative rendering of the abstract in terms of the concrete, in all its human fullness. The power of drama comes in its ability—through poetry and action—to render in fullness, in three dimensions, the contradictions, tensions, and confusions of real life to which concepts themselves cannot do justice.

No doubt one could construct an elaborate scheme of hermeneutic theory to describe the way David reads texts. Yet, an elaborated scheme would put the focus upon theory rather than the text itself, and this would be misleading. In his most insightful moments, David adopts a poetic idiom which does not circumscribe the artistic force of the author, but which points us toward this force, allowing us to see and feel its imprint upon ourselves. One sees David's treatment of the author as artist most clearly in his account of perhaps the two most difficult theoretical minds of antiquity.

Thucydides, for David, was "The Man Who Looked On" at the extraordinary events of the Peloponnesian War and at the achievement of Pericles. Plato, by contrast, is "The Man in the Duststorm," for whom the location of humanity is not history but the logic of truth. The search for a connection between the multiplicity of concrete detail and an immutable and single existence behind them animated Plato's thought. Yet, the reality of ideas did not, for Plato, yield a subject devoid of humanity. Everything, for Plato, is interdependent: "any kind of division of subject matter ultimately proves inconclusive and unsatisfactory. An isolation of one aspect of his thought . . . can only be attained, if at all, when the whole man is imaginatively understood." Plato's intellectual drive is informed by "the sustained passion to hold together a sense of the reality of what man can see, hear, smell, and touch—what he can love, hate, and feel inclination to or revulsion from—to hold together these and an assurance of something beyond such reality that will not render this world trivial but will satisfy an appetite for design, completion, and beauty." David treats Plato under the genus "writer," and for most writers, and especially philosophic writers, the moment of understanding and expression are almost one. "For Plato the illumination and the expression are entirely severed, and the expression is but an intellectual and sensuous experiment to recall the illumination indirectly."[17]

The writer-thinker is one concerned to identify and articulate patterns of reality—not abstractions but generalizations that remain firmly attached to experience. For Thucydides: "the concrete particular, in its completeness, is both the form and the totality of the philosophy." The pattern emerges out of the set of facts, and the artist who is the historian lets the implications spring from the story, not the story from a theory. For David, as for the Greeks, practice comes before and is separate from—indeed frequently calls into question—theory. The pattern that emerges from the concrete particular is never devoid of human form. "The peculiar ironies of chance," David writes of Thucydides, "inspired him with a kind of horror" in which "the disproportion between the people and their fate awakened a human pity which is nonetheless explicable according to his own theory of history and its development."[18] To have the experience and not miss the meaning is the heart of Thucydides' vision.

As the title *Man in His Pride* suggests, David read Plato and Thucydides together as commentaries on the Greek vision of hubris.[19] His described aim was to establish for each "a kind of intellectual personality, complete, alive, and individual," and to articulate in each the "nexus of a human personality" that has tied together both the order of history and the order of logic. Together, Plato and Thucydides and "the polarity of their intellectual configurations" define for David the range and limits of the Western reflection on political man. They are neither fully identified with nor fully estranged from our own world. "They stand consciously in an in-between relationship which acts as a human illumination of the processes of thought without the too-human limitations involved in the more complete historical identification with a particular period."[20]

Far from historicism or psychological interpretation, this reading of Plato and Thucydides was not an attempt to explain the ideas by personal or historical context, but rather to see the fullness of both the ideas and the man by viewing from inside the tensions inherent in the man and the ideas and so to get a clearer picture of their world. David succeeded in making the fifth-century world of Plato and Thucydides "more alive . . . alive in a sense in which the artist and his work have each a place." In doing so, it seemed that "the meaning of human society in fifth-century Athens would be more complete for us than in any other way."[21] In putting flesh on abstract ideas, David rendered these two very different thinkers full and dramatic artists, living actors.

IV

The tensions and reconciliations of the human condition itself, and within particular contingent circumstances, are most acutely felt in that crucible of human experience—the polis. The Irishman's inherent passion for politics aside, David's lifelong interest in politics—or rather political history—derives from the intensity with which political life demands the fullness and complexity of human character, or exposes their absence, in statesmen.

Political ideas do not grow disembodied, and it is only in their growth, in their living presence, however indirectly we must recapture it, that we can understand them. What seems to me vital in our study of the political likenesses and differences between ourselves and the fifth-century Athenians is not so much the consideration of principles as a knowledge of men and situations and men *in* situations. We can learn from knowing them, much as we can learn from knowing our contemporaries. Although the knowledge may grow richer by its very distance, it must, however indirectly acquired, be face-to-face knowledge—in essence like one's understanding of a friend.[22]

Politics fascinates David not as theory but as the realm in which power and necessity converge upon human characters from whom understanding and action are required. As such, political dramas—the Oedipus trilogy or Shakespeare's Roman plays, for example—magnify capacities for self-knowledge and prudent action, as well as their antitheses. The good king and the good dramatist both "discern what is orderly and beautiful in this world, and in their several ways help and encourage it and discourage its opposite."[23] Politics and drama are analogous: political actors are at once themselves and more than themselves, acting out a real and treacherous drama on the stage of history, a stage which is simultaneously public and profoundly personal. Indeed, this is the stage where individual humanity—both real and fictional—is put to the test.

In *The Actor in History*, David focuses on the richness of the stage in uniting politics, poetry, and character. By his poetry, the king or soldier becomes more visible to us, and the experience is one of full sensual enjoyment. "The character we watch on the stage escapes into an area where the sensations with which his acting affects us come also from his histrionic relation to us." The histrionic is distilled in the act—both the actor and the character in the play—which "the poetry has seized and expressed." So, Richard II is constantly "blurring the difference between the actor whose profession it is to render the part for us and the character he represents within the mimic reality of the plot." Because the dramatist is dealing with literary and artistic patterns already familiar to the audience, the stress on the actor's quality in the rendering of reality is all the more striking. Plays capture "various aspects of the theatrical and histrionic in human reality, as human beings apprehend it."[24]

In history plays, the actor's histrionic performance gives an almost immediate, imaginative representation of the historical figure. The poetry is detached from the actor and creates a new reality of which the theater is only an image. The forceful renderings of the person behind historical acts (i.e., the self-conscious, human patterns of historical figures themselves) are enacted by human agents, in history and on the stage. Shakespeare saw the role of the contemporary king "as suggestively similar to the actor in relation to his role." The role grows from himself but is not identical with himself, for "indeed the new self is only understood in the process of representation." Richard II knows "the truth that inheres in acting—in the emotional surrender to a preconceived pattern of fictive passion." For Shakespeare's Richard, reflection on the past is always an imaginative reconstruction "in which that past is given what turn he chose it should have had, and his part in it is changed accordingly. It is always in the form of a play which he rewrites and then plays." The historical consciousness of the English as a people turned English history itself into a kind of self-conscious drama: the Henriad is "a Shakespearian history of England which is itself turning into theater." Yet, there is a conflict between history and drama: "The imagination cannot entirely master the facts—or they will not constitute history."[25] The imposition of a pattern upon the facts is an activity common to the individual, the king, and the actor. Here, the poetry both discloses and carries us beyond the weakness of Richard's character—our delight in the words and images leads us toward an affirmation of the truth of dramatic poetry.

If the Henriad renders the personal as the general and historical, Shakespeare's Roman plays transform the greatness of the history into something more personal: "The objective greatness of the history—of these crises in history—has been transformed by the dramatist into something more personal." Brutus's own struggle, for example, derives largely from the fact that he "continually values the abstract and general over what is alive and personal." The poetry, like the politics of Rome, has been stripped down. Shakespeare's rhythms convey alternately the excitement and the solemnity of Brutus's character, and Shakespeare has him deliver his forum speech in prose, Brutus's only use of prose in the entire play. Here the force of the almost iconic history is made manifest. "The achievement of the Shakespearian portrait is that we finally understand the man." "What we see is illumination, not explanation," and the illumination comes wholly in human terms.[26]

The multiple roles of the actor in history are present in *Measure for Measure,* a play that presents a play of politics in which the Duke-reformer-director contrives and executes the drama. There is something unsympathetic about the self-consciousness with which the Duke goes about his dramatic production. Only human warmth can illuminate the cold demands of justice. What makes sense in the abstract is rendered absurd in the concrete, but only in seeing the foolishness or shocking ugliness of these enfleshed abstractions does the inhumanity of theory become clear. "All these cases involve with mocking emphasis the winning out of what is inhuman, while logical in formulation." Shakespeare's play is alternately so comic and so grim because the "root of comedy is the notion of a stable human nature, and those who try to change it are either fools or knaves." The play itself is totally improbable, yet "the implications of the plot and characters are grimly real." What makes the play a "problem play" to many interpreters is for David the natural expression of the absurdity of trying to fit the crooked paths and lanes of Ireland into a Cartesian grid. The patterns of human reality are themselves crooked paths, and it is from that vantage point that they must be evaluated. *Measure for Measure* on the level of logic leaves us unsatisfied in the end, yet the play also leaves us "full of pity, anger, laughter, and finally a mysterious sense of truth and correctness, the point of its application inexpressible." The images of the play "reach beyond their context and dominate us. The rats drinking after their poison, the monkey playing before the mirror, create a truth for us; the images have seized and frozen a moment of passionate insight."[27]

V

The wisdom that inheres in this moment of passionate insight is forcefully imprinted by poetic expression that is anything but rhetorical window dressing.[28] "The combination of language and physical presence is at its strongest in poetic drama." Our response to this is "only partly analyzable, haunted by echoes verbal and passionate, of things half-known and half-heard." The drama forces us to ask ourselves "with what kind of reality that play mocks us or gives us a glimpse of a new verity." In the end, "the poetry, as it blends the voice and the gesture, hints at a new color that suffuses a new reality, of which the theater is the image." In *Antony and Cleopatra,* for example: "The effect of the poetry is to convince us that here is true greatness, existing in a world exactly suited to bring out its meaning." The play "becomes an ecstasy in which the power of imagination has taken over the world and the world lives only in the power of imagination." We believe in the greatness of the lovers because "the poetry does not illuminate it; it is the greatness itself." The poetry is not only able to disclose reality; it is able to convey to the reality its greatness. If one reads the play or hears it read or sees it acted, "one is supremely aware of the art of poetic theatre. One sees the hint of personality, externally present in body and voice, and through this experiences the greatest things dramatic poetry can do in creating before us impersonal imaginative life." Such experience is of course dependent upon the histrionic art of the actor, but it is Shakespeare's peculiar gift for relating "reality and the imaginative form given it by the player" in the art of acting.[29]

In relating reality and the imaginative form, the artist (the dramatist in particular) identifies and articulates a pattern of reality. The stage is where the patterns of reality are discovered and reenacted nightly in three dimensions. The artist creates the character while the actor, by virtue of his histrionic art, re-creates this creation in turn. "[W]hat remains most in our minds—and perhaps what Shakespeare has emphasized most—is the relation of natural life and the versions of it that the artist in man makes in his images." At the same time, the dramatist and histrionic performer both smooth and roughen the edges of this pattern, conveying in word and voice hints and guesses that the incomplete pattern of reality both is and is not as it seems. In the last plays of Ibsen, Shakespeare, and Sophocles, "art tries to combine a fixed meaning with the fluidity of life, since fluid life carries death. Yet the answer to the question, Which is the truer reality? is a very hesitant one."[30]

What unites the last plays of Ibsen, Shakespeare and Sophocles for David "is the establishment of meaning for the events of a life, looking backward from its conclusion. . . . This is to relate the sequence of acts to some pattern of reality (as far as we can grasp it), so that we can see some things as having led us right and others wrong; so that we believe there was a direction and a significance to our lives." Egotism is the great and characteristic sin in these plays.[31] There is an egotism, also, in possessing too strong a confidence in the pattern of reality one has grasped. The attempt to grasp, to form at least a contingent pattern, itself becomes a datum of experience to be accounted for. The images and patterns from literature take their place in thought and memory as we act out and try to understand ourselves. Literary characters themselves become patterns in our imagination, patterns with which we chart meaning and which in various ways we come to use as patterns of our own thought and in some ways our own action, or, if you will, histrionic performance. It is in some sense our participation in the drama of the stage, and our appropriation of that drama to our own scripting of reality, that render the theater so compelling.

So, too, in history the interplay of event and understanding modifies and passes on patterns of reality that are largely constitutive of our own self-understanding and identity. For Herodotus, the oral tradition he had inherited constituted the imaginative rendering of the past as it mattered to the present. Herodotus's richness comes from his attentiveness to what these imaginative renderings say both about the facts and about the people who convey them, believingly or disbelievingly. As David wrote in his introduction to Herodotus: "The original facts, whatever they were, have taken to themselves a supervening shape—universal, cultural, or, in the deepest sense, religious. It is then that Herodotus thinks they have assumed their closest relation to reality, which is not for him coterminous with what happened in the physical world but rather what was released by the act into the world of thought and feeling and continued thereafter."[32]

The power of the stage is to distill all of these elements—humanity, concreteness, patterns of reality, and their poetic expression—in a single histrionic act. In the case of the novel or historical narrative, the artistry lies in the imaginative verbal expression of these elements. The relation between the stage and the world outside the theater is of course a common trope. We find in the *Tempest* the famous comparison of "the 'real' world and the world of the stage and its creations. Yet it is the 'real' world that wins." The world of the theater gives partial and momentary order; it establishes a fluid but recognizable pattern of meaning against the prospect of unintelligibility. "The dramatist's job (and the actor's) is to invest every detail and gesture of his represented reality with the flavor of significance. When the work is good, it thus re-creates the sensation of the significant discovery which the dramatist himself made in the unordered world of reality outside the theater."[33] Interpretation of all literature is in large part being attentive to and understanding these significances.

The literary imagination for David Grene is the place of intersection between the past and the present in relating the world of thought and feeling to the world of reality, "the myth of the conjunction of time and event."[34] It is a place where meaning is intensely human, in which the concrete particular takes precedence over and reveals the folly of the abstract and theoretical. The literary imagination is a reflection of and reflects back upon human life and participates in the rendering of human judgment—*phronēsis* as well as *dikē*—which is the stuff of existence. This imagination both articulates the human condition and contributes to further patterns of identity and self-understanding. It demands that action be judged not according to abstraction but with respect for its concreteness in human terms. In the realm of politics, imagination lays bare the pride and frailties of our fellows. In religion, pride and frailty assume new shapes against the backdrop of the gods (or God), fate, and the question of transcendence. On the stage, where literature takes on sound and is given life by dramatic enactment, the histrionic art of the actor participates in the fullest expression of the literary imagination, in which he both gives life to and is himself transformed by the power of the language and the action. In all, the histrionic art—in life: improvisational; on the page: impressed upon the soul; on the stage: incarnate beyond imitation—evokes a unity of thought and feeling in "a single-minded attempt to render the highest kind of justice to the visible universe, by bringing to light the truth, manifold and one, underlying its every aspect."[35] Each of these is a theme that David has treated in prose and in conversation, and each runs through the essays collected in this volume with varying intensity.

VI

"In a Drizzly Light," a poem by Brendan Kennelly, introduces the volume. Kennelly paints David Grene's facility with "the ways of words and images," capturing a sense of David's conversation and disposition as a man who is always "advancing into his youth."

Euripides' account of the confrontation between piety and philosophy is the subject of the first essay. Martin Ostwald examines what counted for atheism in fifth-century Greece, looking at Diagoras, Prodicus, and especially Euripides. He argues that customary rituals took precedence over belief; heterodoxy did not evoke the charge of atheism unless the public worship of the gods was called into question. Euripides' treatment of the tension between conventional religion and the intellectualism of natural philosophy ultimately yields a distinctively Euripidean piety. Far from being atheistic, Euripides' vision is the recognition—and to some degree, the reconciliation—of *nomos* and *physis* as effective limits on human desire, yet limits which have the same sacred-philosophical reality underlying them. Euripides, Ostwald writes, "is no longer content to measure the gods by the yardstick of human morality but comes to grips with the phenomenon of religion itself and concludes that the reality underlying it is the object of traditional religion and philosophical inquiry alike."

For Euripides, the wise man resolves the tension between intellectual and traditional piety. In Aristophanes this tension is resolved specifically in the poetic art, for comedy itself permits certain forms of blasphemy, rendering the impious pious. In his essay on poetry and philosophy in Aristophanes' *Clouds,* James Redfield sees the dramatist responding not to the excesses of religion but to the "terror of philosophy." Redfield takes up Aristophanes' portrait of Socrates, noting that the initial unpopularity of the *Clouds* was a failure of the Athenian audience's imagination. By offering the vision of Socrates that he does, Aristophanes represents philosophy and poetry as two kinds of intellectuality, both embraced by the wise. Nevertheless, philosophy represents a new rationalism, dangerous and impious because it substitutes the impersonal forces of nature for the personal gods of Greece. For Strepsiades, the universe is meaningful; for Socrates, it is intelligible. That is, the philosopher is one who discovers, not one who invents, but it is *he* who discovers and so philosophy becomes the worship of self. Redfield writes: "The philosophers worship the discoverable intelligibility of things; that is their hubris." The strange paradox is that this quest for principles of natural necessity should become the pretext for unprincipled behavior. The antipathy between philosophy and the traditional order arises in large part because much of the human world is unintelligible because it is historical. In siding with shared history against nature, Aristophanes sides with myth and with human meaning as manifest in poetic art. Socrates, in this reading, stands as evidence of the failure of Athenian society to maintain a sound cultural tradition.

If Aristophanes finds reconciliation in the convergence of history and myth, Stephanie Nelson's comparison of Homer's *Odyssey* and Joyce's *Ulysses* sees the disjunction between history and myth as the source of the tension that drives heroic striving. In achieving immortality, the hero enters isolation and transcends fellowship with others (for Odysseus, Penelope), the very thing that gives his life meaning. Being a hero negates the individual human being by absorbing him into myth; timelessness annihilates historical man. The identity that Odysseus seeks in refusing Calypso's offer of immortality is his identity as a man, not as a hero. Similarly, Leopold Bloom must find "a new kind of heroism" within time. Both of Bloom's choices in response to Molly's adultery—detachment or revenge—mean isolation from the ones he loves. The hero must confront the awareness of time in memory, which both bars Bloom from his past and binds Stephen to his. Bloom's heroism comes in his finding human significance in the fact that time can neither be recovered nor escaped. The heroic task, then, is to reconcile oneself to time in time. "Only through time time is conquered."

Wendy Doniger takes the theme of time in a different direction, comparing Greek and Indian mythological treatments of the homecomings of Odysseus and Nala respectively. Both of these homecomings reveal "a pattern of approaches to the recognition of signs" after years have obscured the signs themselves but not their memory. Time changes things and people—how is this man or this bed to be identified as this man or this bed rather than a simulacrum? Here, identity is firmly rooted in history. Doniger traces the similarities between Odysseus's return to Penelope and Nala's return to Damayanti. In each case, the unique details of intimacy and mortality permit the abandoned love to recognize the long-absent lover. The real lover is distinguished from an impostor by virtue of "the fragile, ephemeral, conditional, dependent intensity of real life." How do we know one another when time "magically transforms the people we love into other people"? Time both permits and produces doubles, and as Doniger shows, it is self-knowledge that more often than not reveals the correct choice.

Mary Douglas also takes up the riddle of the recognition of signs, though in a very different vein, in her attempt to rethink the Levitical rules distinguishing between pure and impure animals. She takes one clue from Herodotus, who saw animals as riddles which conceal and reveal meanings depending upon the proper knowledge of the context of the signs. Taking on the traditional interpretation of Levitical dietary restrictions, Douglas argues that "the laws of unclean foods should be read as game laws rather than as dietary laws, not as prescriptions for what is healthy or unhealthy for the people to eat, but as rules for protecting animals from human predators." The place of animals and human beings alike in the scheme of creation is the proper context for understanding Leviticus 11. Distinguishing between "unclean" and "abominable" animals, Douglas shows that, in Leviticus, abominable pertains to human actions with respect to animals and not to the animals themselves. Keeping the food laws honors the scheme of creation. The proscription against touching or eating certain animals is not a consequence of those animals' impurity or even vulnerability—they are protected because of their fecundity. That is, they are exemplary of God's promise of fertility and his compassion for all beings. On this view, the Levitical God is merciful and his laws teach people to be kind to living things. Douglas concludes by placing the Levitical rules against the backdrop of sixth- and fifth-century

B.C. theological controversies about the right to take animal life. If Douglas's argument is correct, then many traditionally held opinions about animals would seem to have less to say about the animals themselves than about us as human beings.

The stories that we tell ourselves, and how these confabulations affect self-knowledge, constitute the theme of W. R. Johnson's discussion of Cephalus's self-narration in Ovid's *Metamorphoses*. This tale of misunderstanding and self-deception shows how Cephalus can come to believe as real what in fact has been "slowly constructed in order to cover over a hole in his memory." Neither Johnson nor Ovid have the psychology of repressed memory in view here, but rather the way in which the telling and embellishment of a tale come to take on independent reality in memory. Thus, Johnson's essay picks up the theme of time, memory, and identity of earlier essays by showing how the old man seeks, in David Grene's words, to establish "meaning for the events of a life, looking backward from its conclusion."[36] Ambrose Bierce's definition of "recollect" is "to recall with additions something not previously known." And yet, Johnson argues, despite the restless pride that leads to Cephalus's fictional self-narrations, we decide we finally have some sympathy for him. Cephalus is acting out his own story and reenacts it a little differently each time it is told. Ovid shows us "his profound and playful belief that stories are, for the most part, as polysemic, polycentric, and polymorphous as the worlds within worlds they represent."

Augustine of Hippo's autobiography highlights the importance of memory and imagination for self-understanding in a particularly Christian idiom. My essay examines the theological importance of memory for Augustine before sketching out the several different senses in which Augustine speaks of imagination. Imagination can be a fictive, sensual distraction; the morally neutral, passive collection of images; or the active recollection of images. Ultimately, I suggest, Augustine sees a role for imagination in coming to know—and ultimately to reorder—the data of memory through the narration of stories that array the elements of memory in intelligible patterns. When such literary patterns are rendered intelligible, imagination (the activity of understanding through images) gives way to intellect—pure insight in the absence of mediating images. The *Confessions* both tells and shows us how images, for Augustine, can lead us toward the un-imaged (and unimaginable) disclosure of truth.

The re-presentation of fiction as autobiography is the subject of Seth Benardete's essay on Apuleius's *Metamorphoses*. Benardete reads Apuleius alongside Plato's *Phaedrus,* arguing that "Apuleius's book . . . is Plato's

Phaedrus as rewritten by Phaedrus." This Platonic literary and substantive background allows Benardete to make sense of Apuleius's combination of Lucius the ass, the story of Cupid and Psyche, and Lucius the convert, exploring the relation between *curiositas,* the will to believe, and the "incantatory power of erotic rhetoric." As in Ovid, confabulation actively persuades us to believe certain things about ourselves. The terrors of this self-narration grounded in "the undisciplined imagination" are obvious to Apuleius, for "Apuleius sees that the ultimate consequence of the view that truth is not an issue for rhetoric is the obliteration of experience and its entire replacement by opinion. Freedom from fate is surrender to opinion." Apuleius's "hero," so to speak, must resist slavery to opinion, but how can one's own conversion be more than deceptive self-love or submission to opinion? Ultimately, Lucius reconciles experience and the demands of the moral law by rejecting antinomian eros as vehemently as Phaedrus himself does.

Norma Thompson's essay takes us from a Roman literary interpreter of Plato to a modern English one. Thompson examines several of Iris Murdoch's novels as commentaries on Plato's discussion of the ancient quarrel between poetry and philosophy. Plato's distinction between bardic and philosophic poets reveals Murdoch as a philosophic poet who, like Plato, actively prevents her audience from identifying too closely with any single character. In so doing, she creates a space for her audience to reflect—intellectually and morally—about the literary creation itself and the meaning (or lack of meaning) of what it represents. The poet as bard or rhetorician is engaged in entertainment or image-spawning. Murdoch, by contrast, consistently brings to the fore the Socratic recognition that creative power must resist pursuing the exhilaration of beauty to be in service to what is true and good. Thompson also notes that, in Murdoch's work, the evil character leaves the strongest imprint on us; nevertheless, however intangible, reticent, and unimpressive the good characters might be, goodness in all its weakness neutralizes the evil. The literary experience is not unlike the philosophical experience. We are, in Murdoch's novels and Plato's dialogues alike, consistently stripped of our assumptions and forced back upon our own sentimental expectations. Echoes of the *Phaedrus* resound once again: "our souls strain and fail . . . to see what we most want to see." The magnetism of the good remains, however, as the reader realizes that Murdoch's novels, no less than Plato's dialogues, are "an extended lesson in relearning the skills of the thinking reader."

Soseki's "The Photographer" is an example of a quintessential modern genre, the personal essay. In Edwin McClellan's translation, Soseki offers a snapshot of the modern character—self-conscious, compressed, and hinting at a revelation that is momentary but ultimately, perhaps, not transformative.

The unity of the histrionic art is perhaps best found in Shakespeare. A. P. David looks to the poetic personification of thought, seeing Shakespeare's dramatization of history as mimetic and subversive of the English morality play. The three-dimensional personification of thought (the evocation of pathos in Hal's renunciation stems from the rejection, not of an emblem, but of Falstaff *the man*) reveals "the generative relation between imagination and action." Thoughts take on flesh, and when realized onstage they discover a pathos unforeseen in the premises of those thoughts. That is, the embodiment of thought in character—in poetic imagination and acted out onstage—simultaneously reveals both the fullness of strength and the painful weakness, in human terms, of those ideas. Shakespeare's thoughts, "his protocharacters, are never static emblems of vice and virtue but are instead inherently at variance with themselves." Indeed, Shakespeare's sense of "the theatricality of human reason" shows that thought, like life, is constantly at variance with itself.

The richness, texture, and suggestiveness of English which Shakespeare used to such advantage was itself problematic for Thomas Sheridan, insofar as the variations of vocabulary, accent, and intonation revealed differences in origin and social status. Sandra Siegel argues that Sheridan's initial version of *The Brave Irishman* should be seen as his own attempt to undo the conventions that informed Anglo-Irish social relations. The play itself is not particularly richly conceived as drama, but it illuminates the social world of Sheridan and his contemporaries. Siegel examines Sheridan's place in British social thought and the place of the theater in the complex world of English attitudes toward the Irish. As an answer to Swift's question, "Why do the English laugh at the Irish?" Sheridan conceived his play against the backdrop of Tudor and Stuart "jokebooks" as well as manuals of behavior and decorum. At the heart of the matter is the vexing eighteenth-century dispute as to whether blood or behavior makes a gentleman. Sheridan's play takes this up directly and with the ancillary question, Can an actor be or become a gentleman? The difficulty here lies, in part, in the fact that, blood and education aside, the actor and the gentleman share an ability to act the part, where "to act meant above all to be a master of speaking." Sheridan sought to emulate and thus undermine the popular stereotypical derisions of Irishmen without realizing "that those preconceptions with which he was so familiar applied [also] to him."

By contrast, a later Irishman, Synge, depends upon the verisimilitude of these images and preconceptions of Irish life. Nicholas Grene's essay considers the details of Synge's imagination of place (especially geographical details), looking at how actual and imagined locations play upon one another in Synge's works. Synge's is not realist art. The imagination of place gives realized specificity within which Synge's characters exist in situations vivified by their and his imagination of the world. The imagined places and settings are required as a starting point, providing the required verisimilitude without corresponding in detail to an actual location. Of just what "western world" is Christy Mahon playboy, for example? For the majority of readers, who do not know Synge's geography, the imagination of place conveys more general effects: the social and psychological world of local communities, the elision of immediate actuality (an Irish village) with the imaginary, literary, and mythical past (Scripture, for example), and the imagination of Heaven and Hell. "To the extent that we are taken into the mental landscape of the characters in Synge, are encouraged to imagine the places in which they live and the way in which they imagine the places beyond where they live, the effect is one of dramatic realization, supporting the illusion of the actual."

Mallarmé viewed the capacity of the English language to be at variance with itself as its greatest strength. Françoise Meltzer looks at Mallarmé's famous integrative literary project "le Livre" in the context of his reflections in *Les mots anglais,* examining the importance of English for Mallarmé's understanding of what he himself called *poésie pure,* which emphasized the abstract idea rather than the thing. Compared with the purged purity of French, English thrives upon its history of amalgamation and capacity for continued assimilation: "it is both retrospective and future oriented, and this is its genius." The double lexical wealth of English allows the poet "to state the same thought with two synonyms which do not share a common root," in this way "strengthening both the power of the sentence and its resonances." The richness and etymological variation within English accents Mallarmé's own articulation of poetic truth over against Enlightenment philosophy. Mallarmé emphasized poetic motivation, enthusiasm over reason: "enthusiasm and the imagination emit the seeds of wisdom, which are found in the minds of all men 'like the sparks of fire in flintstones.'"

T. S. Eliot greatly admired Mallarmé and sought to reconcile the Frenchman's poetic vision with a more theistic religious content. David Tracy's essay highlights Eliot's articulation of poetic knowledge, emphasizing Eliot's stature as a religious thinker, notably in *Four Quartets.* Tracy argues that Eliot's religious thought in his poetry is subversive of the stingy orthodoxy of his essays. He sees Eliot against the backdrop of the "dissoci-

ation of sensibility" of modernity and as embracing a classical Neoplatonism and a Christianity of manifestation. Eliot's poetry, for Tracy, is not the
exclusive vision of his Christian apologetics but rather "opens up into a
grounded spiritual vision of great multiplicity, subtlety, and tentativeness."
Thus, Tracy argues that Eliot the poet should be seen as having stronger
affinities with the troubled soul of Simone Weil than with the confidence
of Chesterton or Lewis. Eliot's poetry is, above all, lived poetry which
stands as a reconciliation of the modern splits between thought and feeling, form and content, theory and practice. For Eliot, metaphysical poetry
"elevates sense for a moment to regions ordinarily attainable only by abstract thought." "Eliot learned from Mallarmé that poetry could never
replace the absence of mystical experience nor the thought attendant to
that experience." Tracy explores the impersonal Neoplatonic and Buddhist imagery and structure in *Four Quartets,* examining Eliot's theological
imagination, which understood history as the manifestation of a pattern
of timeless moments. The wondrous power of *Four Quartets* shows how
"philosophy-theology is both a vision of life and a way of life."

The poetic treatment of theological themes returns us to France, and
to rather unlikely sources. Victor Gourevitch's essay takes up seventeenth-
century French debates over theodicy and optimism. Voltaire's theologico-
moral meditation on Providence in his *Poem about the Lisbon Disaster* is an
attempt to reclaim a place for hope in the midst of physical evil. Voltaire
rejects the Augustinian notion of Providence in favor of a mechanistic
view (derived from the new physics) that maintains that "evil is a necessary consequence of inherent limitations matter imposes on intelligence
and will." By contrast, Rousseau in his *Letter to Voltaire* attributes evil
largely to our lack of prudence and to an excess of pride. By maintaining
that Providence is "universal" and not "particular," Rousseau seeks "to
reclaim a commonsense middle ground for the exercise of what might be
called human or personal Providence or prudence." Rousseau's view
leaves room for imagination, because his middle ground is based not on
reason but on "the sweet sentiment of existence." In shifting the focus
from the natural world to our sentiments, Rousseau articulates a refined,
austere Epicureanism that sees the human good as consisting in tranquillity of soul in the face of the apparent disjunction between Providence
and our own well-being.

Much of Rousseau's legacy, of course, dismissed religious impulses
altogether or translated more traditional notions of Providence into secularized visions of progress. Whether human beings can maintain their humanity and hope in the absence of religious belief is of course one of
Dostoyevsky's favorite themes, one that surfaces in his lesser-known novel

A Raw Youth, discussed here by Joseph Frank. Written between *The Devils* and *The Brothers Karamazov, A Raw Youth,* while not Dostoyevsky's best work, takes up the themes of the novels written immediately before and after it. Fathers and sons clash while striving for faith and pondering suicide, engaging the lofty ideas of Populist Socialism in the cauldron of the baseness of the Russian soul. Through his main characters, Arkady and his father, Versilov, Dostoyevsky engages his theme that "the noblest and most sincerely held ideals are ultimately futile if not grounded in an emotive source penetrating the entire personality." The novel itself shows Dostoyevsky's emerging sense that the Populists had now come to share Dostoyevsky's own Christian moral and social convictions, yet lacked the irrational faith which is the only secure buttress of moral values. The sorrow of the world without God is Dostoyevsky's artistic answer to the sublimest secular ideals of socialism. In both Arkady and Versilov we see the love-hate dialectic of characters whose egoism both produces and undermines magnanimity. Dostoyevsky shows how misdirected self-discipline can be turned to a desire for self-sacrifice which is ultimately unsustainable without religious faith. The novel itself is the young Arkady's reeducation of himself through his narration of events.

Henry James takes up similar themes in an examination of self-deception and self-understanding, but in a modern, secular American idiom. Robert Pippin treats James's account of the question, How is one to live well? Or, more specifically in modern terms, what makes for a fulfilling life? James's characters have an American drive for exploration, yet experience an intensely felt sense of limitation on such exploration. Pippin emphasizes the modernity of James's view of the moral life, offering an alternative view to James as neither a high-culture, aristocratic aesthete nor a psychological realist interested in moral questions only as felt. Rather, Pippin sees as a virtue the often-criticized elusiveness of James's psychological meaning, determinate intentions, and stable identities. Pippin examines especially *The Golden Bowl,* following the obscurities of the characters' attempts at self-understanding and understanding of others. This elusiveness, thus, is not just for us as readers but is inherent in James's characters themselves as embodiments of the difficulty of self-knowledge in a specifically modern age. The lack of "human heat" in most of James's characters is attributable to the predominance of opinion in the modern formation of character. James's characters lack views of their own but are formed by their own views of how others perceive them. Pippin works through James's vision of the *"mutuality* of social relations" in charting James's portrayal of the modern moral life. James retains a confidence in "the reality of moral evil, an evil motivated often by egoism and enacted often in deceit," and treats in detail the problem of the sacrifice of one's own happiness and good apart from a moral universe which specifies transcendent duties. Yet, James's account of the conditions of the modern moral life is not answerable in moral terms; James shows simply what is missed when the modern refusal to engage mutual dependence yields only a silence that is not despair or resignation or nihilism or stoicism, but tranquillity in the face of absent gods, both sacred and secular.

Tocqueville observed the tendency of democracy's egalitarian ideal to undermine relationships of mutual dependence, both between individuals and between different generations. Conor Cruise O'Brien sees this latter disruption as at the very heart of the implicit antipathy between Edmund Burke and Thomas Jefferson. Both were on the same side in the American Revolution, but for very different reasons. O'Brien explores these differences by looking at the antipathy between the two over the French Revolution. While Jefferson and Burke did not exchange correspondence, O'Brien argues that a letter from Paine to Burke quoting Jefferson's praise of the French Revolution spurred Burke's fury in the *Reflections on the Revolution in France*. Burke and Jefferson differed with respect to their understanding of liberty (ordered vs. extreme) and with respect to the practical prospects of liberating the world. O'Brien also shows how Jefferson transposed the public argument between Paine and Burke into an American idiom for Jefferson's own political advantage over John Adams. Ultimately, Burke's reverence for ordered liberty clashed with Jefferson's sacred mission of liberation for each generation. In one sense, not surprisingly, their differences are reducible to varying perspectives on tradition. Jefferson's "the earth belongs . . . to the living" is contrasted with Burke's "partnership . . . between those who are living, those who are dead, and those who are to be born."

The restlessness of Americans, their perpetual discomfort with the past and with the present—a discomfort which an eye for the uncertain future only accentuates—has always occupied the American literary imagination. Saul Bellow's reflections on the American literary imagination give a whimsical closing to this volume. The exercise of understanding the past is very much an exercise in self-understanding, and Bellow offers his own account of the intellectual pilgrimage of his youth at the University of Chicago in the Depression. Bellow's account is tinged with a warmth matched by an equally strong sense of resignation and regret for an age of enthusiasm for literature in America that is now past. The "writer describes the inner life of humankind," Bellow asserts, and poetic drama cannot be matched by the prose novel. "But prose fiction is the best we can offer in these times." Bellow embraces Tocqueville in observing that in democracy, the imagination is directed away from the external and focuses on the individual alone. And though, in Tocquevillian terms, American man is Cartesian and antipoetic, there is always a hidden nerve which is full of poetry. It is perhaps this hidden nerve, despite the fact that our mental life is democratically organized (or unorganized), that allows us to see, as Bellow does, a "strange dignity in those who are mad for transcendence or for some impossible idea of nobility." Bellow takes up in the course of these reflections the "weakness for intellectuality" often attributed to him. Modern literature suffers, he says, because "concepts are elaborated but intelligent effective direction is lacking." Bellow opposes certain brands of intellectual writers, demanding that one always "Stand before the bartender and order your Heidegger straight." But at root, as Bellow notes and as his fiction has always revealed, "the ways of imagination are different from those of cognition." Against the barrenness and materialism of modern literature and the modern American mind, Bellow offers a wistful defense of the pleasure of the literary imagination. No one ever understood that pleasure better, or conveyed it more generously to his friends, students, and readers, than David Grene.

Notes

1. See, e.g., the term as used by Robert Alter in *Times Literary Supplement,* no. 4947 (23 Jan. 1998): 15–16.

2. Quoted from David Grene's unpublished memoirs.

3. David Grene, ed., introduction to *The Peloponnesian War: The Complete Hobbes Translation* (Chicago: University of Chicago Press, 1989), vii.

4. Isaac Mathes, "Translators on Translation: An Interview with Wendy Doniger and David Grene," *Chicago Maroon,* 11 Mar. 1994, 17.

5. Ibid., 14.

6. Ibid., 18.

7. Grene, introduction to *The Peloponnesian War: The Complete Hobbes Translation,* xi, viii.

8. *Man in His Pride: A Study in the Political Philosophy of Thucydides and Plato* (Chicago: University of Chicago Press, 1950), later reprinted as *Greek Political Theory: The Image of Man in Thucydides and Plato* (Chicago: University of Chicago Press, 1965); *Reality and the Heroic Pattern: Last Plays of Ibsen, Shakespeare, and Sophocles* (Chicago: University of Chicago Press, 1967); *The Actor in History: Studies in Shakespearean Stage Poetry* (University Park: Pennsylvania State University Press, 1988).

9. Grene, *Man in His Pride,* viii.

10. David Grene, introduction to *Sophocles I,* trans. David Grene, 2d ed., The Complete Greek Tragedies (Chicago: University of Chicago Press, 1991), 7.

11. Grene, *Reality and the Heroic Pattern,* 155, 165–66.

12. Ibid., 97, 100.

13. Quoted in R. F. Foster, *W. B. Yeats, a Life: The Apprentice Mage, 1865–1914* (Oxford: Oxford University Press, 1997), 1:xxvii.

14. Hesiod says that there is no justice between animals, that Zeus has given justice only to human beings, that they might not devour one another as beasts (*Works and Days* 275–78). See Grene's "Response" to Stephanie Nelson's "Justice and Farming in the *Works and Days,*" in *The Greeks and Us: Essays in Honor of Arthur W. H. Adkins,* ed. R. Louden and P. Schollmeier (Chicago: University of Chicago Press, 1996), 37.

15. Sophocles, *Antigone,* trans. David Grene, lines 396–97.

16. Grene, *Reality and the Heroic Pattern,* 116, 117.

17. Grene, *Man in His Pride,* 95, 123–24.

18. Ibid., 74, 76.

19. Alasdair MacIntyre, *Whose Justice? Which Rationality?* (Notre Dame: Notre Dame University Press, 1988), 85, notes (albeit with some complaint) that seeing the *Republic* in terms of Thucydides is "a way of reading defined for recent generations by David Grene's *Man in His Pride,* . . . later mistitled *Greek Political Theory.*"

20. Grene, *Man in His Pride,* vii, ix, x.

21. Ibid., vii.

22. Ibid., ix.

23. Grene, *Reality and the Heroic Pattern,* 94; see also *Man in His Pride,* 92: "If one believed that the history of man politically is a story of greed, strife, and fear, and their working in the society created by them, there was still a time when these passions had for a historical moment been immobilized in a balanced beauty and strength, and Periclean Athens was this historical moment."

24. Grene, *The Actor in History,* 1–2, 5, 7, 3–4.

25. Ibid., 47, 58, 62, 84.

26. Ibid., 97, 93, 114, 115.

27. Ibid., 10, 136, 131, 11, 126.

28. Hesiod's poetry, for example, "is a poetry of vision and rich in physical details; these are the details that pertain to the evolved presence of the object in view, not to the rhetorical or ornamental effect" (Grene's "Response" in *The Greeks and Us,* 42).

29. Grene, *The Actor in History,* 146 (first two quotations), 147, 16, 17, 19, 34, 39.

30. Grene, *Reality and the Heroic Pattern,* ix.

31. Ibid., vii.

32. Herodotus, *The History,* ed. and trans. David Grene (Chicago: University of Chicago Press, 1987), 6.

33. Grene, *Reality and the Heroic Pattern,* 44, 7.

34. See Grene's "Response" in *The Greeks and Us,* 42, where he explains: "The mythological moment exists when past and present are united, not as in the narrative of history, but in already repeated acts. Not, as Eliade has it, to control the outcome by repeating the original act, but to participate in an unknowable certainty."

35. See Joseph Conrad, preface to *The Nigger of Narcissus,* quoted in *The Indispensable Conrad,* ed. Morton Dauwen Zabel (New York: Viking Press, 1947), 705.

36. Grene, *Reality and the Heroic Pattern,* vii.

Prelude

In a Drizzly Light

BRENDAN KENNELLY

February 1996

In a drizzly light outside the Abbey Theatre
David Grene is talking of ancient Greece,
no, not talking

revealing
in that calm attentive smiling style of his
the ways of gods and goddesses
the ways of words and images

cities rivers mountains sacrifices.

Listening
in the drizzly light, I hear him
opening
Cavan Athens Dublin Chicago
small hills actors lovers passionate minds.

I'm in the company of one
who loves adventure
and will pursue it with that laughing brio
to the moment of discovery.

Love is what he finds.

Part One

Atheism and the Religiosity of Euripides

MARTIN OSTWALD

Symbiosis between religion and its adherents and intellectuals who try to explore the world and all that is in it by means of their human resources has often been a rather rocky affair, as the examples of Galileo and Darwin show. The reasons are not hard to find: Galileo's contention that the earth moves around the sun upset too many entrenched sixteenth-century beliefs for comfort, and Darwin's formulation of the theory of evolution threatened a religious establishment that saw its own authority being eroded together with that of a literal interpretation of the Bible.

Galileo and Darwin had their forerunners in ancient Greece. But here the threat came less from scientific thinking as represented by the so-called Ionian natural philosophers than from the sophists, who did much to popularize and apply scientific thinking to everyday affairs. By their very nature, the institutions of the Athenian democracy put a premium on effective speaking: since all important public business was transacted by bodies of which every adult male was actually or potentially a member, persuasion was required to gain not only election to public office but also power to have your pet policy adopted as the policy of the state; since practically all trials took place before a jury, without the power of persuasion you could not obtain the conviction of your opponent or your own

The subject matter of this paper has been touched upon in scattered parts of my *From Popular Sovereignty to the Sovereignty of Law* (Berkeley, 1986), and earlier versions have been delivered as lectures in Rome, Paris, Tel Aviv, and New York. I hope that this first published version will be a worthy tribute to David Grene, the man to whom I am indebted more than to any other for my understanding of Greek tragedy.

acquittal. Training in rhetoric was the road to worldly success, and the sophists were teachers of rhetoric.

In an age that lacked the formal education to which we are accustomed, a teacher of rhetoric also had to be knowledgeable in literature, science, political science, and a variety of other subjects, if for no other reason than to enable his students to pepper their speeches with suitable quotations, to counter arguments from law with arguments from science, and to find analogies from other societies in order to press a point in the legislation they wished to advocate. That the ideas spread by the Ionian scientists and sophists should at some points run afoul of the religious establishment, mainly because they would percolate through to the general public as freely as the ideas of Freud or Marx or Darwin have spread in our society, is part of the story. In particular, I want to examine the interesting effect these new ideas had on Euripides, who was very much a child of his time. In order to put them into focus, a few words are in order on the Athenian religious establishment, which felt itself attacked by these doctrines.

Greek religion demanded of its adherents no more than participation in traditional forms of worship. It was free from dogma, and a concept of faith was alien to it. There was, before the coming of the sophists, no "belief" in the gods in the Christian sense of the term: θεοὺς νομίζειν describes the performance of ritual acts, predicated on the unchallenged assumption that the gods exist and demand veneration.[1] Since the gods are also the guarantors of the stability of the social order, and since their displeasure would disturb it, the state tried to enforce divine worship through its customs, laws, and institutions; but neither the state nor the priesthoods entrusted with the administration of cult and ritual ever displayed any interest in enforcing uniformity of religious belief. Moreover, the gods themselves were thought to be concerned only that men pay them the customary respect owed them and offer the sacrifices that were their due; human morality, so integral a part of the Jewish and Christian religions, remained a matter of indifference to the gods of the Greeks.

This meant that the established religion was intolerant only of attitudes that tended to undermine the public worship of the gods. Dissenting beliefs of individuals were tolerated: Xenophanes was not regarded as a heretic for protesting that the gods of Homer and Hesiod live immorally, for ridiculing anthropomorphism, or for expressing heterodox ideas about the unity of the divine;[2] and Pindar's disgust at the tradition that the gods had feasted on the flesh of Pelops did not make him irreverent.[3] But the doctrines of the Ionian physicists as popularized by the teaching of the sophists could be and were regarded as a threat to the established religion:

obviously they reached an audience wider than that which Pindar or Xenophanes had addressed, and that audience's commitment to public religious observances was regarded as less secure by the religious majority. To assert, as Anaxagoras had done, that the sun is a fiery stone would, if the idea gained currency, detract from the sun's divinity and thus from its worship; and for asserting it Anaxagoras was charged by Diopeithes with having committed a crime against the state.[4] Giving primacy to the human intellect might lead to the agnostic suspension of religious convictions, which the sophist Protagoras, preoccupied with the problem of what is knowable, expressed in the words: "Concerning the gods I am in no position to know either that they exist or that they do not exist, or what kind of shape they have; for many factors prevent knowing, such as the impossibility of attaining certainty and the fact that man's life is short";[5] for this belief, we are told, he was expelled from Athens and his books were burned in the agora. Evidently, the questions he raised were too disconcerting, too prone to undermine the public worship of the gods.[6]

Neither Anaxagoras nor Protagoras can be called "atheists" in the strict sense of the term, which, for us as well as for the Greeks after the fifth century B.C.E., denotes the denial of the existence of gods altogether. There is no evidence that either of them was labeled an *atheos* in his lifetime. And yet, presumably because of their convictions, for which they were put on trial, both appear in lists of *atheoi* compiled in the Hellenistic and Roman periods.[7] Since such lists also include a number of other fifth-century writers who were likewise not marked as *atheoi* by their contemporaries but whose views, held or expressed, ran counter to the conventional piety of the late fifth century, we may infer that their inclusion in such lists goes back to opposition they encountered from the religious majority in their own lifetimes.

Apart from the trials of Anaxagoras and Protagoras, we know the form such opposition took only in the case of Diagoras of Melos, whose name appears on all lists of "atheists."[8] The reason for his prominence is clear: we learn from later sources that Diagoras so maligned the Eleusinian Mysteries that many would-be initiates did not go through with their initiation; and that the Athenians, therefore, published on a bronze stele a proclamation, promising one silver talent to anyone who would kill Diagoras, and two silver talents to anyone who would bring him alive to Athens. (Another source, which dates this incident to 415/14 B.C.E., explains the proclamation as the result of Diagoras's flight from Athens after having slanderously been charged with impiety.)[9]

What precisely Diagoras's offence was we are not told in any ancient source. That it was an especially heinous violation of the Mysteries is shown by the fact that it was still remembered as such by the Athenian public a decade after the proclamation, in Aristophanes' *Frogs* (320). Six years later, the orator Andocides was charged with an impiety "more shocking than that committed by Diagoras"; for while the latter showed his impiety "in speech concerning rites and celebrations not his own, Andocides *acted* impiously concerning the rites in his own city."[10] Evidently, Diagoras had made some kind of public statement that was regarded as particularly offensive because it came from a foreigner, who, we may assume, did not even enjoy the status of a resident alien *(metoikos)* at Athens, and perhaps also because the statement was made at a time when young Athenian intellectuals from the upper classes had been discovered in the illicit *performance*—and thus profanation—of the Mysteries. I refer to the well-known crisis of 415 B.C.E., which, since it happened on the eve of the departure of a huge armada to Sicily, created fear because divinities had been offended. We know that the profaners were put on trial for impiety, but there is nothing in the tradition to suggest that Diagoras was ever actually subjected to a judicial proceeding. On the contrary, what evidence there is speaks against a trial: our knowledge of the measures taken against him comes from the citation of a decree passed by the Assembly, which declared him an outlaw, put a price on his head, and put pressure to extradite him on the people to whom he had fled. This suggests that he was the subject of a resolution of the Assembly, not of a verdict of a jury court. If the proclamation was preceded by a trial, it will have been conducted *absente reo*.[11]

However offensive his disparagement of the Mysteries may have been, there is no evidence of Diagoras's "atheism" in the later sense that he denied the existence of gods altogether. On the contrary, a man who began one of his poems with the words κατὰ δαίμονα καὶ τύχαν τὰ πάντα τελεῖται ("all things are accomplished as divinity and fortune determine")[12] is not likely to have been an atheist. Still, Diagoras seems to have been known in Athens as an "enlightened" poet considerably before the proclamation was issued against him. A reference to Socrates as a "Melian" in connection with the doctrine that Zeus had been supplanted as king by Dinos ("pot") is generally taken as indicating that Diagoras was well known—and perhaps even present—in Athens when Aristophanes produced his *Clouds* (828–30) in 423 B.C.E. But it indicates also that Diagoras was reputed to have absorbed enough of Ionian science, presumably through the sophists, to have been tarred in Athens with the same brush as Anaxagoras. If he enjoyed that reputation as early as 423 B.C.E., any derogatory statement he may have made against the Mysteries in 415 B.C.E. will have evoked the strong reaction on the part of the religious establishment which we see reflected in the proclamation and will explain why it was fear of the people that made him leave Athens before it was issued. It will also explain why and how his reputation as an *atheos* developed and how it was elaborated with fanciful biographical detail in the Hellenistic doxographical tradition.

Diagoras's reputation as an atheist rested on something offensive he had said and on the political response it evoked. The inclusion of the sophist Prodicus in Hellenistic lists of atheists seems to be due to his questioning the existence of gods traditionally venerated by humans. If "atheism" involves merely the refusal to believe in the existence of gods traditionally venerated in a given society, Prodicus was indeed an "atheist." But Prodicus was no theologian. His denial of the traditional gods was only a by-product of his study of the correct meaning and usage of words, in which his rhetorical teaching had involved him. The context in which he discussed the gods is likely to have been an account of the origin of human civilization, a subject in which other sophists had been interested before him. Prodicus seems to have seen two phases in the development of religion. In the first of these, ancient men (οἱ παλαιοί) venerated as gods all those primary natural forces on which their sustenance and well-being depended: sun and moon, rivers and springs, and the like.[13] In the second phase, the appellation "gods" was extended to great human benefactors of the past, whose skills had provided humanity with shelter or taught them the preparation of foodstuffs, such as bread or wine, whose givers were now identified as Demeter and Dionysus, respectively.[14] Whether this kind of outlook deserves to be identified as "atheism" *tout court* remains open to question. Prodicus's denial of the existence of the traditional gods as gods, and his assertion that they were merely deified humans, may indeed have been combined with the expectation that intelligent men such as himself should refuse them traditional worship. Still, the benefactions they had bestowed were real and lasting: would Prodicus have objected to simple folk continuing to recognize their indebtedness by worshiping them as gods? Or would he have disapproved of intellectuals who, against their better knowledge, encouraged divine worship by the masses in the interest of promoting a spirit of cohesion and piety in society?

No statement has survived which suggests that Prodicus worked out the social consequences of his theology, so our questions must remain unanswered. But there is contemporary or quasi-contemporary evidence strong enough to enable us to affirm that, whatever his views of the gods may have been, he enjoyed the respect and admiration of at least some upper-class Athenians to whom the maintenance of traditional piety was important, and perhaps even of the people in general. His frequent visits to Athens in official as well as in nonofficial capacities made him sufficiently well known for Aristophanes to refer in respectful terms to his scientific learning and judgment in three plays, dated respectively to 423 *(Clouds)*, 422 *(Tagenistai)*, and 414 B.C.E. *(Birds)*. These will also have been the occasions on which he met and taught younger members of the upper classes for pay, as all sophists did. Fun could be poked at innocent idiosyncrasies and at his deep, almost inaudible voice, yet he was widely respected as a learned man and as a good teacher, who counted not only Theramenes but also Socrates among his pupils and friends.[15] Nevertheless, the fact that Plato attributes to Laches, an upright, old-fashioned aristocrat, the disparaging remark that Prodicus's talents were more fit for a sophist than for a political leader shows that admiration for him was not universal.[16] Still, nothing disparaging is said anywhere about religious beliefs espoused by Prodicus, and Laches applied also to other sophists what he said about Prodicus. In short, Prodicus's religious convictions were no more detrimental to his reputation among his contemporaries than Xenophanes' were in his time. But his inclusion among the list of *atheoi* a century or two later permits the inference that his views were considered subversive by the contemporary religious majority.

To Euripides, more than to any other author, we are indebted for our knowledge of how widely unconventional ideas about the gods had been spread thanks to the popularization of Ionian science by the sophists. What Euripides' own views were we cannot know.[17] We merely know the views he assigns to the characters in his plays, and we can infer from them that these views were sufficiently familiar to his contemporary audience to be dramatically useful and that they led to success in tragic competition. In other words, Euripides' plays are good evidence for ideas current in Athens in the late fifth century, but they do not constitute evidence for what Euripides himself believed, except that his strong predilection for dramatically exploiting questions raised by the intellectuals of his time makes it hard to believe that he accepted conventional piety with the same resigned acquiescence with which his contemporary Sophocles seems to have accepted it. However, the tendency to credit Euripides personally with the opinions expressed by his characters is an error that some modern scholars have inherited from ancient critics, an error that has earned Euripides inclusion in the Hellenistic list of *atheoi*.

Euripides' close involvement with the intellectual circles of his time is reflected in the student-teacher relationship that his late biographers establish between him, Anaxagoras, Prodicus, Protagoras, and Socrates.[18] Although such statements cannot be taken at their face value, they attest an awareness even in antiquity of the fact that these thinkers influenced Euripidean tragedy, an influence which exposed Euripides to some of the same charges as the sophists. It will suffice here to cite as examples some Euripidean passages which may have been regarded by later generations as suffused with the same kind of "atheism" of which they suspected the natural philosophers and the sophists.[19]

Euripidean criticism of the gods of traditional religion is born of his concern for social justice, which pervades especially his early plays and in his later plays, especially the *Bacchae,* turns into an attempt to come to grips with the problem of religion as such. In all its phases it shows traces of the kind of contemporary thought about the gods which struck later generations as "atheistic." Plays written just before or during the Archidamian War remind of Protagoras's agnostic despair that we can never come to know any truth about the gods (80 B 4) as well as of Prodicus's denial of the existence of the conventional gods: a speech in the *Philoctetes* (frag. 795 [Nauck]; 431 B.C.E.) inveighs against seers who claim to have clear knowledge of divine matters while in reality they manipulate people by persuasion, and a long extract from the *Bellerophon* (frag. 286 [Nauck]; pre-425 B.C.E.) rejects the existence of the heavenly gods not on intellectual grounds, as Prodicus had done, but because wicked and impious tyrants prosper and because small god-fearing states become victims of more powerful impious states. Into this context also belongs the famous and rather ambiguous appeal of *Hecuba* (425 B.C.E.): ἀλλ᾽ οἱ θεοὶ σθένουσι χὠ κείνων κρατῶν / νόμος· νόμῳ γὰρ τοὺς θεοὺς ἡγούμεθα / καὶ ζῶμεν ἄδικα καὶ δίκαι᾽ ὡρισμένοι.[20] The affirmation of divine power in the first of these lines is immediately undercut by the statement that the gods are controlled by norms, the precise nature of which we are not told; and the following two lines suggest that this affirmation has no sanction beyond the *human* conventions which require gods for establishing social norms. Some scholars have seen traces of Protagoras or Archelaus in these lines,[21] others of Prodicus and Critias;[22] but the parallels are too vague to enable us to say more than that Euripides was steeped in the same spirit as other thinkers of his age.

This morally based questioning of the gods recedes in Euripides' later works, giving way to a more ontological attitude. A religious dimension of this can be seen in Hecuba's outcry in the *Trojan Women* (415 B.C.E.): ὦ γῆς ὄχημα κἀπὶ γῆς ἔχων ἕδραν, / ὅστις ποτ᾽ εἶ σύ, δυστόπαστος εἰδέναι, / Ζεύς, εἴτ᾽ ἀνάγκη φύσεος εἴτε νοῦς βροτῶν, / προσηυξάμην σε.[23] Echoes of various philosophers have been detected in this passage, but the religious turn given to their ideas is entirely that of Euripides. It is not concerned with the morality or immorality of the gods but it questions the existence

of the traditional gods by searching for their reality in the powers underlying natural phenomena. A similar sentiment is expressed at the opening
of the *Wise Melanippe* (frag. 480 [Nauck]), which belongs to the same
general period as the *Trojan Women*: Ζεὺς ὅστις ὁ Ζεύς, οὐ γὰρ οἶδα πλὴν
λόγῳ ("Zeus, whoever Zeus is, for I know only by report"), which is said
to have caused such an uproar in the theater that Euripides was compelled
to change the line. But no other work will have made Euripides more
vulnerable to the charge of atheism than the speech of Sisyphus in the
satyr play that bore his name and that was part of the same tetralogy as
the *Trojan Women* (415 B.C.E.). Sextus Empiricus, to whom we owe the
preservation of the fragment, attributes it to Critias as evidence of his
atheism, but the work of Albrecht Dihle has removed any lingering doubts
that it belongs to Euripides.[24]

A considerable number of parallels to the views of contemporary scientists and sophists can be and have been detected in the forty-two lines
that have been preserved.[25] The fragment opens with the theory that men
originally lived "brutish and unorganized" (1–2). Although this theory
appears as early as the middle of the fifth century, it is difficult to attach a
name to it. The idea is not found in any other systematic discussion of the
origins of civilization. Next we find that laws *(nomoi)* were invented to
curb and discipline the excesses of the wicked in order that justice might
be tyrant (5–8). Curiously enough, this is not attributed to an individual
lawgiver, but, as in the account attributed by Plato to Protagoras, to enactment by men *(anthrōpoi)*. The invention of religion, which is of interest
to us here, is credited to "some man, acute and wise in mind," with the
purpose of inhibiting secret wrongdoing (9–11) in action, speech, or
thought (14–15), by instilling the fear of an immortal, powerful, all-
hearing, all-seeing divinity, from whom no thought is hidden (16–24). In
doing so, we are told, the wise man "introduced the pleasantest of teachings, hiding truth with false account," adding that the gods live in a place
where they would most scare and benefit men at the same time: the sky
with its thunder and lightning, but also with its sun and rain (27–36).
"Thus," the fragment concludes, "first I think someone persuaded mortals
to believe that a tribe of spirits exists" (41–42).

If we look for comparable ideas in the surviving contemporary writings of the late fifth century, we shall discover that the atheism expressed
by Sisyphus is either a new conclusion based on contemporary ideas or
constitutes a different and more extreme form of atheism than any we
have so far encountered. The notion that law *(nomos)* cannot inhibit human drives is also found in the sophist Antiphon; but, unlike Sisyphus
(5–8), Antiphon gives no thought to the origin of law at all and takes its

existence for granted.[26] However, like Sisyphus (11), he recognizes that it does not provide a safeguard against secret wrongdoing (B.I.6–23); still, the conclusions drawn from this by the two authors are diametrically opposed to one another. For Antiphon, this deficiency is simply taken for granted and explained as inherent in the artificial character of *nomos*, which constitutes a barrier to the free play of the necessary course of nature; the gods do not enter the argument at all. For Sisyphus, on the other hand, the laws enforce social justice (6), and when they prove inadequate to that task, their deficiency becomes the explanation of the invention of religion by a man of genius (9–16).

The idea that religion was a human invention can also be found in Democritus: "A few intelligent men raised their hands to the place which we Greeks now call 'air' and said, 'Zeus considers (?) all things; he knows, gives, and takes away everything, and he is king over all.'"[27] We do not know what place, if any, this fragment may have occupied in Democritus's theology; but the thought it expresses is sharpened in the Sisyphus fragment in that the invention of the gods is attributed to one single "shrewd man wise in judgment" (12), not in order to explain the majesty of the universe, but to manipulate his less intelligent or more gullible fellow citizens into being more law-abiding. In short, the cognitive purpose of Democritus has been transformed into a socially or politically useful tool. Another piece of Democritean wisdom is the belief that the notion of the gods was implanted in primitive man by the experience of celestial phenomena, such as thunder, lightning, the constellations, and eclipses of sun and moon, and by the fear that they engendered. In the Sisyphus fragment the same phenomena are also associated with fear of the gods, but only in order to account for the wise man's placing the gods in Heaven—the locale of these phenomena—in order to maximize fear of the gods (28) and harness it to socially and politically useful purposes (37–40).

Finally, there is an analogy with Prodicus in Sisyphus's mention of the benefit accruing to humans from the celestial bodies and phenomena, especially sun and rain. Yet Prodicus was concerned with explaining the origin of popular religion by the awe people felt in the face of these benefactions; Sisyphus, on the other hand, not only puts this awe pragmatically into the service of his social and political aims, emphasizing fear rather than admiration, but in doing so also undermines belief even in the kind of "philosophical" gods for which the doctrines of Prodicus and Democritus may still have left room. After all, there is an objective reality underlying the worship of Demeter and Dionysus in Prodicus's theology, and for Democritus the awe inspired by meteorological phenomena is real;

Sisyphus's divinity, however, is purely the contrivance of a human genius and is stripped of any vestiges of anthropomorphic personality: it is all mind and perception (17–21), a vindictive, disembodied master-spy (22–24) to maintain order and discipline in human society.

The Sisyphus fragment as well as the other Euripidean passages we have been discussing will have contributed to shaping Euripides' reputation as an atheist, which is first attested in Aristophanes' criticism of him in the *Thesmophoriazousai* (450–51) a few years after the performance of his Trojan tetralogy, and eventually secured him a place in the Hellenistic list of *atheoi*. While this reputation is presumably based on some contemporary opinion, the reality behind it is even less strong than for his alleged unpopularity. Views expressed by dramatic characters bear witness to familiarity with these views on the part of the contemporary audience: the Sisyphus fragment does not enable us to draw any inference on Euripides' own religious convictions. But it does bear witness to the same profound concern with the phenomenon of religion that we encounter in the *Bacchae;* although this play is only marginally related to the problem of atheism, it is germane to our present discussion in that it includes an attempt to effect some kind of reconciliation between the popular religion of the Establishment and theological ideas that had been propagated by the enlightenment.

That the *Bacchae* is neither the palinode of a converted atheist nor a renewed defiant denunciation of evils wrought by religion can now be taken as established. Ideas and themes that appeared in earlier plays are welded into something that gives a new and profound direction to thoughts about religion and the gods, which had been expressed by Euripidean characters in the 420s. The nature of this direction has been well captured by Jeanne Roux: "it is not a matter of knowing whether the gods are good or bad, just or unjust in terms of human morality, but of knowing that they exist and, in that case, how a man must behave toward them in order to attain happiness and prosperity."[28] Questions raised by human morality are of lesser moment than recognition of the existence of the gods and acceptance, for better or for worse, of the worship they demand. We shall consider two passages that show the transformation contemporary thought underwent in the hands of Euripides to express his peculiar religiosity in the *Bacchae*.

The first of these is spoken by Teiresias in the first encounter he and Cadmus have with Pentheus. The aged seer tries to convince Pentheus to accept the worship of Dionysus by arguing that his worship will spread through the whole of Greece:

δύο γάρ, ὦ νεανία,
τὰ πρῶτ᾽ ἐν ἀνθρώποισι· Δημήτηρ θεά—
γῆ δ᾽ ἐστίν, ὄνομα δ᾽ ὁπότερον βούλῃ κάλει·
αὕτη μὲν ἐν ξηροῖσιν ἐκτρέφει βροτούς·
ὃς δ᾽ ἦλθ᾽ ἔπειτ᾽, ἀντίπαλον ὁ Σημήλης γόνος
βότρυος ὑγρὸν πῶμ᾽ ηὗρε κεἰσενέγκατο
θνητοῖς, ὃ παύει τούς ταλαιπώρους βροτοὺς
λύπης, ὅταν πλησθῶσιν ἀμπέλου ῥοῆς,
ὕπνον τε λήθην τῶν καθ᾽ ἡμέραν κακῶν
δίδωσιν, οὐδ᾽ ἔστ᾽ ἄλλο φάρμακον πόνων.
οὗτος θεοῖσι σπένδεται θεὸς γεγώς,
ὥστε διὰ τοῦτον τἀγάθ᾽ ἀνθρώπους ἔχειν.[29]

The closeness of this passage to concepts of early Greek science and to the thought of Prodicus has often been noted, but it is rarely stated in detail.[30] Greek science is reflected in the significant opposition of dry and wet, which can be traced back as far as Hesiod and informs practically all pre-Socratic thinking about the nature of the physical universe. Considerably more striking, however, is the similarity to Prodicus's two phases in the development of religion, in the first of which men attributed divinity to the celestial bodies and phenomena on which they depended for subsistence, and in the second of which divine status was conferred upon great human benefactors, among whom Demeter and Dionysus are explicitly singled out for mention. The similarity goes even further: we are told that Prodicus believed in the identity of Demeter with bread and of Dionysus with wine, a point which becomes in Teiresias's speech an avowed indifference whether "earth" or "Demeter" is the proper name of the goddess (276), and which results in the identification of Dionysus with his product in line 284. Yet Euripides puts a stamp of his own on Prodicus's view: Demeter, whom Prodicus seems to have regarded as a human who was deified for having discovered how to make bread from grain, becomes in Euripides one of the primary divinities. This is suggested by the opposition of wet and dry that opens Teiresias's argument, and it seems corroborated by the indifference to her name, which recalls similar expressions of indifference to divine nomenclature in the *Trojan Women* and the *Wise Melanippe* which I have quoted before. Not quite consistently with this, Dionysus seems to belong to Prodicus's second phase. This is indicated by the statements that "he came afterward" (278); that he is Semele's offspring (278); that he "invented" the wet drink of the grape cluster, whereas Demeter "nurtures" directly (277); that he "became" a god (284);

and in that he is explicitly named as a benefactor to men (285). But here again there is a peculiar Euripidean twist. While Prodicus concluded from his arguments that the gods of popular tradition do not exist, Euripides puts his arguments into the mouth of a spokesman for the religious establishment, whom we should expect to represent the attitude of conventional piety toward the nature of Dionysus and the problem of admitting his worship into Thebes. If that was Euripides' intent in composing this scene, a strange spokesman Teiresias turns out to be: he uses an argument originally formulated to deny the existence of the conventional gods to show that they—or at least Dionysus—are real enough to deserve recognition and worship. His proof consists in the pragmatic enumeration of some of the benefits derived for men from wine, more of a philosophical than of a popular theology. However, one of the benefits is that Dionysus, "having become a god, is poured as a libation to the gods" (284). The recipients of these libations must be the gods of traditional religion, since there cannot be any other to whom this kind of sacrifice is likely to be poured. This means that Dionysus holds an important key to the performance of traditional worship in that he contributes as a god to swaying the goodwill of the gods of popular religion in our favor. That this strange fusion of philosophical with conventional elements is deliberate is shown in the rest of Teiresias's speech. In the immediate sequel, his rationalistically etymological explanation of the story that Zeus hid Dionysus in his thigh (286–96) is contrived to show that there is a reality underlying an otherwise incredible story; and following that, the entrance of "the god" into the body is given as the source of the seer's craft, in which the "manic" *(maniōdes)* results in the "mantic" *(mantikē)* (298–313). Is this transformation of philosophical "atheism" into a part of traditional religion to be taken as a characterization of the attitude of Athenian aristocrats, whose stewardship of religious cults had been influenced by the sophists? If it is, the dry, abstract tone of Teiresias's disquisition, often remarked on by commentators, may well be intended as a foil to the stark reality of the divine presence that will be demonstrated in the sequel of the play.

The tension between the attempt to comprehend life through the intellect and through direct experience of the divine stands at the heart of Euripidean religiosity in the *Bacchae*. It is most strikingly expressed in the question posed at the beginning of two identical stanzas in the stasimon that separates Dionysus's persuasion of Pentheus to become a voyeur from Pentheus's appearance in Bacchic garb: τί τὸ σοφόν; "what is the wise thing?" That this question dominates the play as a whole has long been seen.[31] Throughout, its common contemporary connotation of intellectual keenness is pitted against another connotation, which sees in the simple unquestioning surrender to the god a higher wisdom: τὸ σοφὸν δ' οὐ σοφία / τό τε μὴ θνητὰ φρονεῖν; "And what passes for wisdom is not wisdom; unwise are those whose thinking goes beyond mortal limits" (395–96). It is the wisdom of the intellect that is consistently found wanting. Dionysus's decision to punish Thebes is motivated by the belief of Cadmus's daughters that the story of Semele's mating with Zeus was merely a *sophisma* ("clever trick") on the part of their father to protect their sister's integrity (30). Teiresias is regarded as *sophos* by Cadmus (179, 186), but his true wisdom is nothing in the eyes of the gods, and the *sophon* of the sharpest human mind cannot countervail against timeless traditions; his own understanding of the nature of divinity is, as we saw, infected with some of the same intellectualism that he condemns as *sophon* in Pentheus (266). Pentheus is of course the chief representative of the human wisdom which the course of the action shows to be deficient in the face of Dionysiac wisdom. Euripides brings this out by the frequent use of *sophon* in an ambivalent sense in the scenes between Pentheus and Dionysus. For example, Pentheus's failure to understand the account the fettered Dionysus gives of himself makes Dionysus describe the gulf that separates them with the words δόξει τις ἀμαθεῖ σοφὰ λέγων οὐκ εὖ φρονεῖν ("a person saying wise things will be regarded by the ignorant as defective in his thinking"; 480). Pentheus, on the other hand, looks upon Dionysus's explanations as *sophismata* ("clever tricks"; 489). In the next episode, Dionysus, having just freed himself, resolves to meet Pentheus's anger with calmness: "it befits a wise man to restrain his feelings and practice self-control," attributing true inner calm to the wisdom that springs from the cult condemned as excessively emotional by Pentheus, a point driven home a few lines later, when Pentheus predicates cleverness *(sophon)* of Dionysus's escape, while Dionysus claims to be *sophos* where it really matters (655–56). Pentheus's tragic end is foreshadowed when he praises Dionysus as "wise" for proposing to dress him up as a woman (824) and when Dionysus approves of Pentheus's plan of investigating the spot where the orgies are taking place as "wiser" than immediately hunting down the worshipers (839).

The kind of wisdom commended by the play is fully articulated only in the choral lyrics, especially in the third choral interlude. The first stasimon, to be sure, differentiates from the *sophon* true *sophia,* which consists in the pursuit of a quiet life, confined to thinking mortal thoughts (389–96), "whose simple wisdom shuns the thoughts of proud, uncommon men," willing to accept "what simple men believe and do" (427–32). But it is only in the third stasimon, just before Pentheus embarks on the errand from which he will not return, that the answer to the question τί τὸ σοφόν—"what is the wise thing?"—appears flanked by two stanzas in which the question is posed:

οὐ
γάρ κρεῖσσόν ποτε τῶν νόμων
γιγνώσκειν χρὴ καὶ μελετᾶν.
κούφα γὰρ δαπάνα νομίζειν ἰσχὺν τόδ᾽ ἔχειν,
ὅ τι πότ᾽ ἄρα τὸ δαιμόνιον,
τό τ᾽ ἐν χρονῷ μακρῷ νόμιμον
ἀεὶ φύσει τε πεφυκός.[32]

In these lines the *nomoi* (traditions) which demarcate the limits of human endeavor imply beliefs as well as practices, and what is traditional *(nomimon)* regards the divine as an object of both belief and worship. If this is so, the *sophon* will resolve the conflict between intellectual and traditional religion by demanding a fusion of the two that resolves at the same time in the field of religion the tension between *nomos* and *physis,* which the teaching of the sophists had injected into Athenian thought. On the other hand, the *nomoi* include the πάτριοι παραδοχαί, the ancestral traditions, which, as Teiresias had asserted (200–203), will resist any human *sophon* as well as the norms and practices of the common simple folk (430–33); but, on the other, they will also include Teiresias's feeble attempt to reconcile the enlightened views of Prodicus with conventional piety, so long as the traditional worship of the gods is not adversely affected. It will not cost the intellect much, this passage assures us, to recognize the divine strength underlying the natural phenomena of our experience, meaning, I presume, that whether or not we identify Demeter with earth or Dionysus with wine, the ἰσχύς (strength) manifested in the very existence of earth and wine demands recognition and worship. The combination of this recognition with the worship it entails will then not only be sanctioned as a *nomimon* hallowed by long tradition but also be grounded in that nature *(physis)* that can be explored by the human intellect.

Seen in this light, the ending of the *Bacchae* is a statement, not on the horrors of religion—*tantum religio potuit suadere malorum* is frequently cited by scholars who believe that it is—but on the dire consequences that failure by the intellect to acknowledge the reality of divine power can bring in its train. It stands in a direct line of development with the tragic perception of Medea and Phaedra in earlier Euripidean plays that life is subject to forces against which rationality cannot prevail. Here, as in earlier plays, Euripides is concerned with and affected by problems raised by the natural philosophers and popularized by the sophists, but, as in the *Sisyphus* fragment, he is no longer content to measure the gods by the yardstick of human morality but comes to grips with the phenomenon of religion itself and concludes that the reality underlying it is the object of traditional religion and philosophical inquiry alike. His attempt to reconcile *nomos* and *physis* in the religious sphere remains unique in fifth-century thought. But it left a less-lasting impression on his contemporaries and on later generations than the fact that Euripides openly grappled with problems raised by thinkers whose views were branded as "atheistic" because they were believed to undermine the traditional worship of the gods.

Notes

1. See in particular W. Fahr, *ΘΕΟΥΣ NOMIZEIN: Zum Problem der Anfänge des Atheismus bei den Griechen,* Spudasmata 26 (Hildesheim and New York: G. Olms, 1969).

2. Xenophanes, frags. 15–16, 17–19, 26–27, 33, in *Poetarum Elegiacorum Testimonia et Fragmenta,* vol. 1, ed. B. Gentili and C. Prato (Leipzig: Teubner, 1979).

3. Pindar, *Olympians* I.25–35.

4. Plutarch, *Pericles* 32.2.

5. Protagoras in H. Diels and W. Kranz, *Die Fragmente der Vorsokratiker,* 6th ed. (Berlin: Weidmann, 1956–59) (henceforth DK⁶), 80 B 4: περὶ μὲν θεῶν οὐκ ἔχω εἰδέναι, οὔθ᾽ ὡς εἰσὶν οὔθ᾽ ὡς οὐκ εἰσὶν οὔθ᾽ ὁποῖοί τινες ἰδέαν· πολλὰ γὰρ τὰ κωλύοντα εἰδέναι ἥ τ᾽ ἀδηλότης καὶ βραχὺς ὢν ὁ βίος τοῦ ἀνθρώπου

6. For details, see Ostwald, *From Popular Sovereignty to the Sovereignty of Law* (Berkeley: University of California Press, 1986), 532–33.

7. See H. Diels, *Doxographi Graeci* (Berlin: G. Reimer, 1879), 58–59.

8. See L. Woodbury, "The Date and Atheism of Diagoras of Melos," *Phoenix* 19 (1965): 178–211.

9. See scholia to Aristophanes' *Aves* 1073 and *Ranae* 320; Craterus in F. Jacoby, *Die Fragmente der griechischen Historiker* IIIb (Leiden: E. J. Brill, 1950) (henceforth *FGH*), 342 F 16.

10. [Lysias] 6.17.

11. See n. 9 above, with Diodorus 13.6.7 and Mubaššir, as cited by F. Jacoby, *Diagoras Ὁ Ἄθεος,* Abhandlungen der Deutschen Akademie der Wissenschaften Berlin, Klasse für Sprachen, Literatur, und Kunst 3 (Berlin: Akademie-Verlag, 1959), 19, with n. 139. Cf. also Woodbury, "Diagoras of Melos," 195.

12. D. L. Page, *Poetae Melici Graeci* (Oxford: Clarendon Press, 1962), no. 738 (2).

13. See Sextus Empiricus, *Adversus Mathematicos* 9.18 (84 B 5 DK⁶). See also Philodemus, *De Pietate* 9.7 (= 84 B 5 DK⁶), as discussed by A. Henrichs in "Two Doxographical Notes: Democritus and Prodicus on Religion," *Harvard Studies in Classical Philology* 79 (1975): 115–23, and in "The Sophists and Hellenistic Religion: Prodicus as the Spiritual Father of the Isis Aretalogies," *Harvard Studies in Classical Philology* 88 (1984): 139–58, esp. 140–45. See also Cicero, *De natura deorum* 1.42.118.

14. See *Papyri Herculaniensis* 1428, cols. ii–iii, as interpreted by Henrichs (see n. 13).

15. Plato, *Meno* 96d, *Charmides* 163d, *Hippias maior* 282c; Athenaeus 5.220b; and scholia to Aristophanes' *Nubes* 361.

16. Plato, *Laches* 197d.

17. See Mary R. Lefkowitz, "Was Euripides an Atheist?" *Studi Italiana di Filologia Classica,* 3d ser., 5 (1987): 149–66.

18. For details, see Ostwald, *Popular Sovereignty,* 279 with n. 304.

19. Several of these passages are also discussed by Mary R. Lefkowitz, "'Impiety' and 'Atheism' in Euripides' Dramas," *Classical Quarterly* 39 (1989): 70–82, in the only recent effort of which I know to cope specifically with the issue of Euripides' "atheism." However, her approach differs radically from that taken here in that she is more concerned with what single passages in Euripidean drama say (or, more frequently, do not say) about their author than with the "religiosity" conveyed by the various plays in themselves.

20. Euripides, *Hecuba* 799–801: "for the gods are strong as is also the law that governs them; for it is the law [= social conventions] that makes us accept the gods and live distinguishing just from unjust."

21. U. von Wilamowitz-Moellendorff, *Aus Kydathen,* Philologische Untersuchungen 1 (Berlin: Weidmann, 1880), 49.

22. E.g., Fahr, *ΘΕΟΥΣ ΝΟΜΙΖΕΙΝ,* 64–65, with 97–101.

23. Euripides, *Troades* 884–87: "O power which mounts the earth and has its fixed place on the earth, whoever you be, hard to guess and hard to know, Zeus, whether you are a natural necessity or human intelligence, I invoke you."

24. Sextus Empiricus, *Adversus Mathematicos* 9.54, with A. Dihle, "Das Satyrspiel 'Sisyphos,'" *Hermes* 105 (1977): 28–42, accepted by R. Scodel, *The Trojan Trilogy of Euripides,* Hypomnemata 60 (Göttingen: Vandenhoeck und Ruprect, 1980). The objections raised against Dihle's attribution by M. Davies, "Sisyphus and the Invention of Religion ('Critias' *TrGF* 1 (43) F 19 = B 25 DK)," *Bulletin of the Institute of Classical Studies* 36 (1989): 16–32, esp. 24–28, do not seem decisive to me.

25. The following is based on the text in B. Snell, *Tragicorum Graecorum Fragmenta,* vol. 1 (Göttingen, 1971), 43 F 19, with some of Dihle's emendations. For a discussion of sources, see also Scodel, *Trojan Trilogy,* 127–28.

26. My discussion is based on the text established by Fernanda Decleva Caizzi in the *Corpus dei papiri filosofici greci e latini* I.1 (Florence, 1989), 183–86 (frag. A) and 192–98 (frag. B). See also M. Ostwald, "*NOMOS* and *PHUSIS* in Antiphon's Περὶ Ἀληθείας," in *Cabinet of the Muses: Essays on Classical and Comparative Literature in Honor of Thomas G. Rosenmeyer,* ed. M. Griffith and D. Mastronarde (Atlanta, Ga.: Scholars Press, 1990), 293–306, esp. 297–98.

27. 68 B 30 DK[6].

28. Jeanne Roux, *Euripide: Les Bacchantes,* 2 vols., Bibliothèque de la Faculté des Lettres de Lyon 21 (Paris: Sociéte d'édition "Les Belles Lettres," 1970), 1:41: "il ne s'agit pas de savoir si les dieux sont bons ou mauvais, justes ou injustes au regard de la morale des hommes, mais de savoir s'ils sont et, dans ce cas, comment l'homme doit se comporter envers eux pour en obtenir bonheur et prospérité."

29. Euripides, *Bacchae* 274–85: "Mankind, young man, possesses two supreme blessings. First of these is the goddess Demeter, or Earth—whichever name you choose to call her by. It was she who gave to man dry nourishment [grain]. But after her there came the son of Semele, who matched her present by inventing liquid wine as his gift to man. For filled with that good gift, suffering mankind forgets its grief; from it comes sleep; with it

oblivion of the troubles of the day. There is no other medicine for misery. And when we pour libations to the gods, we pour the god of wine himself that through his intercession man may win all that is good."

30. For a fairly full discussion, see the commentary on lines 274–85 in R. A. S. Seaford, ed., *Euripides, "Bacchae," with Introduction, Translation, and Commentary* (Warminster, England: Aris and Phillips, 1996).

31. See, e.g., E. R. Dodds, ed., *Bacchae,* 2d ed. (Oxford: Clarendon Press, 1960), 121, 186–88.

32. Euripides, *Bacchae* 890–96: "For one must never attempt to gain insights or to perform acts that go beyond the laws. For it is a light expense to believe that there is strength in whatever is the divine, the divine that has been both an object of belief throughout a long period of time and is forever rooted in nature."

Poetry and Philosophy in Aristophanes' *Clouds*

JAMES REDFIELD

The greatest classical poet on whom David Grene has not written is Aristophanes, which is odd, since Grene shares with that master some important convictions: that it is better to work on the land than to spend one's life hanging about in town, that most fashionable theories are contemptible balderdash, that Aeschylus is a great and wise poet, whereas Euripides, for all his facility, is not. Here I offer to David, who was my own master a lifetime ago, a discussion of one play of Aristophanes which attempts to give an account of that poet's understanding of the wisdom that can be in poetry, and of the share poetry can have in the good life—a life which David Grene has always aimed to live and to teach.

The *Clouds* is a play about a man whose son runs into debt; in seeking to rescue the family the father attempts to learn a style of reasoning which he believes will enable him to defraud his creditors. The old man, however, is unable to learn: when he sends his son instead, the son turns out to be all too teachable and uses the new reasoning against his father. The outcome therefore is perfect poetic justice as the old man is caught by his very attempt to wriggle free. Through the workings of injustice, justice triumphs.

We, however, tend to see the play as a play about Socrates, since we are deeply interested in Socrates (and perhaps not so interested in justice). Since, further, our Socrates is Plato's Socrates, our reception of the *Clouds* is deeply conditioned by Plato's Socrates' remarks about the play. In the *Apology* Socrates says that his real accusers, those who really bring about his conviction, have been working on the Athenians a long time with their slanders; they say Socrates is interested in things above the heavens and below the earth and that he makes the worse appear the better reason. "The worst is, gentlemen, I cannot even tell you their names, unless one of them happens to be a comic poet" (*Apology* 18c–d). "You yourselves have seen the play of Aristophanes, in which he brings on some kind of Socrates saying that he treads the air and other nonsense of which I know nothing" (*Apology* 19c). Aristophanes thus became from Plato's time onward a villain who lied about Socrates, and since we tend not to think deeply about our villains, there are no further questions. Here I ask what Aristophanes intended by this Socrates and what meaning his play had, for its author and for its various audiences, when he wrote it. What did the play mean before Plato gave it the meaning it now has for most of us?

The implication of the *Apology* would seem to be that Aristophanes' play, produced in 423 B.C., was in some large part responsible for the execution of Socrates twenty-four years later. One would certainly not infer from Plato's words that the *Clouds* was a failure. Yet the fact is that the *Clouds* was the one great failure of Aristophanes' dramatic career. It was placed third among the three plays in the competition, and this apparently underrepresents the extent of its rejection. Aristophanes wrote about it in the parabasis, the poet's address to the audience, in the play he produced the following year, the *Wasps:* the chorus protests that although the poet has, like Heracles, defended the people from monsters (by which they mean the demagogue Cleon) and freed the land from taint,

Last year you betrayed him although he'd set out novel ideas
Which because you understood them impurely did not come to fruit.
The fact is (he makes all kinds of libations and swears by Dionysus)
No better comedy has ever been produced before you.
The disgrace is to you for failing to get it at once;
The poet will be thought no worse of by the wise
If while speeding past the competition his invention had a crash. (*Wasps*
    1044–50)

In other words, the play was too good for the Athenians; the "wise," who understood it, will see that its failure casts discredit on the audience, not the poet. It is less clear what he means by "understood them impurely." Purity is, however, a theme of the section; the chorus begins this speech by asking for the attention of those who "care for something pure" (*katharos;* 1015) and claims that the poet is, like Heracles, a *Kathartēs,* a purifier (1043). A little later (1051–58) they say that the audience should welcome and encourage those who have novel discoveries and inventions and should store such notions away in their cupboards; "that way all year your clothes will smell of talent"—that is, clean and fresh. Aristophanes here seems to be talking about the comic catharsis. Whatever was monstrous and unclean becomes in the hands of the poet fresh and pleasant—providing the audience understands it aright. The *Clouds,* as theater people say, "died"; it was a joke that didn't come off, that left a bad taste.

Aristophanes did not immediately admit defeat; he revised the play with the hope of presenting it again. Our text is the revised version; ancient critics, who had seen both versions, tell us that the new version was revised throughout, and the debate between Right and Wrong freshly written, along with a new parabasis and a new ending, wherein Strepsiades burns down Socrates' house. (I here summarize K. J. Dover's careful argument in his introduction to his edition.) This new version was never performed, and the revisions are incomplete; our text, for instance, includes the old parabasis along with the new one. The *Clouds,* in other words, is one of those masterpieces, like *Hamlet* and *The Magic Flute,* transmitted to us in a form that does not represent the intention of the author at any stage of composition.

In the new parabasis the chorus speaks in the person of the poet and tells of the fortunes of the play in the context of an autobiography. Included is how he first produced his plays as the work of other poets—apparently because he was too young to be one of the official poets of the festival. There is reference to the Good Boy *(sōphrōn)* and the Punk *(katapugōn)* of the *Banqueters,* one of the plays thus produced, and Aristophanes' first great success. That play, which is lost, evidently included a contest between a representative of decent, old-fashioned manners and a representative of the new unprincipled style, not unlike the running debate between tradition and philosophy in the *Clouds.* Aristophanes seems to be saying: you liked that play, why not this one? The references to the *Knights* (in which the "simile of the eels" occurred) seem to cut the other way: the *Knights,* which is little more than two hours of character assassination of Cleon, was Aristophanes' play immediately before the *Clouds* and was enormously successful with the Athenian audience. Some evidently asked him: why didn't you do something like that again? The original *Clouds* did include an attack on Cleon (lines 581–94 in our text) but the play as a whole was something quite different. In this new parabasis he wrote for the revision, Aristophanes emphasizes the novelty of the *Clouds* (as does the passage from the *Wasps* quoted above):

You, Audience! It's time for some frank and useful
Talk with you, yes, by Dionysus my patron.
As sure as I want prizes and a name for wisdom

So surely I thought of you as a talented audience
And this, the wisest of all my comedies,
That you deserved first crack at it, as it cost me
The most trouble. The result was, I was defeated
Undeservedly, by mediocrities. It's your fault,
You wise ones, for whom I had worked so hard.
Even so I'll never abandon your talented members.
Since the day my Good Boy and my Punk were applauded
By men it gives me pleasure even to mention
And I—still a maid, not yet allowed to bear,
Exposed the child, and somebody else picked it up—
But you became its patron and raised it in style—
Since then you and I have been sworn allies.
Now, like Electra in the play, this comedy
Comes questing, trying to find a wise audience.
(It'll know its brother's hair if it comes upon it.)
Think what a Good Girl it is—first of all
It didn't come on with a stitched-up leather appendage
Red at the tip, and thick, a joy to the groundlings.
It didn't make fun of baldness, or dance dirty dances,
Nor is there an old man in it who punctuates speeches
With blows of his stick, to cover his bad jokes.
It didn't rush in with torches shouting: Hey!
But came forward confident of itself and its verses.
It's just like me; I'm not the sort of poet
Who relies on orgies or tries to get away with some rehash.
I'm always clever enough to bring on new material,
Never the same things twice, and all of them talented.
When Cleon looked big I smashed him in the belly
But I didn't want to stomp him once he was down.
While that bunch—once Hyperbolus gave them a handle
They keep beating up on the bum—and his mother too.
Eupolis first of all dragged on his Marikas
Remodeling my *Knights* in the worst way,
Sticking in a drunk old hag for her dirty dance;
Then Hermippus made another play from Hyperbolus
And then they all piled up on Hyperbolus
Plagiarizing my simile of the eels.
If you think that's funny you can forget *my* stuff.
But if I and my creations entertain you
By next season you'll be known as the smart crowd. (*Clouds* 518–62)

The *Clouds*, in other words, did not rely on surefire effects and hackneyed themes; it was a new kind of play—at its first production too much of a novelty for its audience.

A claim to "all new jokes" was probably generic in Old Comedy, and usually frankly disingenuous; the special point here, however, is the absence of broad comic effects. The *Clouds*, in its representation of family crisis, does anticipate to some degree the domestic naturalism of the New Comedy of Menander—for example, in Strepsiades' account of his son's achievements as an infant (877 ff.) and of his baby talk (1380 ff.). Perhaps it is this novelty which doomed the play: the Athenian audience was not yet ready for this vein of sentiment. It is true that when Aristophanes went back to the theme of father and son in the *Wasps*, he provided plenty of broad effects: there are orgiastic moments and dirty dancing, much is made of a phallus, and there is an old man who punctuates his remarks with a stick—or at least lays about him with a torch.

However, when Aristophanes revised the *Clouds*, he did not broaden it in this way—except, perhaps, for the burning of the house. It seems that by his revisions Aristophanes was trying to make his novelties work, to persuade his audience of the validity of a new kind of play. Aristophanes, whose plays so often take a retrogressive or reactionary position on cultural and political issues, was nevertheless seen by his contemporaries as an avant-garde poet, classed with that Euripides whom he so often takes as his adversary. And in fact the new parabasis of the *Clouds* precisely makes a claim to progressive art; in it Aristophanes claims for his work and its intended audience just those qualities ascribed in the *Clouds* to Socrates and Mr. Wrong: novelty *(ta kaina)*, wisdom *(sophia)*, and talent *(dexiotēs)*. The play, he says, is wise, and it is (still) in search of a wise and talented audience. It would seem to follow that the *Clouds* is not an anti-intellectual play but rather is intended as a contribution to a debate going on within the community of discourse constituted by the intelligent. In his revision, it seems, Aristophanes seems still to be speaking to that audience and to be clarifying the point that the play is indeed a play against Socrates.

I do not suggest that the *Clouds* was at any stage a play in favor of Socrates; however, as an attack on philosophy the play, particularly as originally constituted, is rather oblique. The plot of the *Clouds* centers on the relationship between father and son, and if it is about a social issue, it is about the failure of one generation to pass on its values to the next. Socrates appears in the context of this issue not so much as a cause but as a symptom. Socrates' Phrontisterion represents the sort of dumb stuff that finds all too ready an audience when society begins to break down. Nor are such doctrines wrong; they are simply not worth knowing. Socrates himself is not represented as contemptible. His accounts of the weather, for instance, are plausible and supported by evidence. His attempts to reform the language may be wrongheaded (such attempts usually are) but they are not stupid. The comedy is generated not by Socrates' teaching but by Strepsiades' failure to rise to its level. Socrates' language in the play is consistently temperate and not infrequently lofty, and he keeps his temper under considerable provocation. It is not even clear in the play that Socrates takes money for his teaching. Strepsiades certainly thinks he does (98, 245–46), but Strepsiades has many erroneous ideas about Socrates. The disciple's account of Socrates' method of feeding his school (175 ff.) is a notorious crux but certainly does not involve the sale of teaching. Strepsiades loses his cloak and sandals to the school (856 ff.), but this is represented as initiatory asceticism, not payment (497 ff.). When Strepsiades finally does give Socrates something, he speaks not of payment but of "showing respect for the teacher" (1147). Socrates' associates are not customers but devoted followers.

Socrates in the *Clouds,* in other words, is not a charlatan; he is a kook, a weirdo who believes his own stuff. His existence is no doubt to be regretted, but mainly as a sign of deep failures within the society, of its incapacity to maintain a sound cultural tradition. Only in the revised version is it made clear that Socrates is a toxic presence who must be eradicated.

The revised ending shows Socrates to be god-hated: on divine instruction Strepsiades burns his house. Mr. Wrong, victorious in debate, personifies Socrates' teaching and is a self-satisfied libertine. However, the social prognosis—that Socrates and Mr. Wrong are the wave of the future—is not in any way palliated. No successful alternative to Socrates is presented in the play—certainly not Mr. Right, who personifies the kind of boneheaded athleticism that caused Strepsiades' son to incur the debts in the first place. At the end Socrates goes down but Strepsiades is left with nothing; his victory feast has turned to ashes in his mouth and he has lost his son, whose last words are of loyalty to Socrates, of impiety, and of contempt for his father (1467–75). There is no reason to believe the Athenians would have liked this version any better than the other; it is too black, lacking that comic optimism which is otherwise to be found, in one form or another, in every one of Aristophanes' surviving plays.

In the *Clouds* Aristophanes lost touch with his popular audience, which he regretted. Such artistic errors must be motivated; I suggest that Aristophanes was pushed to this one by his terror of philosophy, a terror possible only to one wise enough to be tempted by its seductive power.

In these terms Plato (who is surely to be placed among "the wise") may have understood the play better than its original audience. However much the *Apology* misrepresents the social process that brought Socrates to conviction, Plato may still on another level be correct to represent Aristophanes as Socrates' true adversary—just as, in the *Symposium* (212c) it is Aristophanes alone who has something to say when Socrates has finished speaking. I would suggest, in terms of the contrast presented in *Republic,* book 10, that Aristophanes represents the poets as against the philosophers (*Republic* 607b). This is not a contrast between popular and elite values: although the poets (unlike the philosophers) may aspire to a popular audience, they are themselves *sophoi,* wise, and will value most the good opinion of the wise. The contrast, therefore, is between two kinds of intellectuality. For Aristophanes, further, this contrast is internal to poetry, since he consistently identifies the philosophers with Euripides—in the *Clouds* one mark of Pheidippides' conversion to philosophy is his taste for Euripides. (In the first version of the *Clouds* the connection was made vivid through a claim that Socrates was actually writing Euripides' plays: frag. 376 Kock, cf. Telecleides frags. 39 and 40.) Aristophanes thus places philosophy within a more general context of cultural change—from his point of view, cultural decadence. He (his playwriting persona, that is) has his heroes: Lamachus (*Frogs* 1039) and Aeschylus and Simonides and most of all, of course, himself. They all stand for certain values, which are threatened by his cultural adversaries: Theramenes (*Frogs* 967) and Euripides and most of all Socrates. Furthermore, both Socrates and Euripides are charged by the poet with honoring new gods. This issue brings up the question of Aristophanic piety.

The chorus of the *Clouds* is composed of minor divinities; this seems to have been no innovation, as we hear of a number of Old Comedies with titles like *Heroes, Horae,* or *Mousai.* Old Comedy, after all, plays with everything, including the gods; blasphemy, like obscenity and abuse, is a generic feature. The Poseidon and the Heracles of the *Birds* are coarse and stupid; the Dionysus of the *Frogs* soils himself with fear. By this standard the Clouds in the *Clouds* are treated respectfully. The blasphemy, if any, consists in their divinization. This may have been derived from Diogenes of Apollonia, who certainly made much of the Air, or it may be an Orphic touch (there is a late Orphic hymn to the Clouds: no. 21 Quandt), but was more probably Aristophanes' own invention. That the Clouds are divine certainly comes as a surprise to Strepsiades (329–30). It seems, therefore, that Aristophanes commits in the play the very crime of which he in that play accuses Socrates, and of which Socrates was certainly formally accused at his trial: the crime of introducing new gods. Furthermore, Aristophanes has these gods come forward and threaten the judges with bad weather if they fail to vote his play its deserved first prize (1115 ff.). This is the kind of cheerfully unscrupulous self-promotion typical of Old Comedy; Aristophanes has invented some gods and now makes them threaten with divine disfavor those who do not favor the play that invented them. He thus makes these gods his instrument, which is a further blasphemy. He does so, however, in the context of a ritual performance wherein blasphemy was traditional and therefore pious. The contrast between Aristophanes and Socrates in the *Clouds,* therefore, is between a pious and an impious blasphemy; this is another way of approaching the question of the philosophers and the poets.

Within the play this difference is represented as a difference between what Socrates knows and what the poet knows; Aristophanes knows more about the Clouds than his Socrates does, and ultimately the Clouds turn out to be on the side of the poet, not the philosopher. Socrates calls the Clouds "our *daimones*" (253) and says "they provide us with judgment, exposition and thought" (317) but their first words to him compare him unfavorably to Prodicus (359 ff.) and by the end of the play it becomes clear that their apparent admiration for Socrates is feigned; they have been using him to teach Strepsiades a lesson:

We always do that when we see
A man impassioned of wicked behavior:
We get him into deep trouble
Until he learns to fear the gods. (*Clouds* 1458–61)

Strepsiades responds: "Wicked [*ponēra*] of you, you Clouds, but just [*dikaia*]" (1462). Strepsiades deserves what he gets for thinking he might find new divinities who would enable him to escape from his responsibilities as a citizen: to tell the truth and pay his debts. The Clouds in turn are revealed as real Greek gods: untruthful, untrustworthy, and dangerous.

Since the Clouds in the *Clouds* are (according to the play) not false gods but real ones—indeed, they pray to Zeus, Poseidon, the Sun, and their father, Ocean (563 ff.)—the impiety of Socrates consists in the fact, not that he worships them, but rather that he worships them in the wrong way, that he does not understand them. The result is again curiously isomorphic with Meletus's accusation of Socrates at his trial, at least as represented in the *Apology.* Meletus there accuses Socrates of atheism: "he says the sun is fire and the moon a stone" (26d). At the same time he has charged Socrates with introducing "new *daimones*." But *daimones,* Socrates points out in his reply, must be either gods or the children of gods; therefore, Meletus is accusing him of believing in gods but not believing in gods—which is absurd.

This absurdity is at home in the *Clouds,* where Socrates is atheistic: "Gods are not current among us" (247–48); at the end Strepsiades says that he had "jettisoned even the gods through Socrates" (1477). Yet Socrates says the Clouds are "great goddesses" (316); "these are the only goddesses; the rest is drivel" (365). The doctrine seems to be that there are no gods because these are the only gods—along with Vortex *(dinos)* and the other powers by whom Socrates swears: "Chaos and the Clouds and Tongue" (424), "Aspiration, Chaos, Air" (627). To become a philosopher is to abandon the gods of the city for these gods. Socrates' atheism is represented as a specific religiosity.

The *Clouds* in fact reveals to us that the charge ridiculed by Socrates in the *Apology* is not so ridiculous as it is there made to appear. The gods of the philosophers are gods but they are also not gods, which is to say: Socrates treats them as persons (he speaks to them) but he describes them as impersonal forces. Strepsiades had thought that Zeus made the weather as a personal act; the Clouds make it by "necessity" *(anangkē;* 375, 378, 405). Weather, for Socrates, is naturalistically comprehensible; it is the action on a grand scale of the same forces observed in flatulence or cooking a sausage. This is to bring the heavens down to earth. The Clouds are not really gods but Nature. Yet Nature can be sworn by; the Clouds are also inspirational (331 ff.). Socrates, in other words, does not merely inquire into Nature; he adores it. The lesson is learned by Pheidippides: "Vortex is king, he kicked out Zeus" (1471). This is not to replace one god by another but to take as god something that is not god. That is the "hubris against the gods" (1506) for which the philosophers are justly punished by the burning of their house.

The difference may be abstractly stated in these terms: for Strepsiades, for a believer in the traditional gods, the universe is *meaningful;* for Socrates, by contrast, it is *intelligible.* Strepsiades, for instance, thinks that Zeus hurls his lightning at the perjurers (397)—that is, lightning is a *sign* of his displeasure. Socrates replies that lightning occurs by necessity; it is a *symptom* of a natural process. The personal gods disappear; instead, the philosopher claims a personal relation with the impersonal; he rises in his basket and establishes contact with the primal energy.

When in the original parabasis, however, the Clouds complain about the failure of the Athenians to honor them (576), their view of the weather is traditional, not Socratic; we made signs to you, they say, but you paid no attention (581–89). Once again, Socrates is wrong about the

Clouds; the weather is not intelligible but meaningful. The hail is not by necessity but is a communicative act.

In the course of the play, in fact, the Clouds are gradually revealed as in solidarity with the gods of the city; Vortex, a philosophical abstraction, is no doubt a fake, but the real and visible Clouds are real and visible divinities just like the sun and moon. (The Clouds report a conversation with the Moon and bring a message from her; 607 ff.) In the course of the play both Socrates and Strepsiades are punished—one by Hermes, the other by the Clouds—and theological order is restored.

Of course the Clouds are a joke. Aristophanes did not expect that as a result of his play the Athenians would institute a worship of clouds. They are gods only in the fictional world of the play. In the mind of Aristophanes' fictional Socrates, however, they have a different function: they are personified nature worshiped by the philosopher. On this point fiction imitates real life. The gods of philosophers are not a joke, nor are they invented. They are discovered; they are eternal realities in contrast to which the gods of the city appear as a traditional fiction. Whereas the gods of the city are mythical, the gods of the philosophers are empirical; we know of Zeus only the stories we have heard about him, but the action of the Vortex can be pervasively perceived in all the motions of nature. The philosophers worship the discoverable intelligibility of things; that is their hubris.

But it is not immediately clear why the gods of the philosophers should be thought a threat to the city. It is not as though the traditional gods had enforced the moral order; on the contrary, as figures of power rather than righteousness, great but not good, those gods often prove their greatness by their freedom from ethical norms. It is, in fact, one of the rhetorical tricks of philosophy to cite the traditional stories in order to prove that the ethical order need not command our respect. Zeus tied up his father (905) and cheated on his wife (1080), says Mr. Wrong; does this not suggest we would be at least as well off adoring the Vortex? The gods of the philosophers, after all, act by necessity and therefore are reliable, and in this sense truthful.

Philosophy, surely, did not set out to destroy the civic order. It set out rather to discover the sources of order, to reveal those things in the world that are truly eternal. It is a strange paradox that this quest for principles should become a cover for unprincipled behavior—but it is precisely this paradox which Aristophanes intends to set before us. Evidently the first draft did not quite make the point; in the revision the conquest of Right by Wrong showed the connection.

Mr. Wrong destroys ethics by an argument from Nature, according to which actions are not meaningful but intelligible. The man in the street thinks of action as a sign of the person; from good acts we can infer a good person with good intentions. But from the point of view of naturalistic analysis, action is symptomatic and stands to be explained rather than evaluated. Adultery, says Wrong, comes (like the lightning) from "the necessity of nature" (1075); once you can explain it in this way, you can abandon censorship; "use nature, skip, laugh." Having become psychologically intelligible, behavior ceases to be ethically meaningful.

Having abandoned the self to Nature, the liberated individual abandons also the fear of the gods and thus becomes godlike, with the ethical liberty characteristic of the gods. Of the two liberties of Zeus cited to him by Wrong, Pheidippides chooses not the one explicitly recommended to him—adultery—but the other, violence against the father, just like "the roosters and the other brutes" (1427), for to be godlike is also to resemble the beast.

There is a paradox of freedom and necessity in this union of the divine and the animal: once we discover that our impulses are after all completely natural, we feel ourselves free to pursue them. To understand ourselves is to pardon ourselves; therefore, the acceptance of animal necessity, the valuation of the release of the instincts, results paradoxically in a godlike freedom from restraint. The consequences are predictably disastrous. The *Clouds* sets before philosophy a familiar Greek warning: know that you are not a god (nor a beast either: "If you want to imitate a rooster / Go eat manure and sleep up in a tree"; 1430–31). This is a play about the ethical dangers of science; science, by uniting heaven and earth in a single net of necessities, denies us those human motives which alone make action meaningful. We act not out of good or evil but out of necessity. Responsibility for the self is replaced by knowledge of it.

The worship of the discoverable intelligibility of things, furthermore, is really a worship of the self: intelligibility is really there, but the discovery of it is to be credited to us. Nature, after all, simply exists; it has no ideas, although we have ideas about it. To idealize it, to worship it, is always a concealed idealization of our own activity in solving its riddles.

Because philosophy is an activity of the mind, the philosophers tend to think the mind the highest reality. This valuation of the intelligible and of the theoretical activity of the intellect is socially dangerous because it carries with it a practical attitude: that life should be lived not in accordance with what we believe but in accordance with what we know. This involves the illusion that nature exists for our good, or that we can make it so by observing the laws of nature. The myth of the Greek gods, unreliable and recurrently hostile to us, is precisely an antidote to this illusion. Erratically difficult, they embody a world order that is forever hostile to our projects.

The project of science, after all, is not merely knowledge but welfare; science aims, as Nietzsche remarks, not merely to understand the world but to *correct* it. Thus there arises an immediate antipathy between philosophy and the traditional order. That order, like the divinities it transmits to us, is essentially opaque. Much of the human world, after all, is essentially unintelligible because it is historical; all we can say is that things are as they are because that is the way they happened to come into being. A typical example is the irregularities of language. Thus we can understand why so much is made in the *Clouds* of Socrates' attempts to reform the Greek language; such an enterprise is inherently hostile to the city, to the extent that the city is founded on inherited conventions. The point is made most sharply in the original parabasis, where it is shown that calendar reform is hostile to the gods.

Philosophy has always been drawn to the utopian project of founding society on objective science, that is to say nature, rather than shared history, which is to say myth (for history can only be shared in the form of myth). Aristophanes stands with myth; he is a mythmaker who can play with past and future, with real persons mocked and transformed under their own names and linked in plot with imaginary beings, who can degrade and deform honor and righteousness and even the gods, so long as he stays close to his popular audience, so long as everyone can see that his play with tradition is an affirmation of the strength of a tradition that can cheerfully withstand such mockery. In the *Clouds* he lost this moral authority—perhaps because the play is too explicitly intellectual. In its appeal to "the wise," it ended up being pitched over everyone's head. When Aristophanes returned to these cultural themes in the *Frogs*—perhaps his greatest success—he made the spokesman of the new rationalism, not a philosopher, but the most popular of the poets, Euripides, and he provided within the play a spokesman for traditional values, Aeschylus. Socrates in that play makes only one appearance, in the concluding chorus:

Elegance is not to sit
Babbling with Socrates
Casting aside music
And leaving out the greatest part
Of the tragic art.
To pass one's time in idleness

Full of high sentence
And nit-picking nonsense
Is crazy behavior. (*Frogs* 1491–99)

It would seem that, whether or not he misrepresented the historical Socrates, Aristophanes really did think that Socrates personified the problem.

Calypso's Choice: Immortality and Heroic Striving in the *Odyssey* and *Ulysses*

STEPHANIE NELSON

Only through time time is conquered.   *T. S. Eliot*

There are many studies of Joyce's use of Homer, and yet there is still something missing.[1] The overall correspondences have been examined: Bloom and Telemachus as father and son seeking a reunion that can make both whole; Bloom as Odysseus slaying Boylan, the suitor, to regain Molly's affections; Stephen as the dispossessed son seeking his rightful position.[2] So also have the minor, and often very amusing, references: Bloom's cigar as the stake with which Odysseus blinds the Cyclops; the ball which wakens both Odysseus and Bloom in "Nausicaa"; Mulligan's *omphalos* as a reference to Ogygia, "the navel of the sea."[3]

What has gone unremarked is how deeply *Ulysses* reflects the deeper levels of meaning in the *Odyssey*. It is not merely a clever correspondence that Bloom, like Odysseus, ends his journey in bed, nor does it signify simply his conquest of his particular "suitors." Odysseus has regained his bed only by acknowledging his own vulnerability and dependence. So has Bloom.[4] And, more critically for this essay, as Bloom transmutes the role of the hero into ordinary life, so also Odysseus has been able to gain access to his present only by abandoning the heroic code that informed his past. Joyce wrote *Ulysses* about a new kind of hero, an ordinary hero. In a way, so did Homer.

We can gain a much deeper understanding of *Ulysses* by looking at the themes of the *Odyssey*—and vice-versa. Joyce, despite his lack of Greek, understood the *Odyssey* very well. As a result, *Ulysses* brings out Odyssean themes that have often gone unrecognized by scholars. One such theme is that of time. Time, entrapment in time, and the need to escape from time run very deep in Joyce's *Ulysses*. As Stephen famously remarks, "History is a nightmare from which I am trying to awake" (34).[5] Time is as important to Odysseus as it is to Stephen—only his response is rather different. Odysseus is trapped on Calypso's island, in a heroic, fairy-tale world of giants, seductive goddesses, and adventures, gazing always toward Ithaca, longing only for a glimpse of that most transient of things, the smoke from his own chimney (1.57–58). What Odysseus longs for is his wife, his home, and the real-life world of time and change and mortality. For him history is a nightmare that he is striving to reenter.

The Odyssey

HEROIC STRIVING

The aim of the hero is, ultimately, the defeat of time. That is, the hero aims to overcome his own mortality.[6] This appears from a number of directions. A hero overcomes boundaries, and the ultimate boundary is death. A hero seeks self-sufficiency, to act rather than to be acted upon. Like Achilles, or Aristotle's great-souled man, he will not be dependent, except, perhaps, on a friend (*Nicomachean Ethics* 1124b5–30).[7] But the ultimate dependence is our human dependence on time, and the ultimate suffering, our experience of our own mortality. The ultimate independence, then, is our freedom from these human limitations. And, above all, the hero seeks to transcend, to be superior, to achieve the greatest possible *aretē*. In other words, the final aim of the hero must be to become, as Heracles became, a god.

Odysseus's relation to heroism, however, is a paradoxical one. As Achilles is the great hero of the Trojan War, Odysseus is the great hero of *nostos,* of the return home from the war. But that return demands as well an abandonment of the heroic ideal that informed the *Iliad* but that has no place in the day-to-day world of Ithaca.[8] If this is so, and if heroism is defined by its striving for immortality, Odysseus, before he can return to Ithaca, must accept his mortality. He must submit to the world of time.

And so he does. The first choice we see Odysseus make in the *Odyssey* is his rejection of Calypso's offer of immortality. This choice, I will argue, is the focal point of Odysseus's return.[9] Odysseus, like Leopold Bloom, is neither, essentially, a man paralyzed by his loss of heroic identity nor an instrument of justice.[10] He is rather a man who has found a new defining goal for his existence, a goal that necessitates an acceptance of his own vulnerability. In other words, Odysseus is not a lost hero; he is, as Joyce saw, a modern man found.

At the center of the *Odyssey* Odysseus confronts the question of what it means to be a hero. In a sense he confronts it twice, for Odysseus confronts two quite different generations of heroes in Hades. The first is the older generation of heroes, the generation that included Oedipus and Heracles (11.266–80). The second generation is composed of his own contemporaries, the heroes of the Trojan War. The distinction is a traditional one. It is emphasized here by Odysseus's initially confining himself to a description of the women of the older generation. Only at Antinoos's request does he speak of his own comrades.

The last shade that Odysseus meets in Hades defines heroism in its most traditional terms. This is the shade of Heracles, the greatest of the "heroes, those men who perished before" (11.630: ἀνδρῶν ἡρώων, οἳ δὴ τὸ πρόσθεν ὄλοντο).[11] Or rather, as Odysseus corrects himself, he meets his "image / for he himself among the immortal gods / rejoices in feasting, and his wife is sweet-footed Hebe" (11.602–3: εἴδωλον· αὐτός δὲ μετ᾽ ἀθανάτοισι θεοῖσι / τέρπεται ἐν θαλίῃς καὶ ἔχει καλλίσφυρον Ἥβην). Heracles, the ultimate hero, has achieved the ultimate goal of the hero, immortality.

The older generation of heroes can find its archetype in the hero who becomes a god. The heroes of the Trojan War have a different archetype. This is the other great hero that Odysseus meets in Hades: Achilles, the hero defined by his *inability* to achieve divinity.[12] The hero, as he is redefined in Achilles, is mortal. He can achieve his immortality only through *kleos,* through a fame that is undying.[13] Thus, in the *Iliad,* Achilles is faced with the choice between a long, inglorious life and a short, glorious one. He, finally, makes the choice that defines the hero: not return to his home and family, but immortal fame. The complexity of Odysseus's sort of heroism becomes apparent exactly here. Odysseus too is given a choice between immortality and return. He decides for return home, to a world where death comes not gloriously and in violence, but quietly, from the sea.[14]

There is, however, another way to understand Odysseus's rejection of immortality. It is possible, in fact usual, to see Odysseus's decision to leave Ogygia, not as a rejection of heroic values, but as a deliberate pursuit of the heroic ideal. This is the case if Odysseus's rejection of immortality is motivated by his desire for *kleos*—a commodity in short supply on an island that even Hermes finds obscure.[15] It is true that Calypso, the "Concealer," absorbs an identity that Odysseus feels a need to regain, and that he can regain only in Ithaca. But this identity is not simply Odysseus's identity as a hero. *Kleos* is of crucial importance for a hero because it is the only type of immortality a mortal can achieve. As such, it cannot be a sufficient motive for declining immortality itself. No less a hero than Sarpedon, the son of Zeus himself, makes this perfectly explicit:

ὦ πέπον, εἰ μὲν γὰρ πόλεμον περὶ τόνδε φυγόντε
αἰεὶ δὴ μέλλοιμεν ἀγήρω τ᾽ ἀθανάτω τε
ἔσσεσθ᾽. οὔτε κεν αὐτός ἐνὶ πρώτοισι μαχοίμην
οὔτε κε σὲ στέλλοιμι μάχην ἐς κυδιάνειραν·
νῦν δ᾽ ἔμπης γὰρ κῆρες ἐφεστᾶσιν θανάτοιο
μυρίαι, ἃς οὐκ ἔστι φυγεῖν βροτὸν οὐδ᾽ ὑπαλύξαι,
ἴομεν, ἠέ τῳ εὖχος ὀρέξομεν, ἠέ τις ἡμῖν.

Dear lad, if the two of us could, escaping this battle,
Live always unaging and forever immortal
Then neither would I fight among the foremost myself
Nor urge you into battle, where men can win glory.
But now, since the spirits of death stand all about
In their thousands, and no man can flee nor escape them,
Let us go, and either win glory from someone, or have someone win glory
    from us. (12.322–28)

That Odysseus achieves *kleos* by leaving Ogygia is obvious—the poem itself is his renown. But this does not necessarily mean that *kleos* was why he left. Given Odysseus's willingness, if not propensity, to use concealment to achieve his ends, the very least we can say is that his concept of *kleos* is very different from Achilles'. In fact, Odysseus's sense of the importance of *kleos,* like his feelings about the heroic code altogether, will turn out to be deeply ambivalent.[16] Heracles reminds Odysseus of the similarity of their stories (11.617–26). As he does so, we cannot but be reminded of the critical difference, that the hero who tells this story to the Phaiakians has just refused, not *kleos,* but that which *kleos* itself achieves, immortality.

The significance of that refusal appears in Odysseus's meeting with the other archetype of heroism, Achilles. When they meet, Odysseus reassures Achilles that on earth his honor (*timē*) was equal to a god's, and that in death he rules and is not ruled. With these words Odysseus places himself firmly inside a world of heroic values. Achilles' answer appears at first to be an utter rejection of this code. He would, he declares, rather be a *thēs* (a hired servant) to a man without land of his own than king of all the perished dead (11.489–91). The meanest position among the living is preferable to the greatest possible *kleos* among the dead. And to be a *thēs* is the meanest possible position, for as Hesiod rather brutally reminds us (*Works and Days* 602), even a slave has a place and a position, whereas a *thēs,* and in particular a *thēs* to a man who is himself without property, is no more than a vagabond and a wanderer on the earth.

In fact, however, what Achilles expresses is not a rejection of heroism but a rejection of Hades. Although his words to Odysseus seem to reject the ideal of heroism, Achilles' questions about his son and father that follow concern not their lives so much as their honor. It is his father's *honor* that Achilles imagines himself protecting (11.494–503) and his son's *kleos* in which he finally rejoices (11.538–40). Achilles' outburst itself reveals a spirit that still must frame his choices in terms of absolutes. His *thēs* to a landless man is as utterly isolated, at the bottom of society, as Achilles, in life, was isolated at society's summit.

What Achilles has discovered is that the ultimate values of the hero cannot exist among the dead. In choosing a glorious death over a long and inglorious life, Achilles removed himself from a mortal's subjection to time. What he found was that that removal meant, not a greater freedom, but only a greater slavery. A *thēs* may have no status among the living, but he is still an agent. In Hades, a world where there is no change, there is also neither agency nor action.[17] Achilles and Agamemnon are frozen in a world of the past. When we meet them again in book 24 they will be repeating the same stories we heard in book 11. They will go on repeating them throughout eternity. The souls of Agamemnon and Achilles are now just as immortal as Calypso. But this immunity from death is, like the shades themselves (11.215–22, 475–76), a mockery, a shadow that defines, not what is, but what is not. The kind of "immortality" that the soul of Achilles has found has rendered his striving for it meaningless.

What Odysseus has encountered here, at the center of the *Odyssey,* is the essential paradox of heroism. What the hero strives for ends up as the negation of who he is.[18] The hero strives for immortality, but, as Sarpedon declares, it is the fact of mortality that makes even *kleos* of any worth. The hero strives to transcend, but in transcending society he transcends also his own cause and so transcends the very thing that gives his life meaning.[19] Thus, in the course of the *Iliad* Achilles moved beyond his political obligations to Agamemnon, beyond ties of fellowship to Ajax, beyond the ordinary dealing with others in battle, and finally beyond the human altogether, as in his treatment of Hector's corpse. Heracles' striving brought him beyond the human to the divine. Achilles' striving brings him, not closer to the gods, but only further away from other men.[20]

It is here that Odysseus's choice is most truly the opposite of Achilles'. Achilles chose to be a hero. Odysseus chooses instead a place within the ordinary world. It is an either/or situation. To be a hero is to fulfill a role given by society, and crucial to society, that also alienates the hero from society.[21] Odysseus, in striving to overcome his isolation, must also abandon his heroic role. Odysseus is, as the opening lines of the poem declare, "striving to save his own life" (ἀρνύμενος ἥν τε ψυχὴν), his *psychē,* his identity. What he learns in his encounter with Achilles is that this "life" is not one that can be saved by immortality.

RETURN

At first glance there seem to be three different worlds in the *Odyssey:* the heroic world of the *Iliad* (seen now through the eyes of Nestor and Menelaos), the ordinary day-to-day world of Ithaca, and the fantasy world of Odysseus's adventures. In fact there are only two: the magical, heroic world of the past and the mundane reality of the present.[22] The careful structure of the *Odyssey,* dividing the poem between Ithaca and Odysseus's adventures, leaves books 3 and 4 curiously out of place, tottering between the ordinary world of Ithaca and the fantasy world of Ogygia. At first, in Pylos, we seem to encounter simply the old heroic world of the *Iliad,* a world that, although strange to Telemachus, is remembered by Penelope and recalled by Phemius. But as we experience Sparta, the heroic world takes on a more and more fantastic appearance, until finally the worlds of Menelaus and of Calypso have come to look very much alike.

We are led into the association gradually, beginning with Menelaus's fabulous wealth, which Telemachus can compare only to Zeus's, and his power, power such that, while Telemachus can barely convene an assembly, Menelaus gives away entire cities without a second thought (4.174–77). In the world of the adventures Odysseus can be rescued from Circe by Hermes' magic herb. In Ithaca, in contrast, "magic herbs" are so far-fetched an idea that the suitors ridicule Telemachus with the notion that as a last resort he might try to poison them (2.325–30). But there are magic herbs aplenty in Sparta, and from Egypt, the most magic of places. Similarly, in the stories of Troy, Odysseus's disguises and Helen's ability to imitate the wives of all the warriors (4.240–89) are reminiscent of the world of the adventures, where anything is liable to become anything else. Ithaca, in contrast, is a very ordinary place, where Laertes never slept with

Eurykleia for fear of angering his wife (1.438), and where Telemachus finds that the easiest course is to leave home without telling his mother (2.372–76). As we read on, the heroic world comes to blend altogether into the world of magic. Menelaus's raid in Egypt, his encounter with Proteus, and his rescue through Proteus's sea-nymph daughter all seem taken directly from the world of the adventures, while the offer of Elysium made to Menelaus (4.361–70) echoes precisely Calypso's offer to Odysseus, at just the moment that Menelaus reveals to Telemachus that his father is trapped upon a magical island.[23]

Telemachus must go to Sparta to discover that his father is imprisoned on a magical island (4.555–60). Homer sets this discovery against another one—back in Ithaca the suitors discover that Telemachus is gone because Phronios needs his boat back (4.632–37). The placement brings out, humorously, the contrast between the old world and the new. The same contrast is at work in the poem's delight in juxtaposing the wonders of the heroic world with the commonplace concerns of ordinary reality. Gods disguising themselves as mortals are a commonplace of the adventures, as they are of the *Iliad*. In such a world the more mundane problems of such doubling simply do not arise. They arise in Ithaca, however, where Phronios, who saw Mentor/Athene depart for Pylos, is rather puzzled by the sight of the real Mentor still at home (4.653–56). In the *Iliad* Aphrodite whisks both Paris and Aeneas off the battlefield. The nymph Ino saves Odysseus with a magic veil (5.336–50). In contrast, Athene rescues Telemachus rather more mundanely—by borrowing a boat (2.386–87). And as "Mentor" leaves Nestor and Telemachus, explaining that he must set off early to collect a debt "neither recent, nor small" (3.367–68), s/he seems suddenly to forget which world she inhabits—and flies away, in good fantasy fashion, in the form of a sea hawk.[24]

As we turn to the world of adventures, it turns out to be governed by heroic codes. The first adventure, the raid on the Cicones, is detailed like the raids that occupy the background of the *Iliad,* that Odysseus invents in Ithaca, and that both Menelaus and Nestor describe.[25] The central adventure, the journey to Hades, reinforces the association of the magical and the heroic worlds, as does Odysseus's attempt to form a guest-friendship with Aeolus or Polyphemus, or his arming himself (against both reason and Circe's advice) against Scylla. The Sirens' reminder of Troy cements the association. Most important, however, the hero who slaughters hordes of common men before breakfast is a trope out of heroic time and as such is recalled, appropriately, by Achilles in Hades (11.593–96). It is not a rule that applies in Ithaca.[26] It is quite obvious, both to the suitors in the Assembly and to Telemachus, that even if Odysseus could return, he could do nothing against the suitors. No one could fight against such odds, not even a hero (2.246–51, 16.241–44).

What Homer has done is to blend legend with myth and set the result—a new version of the heroic world—against an Ithaca that seems far more reminiscent of the eighth century than of Mycenaean Greece.[27] The result is a reinterpretation of the heroic world with which Odysseus and Achilles, as well as Nestor and Menelaus, are associated. It is now the heroic world as dream world, as a world outside time. In contrast, in Telemachus's world, time proceeds relentlessly. Telemachus grows up. Laertes grows old. Antikleia dies. And the best contrivance Penelope can make against the inevitable wearing away of the memory of Odysseus is her weaving and unweaving of the shroud that Laertes, inevitably, some-day will need.

Odysseus's task is to get from one world to the other. It is, by defini-tion, impossible. It is impossible because the two worlds are not continu-ous; they obey different rules.[28] The heroic world as it appears in the *Odyssey* is a world in mythic time, where stories begin: "Once upon a time. . . ." The human world is our world, whether eighth-century Greece or twentieth-century Chicago. It is a world in historical time, where stories begin: "Yesterday in class . . ." or ". . . in the agora." It is just this impossibility, of passing from one world to the other, that we have been shown in Pylos and in Sparta. Time passes for Nestor and Menelaus as it does for Agamemnon and Achilles, in endless recollections of the past.[29] In the unflattering setting of realism, a world represented by the refreshing common sense of Peisistratus, Nestor and Menelaus, respected, wealthy, and powerful as they are, are not real forces.[30] In a contest with the suitors, Menelaus, for all that he is Zeus's son-in-law, would not be the favorite.

A KIND OF HERO

In the *Iliad* Odysseus seems to serve largely as a counterpoint to Achilles.[31] Where Achilles is isolated, Odysseus is social. The only human tie that Achilles (before book 24) is able to act on is his tie to the dead Patroclus. Odysseus, meanwhile, identifies himself as the agent of Agamemnon, the husband of Penelope, and, uniquely, as the father of Telemachus (2.260). As Achilles becomes more and more isolated from Agamemnon and any conventional social hierarchy, Odysseus, in the embassy of book 9, takes the repetition of Agamemnon's words upon himself. Odysseus, alone among the heroes of Troy, shares his *aristeia,* the Doloneia of book 10, with another hero. Above all, however, the contrast between Achilles and

Odysseus is embedded in their stories. Achilles is the hero destined never to return; Odysseus is the hero whose *nostos* is a given of legend. Achilles is the embodiment of the heroic paradox—he fits neither in the world of men nor in the world of gods. Odysseus's literary destiny will move him (rather unfairly) from the trace-horse of the *Oresteia* (*Agamemnon* 840–41) to the yes-man of later Greek tragedy. He is a different kind of hero.

This is the Odysseus we know when we first hear of Calypso's offer of immortality. It seems obvious, if only for this reason, that Odysseus's decision will be the opposite of Achilles'. Given the choice between divine isolation and human society, the Odysseus we know from the *Iliad* would choose the human. Accordingly the choice is underplayed.[32] The first indication of the choice is snuck into the text in Calypso's conversation with Hermes (5.135–36). It is treated by Odysseus and Calypso as a given of their relationship (5.205–10). It is treated in this way because it is not until Odysseus recounts his wanderings to the Phaiakians, until we have seen him transformed from the team player of the *Iliad* to the man like a savage lion, naked and alone on yet another strange shore (6.130–34), that we can appreciate the significance of the choice. Odysseus has arrived here through a long and gradual stripping away of his comrades. Boat by boat, and then one by one, Odysseus's companions succumb to the Cicones, to the Laestrygonians, to the Cyclops, to the threat of Circe (fulfilled for Elpenor), to Scylla, and finally on the island of Helios. When the last companion is gone, and he has faced the isolation that, in Achilles, seemed to grow from his own nature, Odysseus encounters Calypso and his choice. Odysseus, whose role in the *Iliad* was as the Greek Hector, the hero integrated into his society, is by the time of his choice completely alone.[33]

In his isolation Odysseus has also developed an ambivalence toward the heroic ideal. We see this first in Odysseus's reluctance to reveal his identity, a reluctance very unlike the man who broadcast his name to the Cyclops. We see it again as Odysseus both desires to hear and grieves at hearing Demodokos's accounts of Troy. As in the encounter with the Sirens, where he is invited, desires, and finally resists the temptation to live in the enjoyment of his heroic past, Odysseus seems to both want and not want to identify himself with the qualities of a hero. He has to be goaded into displaying his prowess in games, but when goaded becomes furious at the picture of himself as a merchant (8.145–85).[34] In telling his own story he recounts seeing the shades of famous women in Hades. He does not mention the shades of his companions in Troy until urged by Antinoos.

What lies behind Odysseus's ambivalence may be glimpsed in one of the curious inverted similes that the *Odyssey* occasionally employs.[35] When Odysseus first hears Demodocus sing of Troy he weeps:

ὡς δὲ γυνὴ κλαίῃσι φίλον πόσιν ἀμφιπεσοῦσα,
ὅς τε ἑῆς πρόσθεν πόλιος λαῶν τε πέσῃσιν,
ἄστει καὶ τεκέεσσιν ἀμύνων νηλεὲς ἦμαρ·
ἡ μὲν τὸν θνῄσκοντα καὶ ἀσπαίροντα ἰδοῦσα
ἀμφ' αὐτῷ χυμένη λίγα κωκύει· οἱ δέ τ' ὄπισθε
κόπτοντες δούρεσσι μετάφρενον ἠδὲ καὶ ὤμους
εἴρερον εἰσανάγουσι, πόνον τ' ἐχέμεν καὶ ὀιζύν·
τῆς δ' ἐλεεινοτάτῳ ἄχει φθινύθουσι παρειαί·
ὣς Ὀδυσεὺς ἐλεεινὸν ὑπ' ὀφρύσι δάκρυον εἶβεν.

As a woman weeps, falling over the body of her husband,
Who fell, before the city and the people,
Warding off from the town and the children the pitiless day.
And she, seeing him dying and gasping,
Throws herself over him and cries piercingly. But they are behind,
Beating her with spears on the back and the shoulders,
Stirring her up, driving her on, to have labor and sorrow.
And her cheeks wither with the hard pain of her sorrow.
So Odysseus wept sorrowful tears from under his eyebrows. (8.523–31)

The experience is not that of Achilles, or even of Hector, but of Andromache. Odysseus has come to experience the heroic code, not (as in the poem's introduction) as a sacker of cities, but as the sacked.[36] The implication of the simile, which will unfold throughout the rest of the poem, is that Odysseus has come to see himself not only as the warrior that others depend upon but also as one of the dependent. He is now not only the one who acts; he is also the one acted upon.

Odysseus's ambivalence about his identity as a hero has emerged in the course of his achieving, despite himself, the hero's greatest goal. The goal is independence. When Odysseus lands upon the shore of Phaiakia, his *kleos* extends to heaven (9.20) and there is no one to whom he is beholden. But Odysseus's independence, in the paradoxical way of heroism, is not freedom. It is rather a slavery to circumstance. He has found not pure agency but only isolation. Hence the choice Odysseus makes on Ogygia. Hence, also, the nature of his return.

Odysseus's return, particularly as it is contrasted to Agamemnon's, is the essence of all that is unheroic. It is, of course, exactly for that reason that it is successful. From the mock battle with Iros to the image of Odysseus tormented like a goat's paunch tossing on the fire (20.25–27), Odysseus's homecoming reads more like a parody of epic than like a hero imposing his will on a recalcitrant world. Even the token by which Odysseus is recognized, his scar, betokens not strength but vulnerability. Until, of course, the battle with the suitors. Despite all the care with which Homer rationalizes Odysseus's victory (the bow and arrows, the stance near the door, the use to which he puts his companions), the relief with which Odysseus sheds his beggar's rags is at least partially a relief in taking on once more the power of the hero. Odysseus, splattered like a lion with the blood of the suitors (23.47–48), seems to have resumed his heroic stance along with his heroic simile.

It seems to be for just this reason that the poem cannot end here.[37] Odysseus may conquer the suitors, but it is Penelope who conquers Odysseus. In her unique version of the "bed trick" Penelope recognizes Odysseus—again, not through his strength but through his vulnerability. It is not Odysseus's revelation of the secret of the bed but rather his anger that it has been moved that provides the emotional climax of the *Odyssey*.[38] It does so because Odysseus's anger reveals, finally, where his emotional dependence lies. The secret shared by Odysseus and Penelope is a revelation to the reader. The stable center of Odysseus's world is not the storeroom where his bow lay and which Odysseus has sought so diligently to fill. It is the bed that he himself fixed into the earth.[39] It is to this that Odysseus has been returning, and this to which he will return again. It was for this that he turned down immortality and chose instead a life in time. It was also this, his acknowledgment, in his very core, of his dependence upon another, that enabled him to move from the world of the hero into the world of human life.

Odysseus speaks of his choice between return and immortality twice in the course of the *Odyssey*, once at his first meeting with Antinoos, before he has described his adventures (7.254–58), and finally in bed, as he and Penelope go through with one another the time they have lost (23.333–37). As the *Odyssey* is structured it is only here, the third time we have heard of the choice, that we can truly understand it. To be immortal is to achieve the heroic ideal because it is completely to lose one's dependence on others. In choosing Penelope over Calypso, Odysseus chose rather to lose his independence, and with it his isolation. As it is the bed that he shares with Penelope that is the center and defining point of his existence, it is here, and only here, that the meaning of Odysseus's choice can become clear.

Ulysses

Bed is also the center of Leopold Bloom's world, where, as his epic comes to an end, he rests:

Womb? Weary?
He rests. He has traveled. (737)

Unfortunately, in his case, it is not a bed to which he has exclusive rights.

Bloom is, of course, Odysseus made Everyman. If Odysseus's response to Calypso's choice, his rejection of immortality, is also a rejection of heroic striving, Joyce's *Ulysses* should stress the theme. But on this point the book seems curiously silent. In fact Joyce's parallels are such that there seems nowhere to put it. Bloom cannot choose between Ogygia and Ithaca or between Calypso and Penelope, because in *Ulysses* Ithaca *is* Ogygia, and Calypso *is* Penelope. Where Leopold Bloom ends up at the close of *Ulysses* is exactly the place he started from, 7 Eccles St., with precisely the female he began with, his wife.[40] Leopold Bloom does not have the ability to choose between different worlds. What he has instead is a choice between radically different ways of viewing the one world that modern man, of necessity, inhabits.

The issue first appears as a choice between time and immortality, but in its Christian guise, that is, as a choice between the body and the spirit. Calypso's choice, for Leopold Bloom, is represented by the nymph he has cut out from *Photo Bits* and posted over his and Molly's bed (65, 546).[41] It is her eternal beauty that represents immortality in *Ulysses*. Bloom seems to yearn for it, in Davy Byrne's, in the Library, and obsessively in Nighttown.

The attraction of the nymph is that she represents a way to stop time, and it is time that is inexorably pulling Bloom away from Molly. The thought runs through his head throughout the "Laestrygonians": "I was happier then. Or was that I? Or am I now I? . . . Can't bring back time. Like holding water in your hand" (168). "Two. Pub clock five minutes fast. Time going on. Hands moving. Two. Not yet" (173). "Just a bite or two. Then about six I can. Six. Six. Time will be gone then. She" (174). "She kissed me. I was kissed. All yielding she tossed my hair. Kissed, she kissed me. / Me. And me now" (176). These thoughts of time, and of himself trapped in the stream of time, run directly into a picture of the nymph come to life:

Suppose she did Pygmalion and Galatea what would she say first? Mortal! Put you in your proper place. Quaffing nectar at mess with gods, golden dishes, all ambrosial. Not like a tanner lunch we have, boiled mutton, carrots and turnips, bottle of Allsop. Nectar, imagine it, drinking electricity: god's food. Lovely forms of women sculpted Junonian. Immortal lovely. And we stuffing food in one hole and out behind. (176)

The nymph is spirit and purity and immortality. She is an escape from the threat of time and a removal from what is gross and bodily. Bloom, nonetheless, like Odysseus, finally rejects what she offers.

Bloom, being Bloom, is led on by his meditations to wonder if goddesses require the "hole behind." Being Bloom, he investigates, by examining the statues of goddesses in the library. In their encounter in Nighttown the nymph cites the results of the investigation: "We immortals, as you saw today, have not such a place and no hair there either. We are stonecold and pure. We eat electric light" (551). But Bloom is not, finally, tempted by the eternal purity of the nymph, any more than he is tempted by religion's offer of immortality. What begins as the nymph's rejection of Bloom ends as Bloom's rejection of the "ethereal": "You have broken the spell. The last straw. If there were only ethereal where would you all be, postulants and novices? Shy but willing, like an ass pissing" (553). Bloom's Calypso, along with her spirituality, purity, and immortality, turns out to be, quite literally, merely a cracked plaster saint.[42]

For Bloom, as for Odysseus, the alternative to immortality is life. In Bloom's case the choice between immortality and return has become a choice between the soul and the body. He chooses the body. The Achilles that Leopold Bloom meets in Hades is, of all people, Martha Clifford, his secret correspondent. Our fate after death recalls to Bloom a typo from her letter. She had meant to write: "I do not like that other word." In fact, as Bloom recalls, she wrote: "I do not like that other world." He muses (emphasis mine):

I will appear to you after death. You will see my ghost after death. My ghost will haunt you after death. There is another world after death named hell. *I do not like that other world she wrote.* No more do I. Plenty to see and hear and feel yet. Feel live warm beings next to you. Let them sleep in their maggotty beds. They are not going to get me this innings. Warm beds: warm fullblooded life. (115)

But if Bloom finally rejects "that other world" in rejecting the nymph's offer of a removal from time through the spirit, he also rejects the purely physical escape of sensuality. In "Hades," in the "Laestrygonians," and finally in the "Oxen of the Sun" episode, Bloom, whose sense of the world is nothing if not concrete, encounters the world as purely physical. What he sees, and rejects, most particularly in the conversation of the medical students, is a physicality as impersonal and empty as the spirituality of the nymph or as its direct counterpart, the romantic fantasy of Gertie MacDowell.[43]

Joyce uses the theme of Calypso and of rejected immortality to resolve a division of the physical and the spiritual, of Molly and Bloom, and of Bloom and Stephen that has been developing throughout the book. Bloom himself, the spiritual to Molly's physical, and the physical to Stephen's spiritual, is the resolution. In a fine example of Joycean humor, Bloom is in fact offered immortality in *Ulysses*—when Stephen points out that the soul, as a simple substance, must be incorruptible and so (barring divine practical jokes) immortal. Bloom (unwittingly) rejects the offer, on the grounds that there are few truly simple souls (634). If there are any, Bloom's is not among them. His soul is firmly anchored to his body. Odysseus finds human life in the space between Hades and Ogygia. Bloom will find it somewhere between the spirit and the flesh, between the nymph and *Sweets of Sin,* in Molly's "ample bedwarmed flesh" (61, 734).

BLOOM THE HERO

The promise of the immortal nymph shows up again in "Ithaca," this time in explicitly Odyssean terms. Bloom is contemplating departure:

What universal binomial denominations would be his as entity and nonentity?
Assumed by any or known to none. Everyman or Noman.
What tributes his?
Honor and gifts of strangers, the friends of Everyman. A nymph immortal, beauty, the bride of Noman. (727)

The promise of departure leads, for Bloom, to the promise of return and revenge:

Would the departed never nowhere nohow reappear?
. . . he would somehow reappear reborn above delta in the constellation of Cassiopeia and after incalculable eons of peregrination return an estranged avenger, a

wreaker of justice on malefactors, a dark crusader, a sleeper awakened, with financial resources (by supposition) surpassing those of Rothschild or of the silver king. (727–28)

But, upon further consideration, the possibility is rejected.

Calypso's choice appears in *Ulysses* as the choice between body and soul, between a full physical participation in the world and a rejection of the world of change and decay.[44] As in the *Odyssey,* the choice is underplayed. This is largely because there is no great struggle in making it. For Bloom, as for Odysseus, the choice of life over immortality is not so much a decision that he makes as a revelation of who he is.

The choice that Bloom does make in the novel, although on a more subconscious than conscious level, concerns *how* he will be engaged in the world, whether as an active or as a passive participant. Bloom, in other words, must decide whether or not to be a hero. Bloom knows of the assignation with Boylan. He can either accept Molly's adultery or refuse to accept it. To accept the adultery is to choose rest rather than struggle. To refuse to accept it is the "heroic" choice—the choice of revenge. As a choice between oblivion and struggle, this is, essentially, another version of Calypso's choice. Calypso and Penelope are, in *Ulysses,* the same person. It is natural that they should be, since Molly, by forcing Bloom to choose between passivity and revenge, presents Bloom with both of Odysseus's alternatives.

Revenge is the option favored by Dublin. In *Portrait of the Artist,* Simon Dedalus sings: "What can't be cured, sure, / Must be *injured,* sure, / So I'll go to / Americay" (88, emphasis mine). The Freudian slip sums up the feeling of the city. There is no enduring injury in Dublin; there is only (as is vividly illustrated in *Dubliners*) revenge, frustration, hatred, and isolation. In the carriage to the funeral, in the newsroom, in Davy Byrne's, in the maternity hospital, the Dublin conversation that we overhear in the course of the day is malicious and divisive. The narrator of the Cyclops episode, whose corrosive derision is applied indiscriminately, only sums up an attitude that has occupied the background of the entire book.[45] If Ireland is an old sow that eats her farrow, Dublin is the sow that does so with relish.

Bloom, who refuses the option of revenge, is the exception. When we first meet Leopold Bloom, he is wondering how he looks to the cat (55). Later, unexpectedly, Bloom recalls how he was mocked by the newsboys. As both instances show, Bloom has a quality nearly unique in *Ulysses,* the ability, as he says, to "see ourselves as others see us" (129, 376).

The uncomfortable side of this is expressed by the narrator of the Cyclops episode:

—I'm talking about injustice, says Bloom.
—Right, says John Wyse. Stand up to it then with force like men.
That's an almanac picture for you. Mark for a softnosed bullet. Old lardyface
standing up to the business end of a gun. Gob, he'd adorn a sweepingbrush, so
he would, if he only had a nurse's apron on him. (333)

Bloom refuses the alternative of revenge. In so doing he fully lives up to
Dublin's expectations of him. That he is perfectly aware of this we will
find out only in Nighttown.

In the "Laestrygonians" Bloom sees in the degrading physicality that
surrounds him an epiphany of Dublin: "Every fellow for his own, tooth
and nail. Gulp. Grub. Gulp. Gobstuff. . . . Eat or be eaten. Kill! Kill!"
(170).[46] The alternative that runs through his mind is the welcoming physicality of Molly on Howth Head (176).[47] This is what Bloom, "the new
apostle to the Gentiles" will preach in Barney Kiernan's, love—as he says,
the opposite of hatred (333). This love, or acceptance, is also the opposite
of revenge.

The difficulty lies in the list that follows:

Nurse loves the new chemist. Constable 14A loves Mary Kelly. Gerty MacDowell
loves the boy that has the bicycle. M. B. loves a fair gentleman. . . . You love a
certain person. And this person loves that other person because everybody loves
somebody but God loves everybody. (333)

"You love a certain person. And this person loves that other person" is
precisely Bloom's problem.[48] "Universal love," as the citizen calls it, is fine
for God, but human beings prefer to love someone in particular. It is not
Bloom's relation to the "Gentiles" that he is worried about; it is his relation to Molly.

In one of Joyce's keys to *Ulysses* Bloom's "suitors" are described as his
"scruples," his "bow" as "reason." "Scruples" is a little word for a very
powerful emotion. It is an emotion that Bloom, by avoiding the thought
and the sight of Boylan, has been dodging all day.[49] He faces it in
Nighttown. To choose acceptance rather than revenge means to be willing to be dominated. Bloom's fantasy explores this in the scene with
Bella/Bello Cohen. It also means to be willing to be replaced. The fantasy,
accordingly, casts Bloom, like Odysseus, as a servant in his own home. As
Odysseus passively acquiesces while the servingwomen go out to sleep

with the suitors (20.4–13) Bloom's humiliating acceptance of Molly's adultery is played out in a scene where Bloom, a pandering servant, watches engrossed as Boylan and Molly have sex (565–67).[50]

Bloom is able to work through his fantasy of being dominated by finally rejecting both the physical domination of Bello Cohen and the spiritual domination of the nymph (553–54). Bloom's fantasy of pandering, however, is resolved in a much stranger way, through the blending of his image, adorned with the horns of a cuckold, with the images of Stephen and of Shakespeare (567). To see the significance of this we will have to turn, once again, to the theme of time.

TIME—THE FINAL ENEMY

Bloom's epic, like Odysseus's, is about trying to find the way home.[51] The problem is that neither of Bloom's alternatives, revenge or acceptance, can achieve this. Neither will bring him back to Molly. Revenge, the heroic alternative, is "heroic" because it is a claim to self-sufficiency and independence. For Bloom, "revenge" must mean the mental revenge of bitterness and resentment, an attitude which leads to the alienation pervasive in Dublin. But acceptance of the adultery means also detachment, which must separate Bloom from Molly as surely as remaining on Calypso's island must separate Odysseus from Penelope. Both of Bloom's choices, acceptance or revenge, mean isolation. Like Odysseus, if Bloom is to be a hero, he must find a new kind of heroism.

The problem, essentially, is time. To accept Molly's adultery is also to accept the inevitable flow of time, which is continuously moving Bloom away from his wife, his daughter, his own youth, and the times of togetherness:

Milly too. Young kisses: the first. Far away now past. Mrs. Marion. Reading lying back now, counting the strands of her hair, smiling, braiding.[52]

A soft qualm regret, flowed down his backbone, increasing. Will happen, yes. Prevent. Useless: can't move. (67)

Time is irreversible. On this particular day it is particularly irreversible, as Bloom watches the hour of Molly and Boylan's assignation, the hour that will divide him from Molly, inexorably approaching.[53] The only "solution" arrives, humorously, in the device of his watch—which stops at precisely the time of the adultery (370). It is no solution. It does not bring Molly back; it only freezes Bloom.[54]

Bloom's problem, in a nutshell, is that return is "irrational" because of the "unsatisfactory equation between an exodus and return in time through reversible space and an exodus and return in space through irreversible time" (728). One can return in space, but not in time. As Bloom says about Parnell: "And the coming back was the worst thing you ever did because it went without saying you would feel out of place as things always moved with the times" (651).[55] Bloom learned that lesson this morning, while he was shopping for his doubly unkosher pork kidney. He cannot return to the land of his fathers. That land is dead—present in space, but not in time (61).[56] Bloom's response recalls Odysseus's longing to see the smoke from his own hearth: "To smell the gentle smoke of tea, fume of the pan, sizzling butter. Be near her ample bedwarmed flesh. Yes, yes" (61). There is no return to the past. There is only return to the future.

The solution lies in altogether another revenge piece, not the *Odyssey,* but *Hamlet.* It is Stephen's play rather than Bloom's. Or rather, it is the play where the two, unwittingly, come together.[57] Stephen, quite self-consciously, sees himself as Hamlet the injured son. Bloom, quite unconsciously, identifies himself with Hamlet the wronged husband, the bereaved father, and the returned ghost (152). Stephen argues that father and son are one, that "Hamlet's grandson is Shakespeare's grandfather and that he himself is the ghost of his own father" (18). Accordingly, in Nighttown, the roles combine into the composite picture of Bloom, Stephen, and Shakespeare, and then into Shakespeare's double, the compassionate Martin Cunningham, who forgives his erring wife (96, 568).[58] This should be Bloom's final acceptance of his own detachment—but before we come to a resolution the scene fades into Stephen.

Hamlet is, literally, where Bloom and Stephen come together. The play also provides the key to their relationship. The two Hamlets, father and son, have an inverse relationship: revenge, the solution for Hamlet the father is, for Hamlet the son, the problem. Similarly, Bloom's problem, his inability to recapture the past, is Stephen's solution, while Stephen's problem, his inability to escape the past that has formed him, is exactly the solution Bloom needs. For Bloom, there is no revenge because you can never return again—the ghost is only a ghost and so cannot act. For Stephen, to act at all is to bind yourself into the past and recognize that you are only your father's creature.

Bloom and Stephen, throughout the course of the novel, have unwittingly provided the answers to each other's riddles.[59] Stephen asks his mother, "What is the word known to all men?" Bloom answers, to Alf Bergan, that the word that "everyone knows" is love, the opposite of hatred (333). Bloom asks, "Or was that I? Or am I now I? . . . Rudy" (168). Stephen replies to John Ellington:

. . . through the ghost of the unquiet father the image of the unliving son looks forth. In the intense instant of imagination, when the mind, Shelley says, is a fading coal, that which I was is that which I am and that which in possibility I may come to be. (194)

To Bloom, time carries him inescapably away from himself. For Stephen, "History is a nightmare from which I am trying to awake" (34). Bloom contemplates the impossibility of return; Stephen thinks of Maeterlinck: "If Socrates leave his house today he will find the sage seated on his door-step. If Judas go forth tonight it is to Judas his steps will tend" (213). For Stephen, not return, but escape, is impossible.[60]

Bloom has tried the Maeterlinck solution already, in "Nausicaa," only to run up, once more, against the irreversibility of time: "Curious she an only child, I an only child. So it returns. Think you're escaping and run into yourself. Longest way round is the shortest way home. And just when he and she. Circus horse walking in a ring. Rip van Winkle we played. . . . All changed. Forgotten. The young are old" (377). What he has missed, what he will gain from Stephen, is memory.[61] For Bloom, memory bars him from his past; for Stephen, it binds him to it.

What Bloom cannot see in his own case is immediately apparent to him in Stephen, at the moment that he sees before him a single boy/man, uniting present and past (422). This unity is the key to Stephen's phrase "fabled by the daughters of memory" (24). Memory links the past to the present, showing us the present as the product of the past. But it also "fables" the past, reshaping the past in terms of the present. The child that Bloom remembers, who "frowns a little just as this young man does now with a perhaps too conscious enjoyment of danger" (422), is colored by the young man before him. The charade of Rip Van Winkle played with Molly now has a meaning for Bloom that it could not possess at the time. This power of memory, not to distance the present from the past but to unite the two, is what Stephen gives to Bloom, just as Bloom's sense of detachment from his past is what he can give to Stephen.[62]

This power of memory over time is also shown us by the novel itself. At the very moment that Stephen and Bloom are both, in their different ways, despairing of the possibility of undoing time, Joyce is doing just that. *Ulysses* is as active in re-creating time as it is in re-creating Bloom and Stephen. Time in the novel is elastic; it stretches, as a character's interior monologue extends far beyond the moment he is given for his thought; it condenses, as hours disappear into the breaks between epi-sodes; it doubles back on itself, as Stephen's morning replays itself as Bloom's.[63] Most of all Joyce shows us himself using the novel to re-create himself, for "fabled by the daughters of memory" (the Muses), Stephen and Bloom *are* united, as the past and the present of James Joyce.[64] As the author of *Ulysses* Joyce has quite literally made himself, as God and Shakespeare did before him, his own father: "He Who Himself begot" (197, 208).[65] In so doing he has undone time.

The solution to Bloom's problem is, it turns out, exactly the same as the problem. It is his, and every human being's, dependence upon each other. Bloom's life is involved with all the lives of the novel in ways he cannot even begin to imagine. Bloom does not know this, but he has an inkling. The "scruples" that Bloom slays in "Ithaca" are his own fears about what his acceptance of Molly's adultery means. His weapons are abnegation and equanimity (733). He "justifies to himself his sentiments" (734) through the fact of simple grammatical reciprocity:

the natural grammatical transition by inversion involving no alteration of sense of an aorist preterite proposition (parsed as masculine subject, monosyllabic onomatopoetic transitive verb with direct feminine subject) from the active voice into its correlative aorist preterite proposition (parsed as feminine subject, auxiliary verb and quasimonosyllabic onomatopoetic past participle with complementary masculine agent) in the passive voice. (734)

In other words, "Boylan fucked Molly" is also "Molly was fucked by Boylan." As once "Kissed, she kissed me" (176), Bloom cannot separate Molly from the world, and will not separate her from himself.

Leopold Bloom is, above all, a practical man. Having rejected both of the alternatives offered by his Calypso, either acceptance and isolation or return and revenge, he solves his dilemma in the only way possible— he avoids the need to return by recognizing that he cannot depart (728).[66] In other words he adopts Stephen's problem as his solution. Bloom, who cannot even persuade Stephen to stay the night, cannot become him, nor can he find his satisfaction in the "universal love" that is exclusively God's. What he can do, however, is to kiss Molly's bedwarmed flesh, tell her the story of his day, and sleep in the "dark bed" (737) that he has allowed to remain its center. What he can do is accept the interdependence of all creatures. As Bloom and Molly lie

At rest relatively to themselves and to each other. In motion being each and both carried westward, forward and rearward respectively, by the proper perpetual motion of the earth through everchanging tracks of neverchanging space. (737)

Bloom's motion, *sub specie aeternitatis,* has succeeded in becoming the same as Molly's.

As Penelope tells Odysseus: "The gods granted us misery, / in jealousy over the thought that we two, always together, / should enjoy our youth, and then come to that threshold which is old age" (23.210–12). Time, once past, can never be recovered. But time, equally, can never be escaped; Odysseus's voyages are not yet over and will not be until "death comes to him softly from the sea." What Odysseus chose when he chose dependence on Penelope over the invulnerability offered by Calypso was a life in time. This is also what Bloom chooses—not because the fact of time can bring him back to Molly, but because the fact of time means, as Stephen sees only too well, that he can never leave.

Notes

1. What is missing, as will appear below, is the sense in which both works reverberate reality, and in harmony. It is David Grene—in classes, in readings (he does an exceptional Mr. Deasy), and in conversation—who first showed me this. David, as both a Dubliner and a classicist, has a rather unique authority here. But even more important is David's way of reading literature, attempting to find, as he says, the "center of gravity" of the work and not imposing himself on the text (as he will not impose his sense of a text on his students), but rather developing his understanding from it. This approach has helped me, and so many other students, to develop our own insights with the aid of his knowledge and understanding. This is the greatest debt any of us can owe to our teachers. It is even better than his reading of Mr. Deasy.

2. For studies of the parallels of the overall plot and of particulars, see Hugh Kenner, *Ulysses* (London: George Allen and Unwin, 1980), 19–30, who points out also the distinction between the broad overall pattern and "trivial" correspondences; Joseph Prescott, *Exploring James Joyce* (Carbondale: Southern Illinois University Press, 1966), 28–50, with attention to Joyce's revisions; Stuart Gilbert, *James Joyce's "Ulysses"* (New York: Alfred A. Knopf, 1930), 71–78 and passim; Anthony Burgess, *Here Comes Everybody* (London: Faber and Faber, 1965), 88–93; Daniel R. Schwarz, *Reading Joyce's "Ulysses"* (New York: St. Martin's Press, 1987), 37–44; David Fuller, *James Joyce's "Ulysses"* (New York: St. Martin's Press, 1992), 32.

3. See Prescott, *Exploring James Joyce,* 32; and Gilbert, *James Joyce's "Ulysses,"* 51. See also Gilbert's excellent analysis (48–53) of the significance of the *omphalos* theme—where, however, Telemachus's need to "sever the umbilical cord" with Penelope in the corresponding *Odyssey* scene is not mentioned.

4. "*Ulysses* is a story, and a simple story at that. It is a story about the need of people for each other, and Joyce regards this theme as so important that he has to borrow an epic form in which to tell it" (Burgess, *Here Comes Everybody,* 87).

5. James Joyce, *Ulysses* (New York: Vintage Books, 1961).

6. See, in particular, Seth L. Schein, *The Mortal Hero: An Introduction to Homer's "Iliad"* (Berkeley and Los Angeles: University of California Press, 1984); and Laura M. Slatkin,

The Power of Thetis: Allusion and Interpretation in the "Iliad" (Berkeley and Los Angeles: University of California Press, 1991), esp. 38–52. Schein (17) points to a similar focus in the *Gilgamesh* tradition, while Stephen Scully, in *Homer and the Sacred City* (Ithaca: Cornell University Press, 1990), adds a new aspect to this understanding by seeing the Homeric city, and Achilles himself, as a paradoxical blend of the divine and the tragically mortal. See also Jean-Pierre Vernant, "Death with Two Faces," in *Reading the "Odyssey": Selected Interpretive Essays,* ed. Seth Schein (Princeton: Princeton University Press, 1996).

7. Notice that both Diomedes and Achilles, the two most extreme of the heroes in the *Iliad,* express the wish that they could fight with only a single companion (16.97–100).

8. Cedric H. Whitman, "The *Odyssey* and Change," in *Twentieth Century Interpretations of the "Odyssey,"* ed. Howard W. Clarke (Englewood Cliffs, N.J.: Prentice-Hall, 1983), 90–99, sees Odysseus as representing the old world in the new. See also Anne Armory, "The Reunion of Odysseus and Penelope," in *Essays on the "Odyssey": Selected Modern Criticism,* ed. Charles H. Taylor, Jr. (Bloomington: University of Indiana Press, 1969), 111; and David Grene, "The *Odyssey:* An Approach," *Midway,* no. 9 (1969): 47–68: "The smoke from the chimney, the bed made from the tree anchored in the room, the crooked paths up and down the hills of Ithaca—these are descriptions where the perceived externals fuse with some deeper aspect of meaning. They have nothing to do with the Sirens or the strait between Scylla and Charybdis" (57).

9. For a rare appreciation of the importance of this episode, see Jean-Pierre Vernant, "The Refusal of Odysseus," in *Reading the "Odyssey,"* ed. Schein, 185–89.

10. See Douglas J. Stewart, *The Disguised Guest: Rank, Role, and Identity in the "Odyssey"* (Lewisburg: Bucknell University Press, 1976), esp. 31–74, for the argument that Odysseus is paralyzed by his loss of heroic identity; and Charles Segal, "The Phaeacians and the Symbolism of Odysseus' Return," *Arion* 1 (winter 1962): 17–24, for Odysseus's overall loss of identity. John Peradotto, *Man in the Middle Voice: Name and Narration in the "Odyssey"* (Princeton: Princeton University Press, 1990), esp. 169–72, sees Odysseus as essentially a free agent. Kevin Crotty, *The Poetics of Supplication: Homer's "Iliad" and "Odyssey"* (Ithaca: Cornell University Press, 1994), 170–72, critiques this view.

11. For Heracles, see George E. Dimock, "The Name of Odysseus," in *Essays on the "Odyssey,"* ed. Taylor, 65; Schein, introduction to *Reading the "Odyssey,"* ed. Schein, 13–14.

12. See Slatkin, *The Power of Thetis,* 33–40; Scully, *Homer and the Sacred City,* 121–24. Achilles' need to confront mortality itself seems to stem from what James Redfield calls his "incapacity for illusion" (*Nature and Culture in the "Iliad": The Tragedy of Hector* [Chicago: University of Chicago Press, 1975], 27–28). See also Schein, introduction to *Reading the "Odyssey,"* ed. Schein, 7–8.

13. As Redfield puts it: [Man] becomes a hero because he cannot be a god" (*Nature and Culture,* 101). See also Cedric H. Whitman, *Homer and the Heroic Tradition* (Cambridge: Harvard University Press, 1958), 191–97; Vernant, "Two Faces," 55–57; Vernant, "Refusal," 188.

14. For the parallel of Odysseus's and Achilles' choices, see Dorothea Wender, "In Hades' Halls," in *Twentieth Century Interpretations,* ed. Clarke, 127–29; William G. Thalmann, *The "Odyssey": An Epic of Return* (New York: Twayne Publishers, 1992), 48–50; Gregory Nagy, *The Best of the Achaeans* (Baltimore: Johns Hopkins University Press, 1979), 102. For Achilles' speech in Hades as a retraction of his choice, see Martin Mueller, *The Iliad* (London: George Allen and Unwin, 1984), 31; Schein, introduction to *Reading the "Odyssey,"* ed. Schein, 11–12.

15. See, e.g., Vernant, "Refusal," 185–89; Schein, introduction to *Reading the "Odyssey,"* ed. Schein, 22–23.

16. See Charles Segal, "*Kleos* and Its Ironies in the Odyssey," in *Reading the "Odyssey,"* ed. Schein, 201–22.

17. On the final oblivion of death, as faced by Odysseus in Hades, see Vernant, "Two Faces," 59–61.

18. For example, Achilles, in the *Iliad,* achieves his goal only through the death of Patroclus, a price that completely negates the value of the success (Paolo Vivante, *The Homeric Imagination: A Study of Homer's Poetic Perception of Reality* [Bloomington: Indiana University Press, 1970], 53–60). Stewart compares the position of Achilles in Hades to Falstaff's attitude toward honor: "The point in both cases being that death makes a hero, a man honored for his dying bravery, and thus in a sense there are no heroes; there only have been heroes!" (*The Disguised Guest,* 61). Thalmann points out that the poem's return to Hades in book 24 reinforces the connection of heroism and death and in so doing contrasts this conception of heroism to Odysseus (*The "Odyssey,"* 120–21).

19. Schein sees Achilles as reaching the limits of the human condition itself (*Hero,* 82). The danger here is, as in Aristotle's picture of the great-souled man, that to such a man even honor no longer seems a great thing or a worthy reward (*Ethics* 1124a18).

20. And closer to the lions and wolves that represent him in simile. For the hero's place as between nature and culture, and Achilles' consequent alienation from society, see Redfield, *Nature and Culture,* 99–109, 191–92; Mueller, *Iliad,* 113–15, 120. Charles Segal, in *The Theme of the Mutilation of the Corpse in the "Iliad"* (Leiden: E. J. Brill, 1971), 11–16, 60, comments on Achilles' savagery and his return to humanity in the scene with Priam.

21. Sarpedon points this out, explicitly in describing the hero's role, implicitly in pointing out its implicit demand for the death of the hero (12.310–21). Schein points to the paradox of affirming the value of life through killing (*Hero,* 68, 71–72).

22. The realism of the *Odyssey* has no better witness than the many attempts, notably M. I. Finley's *The World of Odysseus* (New York: Viking Press, 1978), to deduce from it the character of eighth-century Greece. See Schein, *Hero,* 29–30, for the effect of this distinction in the *Iliad.* See Thalmann, *The "Odyssey,"* 131–32, and Anthony T. Edwards, *Achilles in the "Odyssey,"* Beiträge zur klassischen Philologie 171 (Königstein: Verlag Anton Hain, 1985), for the contrast of community values and epic tradition in the *Odyssey.* See Vivante, *Homeric Imagination,* 16–17, for a contrary position that argues for the consistency of scene in the *Odyssey.*

23. For the parallel, see William S. Anderson, "Calypso and Elysium," in *Essays on the "Odyssey,"* ed. Taylor, 73–86, esp. 79–81.

24. See also Grene, "Approach," 61, on Athene's proclivity toward ornithological transformations.

25. Despite Odysseus's intentions at the end of the poem (23.355–58), intentions that the final treaty seems to put an end to, such raids are not part of the ordinary life of Ithaca. Telemachus, in fact, claims that it would be *better* if the people would take his goods, because then he could, in a public and civilized way, demand restitution (2.80 ff.).

26. As Hal says: "I am not yet of Percy's mind, the Hotspur of the north, he that kills me some six or seven dozen of Scots at a breakfast, washes his hands, and says to his wife: 'Fie upon this quiet life! I want work'" (*1 Henry IV,* 2.4.100–104).

27. This is, of course, to put the distinction in purely modern terms. See G. S. Kirk, *Myth: Its Meaning and Function in Ancient and Other Cultures,* Sather Classical Lectures (Berkeley and Los Angeles: University of California Press, 1970), for the modern attempt

to distinguish between myth and legend. The distinction in Homeric terms seems to be simply that the heroic age was seen as part of historical, rather than mythic, time (for which, see below).

28. Grene comments that "the Wanderings belong to the heroic world . . . subject to different criteria and intrinsically different in aesthetic effect from the rest of his story which expresses the real world in which Homer and his contemporaries live" ("Approach," 55). For the distinction between "mythic" and "human" time, see, e.g., Carlo Brillante, "History and the Historical Interpretation of Myth," in *Approaches to Greek Myth,* ed. Lowell Edmunds (Baltimore: Johns Hopkins University Press, 1990), 102.

29. See George E. Dimock, *The Unity of the "Odyssey"* (Amherst: University of Massachusetts Press, 1989), 46.

30. Peisistratus's plea to be allowed to dine without weeping over a past that he (rather ingenuously) acknowledges he never knew (3.190–202), his suggestion that Telemachus wait for dawn before returning to Ithaca (15.49–55), his acknowledgment that his father *is* somewhat long-winded (15.209–14), all stand in contrast to the rather musty wordiness of the older generation. See Grene, "Approach," 60–61; and Whitman, "Change," 90–91.

31. For the traditional contrast of Odysseus and Achilles, see Nagy, *Achaeans,* 53–58; Schein, introduction to *Reading the "Odyssey,"* ed. Schein, 5–6. As presented here, the contrast parallels the contrast of Hector and Achilles, the warrior inside and the warrior outside society, for which see Scully, *Homer and the Sacred City,* 58–61, 116–25. See B. Fenik, "Stylization and Variety," in *Homer: Tradition and Invention,* ed. B. Fenik (Leiden: E. J. Brill, 1978), 71–77, for Odysseus as an exemplar of traditional heroism in the *Iliad;* and Vernant, "Two Faces," 58–59, for the contrast of the two kinds of hero in Hades. Whitman, "Change," 77–78, sees a contrast between Achilles, split between his divine and mortal selves, and Odysseus, who is just himself. For Odysseus as a "centripetal" rather than a "centrifugal" hero, see W. B. Stanford, "Personal Relationships," in *Essays on the "Odyssey,"* ed. Taylor, 19. For this distinction as also distinguishing Bloom from Stephen in *Ulysses,* see W. B. Stanford, *The Ulysses Theme* (Oxford: Oxford University Press, 1954), 215.

32. See Thalmann, *The "Odyssey,"* 66–71. Vivante, *Homeric Imagination,* 168–72, points out that the involuted time scheme of the *Odyssey* is designed to show us Odysseus reemerging out of his past.

33. Stewart describes another aspect of Odysseus's isolation, his suspicion, as the product of his wanderings: "This newer side to Odysseus' character, however, comes not from the general tradition but explicitly from the adventures he has been forced to undergo in his ten years of exile, in this poem (and by this poet)" (*The Disguised Guest,* 50).

34. For the Sirens, see Segal, "*Kleos,*" 191–92. Athene, in contrast, is perfectly happy to present herself as a merchant, first (as Mentes) to Telemachus (1.179–86), then (as Mentor) to Nestor (3.365–70).

35. Thus Eumaius, when he sees (in the company of Odysseus) that Telemachus has returned, is glad to see him, as a son would be to see his father recovered from a long sickness. So also, when Penelope finally embraces Odysseus, she feels like a swimmer who has been ten days in the ocean and finally sees land. See Thalmann, *The "Odyssey,"* 118–20; Helene P. Foley, "Reverse Similes and Sex Roles in the *Odyssey,*" *Arethusa* 11 (1978): 7–26; Segal, "*Kleos,*" 207; and Redfield, *Nature and Culture,* 215, for the same phenomenon in *Iliad* 24 with Achilles and Priam.

36. See Thalmann, *The "Odyssey,"* 63. From the poem's second line, of course, Odysseus has been identified as a hero acted upon as much as acting.

37. As Bloom also sees: "But it's no use says he. Force, hatred, history, all that. That's not life for men and women, insult and hatred. And everybody knows that it is the very opposite of that that is really life" (Joyce, *Ulysses*, 333).

38. See Crotty, *Poetics of Supplication,* 198–99. For the importance of Penelope's deception of Odysseus, and so the revelation of his vulnerability, see Armory, "Reunion," 119; Stanford, "Relationships," 26; and Marylin A. Katz, *Penelope's Renown: Meaning and Determinacy in the "Odyssey"* (Princeton: Princeton University Press, 1991), 165, 176–77.

39. See Katz, *Penelope's Renown,* 179–80.

40. See Richard Ellman, *Ulysses on the Liffey* (Oxford: Oxford University Press, 1972), 33, for the strain; and Kenner, *Ulysses,* 27–28. Bloom's return is, of course, predicted by Stephen: "If Socrates leave his house today he will find the sage seated on his doorstep. If Judas go forth tonight it is to Judas his steps will tend" (213).

41. As in one of Joyce's schemes for *Ulysses;* see Ellman, *Ulysses on the Liffey,* 189; Schwarz, *Reading Joyce's "Ulysses,"* 277. Noting that the nymph looks like Molly when she was slimmer, Ellman sees Calypso as one aspect of Molly, the mistress, as opposed to Penelope, the wife (33–35). In good Joycean fashion Bloom, in explaining metempsychosis, points out to Molly the possibility of being turned into a nymph (65). See also Gilbert, *James Joyce's "Ulysses,"* 128–29; Fuller, *James Joyce's "Ulysses,"* 40.

42. Ellman (*Ulysses on the Liffey,* 143) sees this as one resolution of the spirit/body antithesis that has been building up throughout the novel.

43. Ibid., 125–26, 133–34; Schwarz sees Bloom as rejecting Stephen's tendency toward theory and abstraction (*Reading Joyce's "Ulysses,"* 104–5).

44. In contrast, Schwarz (*Reading Joyce's "Ulysses,"* 106) sees Bloom's "Calypso" as a state of mind that Bloom must reject, involving his own racial past, his mortality, and Milly's and Molly's sexuality.

45. Joyce himself referred to the character as "Thersites" (Ellman, *Ulysses on the Liffey,* 110). See Ellman for a negative and Fuller (*James Joyce's "Ulysses,"* 60) for a more tolerant view of the narrator.

46. Again as the great mediator, Bloom chooses Gorgonzola cheese for lunch, which strikes the balance between the carnivore's and the vegetarian's "wind and watery" diet (166).

47. Schwarz, *Reading Joyce's "Ulysses,"* 131–33.

48. As Fuller (*James Joyce's "Ulysses,"* 59–60) points out, Molly and Boylan are in bed together throughout this episode, and the thought haunts Bloom. Hence, for example, the Freudian slip in "the wife's admirers" (313). Bloom wonders in the case of Parnell: "The eternal question of life connubial, needless to say, cropped up. Can real love, supposing there happens to be another chap in the case, exist between married folk?" (651).

49. For Joyce's scheme, see Ellman, *Ulysses on the Liffey,* 188; and Schwarz, *Reading Joyce's "Ulysses,"* 280. For Bloom's avoidance of Boylan, see Kenner, *Ulysses,* 50–54; and for the slaying of the scruples, Gilbert, *James Joyce's "Ulysses,"* 346.

50. Bloom has already acknowledged to himself that Molly "wears the breeches" in the family (381). This scene is usually, and not wrongly, seen as exhibiting Bloom's hidden desire to be made a cuckold (e.g., Fuller, *James Joyce's "Ulysses,"* 92; Burgess, *Here Comes Everybody,* 161–62). The scene, however, as well as the desire, is motivated as much by fear, and the consequent nagging desire to explore what one fears, as it is by any masochistic tendencies on Bloom's part. On some level Odysseus too "wants" to experience the humiliation, and freedom, of his role as a beggar, but this does not make the experience pleasant to him.

51. Literally, in his persistent planning about the best time to go home and in his worries about having forgotten his key; metaphorically, in his desire to recapture the moment with Molly on Howth Head.

52. Ellman points out that both Penelope and Calypso are weavers (*Ulysses on the Liffey*, 33).

53. See Gilbert, *James Joyce's "Ulysses,"* 123–24, for Bloom's recurrent thoughts of the "Dance of the Hours," which indicates to him the inevitable movement of time and, significantly, was played at the dance where Boylan and Molly met.

54. Joyce develops this point in the Rip Van Winkle theme that runs throughout *Ulysses*. One solution is offered by Bloom's watch, which stops just at the moment of Molly's adultery. But even if Bloom could freeze time for himself, he cannot freeze it for others—its movement, as he sees in Nighttown (542), is slowly and inevitably separating him from everyone he is close to, his father, his son, Milly, and now Molly. The "sleeper awakened" (728)—whether Parnell, Rip Van Winkle, or Odysseus—is no solution to Bloom's problem.

55. Parnell, according to Joyce's key, is Agamemnon, the hero who loses his return by failing to understand that you do not come home to the same home that you left. See Schwarz, *Reading Joyce's "Ulysses,"* 278; Ellman, *Ulysses on the Liffey*, 191. See Schwarz, *Reading Joyce's "Ulysses,"* 50–56, for a more political interpretation of Joyce's use of Parnell. Kenner (*Ulysses*, 131–32) sees Bloom as accepting the role of Captain O'Shea and introducing Stephen as Parnell—hence playing the role of pander.

56. The implied injunction to "stay true" (*Bleibtreustrasse*) to a land he has never seen seems inevitably ironic. See Joyce's scheme; Ellman, *Ulysses on the Liffey*, 189; Schwarz, *Reading Joyce's "Ulysses,"* 277; and Burgess, *Here Comes Everybody*, 91, 107–8.

57. See Fuller, *James Joyce's "Ulysses,"* 38–39, 49–51; and Schwarz, *Reading Joyce's "Ulysses,"* 142–51, for Shakespeare in general and *Hamlet* in particular as the blending of Stephen and Bloom. Hugh Kenner, *A Colder Eye: The Modern Irish Writers* (New York: Alfred A. Knopf, 1983), 196–97, details the *Hamlet* correspondences as they appear to each of the novel's several characters.

58. Schwarz, *Reading Joyce's "Ulysses,"* 22.

59. Hence Joyce's Linati schema describes the last three episodes as "the fusion of Stephen and Bloom" (Blephen/Stoom) (Ellman, *Ulysses on the Liffey*, 186). See Fuller, *James Joyce's "Ulysses,"* 78–79; and Schwarz, *Reading Joyce's "Ulysses,"* 33–35, 103, and passim, especially for Bloom and Stephen as complements. Ellman (*Ulysses on the Liffey*, 146–48) sees Bloom accepting Stephen as a Dantesque salvation of himself. Molly's soliloquy will provide the culmination for this theme of interdependence and interidentification by blending the referents of all her *he*s (Kenner, *Ulysses*, 147).

60. Ellman sees this Vician philosophy as the basis of the "Circe" episode (*Ulysses on the Liffey*, 141–42). The fact that Joyce, in accordance with Vico, sees history as cyclical (Schwarz, *Reading Joyce's "Ulysses,"* 37–44; Kenner, *Ulysses*, 150–51) solves Bloom's problem, but without Bloom's knowledge.

61. See Fuller, *James Joyce's "Ulysses,"* 75–76, 78; Kenner, *Ulysses*, 132–33.

62. Crotty suggests that for Odysseus and Penelope as well their true bond is formed by memory (*Poetics of Supplication*, 199–203). Stephen, of course, gets his understanding of memory from Augustine, whose work Bloom probably never read.

63. See Kenner, *Colder Eye*, 193.

64. A reference necessitated by reintroducing the hero of *A Portrait of the Artist as a Young Man* still as a young man. Comically, only Molly is allowed to notice Joyce's role in

the novel: "O Jamesy let me up out of this pooh" (769). Keri Ames pointed this out to me.

65. See Schwarz, *Reading Joyce's "Ulysses,"* 147–48 (also 12–13, 138–51): "For Stephen paternity is a legal fiction because he believed that as an artist he is the Father—indeed God the Father—of all the reality he creates in his actual and his potential work. And this argument has particular importance to the form of Joyce's art in *Ulysses,* a form which recreates the identity of a younger self."

66. In fact, Bloom has spent much of the day contemplating and then deciding against taking voyages—to see Milly, to Greenwich, to tour Ireland, to the Isle of Man (67, 100, 167, 627, 726). This pattern of frustrated travel plans Bloom himself seems to view as typical ("by a trick of fate he had consistently remained a landlubber except you call going to Holyhead which was his longest"; 626). See also Molly (764–65) on Bloom's naval adventures. For Bloom's disinclination to roam, see Burgess, *Here Comes Everybody,* 168–69; Prescott, *Exploring James Joyce,* 49.

The Homecomings of Odysseus and Nala

WENDY DONIGER

It has been my pleasure and privilege to spend a great deal of my time at the University of Chicago trying to persuade David Grene that Indian texts are as interesting as Greek texts. I win some arguments, lose some. On the occasion of this celebration of all that David Grene has meant to all of us, I thought it best to strike a compromise, to place side by side two epic texts, one Greek and one Indian, on the same subject: the homecoming of a husband after a long absence, and the mutual testing of husband and wife. Since this is a celebration of all the ways in which David has thumbed his nose at time, has gone on and on doing all the things that he loves to do (which include, but are not limited to, teaching for the Committee on Social Thought, riding horses, living on butter cheese meat and gin, and running a dairy farm), far beyond the age at which most people give them up, this seemed a particularly appropriate theme—for it is about the ways in which time does and does not change people, about what remains true in the mind and soul when time plays the body false.

Odysseus and Penelope

Let us begin, as David always begins, with the text—more particularly, as often, the text in translation:

When Odysseus returned to Ithaca after twenty years, disguised as a beggar who claimed to have known Odysseus, his old dog recognized him and with his dying strength wagged his tail but had no strength to move toward his master, who gave no sign of recognition but secretly wept; and then the dog died. When Penelope first saw him, she gave no sign of recognizing him but said to him, "I think I will give you a test, to see if you really knew my husband. Tell me what he was wearing when he was your guest." And Odysseus replied, "Well, it was twenty years ago, but he was wearing a purple woolen cloak, and it was pinned with a clasp of gold, depicting a hound killing a fawn. All the women couldn't tear their eyes away from it [or him, *auton*]." And she recognized the sure signs that Odysseus had showed her.

Then Penelope instructed the old nurse Eurycleia to wash the stranger's feet, remarking to her, "Your master Odysseus was the same age, and probably has such hands and feet now, for mortals grow old quite suddenly in misfortune." And Eurycleia remarked, "I never saw anyone so like Odysseus in form and voice and feet," to which Odysseus replied, "Yes, old woman, that's just what people who have seen both of us with their own eyes always say, that we look just like one another." As she touched him, he turned away from the fire toward the darkness, for he thought she might recognize his scar. And indeed as soon as she washed him she recognized the scar that the white tusk of a boar had made in his leg, above the knee, when he was a young man, at the home of his mother's father, who had given him his name, Odysseus. She knew it by the touch, "by the feel," and she dropped the foot and said, "I didn't know you until I had touched all of my lord." Eurycleia wanted to tell Penelope right away, but Athene and Odysseus forbade her to do so.

After "the stranger" had killed all the suitors, Penelope told him to sleep in the hall or to let the maids make him a bed. But later, Eurycleia told Penelope that the stranger was Odysseus, insisting, "I will quote you a clear sign, that scar from the boar's white tusk long years ago." Penelope went downstairs, but she hesitated; she did not know him because he was wearing such wretched clothes; yet, as she said to her son, "If he really is Odysseus, then we will find other, better ways to know one another, for we two have signs, hidden from others, that we know." And Odysseus smiled and said to his son, "Let your mother test me, and she will understand sooner and better. But now, because I'm wearing such wretched clothes, she won't *say* who I am."

Finally, Odysseus said to Penelope, "You strange woman, the most stubborn of all women. What other woman would hold back like you from her husband when he had come home after twenty years of suffering! Come, then, nurse, make up a bed for me here, for this woman has a heart of iron." Then Penelope replied, "You strange man. I know very well what you were like when you left Ithaca. Come, then, Eurycleia, make up a bed for him here, outside the bedroom; move out the bed that he built himself." Then Odysseus replied in fury, "Woman, who has moved my bed somewhere else? That would be very hard to do, unless a god came to move it. But no mortal man alive, no matter how strong, could move it easily. For a great sign is built into it; I myself made it, no one else. I took a living olive tree and built the bedroom around it and roofed it and added close-fitting doors and trimmed the trunk to make a bedpost and built the bed and decorated it with gold and silver and ivory. Thus I declare this sign to you. But I don't know, woman, if the bed is still in its proper place or if some other man has moved it somewhere else, cutting under the roots of the olive tree." That is what he said, and she recognized the clear signs and burst into tears and ran to him and kissed his head and said, "Don't be angry with me or blame me. I was afraid that some mortal man would come and deceive me with words. Helen would never have gone to bed and made love with a foreigner if a god had not inspired her to do the shameful thing she did; before that, she did not place the ruinous folly in her heart. But now, since you have told me the clear signs of our bed, which no other mortal man has seen, no one but you and I and the maid who kept the doors of the bedroom—you have persuaded my heart, stubborn though it is." And, finally, Odysseus said, "Come, woman, let's go to bed."[1]

I have selected and strung together passages, mainly from books 19 and 23, which reveal a pattern of approaches to the recognition of signs. The so-called Homeric formulae themselves highlight these patterns; Odysseus and Penelope (and Homer) recycle the same phrases, teasing one another and joining together in the very phrases that are ostensibly keeping them apart. Thus, even when Homer says that the stranger's "wretched clothes" kept Penelope from recognizing him, the fact that the stranger uses the very same phrase to reassure their son indicates that he does indeed understand her, and understands that she knows more than she is saying. They call one another "strange" *(daimoni/e)* and agree that her heart is stubborn—an agreement which makes her anything but strange and shows that her heart, however firm, is also soft. Most of all, both of them keep talking about signs.[2]

The word "sign" (*sēma,* pl. *sēmata;* cf. our "semantic," "semiotic," "semaphor," etc.) is used again and again, in a range of related meanings, principally an exceptional mark in its own right (the extraordinary bed) or a sign or token of something else (in this case, Odysseus's true identity). It refers to the details of the golden clasp proving that the stranger did know Odysseus, the hound on the clasp echoing the dog that recognized Odysseus (and, to tease Penelope, the stranger adds the bit about the women admiring Odysseus when he was wearing it). It refers to the scar made by the boar, which the nurse calls a *sēma* to prove to Penelope that the stranger *is* Odysseus. It refers to the ways that, Penelope assures her son, the two of them have of knowing one another.

And, finally, it refers to the marriage bed, whose *sēma* is both a "unique characteristic" (as Richmond Lattimore translates) and a way that Odysseus has of proving that he is the only man who has the right to sleep with Penelope in it. Odysseus refers to the bed twice as a sign, and so does Penelope, four references within forty lines. He says "a great sign is built into it" (which Lattimore renders, obscuring the pattern, "one particular feature") and Penelope speaks of "the clear signs of our bed" (Lattimore, again missing the echo, "these authentic details of our bed"). The bed is a riddle: "When is a marriage bed impossible to move?" Answer: "When it is a living tree." The bed carved from a living tree, and then carefully roofed and gated and bound in gold and silver, is a magnificent metaphor for marriage, which cages and codifies the living force of sexual passion but keeps it alive. Aristotle, perhaps with this scene in mind, quotes Antiphon's statement that if a man buried a bedstead (*klinē;* though Homer called it a *lechos*) and the sap in it took force and threw out a shoot, a tree and not a bedstead would grow.[3] Odysseus knows that if the tree in the bed is still alive, his bond with Penelope is still alive, keeping her from sleeping with anyone else in that bed, and so he himself is still alive. Only after that bed has been tested can Homer give us what Froma Zeitlin has nicely characterized as "that most satisfying of romantic closures: 'and so to bed.'"[4]

Physical, visual evidence does not bear as much weight as words, knowledge, memory. Despite his superficial filth and the fact that Athene has transformed him, the stranger resembles Odysseus first in his feet, then in his "form and voice," then in the scar on his thigh, and finally in his memory of the bed. The nurse recognizes the scar "by the feel" and believes it over the evidence of vision. Later (24.328), Odysseus's father asks for a sign *(sēma)* that he is really Odysseus, and Odysseus tells him about the scar and the boar (24.348), signs that he has offered to others (in addition to the nurse and his father) to aid their recognition of him. But this time he adds something that he did not add for the nurse or Penelope: he names the trees in the orchard when he was a boy (thirteen pear trees, ten apple trees, forty fig trees) and mentions the ripening of things in their season, the seasons sent by Zeus. These living trees function symbolically as offshoots of the living tree from which the marriage bed was made. And Odysseus's father recognizes the sure signs (24.345); indeed, as he hears them he sees them, for he is standing right there in the orchard, probably the very orchard that Oydsseus is talking about, just as Odysseus ends up with Penelope in the same bed with which he had proven himself to her. Thus the bed test in book 23 is framed by the signs in book 19 (the cloak and brooch, the scar) and 24 (the trees in the orchard).

The bed test is also supported by yet another sign, one that is not explicitly called a *sēma* but is an ability, an event, rather than a thing: the sign of the bending of the bow. In book 21, after the conversation about the cloak, Athene inspires Penelope to set the wooers a contest with the bow of Odysseus: "whoever strings the bow most easily and shoots an arrow through all twelve axes, I will go with him and leave this home, which I will remember even in my dreams." Telemachus, ignoring the Oedipal implications, tries to do it and then says that he will let his mother go off with one of the suitors—he'll keep the house (that she will remember in her dreams, those dreams of the return of Odysseus that she always doubts . . .). Telemachus would have succeeded had Odysseus not signaled, with those eloquent brows, for him to stop. Penelope then asks that the bow be given to "the stranger" to try—does she know who he is?—but Telemachus again interferes: he sends her up to her room, saying *he* is the one to say to whom the bow should be given (21.335–52). Astounded, Penelope goes to her room, weeps, and goes to sleep. Odysseus strings the bow and begins the slaughter.

Now, there are very interesting Indian parallels with this scene. In the *Mahabharata*, the text in which Nala appears, the hero Arjuna wins his bride, Draupadi, through a contest with a bow: Drupada, Draupadi's father, says that the man who can string the bow and shoot arrows through the hole in a wheel and hit the mark will win Draupadi. Arjuna strings the bow, takes five arrows, pierces the target, and knocks it down entirely; after that, he takes Draupadi for his wife.[5] And in the other great Sanskrit epic, the *Ramayana*, Rama wins Sita by stringing a bow—indeed, he not only strings it but breaks it in half.

The symbolism of the Indian bow contests is primarily erotic: the arrow moving through the hole needs no Freudian to gloss it, and Rama's cruelty to Sita is foreshadowed when, instead of merely bending and stringing the bow that symbolizes his right to Sita, he breaks it in half, as he will break her. But the *Ramayana* is not unique in the violence of the image: in the other epics, too, *Mahabharata* as well as *Odyssey*, a fight breaks out immediately after the contest as the defeated suitors attack the victor. On the other hand, the *Ramayana* is unique among the three in a way most significant for the question of this essay: the hero is not in disguise. The *Mahabharata* makes explicit what is, I think, implicit in the *Odyssey*: the bow contest proves the identity of the disguised hero. Arjuna and his brothers, the Pandavas, are disguised as Brahmins at the time of the contest; after Arjuna has strung the bow, people begin to whisper, "They must be the Pandavas." So, too, even before the bed trick, the bow trick reveals to Penelope that the stranger is Odysseus.[6]

Odysseus's unfounded suspicions of Penelope may be projections of the fact that he himself has been jumping in and out of bed with Calypso, Circe, and, perhaps, anything that moves. But Penelope, who knows about Calypso (the spiteful Telemachus told her, when it was no longer true, that Odysseus was with Calypso; 17.143) and has good reason to be jealous, has fears about herself as well as about him. In her final speech of recognition and acceptance, she argues that she tested Odysseus because of her fear of being tricked like Helen of Troy. Odysseus's nightmare is that Penelope will turn out to be Clytemnestra (about whom both Odysseus and Telemachus have taken great pains *not* to inform Penelope, perhaps in order not to put bad ideas in her head), but Penelope's own nightmare is that she will turn out to be Helen—who believed her dream sent by the gods, while Penelope, in the famous piece about gates of horn and ivory (a dream about the return of her husband; 19.560), did not.

In fact, in the revisionist history in Euripides' play *Helen,* Helen turns out to be very much like Homer's Penelope, the heroine of "another 'faithful wife' story, of a woman's unflagging fidelity to her knight-errant."[7] Like Penelope, Euripides' Helen fears that her husband, gone so long, is dead, and she is quoting Homer's Penelope when she says, "If my husband were alive, we would recognize one another by symbols that would be clear to us alone" (290). Like Penelope, Helen hears the news that her husband is "in this country, near at hand, a shipwrecked castaway with few friends left" (540). Norman Austin comments, "Here begins what we would expect to be the great recognition scene of all time. . . . Can her secret tokens better Penelope's? The reunion of Odysseus and Penelope pales beside this reunion, since Penelope was never called upon to play a ghost of herself, as Helen is."[8]

Penelope knows that her steadfastness and faithfulness to her husband are not what reveal her to him but what reveal *him* to *her.* Froma Zeitlin describes the bed as "a double-sided sign—of identity for him, fidelity for her. . . . Yet a certain paradox remains in the unequal symmetry between identity and fidelity that dictates to each sex its defining terms. . . . But the ruse works in two directions, because in raising the awful possibility that his bed has been moved, her testing of *his* identity raises the far more important question of *her* sexual fidelity to him."[9] More than that—the trick proves that she is worthy of him not only in fidelity but in trickiness: "in tricking Odysseus into revealing the secret of the bed, she proves herself to be his match in the same qualities that characterize him (and that therefore identify her as a suitable wife for him, his 'other half')."[10]

In Edmond Rostand's *Cyrano de Bergerac,* when Roxane tells Christian how she loved his letters from the war, she says:

Do you suppose
The prim Penelope had stayed at home
Embroidering,—if Ulysses wrote like you?
She would have fallen like another Helen—
Tucked up those linen petticoats of hers
And followed him to Troy![11]

This was Odysseus's fear. But Penelope was not going to fall like Helen. She made sure of that by testing him.

A story that has been called "one of the best known ballads in modern Greece"[12] combines the episodes in which Odysseus is recognized first by Penelope and then by his father:

[The singer says he met a maiden who waits for her husband, gone "these ten long years." The singer says he buried her husband with his own hands, and asks, in payment, for a kiss. When she refuses he says,] "My good girl, I am your husband, I am your beloved man." "My good stranger, if you are my husband, my beloved man, tell me of marks in the courtyard, and then I will believe you." [He tells her of an apple tree and a vine.] "These are marks in my courtyard and everybody knows them; a passer-by you were and passed, you tell me what you saw. Tell me of marks inside the house, and then I will believe you." "Right in the midst of the bedroom there burns a golden lamp; it gives you light while you undress and while you plait your tresses; it gives you light at sweet daybreak, as you dress in your best." "A wicked neighbour it must be, who told you what you know. Tell me of marks on my body, give me tokens of love." "You have a dark spot in your armpit, and between your breasts you wear your husband's amulet." "Good stranger, you are my husband, and you are my beloved man."[13]

The most significant difference from the *Odyssey* is that the woman does *not* recognize her husband; and now it is the woman, not the man, who is recognized by a scar on her body: J. Kakridis notes: "In some variants, among the marks on the body of his wife is also a scar from a bite, but on a different part of the body"; the singer says, "You have a dark spot on your cheek, a dark spot in your armpit, and on your right breast a little scar from a bite."[14] This ballad, like the *Odyssey*, constantly repeats "the identical terms, *sēmata/sēmadia,* as a proof of the recognition."[15] And in yet other variants of the song, the wife is explicitly tested with what is implicitly at stake in the *Odyssey*: she is told that her husband is dead and that his last wish was that she marry the stranger. "When she categorically refuses to, the man is assured about her faithfulness, and he reveals his identity."[16] As in the *Odyssey*, "The formula of the motif of the home-coming husband's recognition requires a double test: on the one hand, the test of the man to prove his identity; on the other, the test of the woman to prove that she has been faithful all these years."[17] This is precisely the double test—I would say the double standard, evoking the gender asymmetry that characterizes all of these texts—that underlies the story of Nala and Damayanti, to which we will now turn.

Nala and Damayanti

The tale of Nala and Damayanti bears a striking resemblance to certain aspects of the story of the homecoming of Odysseus. The Indian story, first told in the great Sanskrit epic the *Mahabharata* in the centuries before the common era and retold throughout Indian history, with many interesting variations, is also a paradigmatic text for Western Indologists, in part because the standard Sanskrit primer (by Charles Lanman) begins with it, so that the opening lines (*asid raja nalo nama,* "There was a king named Nala") plays the same role in Indology that the opening lines of Caesar (*gallia omnis divisa est in partes tres,* "All Gaul is divided in three parts"—another tale of splitting) played for earlier generations of classicists. (How appropriate that the prototypical Roman text is about politics, the prototypical Hindu text about sex—and politics.)

Two episodes of recognition in the story of Nala and Damayanti provide us with parallels to the *Odyssey*. In the first, Damayanti succeeds in recognizing Nala and distinguishing him from four gods who have taken his form on the day she chooses her bridegroom (in a self-choice, or *svayamvara,* a ceremony in which a princess puts a garland over the head of the man she chooses to marry):

Damayanti saw five men standing there, entirely identical in appearance; any one of them she looked at seemed to her to be Nala. She wondered, "How can I know which are the gods, and which is Nala?" She remembered that she had heard, from old people, of the identifying signs [*lingani*] of the gods, but still she saw none of them on the men standing before her. Then she prayed to the gods, by her faithfulness to Nala, begging them to point Nala out to her and to display their own forms so that she could recognize him. The gods were moved by her pitiful request and demonstrated their divine identifying signs. She saw all the gods without sweat, with unblinking eyes, with unwithered garlands, without dust, and standing without touching the ground, and she saw Nala revealed by his shadow, his withered garland, his dustiness and sweatiness, his blinking eyes, and his feet on the ground. She chose Nala for her husband.[18]

Damayanti recognizes her lover by the identifying signs *(lingani)* of his mortality, the normal human flaws that all of us share with him; and she recognizes the divine impersonators by their (abnormal) lack of those signs.

But the gods can manipulate the signs of their own immortality: sometimes they have them, sometimes they do not. In this story, at first they do not, and Damayanti is ultimately able to identify her husband, not by her powers of recognition, dwelling within herself, but by her faithfulness *to him,* the ultimate power of a woman in India, which compels the gods (or at least persuades them) to reveal themselves to her. She is defined only by reference to her man. Or, to take a less feminist tack, she knows him because she knows herself. Her steadfastness and faithfulness to her husband are not what reveal her to him but what reveal *him* to *her,* just as they revealed Odysseus to Penelope.

What is the meaning of the signs by which she recognizes the gods? Some (such as the faded garlands and the dust) are particularly Indian; others (such as the shadow, the blinking, and the feet) occur as criteria in other cultures as well.[19] There is a minor lapse in the text: though Nala is expressly said to *have* a shadow, the gods are not said to lack them. That gods have no shadows may have been such a truism even at this early period that shadowlessness did not even have to be listed among their defining criteria. It is precisely this quality of light and insubstantiality that Damayanti rejects.

There is also a significant correspondence between this scene in which Damayanti states her preference for Nala rather than the gods who resemble him and a scene at the very start of the *Odyssey.* When we first meet Odysseus, he is longing for his homecoming and his wife, but the powerful nymph Calypso, the bright goddess, keeps him back in her hollow caves, longing to make him her husband (1.13–15). Later, when she expresses her disbelief that he should prefer his mortal wife to her, an immortal woman, he replies:

> Mighty goddess, don't be angry with me because of this. I know perfectly well that the thoughtful Penelope is not as good as you are to look at, in appearance or stature, for she is a mortal and you are not merely immortal but ageless. Yet, even so, I wish and hope every day to come home and to see the day of my homecoming. (5.215–20)

And with that, he goes to bed with Calypso. Nothing is said in Penelope's favor other than the fact that she is a part of a home. All else is against her: she lacks beauty, size, immortality, and youth. Setting aside the fact that the man of many wiles would not make Zeus's mistake of praising other women to the woman he is sleeping with at the moment, as Zeus does to Hera (*Iliad* 14.220–25), what endears Penelope to Odysseus is her *lack* of divine characteristics. Had Homer spoken Sanskrit, he would have said that she is a woman whose feet touch the ground and who casts a shadow.

Let us turn now to the second half of the story of Nala and Damayanti:

Nala and Damayanti married, and she gave birth to twins, a boy and a girl. But the demon of gambling and bad luck, Kali, entered Nala when he neglected to wash his feet; he gambled away his kingdom, and he and Damayanti were forced to go to the forest. When birds, incarnations of the dice, stole the clothes he had been wearing, Damayanti wrapped him in the other half of the single cloth that she was wearing. One night, in despair, he cut in half the piece of cloth as she slept, leaving her with one half, and he abandoned her there. The Kali in him wanted to leave her, but the husband wanted to stay with her; he was like a swing that goes back and forth. After a while, a snake magically transformed Nala into a dwarf named Bahuka ["Short-armed" or "Dwarf"], and he became the charioteer of a king, for Nala had been an expert horseman.

Damayanti became the servant of a queen. Her parents searched for her and a messenger recognized her by a tiny birthmark, a mole between her eyebrows; it was hidden by dust, but he recognized the mark [*cihna*] and her, and brought her home. They washed the dust off the mole and her parents embraced her. For years Damayanti searched for Nala, sending out a messenger to recite the words, "Gambler, where did you go when you cut our cloth in half and abandoned me?" One day, she learned that Bahuka had said, in reply, "Faithful wives should never get angry, even if their husbands desert them—especially if birds stole away the husband's clothes." To bring Nala to her, Damayanti sent a message to the king whom Nala served, announcing that she would hold a second ceremony of self-choice on the very next day.

When Nala in the form of Bahuka heard this announcement, he thought, "Maybe she is doing this as a scheme for my sake. But women are fickle by nature in this world, and I did do a terrible thing. Still, how could she do such a thing, when she has had [my] children? I will go there to find out if this is true or not." He drove the king's chariot so swiftly that they were able to cover the hundred leagues in a single day, and the king began to suspect that, despite his appearance, the charioteer might be Nala; for who else could drive horses so well? "And great men, driven by the gods, sometimes live in disguise, so that it is hard to recognize them." As Bahuka drove the horses into the city, the chariot roared in a way that Nala's old horses in the palace stables recognized; they became excited, and so did Damayanti. But when she saw the deformed charioteer she did not recognize him, and she thought that Nala must have taught him to make the chariot roar like that.

Still she had him questioned by her woman, Keshini, who asked him about Nala. Bahuka said, "King Nala left his two children here and went where he wanted. No one knows where Nala is; he is disguised and deformed. Only he himself knows Nala—and she who is closest to him. For Nala never announces his identifying signs [*lingani*] anywhere." Then Keshini said, "When Damayanti's messenger said, 'Gambler, where did you go when you cut our cloth in half and abandoned me?' you made a reply. Damayanti wants to hear what you said then." And Bahuka wept and replied, "'Faithful wives should never get angry, even if their husbands desert them—especially if birds stole the husband's clothes.'" Keshini told Damayanti what he had said, and how he had wept and revealed his emotional transformation [*vikara*].

Then Damayanti suspected that this must be Nala, and she sent Keshini to observe him, and especially to note any divine sign [*nimitta*, "cause" or "omen"] that she saw in him. Keshini went and noted the charioteer's identifying signs and the divine sign that she had seen while he was cooking the king's meat: low doorways grew tall as he approached them, and narrow openings opened wide; when he looked at an empty pot, it became full of water; when he held up a handful of grass, it burst into flame; when he touched fire, he was not burnt; and when he held flowers in his hands and pressed them, they blossomed and smelled sweet.

Damayanti suspected that he must be her husband Nala, revealed by his actions and behavior though he had taken the form of Bahuka. She sent Keshini to bring her some of the meat that Bahuka had cooked, and as soon as she tasted it she knew that the cook was Nala, for in the old days she had often tasted meat cooked by Nala. Then she sent Keshini to him with the twins, and Bahuka recognized them and took them on his lap and wept and said to Keshini, "They look just like my own pair of twins; that is why I am crying. But if you keep coming to meet me, people will get the wrong idea, for we are foreigners here. So you had better go."

Then Damayanti told her mother, "Suspecting that Bahuka was Nala, I tested him in various ways. The one remaining doubt is about his appearance." And with the permission of her father and mother, she had him brought to her room; she was wearing a red garment and her hair was matted and she was covered with mud and dirt. When he saw her he burst into tears, and she said to him, "Bahuka, did you ever see a righteous man who abandoned his sleeping wife in the forest? Who but Nala? And how had I offended him, to deserve this? How could he abandon me who had chosen him, rejecting the gods who stood before me? Me, his faithful and passionate wife, who bore him children?" She wept, and he wept again and told her all that had happened to him, concluding, "But how could a wife ever abandon a devoted and loving husband and choose another, as you are doing?" Then she told him that she had announced the self-choice only as a scheme to bring him there, purposely announcing it only in Nala's city and stating that it would take place in a day's time. "Who but you," she asked Nala, "could travel a hundred leagues in a single day?" Still Nala hesitated, but she called the elements to witness that she had done nothing wrong, even in her mind, and the Wind spoke from the sky, so that everyone could hear, affirming that Damayanti had been faithful to him even in her mind.[20]

There are important symbolic bonds between this part of the story and the earlier episode; the second choosing of a bridegroom is the mirror image of the first. The disguises and recognitions in this part of the story balance those in the first part. Where, for instance, Nala's feet were one of the things that revealed his humanity (just as Odysseus's feet revealed his identity), here his feet prove the weak spot through which disaster enters him. And where, in the earlier episode, Nala speaks with the gods' voice and they look like him, here it is the voice (more precisely, the voices of his horses and chariot) that reveals him to Damayanti even when he does not look like himself. (The horses are the first to recognize him, as Odysseus's dog recognizes him; and both the king and Damayanti recognize him by his skill with the horses.) In their final confrontation, Damayanti assumes the red garment, matted hair, and mud and dirt that characterize the renunciant and exile, the form she had when he abandoned her.

Damayanti herself is hidden under ashes, like Cinderella, but is quickly recognized by a partially obscured birthmark. Then it is her turn to recognize him. Whereas Nala was mistaken for someone higher in the first episode (which Damayanti throws back in his face at the end, in her final accusation: I rejected gods for you, and then you rejected me), here he is mistaken for someone lower, literally smaller, a dwarf, as his name indicates. Nala is, like Odysseus *polumetis,* a man of many disguises. The dwarf, however, is also the most famous disguise of the god Vishnu, who took three expanding steps to trick the demons into giving him (back) the triple universe;[21] the dwarf Nala, like the dwarf Vishnu, has powers of expansion: low doorways rise before him.

There are several sorts of signs by which Damayanti recognizes Nala, tests by which he proves who he is, and there are two different terms for them in the Sanskrit text: there are the identifying signs *(lingani)* of Nala as an individual, the same term that was used for the signs that identify the gods as a class (the related term *cihna* is used for Damayanti's identifying mole); and there are the divine omens *(nimittani)* that identify Nala as a human who is not merely a human. (These supernatural signs play a less important role in the more realistic corresponding scenes in the *Odyssey,* but they are there, too.) The identifying signs are intended specifically for Damayanti to unravel, for, as Nala tells Keshini, only "she who is closest to him" will know the identifying signs that he never makes public. They are multiple, a chain of tests that dwarf even the gamut that Odysseus and Penelope make one another run in the parallel situation.

First is the riddle of abandonment, the riddle of memory, the words that refer to something that only the two of them knew about. The riddle is broken in half like the two halves of the cloth that Nala split when he left her, the cloth that the riddle is made of: her message is the first half, the accusation ("Gambler, you cut the cloth in half and abandoned me"), and his reply is the exactly parallel second half, the excuse ("Forgive me for abandoning you; the birds/dice stole my own clothes"). The riddle occurs three times, twice in exactly the same words and, at the end, in paraphrase, without the cloth or dice/birds: "Why did you abandon me?" "Why did *you* abandon me, by deciding to remarry?"

Then Damayanti recognizes Nala by a series of his actions and skills, beginning with his horsemanship and his cooking. Though Nala as Bahuka passes both tests (horsemanship, equated with non-remarriage, and cooking, a sign of intimacy), neither is definitive: he might have learned the horsemanship from the real Nala, and even after she recognizes his cooking, she worries about his changed appearance. But the announcement that the remarriage ceremony will take place on the very next day restricts the field of possible suitors to Nala alone, by calling upon his unique horsemanship, and this sign then rebounds back for Damayanti when she uses it to prove not her own identity (which he does not doubt) but her fidelity (which he does). It proves simultaneously who he is (a unique horseman) and that she has been true to him in bed (because she worded the wedding invitation to limit the field to the unique horseman).

Another aspect of his behavior is also suggestive, though not finally persuasive: the emotional transformation that comes over him when he weeps. And, finally, Damayanti recognizes Nala through his own recognition of their children, the inevitable twins of doubling parents, who look just like one another even as they "look just like" Bahuka's own twins. (Telemachus's resemblance to his father plays an important, though rather different, role in the mutual recognition of Odysseus and Penelope.) On this final occasion, Nala relaxes enough to tease Keshini about her repeated visits to him ("We can't go on meeting like this"—just as Odysseus teases Penelope with his remark about the women who admired Odysseus when he was wearing the clasp with the hound), implying that she will be accused of being a messenger who woos for herself—just as he was when he first wooed Damayanti for the gods. Now, at last, when he is in disguise, he can woo for himself.

A version of the story was recently recorded in Rajasthan by Ann Grodzins Gold and Lindsey Harlan,[22] an entirely realistic version, in which Damayanti must choose Nal from among kings, rather than gods, and he is made unrecognizable not by magic (as in the *Mahabharata*) but simply by misfortune. In the end, there are two queens, for Damayanti is doubled, and when both the mother and the stepmother claim the child, there is a test to discover who is the real mother: the stepmother puts on a silk blouse, and Damayanti puts on a wooden breastplate, but Damayanti's milk squirts through the wood. As usual, Damayanti recognizes Nal by his good cooking (in this case, by its smell), and, as usual, she must find Nal in order for him to find himself.

Damayanti is also doubled in the Dhola epic of Braj Kshetra, in contemporary eastern Rajasthan and western Uttar Pradesh, a text recorded and interpreted by Susan S. Wadley. Let us join the story after Damayanti has rejected the gods, including Indra, king of the gods:

> In envious fury, Indra cursed Nal to have bad luck for twelve years; one day Nal and Damayanti became separated in the forest. After a while, Damayanti arranged another self-choice and invited the kings of fifty-two kingdoms. When the invitation came to the king whom Nal was serving in disguise, he asked Nal to drive the chariot to the self-choice in six days. Nal (who had received, in a previous adventure, Jaldariya, Indra's magical horse) wasted much time buying the most decrepit horses imaginable, and they had to make the journey in only an hour and a half. Damayanti knows that Nal will have come in an hour, so she sends a servant to ask how long it took each king to arrive. Then she asks each to cook, but there is no fire anywhere in the kingdom and only Nal can light the dung for cooking. Finally, she adorns him with the garland, only to have Indra protest (again) and force her, once again, to identify Nal while he is disguised by Indra. Instructed by the goddess whom she worshiped at her home shrine, she recognizes him as human by his shadow and by his ability to cook without coals.[23]

Here the episode of the self-choice is repeated, together with the criterion of the shadow, in combination with the tests that occur only in the second episode in the *Mahabharata*: the cooking (now reduced to the simple ability to light the dung without fire) and the horses who are magically swift (the journey now reduced to an hour and a half instead of twenty-four hours).

The Dhola epic prefaces these two episodes with an entirely new story, about Nal and another woman, the goddess Motini, which involves other tests of identity that also occur in the second half of the *Mahabharata* story:

When Nal's mother was pregnant with him, her co-wives plotted against her and persuaded the king that the child, when born, would kill his father. With great sorrow, the king sent a servant to kill the queen, but the servant killed a deer instead and took back the deer's eyes to prove that she was dead. She gave birth to Nal, and a merchant adopted her as his daughter and raised Nal as his grandchild.

A goddess named Motini fell in love with Nal. She was worried about his caste when he said he was a merchant: "When she sees his beauty, she is like water; when she thinks of his caste, her body burns." So she invited him to play dice in order to discovery his identity. He declined at first, saying that it was a game only for those who wear turbans [i.e., kings]; but when he won, it was clear that he must be of royal blood.

Motini and Nal married, but she said, "I may bring you only unhappiness. I am a *devi*'s [goddess's] daughter and your kingdom will be destroyed because I cannot carry a child in my womb. Your lineage will be destroyed. If you marry a human, you will have children and your throne will survive." Motini came to the court of Nal's father, who fell in love with her, but she refused to marry anyone unless the *Nal Katha* [the story of Nal] were told.

Now, the daughter of the snake Vasuki had given Nal a flower that transformed him into a man a hundred years old. So transformed, he had said, "I don't think that I'll be recognized by my love. . . . She will say, 'Where has this old man come from, almost dead.' She will kill me." She then gave him a second flower to restore him to his form as a handsome young man and told him to keep both flowers. Now Nal, as an old man, came to the court and told the *Nal Katha* [i.e., his own story up to that point]. Nal was recognized and reunited with his wife Motini. They sent for his mother, too. He was himself again. But since Motini could not bear children because of her nonhuman birth, she departed for Indra's heavenly kingdom so that Nal could marry again, returning to earth to intercede when he got into trouble.

[Then Nal married Damayanti . . .]

Here the character of Damayanti has been split into two nonhuman women, Motini and Vasuki's daughter, a goddess and a serpent woman, who devise new solutions to new variants of the old problems. Several clues to Nal's identity are expansions of themes that we know from the Sanskrit epic: where he identified himself there by half of a riddle, here he identifies himself by telling his entire life story (as Odysseus tells his in the *Odyssey,* to *conceal* his identity). Other clues are inversions of themes from the Sanskrit epic: now dice are no longer the problem but part of the solution, part of his identification; and the male snake who helps Nala in the Sanskrit epic becomes the daughter of the serpent king, who gives him the gift of transformation into someone first old, then young (and who apparently does not mind when his first concern is that his other woman might not love him so transformed).

The theme of divine/human intermarriage occurs in both gender variants here: a goddess (Motini) falls in love with Nal, and then a god, Indra, falls in love with Vasuki's daughter. Motini explicitly raises the problem of class on two parallel levels, the tension between mortal and immortal and between low caste and high caste. At first, Motini fears she is too distant from Nal, of a higher class than he, until Nal's skill at dice reveals his true social class (to her at least, if not to himself); his knowledge is his identity. This apparent conflict between Nal's apparent and real castes causes Motini to experience the dramatic ambivalence that Nal experiences in the *Mahabharata:* where he was torn in half, pulled and pushed, she is caught between cold and hot. The conflict between the larger classes of mortal and immortal, however, proves the more serious problem. Damayanti's preference for a mortal husband is here transformed into Nal's preference for a mortal wife, and the reasons for this are spelled out in this text: a goddess cannot bear children.

Comparison: Damayanti and Penelope

There are interesting correspondences and differences between these two texts. Some of the tests that Damayanti and Nala use on one another are of a different order from those that Odysseus and Penelope use in the parallel situation. Telemachus's resemblance to his father, Odysseus, plays an important role, though very different from that of the twins of Damayanti and Nala, in the mutual recognition of Odysseus and Penelope: Nala's recognition of his twins helps Damayanti to recognize him, whereas Telemachus announces that although his mother says he is Odysseus's child, no one knows his father for sure (1.215–16). Yet Damayanti's children play a minor role in the story as a whole in comparison with the role played by Telemachus.

Supernatural signs are less important in the more realistic corresponding scenes in the *Odyssey,* but they are there, too. Where Nala's feet identify him to Damayanti, Odysseus's telltale feet, together with the scar on his leg, identify him—not to Penelope, whom he does not yet trust—but to his old nurse, whom he does trust. And just as the folk tradition in India changed the force of the sign of the second marriage by having Nala marry some other woman, so the folk tradition in modern Greece reversed the force of the sign of the scar by having Odysseus recognize Penelope by the telltale marks on *her* body.[24]

Froma Zeitlin likens the two mutual bed tests set by Penelope and Odysseus to the two once divided and now reunited halves of a literal symbol, the *symbolon*[25] that was broken in half (like the two pieces of a thousand dollar bill in an espionage contract) to be rejoined as proof of identity; but Nala literally tears the two halves of the bed in half when he leaves Damayanti, since her cloth, which covers them both, is all the bed they have that night; and it is Penelope who unilaterally fits it back together with the riddle of the bed that is a tree.

Like Penelope, Damayanti uses the ruse of a proposed remarriage to smoke her husband out; as Zeitlin points out, "To accept a second marriage is not, after all, equivalent to adultery. . . . There is a distinction between acquiescence to courtship, no matter how unwelcome, and actually sleeping with the enemy."[26] Like Damayanti, Penelope is apparently free "to choose the man for her husband whom her heart desires."[27] But the two women also force their husbands to reveal themselves by appealing to their pride and vanity, tempting them to reveal their skills—Nala his horsemanship, Odysseus his carpentry (he is a fine raft-builder, as we know). The twenty-four-hour test that Damayanti sets is like the bed test that Penelope sets for Odysseus, forcing his hand, forcing him to show his sign of identity even if he wishes to remain in disguise. (This, too, is a more widely distributed trope in both ancient India and ancient Greece: Arjuna, in hiding, reveals himself when he cannot resist bending the bow and shooting the targets in the contest to win Draupadi;[28] Achilles, hiding in drag on Skyros, is tricked by Odysseus into revealing himself when he cannot resist reaching out for shining weapons.[29])

And this sign then, in both cases—horsemanship and bed-carpentry—rebounds back for the woman when she uses it to prove not her own identity (which he does not doubt) but her fidelity (which he does). Both tricks prove simultaneously who the man is and that his wife has been true to him in bed. His identity and her fidelity are implicitly equated and essentialized: he must prove who he is, and she must prove that she is his. Damayanti does this twice: before they are married she forces the gods to reveal their (and Nala's) identity when she swears by her fidelity to him, and then, years later, she proves her fidelity to him when she has successfully tested him for his identity.

Thus, the two texts are arguing simultaneously for the choice of the mortal over the immortal and for the ability to see the true husband through the disguises of age—of mortality. This apparently "wrong" choice is one that opts for a kind of continuous connectedness that is our symbolic immortality, the fragile, ephemeral, conditional, dependent intensity of real life, the emotional chiaroscuro, the sense of impending loss that makes what we have so precious while we have it, more precious than the security of an eternity without that immediacy and intensity. The Greek and Sanskrit texts share this insight.

Yet the two cultures reverse the genders of those who choose mortals over immortals. The Hindu woman (Damayanti) and the Greek man (Odysseus) choose the mortal spouse over the immortal surrogate, though in both cases it is the wife who must recognize her changed husband. In this sense, though Nala and Penelope recognize their spouses, who return the compliment by recognizing them, Damayanti and Odysseus choose their spouses twice: over against both divinity and youth. The Hindu text thus doubly affirms the virtue of the woman, while the Greek text doubly affirms the man.

In both epics it is the woman, not the man, who has the more serious doubts—not about chastity but about identity. Yet the women have far better reason than the men to doubt the chastity of their spouses: Penelope is the one who has good reason to be jealous. So, too, Nala suspects Damayanti of infidelity, though he is the one who has been to blame, as she well knows; his unfounded suspicions of her are projections of his own abandonment of her. Though Nala in the Sanskrit version is not explicitly unfaithful to Damayanti, in the Dhola epic, Nal does take a second wife.

The women themselves manipulate the signs; truly they have agency. Mihoko Suzuki has pointed this out with reference to Penelope, taking Claude Lévi-Strauss's formulation that men exchange women like words or signs[30] and remarking that Penelope (and, I would add, Damayanti) "insists upon her status as a [speaking] subject, a generator of signs,"[31] especially the sign of the bed. The Hindu woman has a power over her husband that the Greek woman lacks and takes a more active role in planning the recognition scene: Damayanti sends messengers to seek Nala, while Penelope treads water, unweaving what she has woven. Penelope is far from her home, and alone, and under pressure by the people around her (the suitors) to remarry, while Damayanti is in her base of political power, with the support of her parents, and presumably under strong pressure *not* to remarry. Yet despite the fact that Damayanti is more active than Penelope, even Damayanti is still defined, like Penelope, by her fidelity to her husband. In the end, all four of them—Nala, Damayanti, Odysseus, and Penelope—must recognize both the identity and the fidelity of their partners.

◦⟡◦⟡◦⟡◦

Differences between the true husband and his impersonator, or between two forms of the same person, are often accounted for by the passage of time, the aging that produces natural changes. Natalie Zemon Davis's reconstruction of *The Return of Martin Guerre* tells of a man who, like Odysseus and Nala, but in recorded history, returned to his wife after a long absence in a war and had to prove to her that he was her husband, despite the changes wrought by time and suffering.[32] (In the American film version of that story, *Sommersby,* the hero returns from the American Civil War.) In those stories, the man is an impostor who pretends to be the man who left for the war long ago; the fact that age changes faces is used to justify the differences between the substitute and the original: "time has passed." But in the tales of Damayanti and Penelope, the true husband is pretending to be someone else, and time is called upon to account not for the trick of imposture but for the truth of change. The enemy of both identity and fidelity is time, which magically transforms the people we love into other people. Scientists tell us that our bodies are entirely regenerated, cell by cell, every seven years (the period also traditionally regarded as the limit for sexual fidelity, the so-called seven-year itch). How do we recognize one another, and ourselves, despite the ravages of time? Ask Penelope. Ask Damayanti. Ask David Grene.

Notes

1. Homer, *Odyssey* 17.300; 19.215–25, 250, 358, 381, 385, 389, 409, 468, 475, 516, 594; 21.218; 23.7, 73–75, 95, 113–15, 166, 202, 206, 225, 229, 254, 310.
2. See Gregory Nagy, "Sēma and Noēsis: The Hero's Tomb and the 'Reading' of Symbols in Homer and Hesiod," in *Greek Mythology and Poetics* (Ithaca: Cornell University Press, 1990), 202–22.
3. Aristotle, *Physics* 2.13–16.
4. Froma Zeitlin, "Figuring Fidelity in Homer's *Odyssey,*" in *Playing the Other: Gender and Society in Classical Greek Texts* (Chicago: University of Chicago Press, 1996), 19–52 (quotation on 20).
5. *Mahabharata* 1.176.10–12, 179.15–25.
6. I am indebted to Stephanie Nelson for pointing out to me the relevance of the bow contest to Penelope's testing of Odysseus.

7. Norman Austin, *Helen of Troy and Her Shameless Phantom* (Ithaca: Cornell University Press, 1994), 140.

8. Ibid., 161.

9. Zeitlin, "Figuring Fidelity," 23–25.

10. Ibid., 48.

11. Edmond Rostand, *Cyrano de Bergerac,* trans. into English verse by Brian Hooker (New York: Bantam Books, 1950), 160.

12. Johannes T. Kakridis, *Homer Revisited,* Publications of the New Society of Letters at Lund 64 (Lund: Gleerup, 1971), 154.

13. Ibid., 152–53, citing the variant given by Nikolaus Politis (no. 84).

14. Ibid., 154.

15. Ibid., 155.

16. Ibid., 160.

17. Ibid., 161.

18. *Mahabharata* (Poona: Bhandarkar Oriental Research Institute, 1933–69), 3.52–54.

19. Wendy Doniger, *Splitting the Difference: Gender and Myth in Ancient Greece and India* (Chicago: University of Chicago Press, 1999).

20. *Mahabharata* 3.68–75.

21. See Wendy Doniger O'Flaherty, *Hindu Myths* (Harmondsworth: Penguin, 1975), 175–78.

22. Ann Grodzins Gold and Lindsey Harlan, "Raja Nal's Story," paper presented at the Annual South Asia Conference, Madison, Nov. 1993.

23. Susan S. Wadley, "Raja Nal, Motini, Damayanti, and the Dice Game: Some Preliminary Thoughts," paper presented at the Annual South Asia Conference, Madison, Nov. 1993; Susan S. Wadley, "Bubbling Kings and Trickster Goddesses in the North Indian Epic Dhola," paper presented at Columbia University, Apr. 1996. My summary here has been supplemented by personal communications from Wadley.

24. Kakridis, *Homer Revisited.*

25. Zeitlin, "Figuring Fidelity," 24.

26. Ibid., 31–32.

27. Ibid., 43.

28. *Mahabharata* 1.181.

29. Ovid, *Metamorphoses* 13.162.

30. Claude Lévi-Strauss, *The Elementary Structures of Kinship,* trans. J. H. Bell, ed. Rodney Needham (Boston: Beacon Press, 1969), 496.

31. Mihoko Suzuki, *The Metamorphoses of Helen: Authority, Difference, and the Epic* (Ithaca: Cornell University Press, 1989), 88.

32. Natalie Zemon Davis, *The Return of Martin Guerre* (Cambridge: Harvard University Press, 1983).

A Bird, a Mouse, a Frog, and Some Fish: A New Reading of Leviticus 11

MARY DOUGLAS

The Bible commands the Jewish people to abjure certain animal foods, which are termed "unclean." The word "unclean" has been interpreted to mean "dirty" in the common sense, though it is in no common sense that the evil power of contagion is liable to contaminate the sanctuary. At its crudest, the argument proposed here is that the laws of unclean foods should be read as game laws rather than as dietary laws, not as prescriptions for what is healthy or unhealthy for the people to eat, but as rules for protecting animals from human predators.

The topic seems right in several ways for a volume in honor of David Grene, partly because its controversial character salutes him as an Irishman and compliments a countryman's interest in fish and animals. Also, Herodotus comes into the story, thanks to vividly remembered discussions we had about the translation of *The History* that he was making in 1981–85. Furthermore, Leviticus, another antique work of supreme literary skill, bristles with translation problems worthy of the interest of an accomplished translator.

What I offer here is part of a new reading for Leviticus 11, the chapter that describes the forbidden animal foods. My study of Leviticus develops all the time, and details are quickly superseded, though the main argument

I am grateful to Wendy Doniger, Walter Houston, Jacob Milgrom, and Robert Murray for reading an early version of this chapter and helping me with this argument, which will be published in *Leviticus as Literature* (Oxford: Oxford University Press, 1999).

has not changed.[1] I make the case that the listed species are not forbidden because they in any way arouse revulsion or because their nasty habits serve for moral allegories. Rather, the list must be read as part of a larger doctrine about living beings, human and animal, and their place in the scheme of creation. Comparative religion shows that usually when gods impose dietary rules upon their worshipers, an animal is not forbidden as food because there is anything wrong with the animal, anything abhorrent or disgusting about it. Rather, the animal turns out to have featured in the mythology as a strong or talented being which has rendered a service to the god, or in some prehistoric exchange a human ancestor incurred a debt of great magnitude to the ancestor of an animal species. They formed a pact of everlasting friendship, and in consequence the human descendants of the original beneficiary are forbidden to eat the animal descendants of the original benefactor. I write as an anthropologist of a generation taught about the philosophical principles underlying totemism and animal classification by Claude Lévi-Strauss, and expecting the whole structure of the universe to be involved in their explanation.

This essay focuses mainly on the category of creatures which Leviticus calls "swarmers," whether on land, in the water, or in the air. In Leviticus, creatures that swarm can be recognized by the way they glide about on their bellies. They do not have proper legs, they cannot walk or jump, but they crawl, slither, wriggle, or creep along; above all, they are abundantly fertile. Land swarmers are moles, lizards, worms, snakes, ferrets, and mice. Water swarmers are all the creatures that lack fins and scales— eels, mollusks, octopuses, crabs, lobsters, etc. Air swarmers are mostly insects. As the forbidden birds are named but not described, and so cannot be identified, I shall leave them out and concentrate on water and land swarmers.

Many scholars have tried to make sense of the biblical rules.[2] As most focus on a selected few of the classified beasts, the solutions tend to be piecemeal. They invoke, for example, an instinctive phobia against snakes, or they appeal to the mythology of the Garden of Eden: going on the belly figures in the curse that God put on the snake, so all belly-runners are cursed and therefore not to be eaten. Or the explanations are trivial, for example, supposing that revulsion for creepy-crawlies or at finding a fly in the soup explains the rules. Other explanations refer to the pastoral life of early Israel or postulate that the animals are allegorical of temptations to gluttony or lust or are forbidden simply because they are indigestible, unwholesome, or poisonous. A modern minimalist approach is to translate *ṭame',* not as "unclean," but as "impure," used in a technical and strictly ritual sense. In Mesopotamia the term *nig-nig* corresponds closely to the idea of biblical uncleanness in the sense of setting bounds to human action.[3] "Impure," *tame'*, as it is used in the Book of Leviticus, means not permitted to approach the altar, unbefitting the cult, dangerously contagious. Ritual impurity has always been a central idea in the religions of the eastern Mediterranean region and its hinterland.

In each religion purity has to do with whatever is understood about the emanation of power and danger from the awful majesty of God, and impurity often has something to do with demons. The idea that ritual impurity means unclean in the sense of dirty is so inadequate that it makes the coherence of Leviticus problematic. Such an egregious misinterpretation is worthy to be set beside Herodotus's story of a fatal misreading of a riddle about animals.

A Bird, a Mouse, and a Frog

The Persian king Darius thought he could easily conquer Scythia, and he sent his herald to the Scythian kings to tell them he would accept gifts of earth and water to signify their submission. In reply the Scythian kings sent

a bird and a mouse and a frog and five arrows. The Persians asked the bearer what was the meaning of these gifts. But the man said that he had no instructions given him save to give the gifts and get back home again with all good speed; the Persians, he said, if they were clever, would know the meaning of the gifts.

Darius interpreted the message as a surrender:

He formed his conjecture this way: that the mouse is a creature of the earth and eats the same fruits of the earth as man; that the frog lives in water; that the bird is the likest to a horse; and that the surrender of the arrows was the surrender of the people's own valour.

In other words, he assimilated the meaning of the gifts to the terms of his own message. He rejected an alternative opinion, which was as follows:

If you do not become birds and fly away into the sky or become mice and burrow into the earth or become frogs and leap into the lakes, there will be no homecoming for you, for we will shoot you down with our arrows.[4]

Darius grossly mistook the kind of culture he was dealing with. He took it for granted that they did not want to fight. He referred the animal symbolism to his own territorial interests and missed the reference to the animals' habits in response to danger. He also mistook the direction of the riddle, thinking it signified a submissive posture in the face of his attack, whereas it was a gesture of defiance, and so he misunderstood the five arrows. He misread the message because it was from an alien culture; the misreading was nearly disastrous, and rather than conquering the Scythians, his army barely escaped.

"Unclean" in Leviticus

The ancient list of animals forbidden in the Mosaic dietary code is like a riddle which gives a few characteristics and leaves the connection between them to be guessed. Presumably it was no riddle to the people to whom the writing was addressed. Leviticus states that some animals can be eaten, others are unclean *(tame')* and must not be eaten or their carcasses touched, and others are abominable *(sheqets)* and their carcasses not to be touched. But what makes some of them unclean? And what makes the others abominable? What do such diverse creatures have in common to come under the same rubric, opposed to holiness? Everything depends on what *tame'* means, or *sheqets*. The clues that Leviticus gives serve to identify the species, especially mentioning the legs and feet of land and air animals, and the fins and scaly covering of fish. Nothing is said about how they behave or what they eat.

The riddling style of these laws has left scope for debate and allowed a shift of the meanings of ritual impurity from the antonym of holiness toward material dirtiness. As dirt tends to do in real life, the concept of dirt has contaminated the conceptual field; the idea of disgust at eating unclean things dominates all the other rules. This was the case when the first-century rabbis debated the interpretation of the laws, and to this day it is common to explain ritual purity by natural reactions. A very distinguished Bible scholar supplies a perfect sample of this reasoning: "Many people wince at having to pick up a dead animal; most people (except two-year olds) try to avoid touching defecation; corpses inspire a natural feeling of awe, and we hesitate to touch them; washing off semen and blood is almost natural."[5] The kitchen, medical, and bathroom senses understandably intrude on interpretations of Leviticus since the book seems to play upon disgust at bodily exudations in its long disquisition on the meaning of atonement in chapters 12–15. But if you go by the secular idea of uncleanness, there is nothing self-evidently more unclean about pork to pork eaters than there is about beef to beef eaters; as for hare or camel or hyrax, there is nothing natural or obvious that makes these animals inedible and their carcasses not to be touched. This is the riddle. You cannot work it out from the description; you have to consider the other meanings in which these are enclosed.

The first step toward a solution is to read the text carefully again. There we find something unexpected: "impure" *(ṭame')* only applies to certain land dwellers. Creepy-crawlies from the air and the water are abominable, but they do not convey contagious impurity. This is a surprise, considering how strongly the idea of bugs and insects has come to dominate the interpretations of uncleanness. Jacob Milgrom found that Leviticus divides unclean animal foods into two sorts, one called *ṭame'*, the other *sheqets,* with completely different actions prescribed for each.[6]

Uncleanness or impurity is a contagious condition of a person, place, or thing and is incompatible with the service of the cult. When impure contact is discovered, something specific has to be done to cancel it: washing, waiting till nightfall, or a sacrifice. If nothing is done to cancel it, it will contaminate the sanctuary, with untoward consequences. Abomination occurs when a corpse is touched, but if there is contact and the corpse is not an animal in the "unclean" category, nothing has to be done and no penalties will befall. After touching the corpse of an unclean animal, the person has to wash and remain unclean until evening. Contact with the corpse of a water swarmer (Lev. 11.9–12) or air swarmer (Lev. 11.20, 23) is not unclean, it is off-limits; touching it is an "abomination," but no action is required. Water creatures, and nearly all insects, are counted as abominable but they are not called unclean.

Deuteronomy 14 treats "abomination" as a synonym for "uncleanness." The traditional reading of Leviticus, chapter 11, follows Deuteronomy. There are so many differences between Deuteronomy and Leviticus, however, that it would be poor practice to elide them and settle on a common denominator. Within Leviticus, but not within Deuteronomy, abomination *(sheqets)* and impurity *(ṭame')* belong in different systems of action, so they must be treated to that extent as different concepts. Since this essay is mainly about the rules for air and water dwellers, let us deal briefly with the impurity of land dwellers and then proceed to the abominations of air and water. Only the carcasses of certain land animals can convey impurity. Only ruminants with split hooves are pure. When the other types of land animals have all been listed as impure, look round and see what land animals are left—none.

Land Animals

Ruminant	Nonruminant
a. Split hooves (vv. 1–4)	*c.* Split hooves (pig; v. 7)
b. No split hooves (camel, etc.; vv. 4–6)	*d.* Solid hooves (horse, mule; v. 26)
	e. Paws (v. 27)
	f. Land swarmers (vv. 29–38)

All land animals are either clean or unclean (pure or impure). This was not apparent with older translations of verse 26, but when, as in the Jewish Publication Society translation, the verse is clearly taken to refer to animals with solid hoofs, we have a comprehensive typology of land animals:

a.   Animals of the flocks and herds, ruminants, split hooves
b.   Ruminants without split hoofs (camel, daman [Syrian hyrax], hare)
c.   Nonruminants with split hooves (pig)
d.   Nonruminants with solid hooves (ass, horse)
e.   Nonruminants with paws (e.g., lion, civet cat, dog, hyena)
f.   List of eight nonruminant quadrupeds that go on their bellies: mole, mouse, great lizard, gecko, land crocodile, lizard, sand lizard, and chameleon

Only the members of category *a* (split-hooved ruminants) are clean or pure; all other land animals are unclean or impure. In addition to the above six categories, there are land dwellers indicated as "swarming things that go on the belly, go on all fours, or with many feet" (v. 42) (tradition assumes these are insects, snakes, worms, spiders, and centipedes). The land swarmers are both impure and abominable. The people must not defile themselves by contact with their carcasses (vv. 43–44).

The zoological criteria are exhaustive for land animals. The classification neatly puts the domestic flocks and herds in one class, as ruminant ungulates. Two concentric circles organize land dwellers such that the domesticated beasts on whom the people of Israel depend for their livelihood are selected out of all other land animals and identified for consecration to God. The land of Judah is the center of the universe, and the temple is the center of the land of Judah and of the universe. Both the selected land and the selected quadrupeds correspond to the people of

Israel, who were selected from all other peoples for a consecrated destiny.[7] The effect is to make the flocks and herds a zoological parallel to the concentric microcosm of Israel in the universe. Eating only the consecrated animals brings the human body into the microcosm as a figure of the altar, on which only these same animals are acceptable. The land animals that are clean are consecrated to the altar, recalling the covenants of Noah and Abraham. They are the flocks and herds that come under the covenant, their firstborn belong to God, they keep the Sabbath. The effect of counting the other land animals as impure is to protect them from human predation.

Impurity is about unfitness to be consecrated; it is about the approach to the altar. If someone has gone further than just touching but has actually eaten a clean beast that has "died of itself" (i.e., died without being consecrated), the sanction is still mild: "Anyone who eats its carcass shall wash his clothes and remain unclean until evening; and anyone who carries its carcass shall wash his hands and remain unclean until evening" (v. 40). Of all land animals, only the carcasses of the clean domestic flocks and herds can be touched, carved for placing on the sacrificial altar, cooked for food, skinned for leather garments, bags, and containers, and have their horns removed for trumpets or drinking vessels. Whether the rule is meant to stop furriers, taxidermists, and carvers of bone or ivory ornaments, dice, or horn cups from practicing their trade, or whether they are merely expected to wash and be unclean until evening, we cannot tell. By the end of the chapter every living thing on the land has been included: ruminants and nonruminants, going on hoofs, going on paws, gliding on the belly. What else is there?

Leviticus divides land animals into two classes: the clean, which are the consecrated herds of the people of Israel; and the unclean, which includes land swarmers. The negative meaning of "unclean" for land animals is to be unqualified for consecration. It says nothing about nasty characteristics. In each of the three environments there is a permitted type for eating (split-hooved ruminant quadrupeds on land, birds with wings and two legs in the air, and fish with fins and scales in the water) and an unacceptable type (the swarmers). The air and water swarmers are abominable, not impure.

The Swarmers

In the water, true fish are allowed as food, but all the rest, which have no fins or scales, are disallowed (Lev. 11.9). A popular explanation for the law forbidding the touching or consumption of the carcasses of water animals without fins or scales is that they are scavengers. This idea derives from the English translation of the Hebrew word as "unclean" and has absolutely no justification in the text. What Leviticus specifies is that nothing may be eaten that lives in the waters and lacks fins or scales, and their carcasses must not be touched: "They shall remain an abomination to you; of their flesh you shall not eat, and their carcasses you shall not touch" (Lev. 11.11, also 12). It does not say there is anything inherently abominable about shrimps, crabs, eels, or octopuses, or even that they are universally to be abominated. They are just an abomination to the people of Israel. In the air, "all winged insects that go on all fours are an abomination to you," except those that "go on all fours that have legs above the feet with which to leap on the earth" (11.20–23). Some locusts pass the test. What about spiders and centipedes? "Going on all fours" is a graphic description of creeping or crawling, a concept associated in the text with swarming in any environment.

Every swarming thing that swarms upon the earth is an abomination; it shall not be eaten. Whatever goes on its belly and whatever goes on all fours or whatever has many feet, all the swarming things that swarm upon the earth, you shall not eat; for they are an abomination. (11.41–42)

You shall not defile yourselves with any swarming thing that crawls on the earth. (11.44)

Clearly it is a very solemn and important law. The peroration of the chapter connects avoidance of swarmers with holiness:

For I am the Lord, who brought you out of the land of Egypt, to be your God; you shall therefore be holy, for I am holy. This is the law, pertaining to beast and bird and every living creature that moves through the waters and every creature that swarms upon the earth, to make a distinction between the unclean and the clean and between the living creature that may be eaten and the living creature that may not be eaten. (Lev. 11.45–47)

The key words in English are "swarming" and "creeping"; in Hebrew, *sherets* and *remes*. To the editors of Leviticus a connection between eating swarming, creeping things and unholiness would seem to be as obvious as the message with the bird, the mouse, and the frog was to the Scythian kings. Before answering the question of why eating or touching the corpses of swarmers should be forbidden, three preliminary questions must be resolved.

One is why the word "abominable" *(sheqets)* should be used for these creatures. It is just not plausible that the merciful creator who in the first chapter of Genesis made the swarmers and blessed them and told them to go forth and multiply should turn round in Leviticus and tell his people that the animals are abominable. So the first question is why he should have made animals he detested. The answer proposed here is that he neither detests nor tells his people to detest the swarmers. The problem is in something about the English translation of *sheqets* as "abominable." Then the second question follows: "What is peculiar about the swarmers that they should be singled out?" The answer proposed has to do with their fecundity, which is recognizable in English if the Hebrew word *sherets,* often translated as "swarming," were always to be given the equally legitimate translation "teeming." The third question concerns the connection between teeming/swarming and moving/creeping/crawling. The answer to this question also answers the first and second and leads to another consideration altogether.

The argument here proposed is that the swarmer is not abominable at all. What is abominable is some action against it—eating it or even touching its corpse—which rules out butchering it for cooking or other uses. The confusion has arisen from the elision of *to'eba,* Deuteronomy's word for "abominable," with Leviticus's word, *sheqets.* In Deuteronomy it is usually an action that is abominated, such as worshiping idols or, for example: "You shall not do so to the Lord your God; for every abominable thing which the Lord hates they have done for their gods; they even burn their sons and daughters in the fire to their gods" (Deut. 12.31). The word in Leviticus that is translated "abominable" is taken to mean the same as the other term in Deuteronomy, *to'eba,* "abhorrent," "hateful," "detestable." The word *sheqets* is rare outside Leviticus and so is evidently a special priestly term. Breach of the law makes a person "abominable" (Lev. 11.41–45). In English we can say that cannibalism is detestable, but this does not mean that the victim is detestable. For Leviticus I would like to argue on the same lines that it is not a certain animal but the harming of it that is abominable. (The word in Deuteronomy, *to'eba,* which actually starts the list of unclean land animals, "You shall not eat any abominable thing" [Deut. 14.3], is generally used in translation as if it were exactly the same as *sheqets* in Leviticus, but it is a different word. The one book should not be used to interpret the other.)

A law code does not normally enjoin emotions like abhorrence. To be correctly translated, we could expect the law codes in Deuteronomy and Leviticus to consist of behaviorial injunctions: so, when the word for abominable is shorn of emotional quality, the law would be telling the people that they must shun or avoid these animals. My argument is that the impact of the law in Leviticus is simply to forbid doing harm to the creatures.

Why particularly avoid harm to the swarmers? My first idea was that the ones singled out for protective care are the most vulnerable, but on further reflection I now believe they are protected precisely because of their fecundity and abundance of life.

Fertility

The word *sherets,* translated as "swarming," has a strong connection with fertility. Levine says that it means "to come to life, crawl, swarm."[8] In Genesis the word is used for God's command to the waters to bring forth:

God said: Let the waters *bring forth swarms* of living creatures. . . . God created the great sea monsters and every living creature that *moves* [creeps, in some translations] with which the waters *swarm,* and all the winged creatures of every kind. And God saw that this was good. (Gen. 1.20–21)

After the Flood, when he made his covenant with Noah, he again told the living creatures to be fruitful and multiply, to "*bring forth abundantly* [*sherets*] on the earth and multiply in it" (Gen. 9.7). When *sherets* is used in Genesis it means benign fecundity. The same word in Leviticus has been translated so as to shed its connection with proliferation and bringing forth. It merely suggests a large, invasive crowd. This is part of the problem. Bringing forth abundantly has acquired an unwarranted pejorative sense in Leviticus.

Now turn to the word that is translated as "creep" or "crawl" *(remes).* Leviticus has said: "You shall not defile yourselves with any swarming thing that *crawls* [or creeps] on the earth" (11.44). Evidently swarming and crawling (or creeping) are associated in Leviticus as they are in Genesis. A biblical commentary says that *remes* is a general term for creatures whose bodies move close to the ground, such as reptiles, creeping insects, and very small animals.[9] Thus the creeping movement becomes a criterion to identify swarmers, and the verb "to creep" is assimilated to the notion of swarming. But again, creeping does not necessarily have a negative sense. In English, we can say that the flesh creeps; in Hebrew, the ground can creep, or an animal. The Hebrew dictionary cites Genesis, "all with which the ground creeps [teems]," "creep," "move lightly," "move about," or "move lightly" or "prowl" on land or "glide about" in the waters. In Genesis the word refers to any breathing thing, anything with the breath of life in it:

And to every beast of the earth and to every bird of the air and to everything that *creeps* on the earth, everything that has the breath of life. (Gen. 1.30)

And all flesh died that *moved* [*remes*] upon the earth, birds, cattle, beasts, *all swarming* [*sherets*] *creatures that swarm* upon the earth, and every man, everything on dry land in whose nostrils was the breath of life. (Gen. 7.21–22)

But the Leviticus translations have lost the main idea of the Hebrew word, the idea of life.

In English the meanings of the two words "swarm" and "creep" are so close that "teem" is found in the dictionary definitions for both. Only when we recognize that "swarming" connotes a fertility principle and that "creeping" connotes the life principle that is expressed by reference to movement does it make sense that swarmers are entitled to special protection in the Levitical laws.

We have posed the puzzle about the forbidden animals in terms of a paradox: how could the loving creator God tell his people to detest or abominate his creatures? What sense does it make? Do we have to be satisfied with a reading of Leviticus in which this paradox is unresolved? There is a common idea that the priestly editors of the Pentateuch and especially of Leviticus and Numbers lived in a privileged, secluded world of their own and promoted a view of religion that downplayed God's compassion, so praised by the prophets, in favor of finicky rules of purity. A wedge driven between the priestly and the prophetic teachings explains much of the misreading of the purity and abomination rules.

Jacob Milgrom has confessed to doubting that the God of the Bible would have rejected his animal creation. His view is that the Mosaic dietary system teaches reverence for all life by restricting wanton killing of animals.[10] In the same article he discusses rabbinical commentaries to that effect:

Rabbi Judah said in the name of Rab: "A man is forbidden to eat a thing until he had fed his beasts." But lest an individual opinion be regarded as too selective evidence, let us cite a Talmudic law: "To relieve an animal of pain or danger is a Biblical law, superseding any rabbinic ordinance." The same Rabbi Judah was painfully afflicted for his callous comment to a calf being led to the slaughter:

"Go, since for this you were created." And the Talmud continues: "After that a reptile ran past his daughter and she wanted to kill it. He said to her: Let it be, for it is written, His mercies are over all His works."[11]

Milgrom did not use that story to explain the specific impurity or abomination of the listed animals; on the contrary, he suggested that the riddle is insoluble. My own attempt to explain it starts from the point at which he stopped: the swarmers and creepers are all part of God's excellent creation, and what is defiling and abominable is to attack any of them. The negative verb "do not touch" is often used in the Bible in the sense we use it in English, as in "Don't you touch a hair of his head" or the standard cockney disclaimer "I ain't touched nuffink." In Genesis when King Abimelech commands his followers not to harm Isaac, he says: "Whoever touches this man or his wife shall be put to death" (Gen. 26.11), and a little later he says to Isaac, "We have not touched you and have done to you nothing but good" (26.29). In this light the prohibition on touching the carcass is quite different from the prohibition on eating. It has priority over it. It is about protection, not about cleanliness.

Leviticus and Deuteronomy agree that God's promise of fertility is the fundamental meaning of the covenant to the people of Israel. According to Deuteronomy, God has promised to multiply the people of Israel in return for their obedience:

And because you hearken to these ordinances and keep them, the Lord your God will keep with you the covenant and the steadfast love which he swore to your fathers to keep; he will love you, bless you, and multiply you; he will also bless the fruit of your body and the fruit of your ground, and your wine and your oil, the increase of your cattle, and the young of your flock . . . there shall not be male or female barren among you, or among your cattle. (Deut. 7.12–14)

The promise of fertility demonstrates God's compassion for his people; it is the reward of covenanted obedience and loyalty: "that the Lord may turn from the fierceness of his anger and show you mercy and have compassion on you and multiply you as he swore to your fathers, if you obey the voice of the Lord your God, keeping all his commandments" (Deut. 13.17–18). This would have been the traditional context in which the priestly editors described the creation in Genesis 1.20–23 and took such pains to mention the swarmers.

With fertility in mind, turn again to the criteria for fish which qualify as edible water dwellers: the scaly covering is a protective armor and the fins are a means of guided locomotion. Consider the octopus or the eel.

Without scales their soft skins are as vulnerable as shoals of young fish. I suggest that the swarmers are species in which the adult members have characteristics in common with the young of other species. Equipped with scales and fins, the fish would be able to look after itself. In other religions, including that of Mesopotamia, taboos often work like game laws, restricting the devastation of poachers.

Herodotus would have turned the argument into a wonderful story, pitting the commentators against each other, denouncing their errors, and presenting his own opinions. First, he would have the priestly editor ask, Is it not reasonable to assume that all the water creatures without fins and scales are swarmers, and that as such they exemplify the principle of fertility, and that their protection is the object of the law? Then Herodotus would have an opponent protest that it is far-fetched to relate the dietary laws to God's promise in Genesis to promote fertility on the land, in the air, and in the waters. Another opponent would add that the P source is quite a distinct source in the Pentateuch, and the priests do not see God as loving and compassionate, only as strictly insisting on formal correctness and purity. Another opponent would defend the traditional view that dirt is dirt and uncleanness is against holiness; swarmers are dirty, and why would God want to protect them? Herodotus would sum up by pointing out, on behalf of the Leviticus editor, that those interpretations depend on a very prejudiced view of the priestly writings. Then he might mention his own reports on the religion of the Egyptians, also priest-dominated, where animal life was held to be sacred:

Egypt . . . is not very populous in wild animals. But those that are there, wild or tame, are all considered sacred, both those that have their living with mankind and those that do not. (Herodotus 2.64–66)

Here is a people for whom the sacrifice of beasts themselves is unholy, except for pigs, bulls, bull-calves—that is, such as are pure—and geese. (2.45)

God's Compassion for His Creatures

The one concept that consistently relates the uncleanness rules to the abomination rules against touching swarmers' corpses, and relates these rules to the command of holiness, is God's compassion for living things. Can we suppose lightly that the priestly editors did not see God in the same light as the psalmist who says:

For he delivers the needy when he calls, the poor and him who has no helper. He has pity on the weak and the needy and saves the lives of the needy; from oppression and violence he redeems their lives. (Ps. 72.12–14; and see Pss. 145.8–9 and 104.24–29)

For anyone who might harbor an initial prejudice against priests (say, a congregation trained in the Deuteronomic School) it might appear that the priestly editors had a harsher theology. Deuteronomy forbids boiling a kid in its mother's milk, a rule taken to be a sign of sensitivity to the sufferings of animals. This famous rule has no place in Leviticus, but on the same score the latter has the rule allowing a newborn bull or sheep or goat to remain with its mother seven days (Lev. 22.26 ff.), which can be read in the same way. Reading the priestly writings so much later, when the old animosities have died down, we can ask whether the two schools were not in fact teaching the same central doctrine. Let us now accept that the God described in Leviticus is also merciful and that the laws he gave to Moses teach his people to be kind and to respect life.

We read what we are expecting to read, as Darius, in the riddle of the bird, the mouse, and the frog, only saw what he was expecting to see. The books of Moses (Exodus, Leviticus, Numbers, and Deuteronomy) give the impression of the people of Israel confronted by their God alone in a vast desert; no one else is there except hostile Canaanite armies, whom God keeps at a distance. But these same books are also emphatic on the danger of the people of Israel being seduced by other religions. Wherever priests think it necessary to put their doctrines into writing, they are likely to be in confrontation with other religions. There are always rival preachers seeking to attract the faithful to other shrines. A competition in holiness would be the context we should expect.

In the sixth and fifth centuries, when the priestly books are supposed to have been edited, the whole world as it was known to those who lived in the region from the Mediterranean to the Aegean and on through Asia Minor to the Himalayas was engaged in theological controversy about the right to take animal life. This philosophical context cannot be ignored in Bible interpretation. Empedocles in Sicily (490–430 B.C.) wrote poems about an idyllic golden age when the Goddess of Love prevailed and humans neither ate nor sacrificed animals. He taught that we are kin with animals and to kill and eat them, or to sacrifice them, is a crime.[12] We cannot assume that the priestly editors did not know the old oriental controversies about the sanctity of animal life. After all, there had been millennia of waterborne and land traffic over the region. They were not recluses; they had been to Babylon, they had been to Egypt, they would have been familiar with the Egyptian reverence for animals described by Herodotus. They would have met or heard of various ascetic religious groups. Though they would not have agreed with him, they might have had news of the dietetic precepts of Empedocles. There is no reason, either, to suppose that Empedocles was the first to teach the iniquity of killing animals.

Holiness is very often a competitive business, and in those days kindness to animals would be one of the obvious ploys in the spirituality stakes. In addition to protecting human life, Hinduism protects cows; Buddhism goes one better and protects all animals. Oriental ascetic movements which make a point of not killing often make respect for insect life the test case. "*We* are forbidden to kill insects!" is a winning strategy in competitive claims to spiritual worth. If animals are to be ranged according to their vulnerability, insects score highest. Individually, insects are the easiest living beings to kill, the most provocative and likely to be attacked, with power to annoy but not to protect themselves. The spies sent by Moses to scout out the Promised Land returned saying it was peopled with giants compared with whom they seemed to themselves as grasshoppers (Num. 13.33). Being likened to insects struck fear into the hearts of the people of Israel.

Jainism is supposed to have been founded in the sixth century and, along with Buddhism, claims to have links with more ancient pre-Vedic movements. This is the religion which requires its followers to look carefully where they walk, to sweep the path in front of them, and to examine the place where they are going to sit, lest they carelessly crush a living insect.

A monk should remain undisturbed even if bitten by insects. He should not scare them away nor keep them off. He should not kill living beings.[13]

After inspecting his cloth, the Jain monk should fold it and remove any living organisms that are there with his hand:

[O]ne who is careful in his inspection protects the six kinds of living beings, e.g. the earth bodies, the water bodies, the fire bodies, the wind bodies, plants and animals.[14]

[I]f crawling animals feed on his flesh and blood, he should neither kill them nor rub the wounds; even if these animals destroy the body, he should not stir from his position.[15]

Herodotus mentions some Indians situated very far to the south of the Persians, perhaps a religious community:

There are other Indians again, and another style of life. These will not kill any living thing, nor do they sow anything or possess houses; and what they eat is herbs. (3.100)

There is no reason to suppose the earliest written accounts of extreme ascetic movements coincided with the origin of asceticism. We should not conclude that this ascetic community only started when Herodotus reported it, or that it was unique. Such movements could have been contemporary with the beginnings of early Israel.

The priestly books could well have been composed partly as retaliation against other seductive religious doctrines. If the priests had not been conscious of competition, they would not have inveighed against idolatry. In the Middle East, devotees of dozens, or hundreds, of competing religious sects would have been scoring against each other with more and more exacting paths of renunciation.

However, the religion of Leviticus was a religion for all the people of Israel, not for a class of devoted monks. It was for practical life. Consequently, it is not surprising that the book does not forbid all animal killing. The cereal offerings of Leviticus have recently been analyzed, with the conclusion that they were equally important, if not more important, than the animal offerings.[16] If this is right, any tension there may have been within the cult between vegetarian and blood sacrifice is boldly resolved by presenting animal sacrifice as the linchpin of the covenant between God and his people. In this context of rival religions and pressures to vegetarianism, the Levitical prohibitions on animal foods were part of the total apologia, including the lessons on the meaning of blood. It is worse than anachronistic to read the injunctions about swarming and crawling creatures as expressions of disgust. On the contrary, at that time the rule about swarming things, "Do not eat them; it is abominable to touch their corpses," would be understood to express responsibility for the smallest of God's creatures.

Notes

1. Mary Douglas, "The Forbidden Animals in Leviticus," *Journal for the Study of the Old Testament* 59 (1993): 3–23; Mary Douglas, "Holy Joy: Rereading Leviticus," *Conservative Judaism* 46 (1994): 3–14.

2. Walter Houston, *Purity and Monotheism: Clean and Unclean Animals in Biblical Law,* Journal for the Study of the Old Testament, Supplement Series 140 (Sheffield: JSOT Press, 1993).

3. Mark Geller, "Taboo in Mesopotamia, a Review Article," *Journal of Cuneiform Studies* 42, no. 1 (1990): 105–17.

4. Herodotus, *The History,* trans. David Grene (Chicago: University of Chicago Press, 1987), 327–28.

5. E. P. Sanders, *Jewish Law from Jesus to the Mishnah: Five Studies* (London: SCM Press, 1990), 145.

6. Jacob Milgrom, "Two Biblical Hebrew Priestly Terms: *Seqes* and *Tame,*" *Maarav* 8 (1992): 107–16.

7. Mary Douglas, "Deciphering a Meal," in *Implicit Meanings* (London: Routledge, 1975), 210–30. Originally published in *Daedalus* 17 (winter 1972).

8. *Leviticus: The Traditional Hebrew Text with the New Jewish Publication Society Translation/Commentary by Baruch A. Levine* (Philadelphia: Jewish Publication Society, 1989), 67.

9. *Genesis: The Traditional Hebrew Text with New Jewish Publication Society Translation/Commentary by Nahum M. Sarna* (Philadelphia: Jewish Publication Society, 1989), 11.

10. Jacob Milgrom, "The Biblical Dietary Laws as an Ethical System," *Interpretation* 17 (1963): 291.

11. Ibid., 299.

12. Richard Sorabji, *Animal Minds and Human Morals: The Origins of the Western Debate* (London: Duckworth, 1993).

13. Kailash Chand Jain, *Lord Mahavira and His Times* (Delhi: Mitilal Banarsidass Publishers, 1974), 133.

14. Ibid., 140.

15. Ibid., 151.

16. Alfred Marx, *Les offrandes végétales dans l'Ancien Testament: Du tribut d'hommage au repas eschatologique* (Leiden: E. J. Brill, 1994).

Confabulating Cephalus: Self-Narration in Ovid's *Metamorphoses* (7.672–865)

W. R. JOHNSON

Und so erzähle ich mir mein Leben.   *Nietzsche*

Not a little of the fun, the elegance, and the power of David Grene's thinking derives from his skill and pleasure in the art of telling stories, so perhaps a brief essay touching one facet of that art will not be out of place in this collection. The essay deals with a Latin storyteller, it is true, and not one of Mr. Grene's beloved Greeks, but this impropriety he may allow, for the storyteller in question is invariably on most lists of the best in the West, and he is certainly among its wiliest.

That wiliness works for him nine times out of ten, but occasionally it doesn't. The tale of Cephalus and his dead young wife is one of those that cause their audiences to be vaguely dissatisfied and to start explaining to themselves why they feel what they are feeling when the story ends. In this case, most or at least many of Cephalus's listeners, the moment he has finished his tale, begin explaining to themselves why they feel as they do toward this man who, of course, has been telling a story that explains to himself and his listeners (among whom we are) how he feels and why he feels as he does about himself and his vanished Procris. Is he innocent or guilty? If there is any guilt (or innocence), is any of it hers; or hers as well as his? In its fluttering indeterminacy and its shifting pathos, in its teasing discords, the story is haunting, irritating, unforgettable. What I want to do here is not to explain away the tale's uncertainties but to try to describe something about how, as Auden would put it, "the contraption works."

On the surface, the story is simple enough. Cephalus, a young man recently and happily married, goes off one morning for a day's hunting. He is soon spotted by Aurora, goddess of the dawn, who whisks him off and has her way with him until his protestations (I love my wife) begin to annoy her and she sets him free. On his way home he begins to wonder if Procris, his wife, has been faithful to him. He decides to test her, and, having changed his appearance (with Aurora's help), he attempts to seduce her. Procris resists his blandishments easily, but finally he makes an offer for her virtue that she cannot (or will not) refuse. He throws off his disguise and accuses her of intended infidelity. Furious, she flees him for the solace and protection of a life in the wild, in the service of the virgin goddess Diana. But he cannot live without her, he pleads with her to take him back, admits that he too would have yielded if he had been tempted as she had been tempted by him. His suit is successful. She returns to him, giving him, as an earnest of her faith in their reunion, two gifts, a spear that never misses its mark and that also returns, having accomplished its task, to the hand that hurled it; and, no less wonderful, a dog that Diana had given her, a dog that was faster than any other in the world.

For a while (the length of time is left vague) they are happier than ever before. He goes back, naturally, to his second love, hunting, and gets into the habit, when he's tired out by the morning's exertions, of lying down and letting the breeze blow over him and cool him off. This ritual seems to involve his actually invoking the breeze, coaxing it, whispering to it, and speaking its name, Aura. Some busybody rushes off to Procris and tells her what her husband and Aura are up to. She struggles against believing this report's veracity, but at last she yields to her jealous suspicion and goes off to lie in wait for the hunter, to catch him in the act. The inevitable happens. She hears him call for Aura, she groans. He hears another sound (a leaf falling) and casts his spear into the foliage; he hears her cry out and rushes to find her dying, trying to pull the spear from her wound. She begs him not to let Aura take her place in his affections. He explains her mistake to her, and this seems to comfort her somewhat, and she dies *vultu meliore mori secura videtur* ("she seemed to die untroubled, with a better expression on her face"; maybe a slight smile?).

Cephalus, the teller of his own tale, is an old man at the time of the telling.[1] He has come from Athens to ask King Aeacus that he ally Aegina with Athens against the threats made to it by Minos, king of Crete. When his request is granted and preparations are being made to send troops to Athens, Phocus, youngest of the princes of Aegina, asks him about the remarkable spear he is carrying with him. With some hesitancy, tearfully, the old man complies and begins to tell its/his tale to Phocus and to

Clytus and Butes, two young nobles who have accompanied him from Athens and who have doubtless heard this story before (missing from this situation of discourse are Aeacus, who is asleep, and his elder sons, who are off mustering their troops). In trying to assess the accuracy of his version of his tale, we should not underestimate Cephalus's age (in addition to the epic garrulity of the aged, defects of memory also matter), nor, probably, should we discount the information we received at his first entrance, back at 496–97, about how he looks, for the remnants of his former good looks *(veteris pignora formae)* are so vivid that he remains even now *spectablis*. The narrating I is a handsome, fading echo of the yet more handsome narrated I, and those fabled, hunky looks are central to his tale.

But before we start the search for that shifting and unstable center, we might do well to face up, at the outset, to his story's major inconsistency. The first thing we learn about the spear (683–84) is that it hits what it is aimed at, that contingency cannot obstruct it, that it returns, bloody and of its own accord, to the hand of its hurler *(consequitur quodcumque petit, fortunaque missum / non regit, et revolat nullo referente cruentum)*. Yet at his story's close, just after he has summoned his breeze *(aura, veni, veni, optima)* and hears (or thinks he hears, *videbar*) groans that interrupt his summons *(inter mea verba)*, he hears (or thinks he hears?) the rustle of a falling leaf (as he now understands), which he interprets as the presence of a wild animal, and lets fly a spear in that general direction (he need not have the beast in view, for the spear will not miss its mark). Procris cries out, and of course he recognizes her voice and runs to her *praeceps amensque* (844). The spear has penetrated the middle of her chest (he supplies this detail before he narrates his finding of her; he has transferred it back to the moment before he discovers her) and he comes upon her *(et sua, me miserum, de vulnere dona trahentem)* trying to dislodge her gift to him from the wound it has made in her. He does not tell us how, but somehow the spear is removed, and he props up, in gentle arms, the body dearer to him than his own *(corpusque meo mihi carius ulnis / mollibus attollo)*, then tries to staunch the blood and to bandage the wound as he begs her not to die and leave him guilty of her death *(neu me morte sua sceleratum deseret, oro; 850)*. That is not quite yet the closure he fashions for the story of his narrated I and his griefs, but before we look at that final moment, we need to consider what he says about his magic spear.

The easiest thing to say would be: Ovid forgot what he said about the spear's boomerang feature (as an advertiser might call it) when he depicts Procris in the act of trying to pull out the spear. The spear should have done its deadly work and flown back *(revolat)* to the hand of its new owner, but perhaps this is a section of the poem that Ovid failed to revise (maybe he had noticed the lapse but never got around to fixing it: this is somewhat preferable to positing his sheer forgetfulness or outright, ignorant blundering).[2] Or we might suppose that Clytus or Butes, whichever of the two it is that describes the properties of the spear (*Actaeis e fratribus alter;* 681 ff.), was exaggerating a little in order to impress another teenager (his teenage host), but that seems rather far-fetched. Or one could suppose that the spear itself, dismayed to find it had mortally wounded its previous owner, began to malfunction. Perhaps there are other explanations as well. The one that I find attractive is that Cephalus has invented this last scene, that he has become so locked into believing it (desperately) that its huge discrepancy never occurs to him (in the language of our day, he "denies" it); and his audience (this one, along with all the others that have listened to his story over the years since the event it represents took place) either misses the discrepancy or it ignores it, lets it go.

What did happen in those last few seconds of Procris's life? What I piece together from the fragments that Cephalus (or his memory) has collected (and invented) and assembled is something like this: she followed him that last morning (someone had told her about Aura), and when he stopped to rest, she stopped too and hid in the bushes and waited; he summoned Aura, Procris groaned (for she discovered the bad truth that he was unfaithful), he responded "automatically" to the sound he heard and launched his (her) spear; it killed its prey (perhaps she screamed) and returned, bloody, to the hand of Cephalus; he went to see what he (or it) had killed; he found her there dead.

Is he lying then? No, he is confabulating.[3] He believes, he has come to believe, he has learned to believe, that he remembers what he has in fact slowly constructed in order to cover over a hole in his memory, a hole that once held what he could not bear to remember, to believe, to know, what he had begged her not to let him be left with when, in his perfected version of her death, he asks her not to die and make him guilty of her death. He is, of course, innocent of her death, as even the most hostile dismantling of his version will end by admitting. But, of course, he is also guilty of her death, as another style of dismantling his version will show, for what confabulation—his sincere belief in the texture of his lies—has imperceptibly pieced together for him, year after year, as the story was retold and retold and retold, is a tale of his innocence, an innocence that hides his guilt.

But in what would that guilt consist? He cannot be (but can he feel?) guilty of her death (for as regards that unlucky cast of the fatal spear, his real innocence more than balances any formal responsibility). Perhaps he feels not so much guilty for what he did (a particular action, a particular set of actions) as for what he is (or was: the narrating I, after all, is still constructing his palimpsest of his narrated I's). Let's investigate that, the kind of person, the kind of husband, he was.

One thing he emphasizes about himself is that he was a happy (and lucky) person. As a prelude to the first section of his narrative (Aurora's attentions and their aftermath), he states that he was held to be *felix* and in fact was so in getting Procris as his wife *(felix dicebar eramque);* but his luck didn't last, because the gods were against him *(non ita dis visum est, aut nunc quoque forsitan essem;* 699–700), or he would be happy still. When beginning the second section of his narrative (after his reconciliation with Procris), he speaks of the early years of their marriage (he has erased the rupture) as blissful: *primos rite per annos / coniuge eram felix, felix erat illa marito* (798–99). Husband and wife, each was the other's happiness. That blessed mutuality he seems to understand well enough to be able to distill it into a superb and memorable line: *mutua cura duos et amor socialis habebat* (800). But then a curious hyperbole weakens our trust in his assertion. Procris would not have yielded to Jupiter himself, nor could any female have won him away from Procris, not Venus herself *(non si Venus ipsa veniret;* 802), so absolute was their fidelity to one another *(aequales urebant pectora flammae,* "identical flames burned our breasts"; 803). But *flammae* and *curae* (together with their *amor socialis*) are not the same thing. The flames are sexual and they are erotic (physical drive and imaginative elaborations of that drive), and they do not necessarily include the concerns, the regard, the worry, or the affection that committed, contented, ordinary, domestic "wedded bliss" entails. That process of happiness (it is not, except for purposes of logical reflection, a state), the dynamics of a stable relationship, whether inside or outside marriage, includes the erotic and the sexual, but it subordinates them to a more complicated and less flexible or less capricious design than the one that Cephalus really values. He liked perhaps the idea of being married (he, the narrated I at the time of the narration), but he didn't like, or to be fair, he didn't understand, the peculiar constraints that *cura* and *amor socialis* put upon the erotic imagination ("he just didn't get it"). That does not make him guilty, of course, but some part of him knows (and the more he tells his story, the more that part of him knows) that Procris is dead because his erotics could not or would not yield to the claims of *cura* and *amor socialis*.

He is very beautiful, and interesting things tend to happen to him when he's out there all alone in the wild, hunting (and being hunted). After he is reconciled with his wife and their happy marriage is resumed (its rupture, not unreasonably, unremembered), it is slightly disconcerting to find him heading out once again, again all by himself, into the very place that brought him such grief before. He does not say that he was without companions when he encountered Aurora, but every indication suggests that he was. Now, once again happily married, he is up at dawn, day after day: *venatum in silvas iuvenaliter ire solebam, nec mecum famili . . . tutus eram iaculo* (805–8). "It was my custom to go hunting every day, alone, into the woods, with the kind of zest that young men have for their hunting." The adverb is a charming touch. It is the narrating I's nostalgic admiration for his narrated I, an old man's wise condoning of youthful folly. Was he safe by himself, that impulsive young man, safe with his spear (his fatal spear)? Ought he to have wandered around in the dangers of the forest alone? The old man thinks not, but he knows, he remembers, what it was to be young, passionate, greedy for life's good things—one must not be harsh, judgmental.

But perhaps the old man should not be so indulgent. He knows that the narrated I is once again entering the lovely wild (it is where, throughout this poem, bad things happen to good young people, and the narrating I knows those conventions as well as the poem's protean narrator who narrates him), and he also knows that what happened to him before is going to happen to him again, *eadem sed aliter:* that is to say, once again he is going to lose his wife.

There are various ways of describing the wild and how it functions here and elsewhere in the poem. I want to focus on it as the site of the narrating/narrated I's shared erotic imaginations (the old man's structuring memory of the young man's sense of his erotic self). Cephalus is very beautiful, and he is (by choice) all by himself in the wild (for the moment, I leave aside his hunting and his prey and his phallic spear though they are doubtless part of his erotic fantasmatic).[4] Perhaps there were erotic moments, real or imaginary, in the first two months of the marriage (700) that the old man chooses to discard or conflate, but on his first (recorded) visit to the wild, the young husband's beauty brought him the attention of an amorous goddess. When we find him in the wild once again, he has developed the habit of wooing (and winning?) the ministrations of another (now, imaginary) goddess whose name faintly echoes his first (real) goddess.[5] This habitual dalliance with an imaginary lover finally comes to light when its random witness reports it to Procris (the *nescio quis* of 822). If chance or cruel fate had not sent the busybody into the wild, Cephalus would not have lost his wife, and neither would he have lost (and lost them he has, for grief has ruined them) the dalliances, the delicious isolation, the imaginary Aura and the memories of the real Aurora that his conversations with the breeze freshen and magnify. They want him, he is beautiful, he is alone and inviolable, and only the goddesses can have him, because they cherish him and solace him and serve him, because they worship his perfection.

If Procris had not died, Cephalus would have continued going into his world of dream erotics and he would have continued to be a normal, blissful husband. He would, without quite knowing it, have continued leading this double life till the day he died. But because the busybody sent by destiny intervened, the imaginary world that was real to him (the erotic wilderness of Aurora and Aura and his own celebrated beauty) collapsed in upon the "real" world that he could never quite grasp and keep his mind on (Procris, himself as an ardent young husband). The young Cephalus did not understand what happened to him and how and why it happened, nor (consciously) do the various versions of the young Cephalus that his older narrating selves keep reinventing as they palimpsestically replace one another: indeed, they are fervently united in the purpose of trying to make sure that this complexly innocent "he" will never find out (or "recollect") what happened (in his *Devil's Dictionary,* Ambrose Bierce defines "recollect" thusly: "to recall with additions something not previously known"). Guilty though he is (guilty, we now see, in every way), they labor, endlessly revising their revisions, to make sure he will be, in his own eyes and in theirs, forever innocent, forever young, and forever *felix* as well, had wicked heaven relented and been kind.

And Procris, what of her? What was she guilty of, and in what degree?[6] In various other versions that Ovid displaced or reshaped or suppressed in order to create a story for his Cephalus to narrate, her guilt is huge or at least equal to her husband's. She is, in these stories, promiscuous or jealous or vindictive or all of the above. But as one unpacks the Ovidian version, these earlier, other Procrises are erased along with their guilt. Crucial here (both to her innocence and to Cephalus's representation of his own innocence) is what he has to say about the infidelity she had been willing to commit when the price became right (*dum census dare me pro nocte loquendo / muneraque augendo tandem dubitare coegi;* 739–40). After numerous attempts to seduce her had failed (and he admits that their failure should have satisfied him), he finally got her to hesitate (between yes and no) by increasing the promised fee for her favors until she could no longer say no. "I forced her to hesitate"; that's what he says. But how did he know? She apparently said nothing. Did he read it in her face, in her hands, her posture? But suppose he misread her. Suppose in his eagerness to trap her (what he remembers now is his initial joy in finding her at first inviolable) he had become impatient and had mistaken her irritation (she was perhaps about to order him to leave) for the beginnings of compliance (she was angry, stammering, pale, blushing, "not herself"?).

In any case, she rushes off, furious, to the wild and to Diana. That irrational flight seemed then a proof of her guilt (lust in the heart) even though he himself now (in telling the story, as then when it "happened") feels guilty for having doubted her, for having tricked her (743–46). (So he says: but she did in fact, he also says, capitulate: so she was also unfaithful. They are equal now in infidelity.)

What actually happens next in the story (that Cephalus is trying to tell, trying not to tell) is unclear. She has gone off to the mountains. He tells his audience that her absence made his heart fonder, that he went to her and confessed his guilt in treating her as he had, that he begged her pardon, telling her that he himself might have succumbed had he been tempted as she had been tempted (747–50) (but in fact he had succumbed to Aurora). Did he go to her, or did she return? In the most plausible version of this section of "the basic tale," Diana, though she loves Procris, must send her back because she is not a virgin, but the goddess gives her the spear and the dog which she in turn will give to her husband. So it is possible that Procris returned to him rather than he went to find her. It is also possible that they came looking for one another, that they came together in mutual need and mutual desire. In his version, he comes off very well: he blames himself even though he is more innocent than she is (he is guilty only of a true lover's desperate subterfuges, but she, of greed and adulterous tendencies—and she exacted revenge from him by abandoning him, *laesum prius ulta pudorem,* 751). Moreover, he had the courage to admit his mistake, and he really loved her, and all that adds up to a pretty nice guy.[7]

Once Cephalus has recounted his reunion with his wife, the story could (and maybe should) move on to its closure, for it was Phocus's question about the spear that had generated the narrative (685–86), and Cephalus's adumbration of its tragic history (688–93) has given the tale its focus and its goal. But Cephalus is (as we have begun to guess) in no hurry to get to that final image. He has chanced to mention the *canem munum* that came along with the spear. Would Phocus like to hear about the dog as well as the spear (*muneris alterius quae sit fortuna, requiris?* 757)? As we presently see, what really interests Phocus is the spear, but he is polite and raises no objection to hearing the wonderful tale of Laelaps, the fastest dog in the world, who was turned to marble along with the horrific monster he was chasing in circles until a god, perhaps to end their perplexities, transformed them from unshaped marble into shaped marble (i.e., statues; 792–93). One might think that a young man might like listening to a miraculous hunting tale very well told by a famous hunter, but Phocus is obsessed with the spear (a nice touch of Sophoclean irony this, considering what is going to happen to him: death from a spear tossed by Peleus, who is now busy elsewhere, collecting the soldiers for the Athenian cause).[8] When Cephalus finishes the story of Laelaps, he falls silent (as if, almost, he were not going on to tell about the spear), but Phocus is ruthless in reminding him of his obligations to his audience: *iaculo quid crimen in ipso est?* (794).

Cephalus begins again (but the momentum of *her* story is broken in a way that an effective "transparent" and primary narrator would be less likely to let happen); this secondary narrator, husband of the dead woman, delays his movement to the fatal scene. He lingers on their initial bliss (*iuvat o meminisse beati / temporis . . . quo primos rite per annos / coniuge eram felix, felix erat illa marito;* 798–800). Here he emphasizes, as we have seen, the perfected mutuality of their union. Then he describes, innocently, easily, his habit of summoning aura (Aura, Aurora), giving no indication whatever that he recognizes anything strange in this repetition (and the compulsions and repressions that engineer it). He sketches what the unknown *temerarius index* (824) deduces from what he chances to overhear and describes how the *index* takes this story of the young hunter's passion for a nymph straight to his wife (*linguaque refert audita susurra;* 825).

Then Cephalus does a curious thing, curious but natural. He puts to good use an old saw (*credula res amor est* [826], "love is not skeptical"—of good signs, of bad signs?) which valorizes his focalization of Procris, his representation of what his wife felt and thought on hearing this whispered slander. First she fainted, overwhelmed with emotion *(subito conlapsa dolore . . . cecidit),* "so I am told" *(ut mihi narratur).* This is his warrant for representing a complex compound of emotions and thoughts that his source can hardly have been privy to (unless it was, here suppressed, one of those ubiquitous nurses from tragedy, eavesdropping on Procris's soliloquy). But maybe Cephalus is doing more here than filling in the blanks his informant left. Maybe there was no informant; maybe he is "making it all up" (826–34):

And love is credulous. Struck down by grief—
so I am told—she fainted. When she gained
her senses—slow in coming back—she wept,
said she was wretched; and her long lament
mourned her betrayal; in her misery
over a sin that never was, she feared
a nullity, a name without a body;
poor Procris grieved as if she had indeed
a rival. Yet from time to time she felt

some doubt and hoped that she had been mistaken;
she would reject the tale of her informer,
refusing to condemn her own dear husband
if she'd not seen him sin with her own eyes.[9]

He is making it up (or goes to extreme lengths in elaborating what he can only guess at) both because he is a good (competent, not necessarily reliable) storyteller and wants adequate motivation for his wife/heroine and because her conflicted jealousy echoes and mirrors his jealousy in part 1 of his story. That echoing mirror vindicates him once again: he was wrong to be jealous of her (but his jealousy proved his love) just as she was wrong to be jealous of him (but her suffering and her decision to prove herself wrong are the indices of her noble passion). His inferences, to be sure, are logical, but (to take one other version among others), she may have assumed that her source had misheard the name Aura and that he had taken up with the dawn goddess, Aurora, again; she may have gone off to catch them in flagrante and then give to both of them a piece of her mind and to him his walking papers, once again and this time for good. And, of course, she may not have fainted at all. Either the hero's source might have added that (obligatory and gendered) detail (she was hysterical) or Cephalus may have had no source whatever and may have tossed it in for the sake of "the illusion of reality." There are all sorts of ways of representing what she may possibly have felt on hearing about Aura.

And there are as well all sorts of ways of representing how she died. What Cephalus gives his audience is a sort of lyrical death. He comes upon her in her agony, he lifts her up, he tends to her wound, he begs her not to die (and thus abandon him, leaving him looking guilty of her death; 850). Her strength has failed her rapidly, but just on the point of death she forces herself to say a few last words (*viribus illa carens et iam moribunda coegit / haec se pauca loqui;* 851–52). She begs him *(supplex oro)* by the vows of their marriage bed, by the celestial gods and her own personal gods, by her love for him that has been fatal to her, she begs him to promise he will not marry Aurora. When she says this, of course, he realizes what her mistake has been and he quickly corrects it *(et sensi et docui),* but he realizes that the truth is not useful here. She slumps as he holds her; her vital powers trickle away with her blood. But as long as she can see, she looks up at him and breathes out her unhappy spirit into him, in his mouth (note the awkward slippage of prepositions and the strange shift of pronomials, *et in me infelicem animam nostroque exhalat in ore,* 860–61, "into me," "in our mouth," as if the event or the memory of the event resists intelligibility and defies spatial imagination).[10]

But at the instant of her death something unhoped for has happened: *sed vultu meliore mori secura videtur* (862). She seemed to die without a care, literally, "with a better face." So, after all, she has lived just long enough to understand his correction, to see her stupid mistake, and can therefore die *secura,* with a faint smile on her face, at the very least without stress that would disfigure the beautiful face, which looks its last look at him, understanding it all, forgiving him, loving him (*flentibus haec lacrimans hero memorabat;* 863). The weeping hero recounted these things to an audience he had reduced to tears.

Cephalus puts his grief aside and steps back into the public world. The swift closure of the story and of book 7, which contains it, gives us no chance to reflect on it until we have closed the volume and reviewed the story in our minds (or reopened the volume, reread the death scene, then continued to read the story backward to its poignantly innocent inception), continuing to pick at its knots until, recalling that the spear behaved improperly (perhaps we noticed that impropriety and let it go for the sake of suspending disbelief), we find we are not happy with the teller's version of his own tale, that we are not at ease with its beautiful death and, it may be, its beautiful lie. We may finally decide that we understand why he has spent his life inventing this fiction (and why he likes telling it); we may finally decide that we have some sympathy for him.

But mostly what his story has moved me to do (in this reading of it) is to try to reconstruct from its countertale, here, the story embedded in the fissures of his story (her story).[11] Not a little of what commends Ovid to us, of what has charmed centuries of readers (at whatever spot they fixed him in the shifting hierarchies of the canons), is to be located in his feeling for the underdog, his desire to help the losers have their say, his skeptical perspective on the victors' versions, his profound and playful belief that stories are, for the most part, as polysemic, polycentric, and polymorphous as the worlds within worlds they represent and as the listeners that desire them.[12]

Notes

1. For another view of Cephalus's age, see the useful observations of Frederick E. Brenk, "*Tumulo Solacia* or *Foedera Lecti:* The Myth of Cephalus and Procris in Ovid's *Metamorphoses,*" *Augustan Age* 2 (1982): 21 n. 6.

2. See W. S. Anderson, "The Example of Procris in the *Ars Amatoria,*" in *Cabinet of the Muses: Essays on Classical and Comparative Literature in Honor of T. G. Rosenmeyer,* ed. M. Griffith and D. J. Mastronarde (Atlanta: Scholars Press, 1990), 131–45. As Anderson

points out (133, 139), Ovid does correct this "infelicity" when he comes to rewrite the story in his revision of the *Ars Amatoria*, adding, according to a newly suggested chronology, a third book to the previous two (131–32).

3. See Daniel C. Dennett, *Consciousness Explained* (Boston: Little Brown and Co., 1991), 250. The confabulation is perhaps structured by *Deckerinnerung*, by a screen memory wherein a more dreadful image is displaced (or hidden) by one somehow less dreadful. Here, his feckless habits with the magic spear (all his irresponsibilities) are dissolved into, disappear into, the pathos of his futile efforts to undo her death.

4. See Kaja Silverman, *Male Subjectivity at the Margins* (New York and London: Routledge, 1992), 3–10 and passim. "The fantasmatic . . . [is] the unconscious prototype for all dreams and fantasies, . . . the structuring scenario behind symptoms, transferences and other instances of repetitive behavior" (3). See also Jean Laplanche and J. B. Pontalis, *Le vocabulaire de la psychanalyse* (Paris: Presses Universitaires de France, 1967), 153–59.

5. For an insight into the "aesthetic thrill" of these complex mirrorings, see Leonard Barkan's observations on the link between Petrarch's Laura and Ovid's Aurora/Aura in *The Gods Made Flesh: Metamorphosis and the Pursuit of Paganism* (New Haven: Yale University Press, 1986), 208–9.

6. A precise and eloquent argument for her innocence is made by Joseph Fontenrose, "Ovid's Procris," *Classical Journal* 75 (1980): 289–94, which specifically answers the accusations against her by Peter Green, "The Innocence of Procris," *Classical Journal* 74 (1979): 15–24 (among them, that she is "a conniving little trollop," 24). For rumors of her guilt that a (chivalrous?) Cephalus "suppresses," see Sara Mack, *Ovid* (New Haven: Yale University Press, 1988), 131–34.

7. For acute observations on the complexities of line 751, see R. J. Tarrant, "The Silence of Cephalus: Text and Narrative Technique in Ovid, *Metamorphoses* 7.685 ff.," *Transactions of the American Philological Association* 125 (1995): 106–7.

8. By Peleus or by Teleamon. Ovid opts for Peleus in lines 267 ff., but there are a number of variants as regards both weapon and perpetrator. A fatal discus is traditional, but death at a boar hunt (by spear?) is among the possibilities. See Sir J. G. Frazer's note in his edition of Apollodorus, *The Library* (Cambridge: Harvard University Press, 1989), 2:57–59. For the situation of discourse, see Betty Rose Nagle, "Ovid's *Metamorphoses*: A Narratological Catalogue," *Syllecta Classica* 1 (1989): 110–11.

9. The translation is that of Alan Mandelbaum, *The Metamorphoses of Ovid* (San Diego: Harcourt Brace, 1993), 243.

10. See F. Bömer's commentary, *Metamorphoses* (Heidelberg: C. Winter, 1976), 3:375, for the syntactic anomalies of the verse; see Hermann Frankel, *Ovid: A Poet between Two Worlds* (Berkeley and Los Angeles: University of California Press, 1945), 215–16, for a discussion of how the narrator's use of *anima* functions here to complete a "triple entendre" that effects "a tragic irony of the pathetic type," but the pathos is Cephalus's and the irony is that of the narrator who narrates him.

11. For the principle involved here, see Pierre Macherey, *A Theory of Literary Production*, trans. Geoffrey Wall (London: Routledge, 1978), 85–89, 132.

12. The perspective has similarities with that of Nietzsche in *Twilight of the Idols*, "Reason in Philosophy," 1; "Morality as Anti-Nature," 6; "Expeditions of an Untimely Man," 10. For a valuable discussion of variations in styles of readings and of readers (and their changing texts), see John Frow's description of fashions in English Homers in his *Marxism and Literary History* (Cambridge: Harvard University Press, 1986), 170–78.

Memory and Imagination in Augustine's *Confessions*

TODD BREYFOGLE

Memory, like love, is an act of imagination, an abandonment and a possession.
Susan Dodd, Mamaw

Augustine's *Confessions* is at once an autobiographical remembering and an imaginative presentation of the spiritual life of an author of enormous literary consciousness and ability. Of all the works of the Augustinian corpus, few have received as much attention as the *Confessions*. One is tempted, thus, to paraphrase Isidore of Seville—who remarked that anyone who claimed to have read all of Augustine's works is a liar—and say that only a liar would claim to say something new about the *Confessions*. I have no desire to be called a liar. I do, however, wish to offer some provisional thoughts and suggestive remarks on an apparently central topic which has been little discussed: the relationship between memory and imagination in Augustine's *Confessions*.[1]

I

Augustine's theoretical treatment of memory, which has of course received extended treatment, occurs in book 10 of the *Confessions*. We cannot engage the vexing debate regarding the relationship between the first

I am pleased to offer this essay in gratitude to David Grene, who understands, with Augustine, that the stories we read often tell us as much about ourselves as they do about those who write them. In deference to the story itself, and to David, I have kept notes and scholarly argument to the barest minimum.

nine and final four books of the *Confessions* here. Suffice it to say that in writing the thirteen books of the *Confessions* Augustine saw them as an integrated whole. It is not surprising, then, that after nine books of confessional remembrance of his life's events and their meanings that Augustine should turn to reflect on the faculty of memory itself.

The real continuity between book 10 and the narrative that precedes it lies in the fact that the *Confessions* as a whole are an ascent to God. That is, they are the record of a heart's journey to God. The narrative of book 9 ends with remembrances of Augustine's mother, Monica, whose life had been so instrumental in her son's conversion and with whom Augustine had shared a mystical ascent to the divine shortly before her death. The shift from the content of memory to memory itself in book 10 is thus a natural one. If we ascend to God by means of remembrances, Augustine's argument would seem to run, perhaps we may ascend higher by understanding more fully memory itself. In introducing the topic of memory he writes: "I shall pass on, then, beyond this faculty in my nature [i.e., sense perception] as I ascend by degrees toward Him who made me. And I come to the fields and spacious palaces of memory" (10.8).

The shift to memory is thus also a shift from material to spiritual reality. To be sure, memory is a "treasurehouse," a "great harbor" of images brought to us by sense perception. But it stores only images, not the material things themselves.[2] A "boundless subterranean shrine," memory is the place which is no place. Thus, memory is part of Augustine's shift—which he attributes to the writings of the Platonists, probably Plotinus—toward recognizing the reality of nonmaterial substances.

Memory is more than just a storehouse of images derived from sense perception. For example, Augustine contends, in storing the liberal sciences learned at school, memory does not possess images of the knowledge but the knowledge itself. Further, there are things in memory that do not impress their images upon us from outside. The laws of number and dimension, for example, have their reality apart from a body. It would appear then, for Augustine, that they are known innately, from within. He writes:

Touch says, "If the thing is not a body I did not handle it, and if I did not handle it, I gave no information about it." From where, then, and how did they enter into my memory? I do not know. For when I learned them, I was not taking them on trust from some other mind; I was recognizing them in my own mind . . . even before I learned them, but they were not in my memory. Then where were they? Or how was it that, when I heard them spoken, I recognized them and said: "That is right. That is true," unless in fact they were in my memory

already, but so far back and so buried, as it were, in the furthest recesses that, if
they had not been dragged out by the suggestions of someone else, I should
perhaps not have been able to conceive of them? (10.10)

Here Augustine approaches the Platonic teaching of *anamnesis,* that
knowledge is the recollection of impressions made by eternal forms upon
the unincarnate soul. But Augustine does not embrace the Platonic teaching. At this point, his interest is more descriptive than metaphysical. Some
of the things we know, he says, appear to be already within our memory,
if only in "wonderfully secret hiding places" where they wait to be discovered.

Memory does not only house true things, for contained in the memory are false opinions, along with the distinctions by which memory
judges them to be false. Memory also contains the feelings of the mind,
of past fear or joy or surprise. But the mind can be happy while the
memory contains something sad. There can be, therefore, no one-to-one
correspondence between memory and mind. The memory, as it were,
opens wider than the mind, containing past states of mind which can
coexist with the mind's present state. Memory, in some sense, is the locus
of the mind.

How then are memory and mind connected? Augustine, as he frequently and artfully does, resorts to metaphor:

. . . the memory must be, as it were, the stomach of the mind, and happiness and
sadness like sweet and bitter food, and when they are committed to memory it
is as though they passed into the stomach where they can be stored up but cannot
taste. A ridiculous comparison, perhaps, [he concludes,] and yet there is some
truth in it. (10.14)

What Augustine does not develop is the means by which we recall
stored memories and experience them again, though as memories and not
the things themselves. The mind is not just the portal through which images proceed, it is also the place where, as it were, we chew the mental
cud. More precisely, memories are viewed by the mind, from which proceed images of memories and of the new feelings those memories
provoke.

The storage of memories takes place both by means of and apart from
images. Those people who are not healthy, Augustine says, still retain
through the force of memory an image of health (10.15). Yet, when I
name the numbers, he continues, it is the numbers themselves and not
their images that are in my memory. What happens when we remember

memory itself? Do we remember an image or the thing itself? Augustine writes: "I say 'memory' and I recognize what I mean by it; but where do I recognize it except in my memory itself? Can memory itself be present to itself by means of its image rather than by its reality?" (10.15). The answer, as far as it goes, is no; memory can only be present to itself in its reality. Forgetfulness, on the other hand, is the privation of memory and as such must be retained in memory not in its reality (for then we would not remember it) but in its image (10.16). Like evil, forgetfulness is a privation of being.

As part of his ascent, Augustine tries to go beyond the power of memory itself but recognizes that he cannot. One cannot strip memory away the way one can in thought close off sense perception. Memory thus becomes not only the locus of stored sense perception but also the field in which we carry on our spiritual striving for God. We can go no further than memory. Or can we? Even beasts have memory, Augustine notes, or birds would not be able to find their nests. How then does our memory differ from that of beasts, and what separates human beings from four-footed animals? At this point in the discussion, Augustine is not compelled to give an answer.

The first half of Augustine's account of memory, as we have seen, concerns the functioning of memory and the character of its contents. Beginning at chapter 20 of book 10, however, Augustine moves to consider in more detail the problem of *anamnēsis*. This second half of his account is devoted to the question of whether we seek something by remembering or by learning something unknown. "How, then, Lord do I seek you?" he writes at 10.20. The cry recalls the initial movement and continuing theme expressed at the very beginning of the *Confessions:* "Grant me, O Lord, to know and understand which should come first, prayer or praise; or indeed whether knowledge should precede prayer. For how can one pray to you unless one knows you?" (1.1). We seek God, but how? Is he present in my memory, and if so is he there in image or reality? And how did he get there? These questions Augustine does not ask straightforwardly, but one can hardly avoid their nagging presence in the context of Augustine's reflections.

Augustine begins with a simpler question. When we seek God, he writes, we seek the happy life. All have knowledge of the happy life. Man would not love the happy life unless he had some knowledge of it. Do we seek the happy life by remembering or by learning something new? Perhaps it is in our memory, Augustine suggests, whence it is left over from some previous experience of the happy life. Augustine's orthodoxy does not permit him the fully Platonic route—namely, the transmigration of souls—but he does not seem overly perplexed by the precise origin of our knowledge of the happy life. Simply, Augustine concludes, it is the case that all men desire to be happy: "And this would not be so unless the thing itself, signified by the word, was contained in their memory" (10.20). When memory possesses the good life—as when it possesses number—it grasps not the image but the reality itself.

Similarly, men have some knowledge of truth. For if all men desire to be happy, they desire a state of joy not in deception but in truth. Augustine writes:

For they love truth also (because they do not want to be deceived) and in loving the happy life (which simply means joy in truth) they must certainly love truth too, and they would not be able to love it unless there were some knowledge of it in their memory. (10.23)

Memory then, contains innately and in reality the knowledge of the happy life and of truth. But where does this lead in our seeking after God? The rhythm of Augustine's prose intensifies:

See what a distance I have covered searching for you, Lord, in my memory! And I have not found you outside it. Nor have I found anything about you which I have not kept in my memory from the time I first learned you. For from the time I learned you, I have not forgotten you. For when I found truth, then I found my God, truth itself, and from the time I learned you, you stay in my memory [*itaque ex quo te didici, manes in memoria mea*], and there I find you whenever I call you to mind and delight in you. (10.24)

God too is there in memory. But was he always there? Augustine's strange mixture of tenses suggests that the answer is yes. Indeed, he has already conceded that truth is innately in memory—to be discovered, as it were. God is truth and when he found truth he found God. God resides and is sought in memory. In true Plotinian fashion, God is to be sought within. But how does one seek God? How does one go about discovering God in one's memory? Augustine tells us all he can; he tells us how he himself found God—he narrates, in books 1 through 9, the confession of his conversion.

II

What then of imagination? Imagination in Augustine has received little attention. This is so partly because Augustine has no explicit or developed theory of imagination (the way, for example, Coleridge does).[3] Indeed, one must take care not to read back into Augustine a later formulation of a notion of imagination. Further, there would seem to be—as is frequently the case with Augustine's terminology generally—a shift in his understanding of imagination over time. The most perplexing problem is that Augustine uses the word *imaginatio* in at least three different senses.

In the first place, Augustine uses *imaginatio* in a pejorative sense to denote images and thoughts which distract the soul from truth and focus the mind upon fleshly, rather than spiritual, things. The most explicit use of imagination in this sense comes in *De vera religione,* composed around 390. Here, imaginations are derived from things perceived by the senses and are barriers to proper contemplation.

Obstinate souls! Give me a single man who can see without being influenced by imaginations derived from things seen in the flesh [*sine ulla imaginatione visorum carnalium . . .* in imagination [*figmento cogitationis*] I go where I like, and speak to whom I like. These imaginary things are false, and what is false cannot be known. When I contemplate them and believe in them, I do not have knowledge, because what I contemplate with the intelligence must be true, and not by any possibility what are commonly called phantasms [*phantasmata*]. (*DVR,* 64)

Imagination clouds the mind with illusions and fantasies. Near the end of the work he utters a stern warning: "Let not our religion consist in phantasms of our own imagining. Any kind of truth is better than any fiction we may choose to produce" (*DVR,* 108).

That imagination leads us into falsehood and distraction is a theme found also in the *Confessions.* Here, however, it is a criticism reserved primarily for non-Christian literature. Augustine denounces "Homer's fictions" (1.16–17) and condemns the stage plays whose fantasies evoke false emotion: "I used to sympathize with the joys of lovers, when they wickedly enjoyed each other, even though all this was purely imaginary and just a stage show [*quamvis haec imaginarie gererent in ludo spectaculi*]" (3.2). Such imaginings, moreover, distracted him from the state of his own soul: he wept at the death of Dido yet bore with dry eyes his dying heart (1.13). Imagination in this first sense draws the mind away from what is truly real.

Augustine seems to have modified his consideration of imagination in the time between the writing of *De vera religione* and the *Confessions*. In several letters exchanged with his friend Nebridius in the early 390s, Augustine moves to a distinction between *phantasia* and *imaginatio,* the two of which had been convoluted in the formulations of *De vera religione*. Nebridius (letter 6) poses a question for Augustine concerning the images present in memory. These he calls *phantasiae*. In his reply Augustine prefers to use the several variations of the word *imaginatio* to refer to "what you have proposed to call by the name of *phantasiae*" *(quae phantasiarum nomine appellare voluisti)* (letter 7). In distinguishing between *phantasia* and *imaginatio,* Augustine accords a strong degree of reality to images present in memory, something he was not willing to do in *De vera religione*. The distinction seems to have been lost on Nebridius. In letter 8 Nebridius persists in the use of *phantasia,* and Augustine in letter 9 gently admonishes his friend to reread the letters, for he has not fully understood them.

This shift is borne out in the *Confessions* where *imaginatio* comes to have a second sense—namely, the formulation of mental images more generally. Thus, the mind can imagine the sun rising and the memory can contain "images" of the happy life or of truth. In contradistinction to the images produced by literary fictions, imagination now has a positive connotation.

Third, imagination takes on, in the *Confessions,* the sense of expectation or "prediction." This sense can only be understood in conjunction with Augustine's views on the relationship between memory and time. People, Augustine remarks in book 11, frequently speak of time in terms of past and future. But how can this be? Augustine asks. Things that have happened in the past have passed away and consequently no longer exist; things that will happen in the future do not yet exist. How then, Augustine queries, do we speak of past and future as though they exist? Augustine's answer is this: past and future exist only in the present by means of memory.

Augustine gives the following example of imagination as expectation:

I am looking at the dawn sky and I foretell that the sun is going to rise. What I am looking at is present; what I foretell is future. What is future is not the sun, which is already in existence, but its rising, which has not yet taken place. Yet unless I could imagine in my mind this rising [*tamen etiam ortum ipsum nisi animo imaginarer*] (as I do now in speaking of it), I should not be able to predict it. (11.18)

Augustine's point is not that if he imagines something in the present it will happen. Rather, he is contending that the future exists (for the finite human mind) only insofar as it exists in the present imagination, expectation, or intention. Later, Augustine will come to see imagination and will as occupying symmetrical roles mediating, respectively, between sense and intellect, and memory image and inner vision.[4]

Imagination, then, "fills gaps" so to speak in the memory by picturing what one can expect in the future. Imagination thus has a creative power—not creation ex nihilo (which will characterize the individual creative genius of later Romanticism) but rather creative in the sense that *imaginatio* actively combines existing images in memory to form new images which reside in memory.[5] The ability of imagination to perceive similarities and to effect combinations of existing images is at the heart of analogical thinking for Augustine. At least one example suggests that imagination could also supply information missing from the past. In book 1 Augustine notes that he has no memory of his infancy. Yet, he can infer from his knowledge of other infants what his own infancy must have been like. Augustine does not explicitly call this inferring "imagination," but for us to do so would be consistent with Augustine's other uses of the term. Imagination thus supplies images of things that do not yet or no longer exist. Augustine—to repeat—does not have a theory of imagination, but he does appear to have a coherent threefold use of the word *imaginatio* meaning "fantasy," "simple mental image," or "a mental image produced by an intentional act of combination or analogical reasoning."

A fourth meaning may also be implicit in Augustine: the sense that imagination orders the content of memory. The crucial passage comes at book 10, chapter 11:

We find, therefore, that to learn those things which we do not draw into us as images by means of our senses, but which we perceive inside ourselves as they actually are without the aid of images means simply this: by the act of thought we are, as it were, collecting together things which the memory did contain, though in a disorganized and scattered way [i.e., imagination in the second and third senses], and by giving them our close attention we are arranging for them to be as it were stored up ready to hand in that same memory where previously they lay hidden, neglected, and dispersed, so that now they will readily come forward to the mind that has become familiar with them.

By act of thought—the word Augustine uses here is *cogito*—we are able to discover and apprehend true realities in our minds *without* the aid of images. Augustine uses *cogitatio* and *imaginatio* synonymously at least once in the *Confessions* (5.3, though the use is pejorative, as is also the case in *De vera religione*, 64). However, in book 12 of the later *De Genesi ad litteram,* Augustine systematically uses *cogitatio* synonymously with *imaginatio* in its ordering capacity, lending some credence to the assertion that the arrangement of memory is indeed a fourth aspect of imagination in the *Confessions.* Imagination in this sense orders images in such a way as it sometimes disposes the mind to the unmediated, imageless vision of pure intellect.

If this is true, then the cultivation of the imagination becomes central to the whole of Augustine's enterprise, for to ascend to God by means of memory is to ascend to God by means of memory rightly ordered by imagination in accordance with the truth. Truth cannot come forward in memory until the things stored there are arranged by "close attention." To be in a state of sin is to have a disordered memory. But the extent of the disorder is known only after the fact by memory. That is, the disorder is recognized in retrospect. Thus, Augustine can write that Alypius's future healing was being "stored up in his memory" (6.9).

Memory and imagination are part and parcel of what E. R. Dodds has outlined as Augustine's therapeutic activity in the *Confessions.*[6] The awareness of sin is the awareness that one must need healing, which in turn leads to a call for the medicine of grace. God, to Augustine, is constantly "my Physician" in the *Confessions,* but the medicine of grace is administered through memory. "*Noverim me, noverim te:* I would know myself that I might know you God," writes Augustine. Augustine continues to undergo conversion as he re-collects the working of God's grace. Indeed, to some extent imagination is identified with the act of confession itself, for, as Augustine acknowledges, his confessions are an arranging of his memories and their meanings. The narration and reiteration of conversion thus become a function of imagination, the ordering of memory. The *Confessions* is thus a means of therapy by which Augustine, through the ordering of memory, seeks an understanding of the meaning of his past and, consequently, of his present. The Christian, for Augustine, is never fully healed on this earth. Writing the *Confessions* was part of that process of healing. Thus Peter Brown writes of Augustine's reflections on memory: "The amazing Book Ten of the *Confessions* is not the affirmation of a cured man: it is the self-portrait of a convalescent."[7]

Augustine's act is not a solitary affair. He is very much conscious of his wider audience. "Why then," Augustine writes at 10.3, "do I bother to let men hear my confessions?" There was a need in the growing Christian community for the *servi Dei* to explain and justify the dramatic changes in their lives. The ordering of memory in the act of confession thus takes on communal importance. Augustine writes:

So in confessing not only what I have been but what I am the advantage is this: I make my confession not only in front of you, in a secret exultation with trembling, with a secret sorrow and with hope, but also in the ears of the believing sons of men, companions in my joy and sharers in my mortality, my fellow citizens and fellow pilgrims—those who have gone before and those who follow after and those who are on the road with me. These are your servants and my brothers; those whom you have willed to be your sons, my masters whom I am to serve if I wish to live with you and of you. (10.4)

Indeed, Augustine recognized that biography had played a substantial role in his own conversion. Victorinus's conversion and Ponticianus's recounting of the conversion of two imperial officials profoundly affected Augustine's own approach to Catholic Christianity:

This was what Ponticianus told us, [Augustine writes]. . . . But you, Lord, while he was speaking, were turning me around so that I could see myself; you took me from behind my own back . . . and you set me in front of my own face. (8.7)

Stories—or what are now called more professionally (and often sterilely) "narratives"—thus serve as mirrors in which Augustine wishes us to see ourselves and so to turn to God.

Is there any relationship between imagination and knowledge? The critical passage from book 10, chapter 11, would suggest that there is. The aim, Augustine says, is to apprehend the realities in themselves and not their images. That is, the grasping of a number itself is "more real," so to speak, than the apprehension of the image of the sun rising. There are things, Augustine tells us in *De doctrina christiana,* and there are signs. Things stand for themselves; signs point to what lie behind the signs. When we have the memory of the sun rising, we possess the image, the sign; in the case of number, memory contains the thing itself.[8] Augustine's aim is to achieve an imaginative rendering not of the sign but of the thing itself. The sign *points to* what lies behind it.[9]

The most obvious and conventional signs are words. Thus, part of the operation of imagination is to effect the apprehension of the things themselves without words, without mental images. The ascent to God through memory thus reaches its highest stage through that act of the imagination by which the intellect is disposed to apprehend things without the aid of signs. Thus, we get the famous mystical vision at Ostia, based on Plotinian ecstasy. In that extraordinary account of the beatific vision, earth and heaven grow silent, images and signs pass away, "and in a flash of thought" Augustine and Monica make "contact with that eternal wisdom which abides above all things" (9.10).

Less mystically, perhaps, Augustine elsewhere speaks of breaking through "the knots of language" (1.9) and of making his confession not "by means of the words and sounds of the flesh, but with words of the soul and the crying out of my thought which your ear knows" (10.2). In book 12 Augustine regularly speaks of the "inner eye" and the "inner ear," with which we perceive truth without sensory or mental images. Indeed, Augustine tells us, "the poverty of human understanding [*intelligentia*] shows an exuberance of words, since inquiry has more to say than discovery, asking takes longer than obtaining, and the hand that knocks does more work than the hand that receives" (12.1). The more words, the further we are from the reality of the thing itself. Augustine's ascent to God thus has a firmly apophatic character.

Augustine speaks of understanding *(intelligentia),* not knowledge *(scientia),* and the difference is of some importance here. "Grant me, O Lord, to know and to understand [*scire et intellegere*]," Augustine writes in the opening paragraph of the *Confessions.* The two go hand in hand but are somehow different. Augustine achieved rational certainty of the truth of the Catholic faith, but his soul refused to act:

I lashed my soul on to follow me now that I was trying to follow you. And my soul hung back; it refused to follow, and it could give no excuse for its refusal. All the arrangements had been used already and had been shown to be false. There remained a mute shrinking; for it feared like death to be restrained from the flux of a habit by which it was melting away into death. (8.7)

The will does not always follow the reason. Rational knowledge is thus necessary for Augustine but not sufficient for commitment. One's memory can contain the truth and even be recognized by mind; this is knowledge. But in understanding, the truths in memory are properly arranged, inclining both the mind and the heart to certainty. What is required is the ordering of one's heart, one's entire being, toward God. The connection between heart and memory is strong for Augustine: "My heart and my memory are open before you [*coram te cor meum et recordatio mea*]" Augustine writes (5.6). Reason brings the soul to knowledge; imagination orders the memory and disposes the heart to an understanding which grasps the reality that reason can apprehend only in signs.

III

The *Confessions* takes up many of the issues with which Augustine wrestled in his early writings, and upon which he continued to reflect during the remainder of his prolific career. In *Contra academicos,* composed at Cassiciacum in November of 386, three months after his conversion, he wrestled with the questions of knowledge, certainty, and doubt. In *De libero arbitrio,* begun in 388 but not finished until 395, Augustine confronted the problems of evil and free will, and with them the questions of God's existence and our knowledge of truth. From 396 to 397 Augustine struggled (for the second time, the first was in 389 in *De magistro*) with the problems of signs, reality, and interpretation in *De doctrina christiana.*

Some time in 397, Augustine interrupted his work on signs in *De doctrina christiana* to compose the *Confessions.* Augustine's shift from dialogues and treatises to the unquestionably unique narrative genre we call the *Confessions* may well have grown out of his consideration of signs and representation. The fact that he did not resume work on *De doctrina* until 426 suggests that he may have considered the *Confessions* its completion. The *Confessions* is unique because it represents, not a discontinuity of content, but rather a discontinuity of form and style. That is, it is an attempt to treat artistically and dramatically the persistent questions of knowledge, God, doubt, truth, and signs.

To a large degree, the *Confessions* incorporates the other genres of Augustine's production. The work is, but not merely so, a historical narrative of a man's life. It is deeply philosophical, as we have seen, and controversial (e.g., anti-Manichean), like his antiheretical tracts. Further, it is exhortative, like his sermons, and as personal as letters, as well as being a dialogue of sorts. Above all, the *Confessions* is literary, full of rich imagery and fine rhetorical style. The contemporary authority on Augustine's aesthetics has described the work as "a symphony" and has demonstrated the truly poetic character of the composition—after all, we know that Augustine wrote elegant and prize-winning poetry. Consider Robert J. O'Connell's rendering and translation of several passages from the *Confessions* into free verse.[10] First, the "rhythmic evocation of silence" at Ostia (9.10):

Si cui sileat tumultus carnis
sileant phantasiae terrae et aquarum et aeris,
sileant et poli
et ipsa sibi anima sileat
et transeat se non cogitando . . .

et loquatur ipse solus non per eas
sed perseipsum,
et audiamus Verbum ejus.

If to anyone the tumult of the flesh were hushed,
hushed the images of earth, and waters, and air,
hushed as well the very heavens;
did the soul, indeed, fall silent to itself,
and mount, by not thinking on itself, beyond itself . . .
and He alone spoke, not through these things
but through His very Being
that we might hear His word.

Or this passage from 10.27:

Sero te amavi,
pulchritudo tam antiqua et tam nova,
sero te amavi.
. . . . . .

Vocasti et clamasti et rupisti surditatem meam,
coruscasti, splenduisti, et fugasti caecitatem meam,
gustavi et esurio et sitio,
tetigisti me, et exarsi in pacem tuam.

Late have I loved Thee, Beauty,
ever ancient, ever new,
late have I loved Thee!
. . . .

Thou didst call, cry out to me, and shatter my deafness;
Didst flash forth and shine to me, and scattered my blindness;
Didst send forth Thy fragrance, and I drew in breath and now pant for Thee.
I have tasted, and now hunger and thirst for Thee;
Thou hast touched me, and I burn for Thy Peace.

Indeed, the moving cadence of the Latin would have been like music—
we must remember that the book would have been read aloud, not silently.

   Memory and imagination lie at the heart of the *Confessions,* for together they overcome the problem raised implicitly by *De doctrina chris-*
tiana: leaving behind the signs to apprehend the things themselves. Signs,
even in memory, risk being conceived of corporeally. Augustine's poem-

like narrative of prayer and recollection serves as a complex of signs, the reality behind which cannot be thought of corporeally. Augustine gives us a life, a memory whose process of being ordered points the reader to God even as Augustine's own discovery of God is being reenacted. Augustine "does not tell us what to do or how to speak theologically, but [rather] by showing us how God is related to all creatures through the story of his own experience of coming to belief."[11] By imaginatively entering into Augustine's life and witnessing the arrangement of his own memory, we are invited to do the same in our own. All exists in the present by means of memory. What we are and what we will be are defined by memory. More precisely, we are defined by how we order our memory. In this way, imagination becomes the center of man's whole rational, intellectual, and spiritual existence. Coleridge's understanding of imagination is unmistakably modern, yet it has some affinities with Augustine's qualified appreciation of imagination. Although one must keep in mind his Romantic differences from Augustine, Coleridge nonetheless captures the Augustinian spirit well when he writes:

> Religion necessarily, as to its main and proper doctrines, consists of ideas, that is, spiritual truths that can only be spiritually discerned, and to the expression of which words are necessarily inadequate, and must be used by accommodation. Hence the absolute indispensability of a Christian *life,* with its conflicts and inward experiences, which alone can make a man to answer to an opponent, who charges one doctrine is contradictory to another,—"Yes! it is a contradiction in terms; but nevertheless so it is, and both are true, nay, parts of the same truth."[12]

Augustine sees a role for imagination in coming to know—and ultimately to reorder—the data of memory through the narration of stories which render the elements of memory in intelligible patterns. When such literary patterns are rendered intelligible, imagination (the activity of understanding through images) gives way to intellect—pure insight in the absence of mediating images. The *Confessions* both tells and shows us how images, for Augustine, can lead us toward the un-imaged (and unimaginable) disclosure of truth. Articulations of this disclosure are halting—we see through a glass darkly—and contradictory. Ultimately, for Augustine, such images of truth are reconcilable and rendered intelligible not abstractly but in a human life. And so, in trying to tell us of the truth, Augustine finds himself simply showing us the truth by presenting us with his life. "Only a life sufficiently large and alive," wrote Baron von Hügel, "a life dramatic with a humble and homely heroism which, in rightful contact with and in rightful renunciation of the Particular and Fleeting, ever seeks and finds the Omnipresent and Eternal; . . . only such a life can be largely persuasive, at least for us Westerns and in our times."[13] Augustine, in the *Confessions,* gives us such a life and in so doing renders a compelling conjunction of the literary and theological imaginations.

Notes

1. This essay is a slightly revised and expanded version of an essay previously published in *New Blackfriars* 75, no. 881 (Apr. 1994): 210–22, and reprinted here by kind permission of the editor of that journal. Earlier versions of the paper were read at Fisher House, Cambridge (at the kind invitation of Marcus Hodges, O.P.), and at the 1993 Patristic, Medieval, and Renaissance Studies Conference at Villanova University. English quotations from *Confessions* are from the translation by Rex Warner (New York: New American Library, 1963).

2. In this, as we might expect, Augustine rejects Lucretius's material theory in which memory is constituted by the collection of many "thin films" that come to rest there. Whereas Lucretius's scheme gives an explanation for the presence of images in memory, Augustine confesses that he does not know how these images are formed. Nonetheless, the images are present to be brushed aside or called up when needed.

3. The most recent theoretical treatments of Augustine's understanding of imagination are Gerard O'Daly, *Augustine's Philosophy of Mind* (Berkeley and Los Angeles: University of California Press, 1987); Gerard Watson, *Phantasia in Classical Thought* (Galway: Galway University Press, 1988); and Eva T. H. Brann, *The World of the Imagination: Sum and Substance* (Savage, Md.: Rowman and Littlefield, 1991). Murray W. Bundy's *The Theory of Imagination in Classical and Medieval Thought* (Champaign: University of Illinois Press, 1927) remains very useful. Robert J. O'Connell's *Soundings in St. Augustine's Imagination* (New York: Fordham University Press, 1994) and *Art and the Christian Intelligence in St. Augustine* (Cambridge: Harvard University Press, 1978) are perceptive and admirable accounts of Augustine's understanding of art and his use of images. Readers of O'Connell will note my departures from him, especially in that I remain less confident than O'Connell that Augustine had an explicitly developed (and essentially negative) theory of the imagination.

4. Notably in *De Trinitate* 11 and *De Genesi ad litteram* 12.

5. See also *De libero arbitrio* (especially book 2), where Augustine says that one can only conceive of things that actually are.

6. E. R. Dodds, "Augustine's *Confessions*: A Study of Spiritual Maladjustment," *Hibbert Journal* 26 (1927–28): 460.

7. Peter Brown, *Augustine of Hippo: A Biography* (Berkeley and Los Angeles: University of California Press, 1969), 177.

8. In many ways, the centrality of numbers in Descartes's discussion of certainty (in the *Meditations*) is an Augustinian impulse.

9. Augustine's understanding of sign in this sense has profound affinities with Jean-Luc Marion's discussion, in quite a different Greek patristic/postmodern context, of the "icon"; see Jean-Luc Marion, *God without Being,* trans. Thomas A. Carlson (Chicago: University of Chicago Press, 1991).

10. O'Connell, *Art and the Christian Intelligence,* 119, 215.

11. Sallie McFague, *Speaking in Parables: A Study in Metaphor and Theology* (Philadelphia: Fortress Press, 1975), 165.

12. S. T. Coleridge, *Literary Remains* (New York: AMS Press, 1967), 4:63 (emphasis mine).

13. Baron F. von Hügel, *The Mystical Element in Religion,* 1st ed. (London: J. M. Dent, 1909), 1:368.

Metamorphosis and Conversion: Apuleius's *Metamorphoses*

SETH BENARDETE

In a book called *Transformations,* which we learn is a "Greekish tale" *(fabula Graecanica)* told by an educated Greek in poor Latin, the two biggest surprises are the almost simultaneous revelations that the narrator is the North African author and a convert to the religion of Isis (11.28).[1] Any interpretation must focus from the start on the apparently superfluous eleventh book: how do corporeal transformations end up in a spiritual turnaround that involves the re-presentation of fiction as autobiography?

The narrative's forward motion seems to be suspended for almost two books (4.28–6.25) while Lucius the ass and the girl Charite listen to an old woman tell the story of Cupid and Psyche. The story is meant to divert and console. Whatever the story's intermediate origin might be, its ultimate source is Socrates' second speech in Plato's *Phaedrus.*[2] Since the unifying theme of the *Phaedrus* is itself so hard to make out, Apuleius all but tells us that our understanding of the unity of his work depends on his understanding of his model. To put together the three parts of his tale—Lucius the ass, Cupid and Psyche, Lucius the convert—is to put together something like the beautiful animal that the *Phaedrus,* like every Platonic dialogue, is. The first clue to our finding the beauty in this monster is supplied by the *Phaedrus* itself. At the conclusion of Socrates'

In *Man in His Pride*, David Grene called attention to the tension in Plato between justice and eros. The present essay is offered as an account of another who saw and reflected on that same tension.

speech, the issue becomes one of writing, and when Socrates asks whether the premise for things to be well and beautifully spoken must be that the thought of the speaker knows the truth about what he is to say, Phaedrus asks in turn whether the speaker has to know more than the opinions of the many. Socrates then asks: "Were I to persuade you to ward off an enemy by the acquisition of a horse, and we should both be ignorant of a horse, but I, however, should happen to know about you that Phaedrus believes that of tame animals the one with the longest ears is a horse—

PHAEDRUS: It would be ridiculous, Socrates.
SOCRATES: Not yet. But when I should persuade you in earnest, putting together a speech in praise of an ass, calling it a horse and saying how the beast is a worthwhile possession at home and on campaign, useful to fight from, capable besides of carrying baggage, and useful in many other respects—
PHAEDRUS: Now it would be completely absurd.

Since Socrates chooses to illustrate the question of truth with the example of an ass being mistaken for a horse,[3] we are forced to ask what difference it would make in his own myth if the winged horses had been winged asses. That the image would have been funnier can be granted; but it would not have been more monstrous; and the only real loss would have been that the myth requires that the chariot of the soul be a war-chariot (248a6–b1). The ascent of the soul in following an Olympian god is coupled with its fighting against other souls. Love is a form of war. Now let us suppose that Phaedrus, who believes it makes no difference whether the speaker knows the truth or not, was the teller of Socrates' myth. His Latin name would be Lucius, and he would without knowing it speak of asses while saying "horses." He would fail to understand the need to separate the account of love from the account of warfare and therefore not surprisingly speak of his forthcoming sexual encounter with Fotis as an undeclared war (2.16–17).[4] Apuleius's book, then, is Plato's *Phaedrus* as rewritten by Phaedrus. He becomes the writer of a book that he does not understand but that bears his name and fulfills the prophecy of Diophanes that he should become a book or books (2.12).[5] Lucius wanted to become a bird; he wanted the wings of Eros (3.22); he became an ass instead and ended up seeing himself in his longing in a parade that precedes the procession of Isis. The eleventh item in that parade was "an ass with wings glued on, walking by the side of some weak old man; you would call him Bellerophon, the other Pegasus, and you would laugh at both" (11.8).[6]

Apuleius seems to have identified the unifying theme of the *Phaedrus* as that of writing[7] and imagined what it would be like if Phaedrus were the author of himself and became his own image. Such a collapse of story-teller into the story, whereby the necessity to suspend disbelief vanishes, would seem to be a way of asserting the total triumph of the law, whose success consists in its being no longer an injunction but a description. As Papinian says, "Any acts which offend against our piety, reputation, or shame must be believed to be acts which we not only ought not, but cannot, do."[8] Apuleius's version of this rule is for Lucius to reject anti-nomian eros as vehemently as Phaedrus does and become at the end a successful lawyer (11.15; *Phaedrus* 258e1–5).[9] We are thus brought back to the beginning of the *Phaedrus,* where Socrates hears Phaedrus recite an antierotic speech by Lysias, the first Athenian to write forensic speeches for pay.

The first words that Apuleius's narrator quotes—we do not know he is Lucius until a friend greets him (1.24)—have to do with lying: "Spare me! Stop lying with such absurd and monstrous language." A traveler ad-dresses these words to his companion as they are going toward Hypata in Thessaly; he goes on to say that the story he heard is as much a lie as if someone should say that by magical incantations rivers go backward, the sea ceases to be restless, the winds breathe their last, the sun stands still, the moon foams, the stars are plucked out, day is removed, and night never ends. The scoffer speaks of nothing but perceptible things; but when his companion goes on with his story and has someone speak of a witch's power, the list, which also has eight items, is quite different: to take down the sky, lift up the earth, harden the waters, dissolve mountains, raise ghosts, sink gods, quench stars, and light up Tartarus itself.[10] Gods and souls *(manes)* replace the moon and winds; the identity of the moon and Isis is thus foreshadowed, and the etymological link between soul and wind hinted at: in the first list the winds by magic become *inanimes,* no less breathless than lifeless.

Apuleius thus indicates that the book is about belief, and Lucius's *curiositas* is guided primarily by the will to believe. Apuleius, moreover, by noting that the difference between what we might call nature and religion turns on god and soul, recalls the beginning of the *Phaedrus,* where Phaedrus questions Socrates as to his belief about the story of Bor-eas, the North Wind, and the rape of Orithyia. The rationalized account, according to Socrates, denies that Boreas is a god and thus turns a story of love into a story of violent death; but even the myth implies that love is always violent, for the radical difference between lover and beloved cannot be overcome without violence. Persuasion by speech, however, does imply that there is a mean between modern rationality and ancient

violence. Different kinds of beings can form alliances, for speech is powerful enough to bring them about. Persuasion of necessity, in Timaeus's
phrase, is possible if psychology is the core of cosmology. Magic would
simply be a weaker version of that power which originally put the cosmos
together (2.12).

Before Lucius's own adventures begin, he hears a complicated story
whose final episode concerns the death of "Socrates" beside a plane tree
and a stream (1.5–20).[11] This allusion to the *Phaedrus* reinforces the view
that the *Metamorphoses* as a whole is built on the *Phaedrus* and at the same
time suggests that its own possibility depends on Socrates' defeat by magical forces that he somehow provoked and could not control. The historical scheme Apuleius has in mind is this. The monstrous gods of Egypt
represent the pre-Olympian religion of the ancient world. That religion
was suppressed but not destroyed by the Greek poets, sculptors, and painters who succeeded in presenting the gods as so beautiful that we could be
indifferent to the issue of their reality.[12] Plato, then, through his spokesman Socrates, argued that the beautiful gods of Homer were nothing but
so many representations of a certain longing of the human soul. The truth
of the beautiful gods is human eros. The historical consequence of this
revelation was the destruction of the Olympian gods and a return to the
magical religion that preceded it, but with a difference. The old religion
became infused with the Platonic interpretation of things, so that it underwent the spiritualization that the religion of Isis represents: in the procession that inaugurates her own, a monkey represents Ganymede (11.8).
This spiritualization is of such a kind as to allow for its combination with
Roman law. The way in which the pre-Olympian religion gets transformed is supplied by the notion of persuasion. The incantatory power of
erotic rhetoric, so that the beloved is made to undergo supposedly the
same experience as the lover did through sight, is taken over by Apuleius
in the form of Thessalian witchcraft becoming in time the experience of
his own religious conversion, in which there are dream visions to take the
place of the Olympian gods (11.3, 25, 30). Apuleius's book is meant to be
a history of the world from its preliterate beginnings up to his own day.
This history is told through the experiences of Lucius, who in aspiring to
be a bird became an ass, the symbol of Set, and ends up as the worshiper
of Isis, the enemy of Set (11.6). The Greek name for Set is Typhon. He
is a kind of wind, whom Hesiod represents as the last of the pre-Olympian
gods and capable of imitating all sounds and voices.[13] Socrates' attempt at
self-knowledge, which would settle the question whether one can believe
or not in the possibility of the god Boreas, turns on the question whether
he himself is a beast more complex than Typhon or is a tame and simpler

animal (*Phaedrus* 230a3–6). Whatever the *Phaedrus* might disclose about Socrates, we already know all about Lucius.

The connection Apuleius makes between pre-Olympian gods and Egypt is not his own; it can be traced back to Herodotus, who says that the poets Homer and Hesiod are responsible for transforming Egyptian gods into the beings the Greeks worship (2.53). There is, moreover, a connection between Egypt and Plato's *Phaedrus,* for Socrates assigns to Theuth the invention of writing (274c5–275b2).[14] The hieroglyphs show images of animals that represent sounds. They are, as it were, the very expression of Socrates' teaching that a perfect writing must be like a living animal, for the consonantal alphabet of Egyptian can only be read if spoken with its nonrepresented vowels. The reader must give life to the writing. Apuleius hints at this by asking his reader not to scorn to look at an "Egyptian papyrus inscribed by the acuity of a Nilotic reed." Tentatively, then, we can say that the Olympian gods are to the Egyptian gods as living speech is to writing, and this proportion represents the movement of the *Metamorphoses* from classical paganism to a new kind of religion that involves a book (11.17, 22).[15]

The defeat of Socrates in the new order is represented by his death becoming known only when he returns to the triumphal setting of the *Phaedrus.* The narrator of the story to Lucius is Aristomenes, while "Socrates" himself is legally dead and a ghost ("larvale simulacrum"; 1.6) even at their first encounter. Aristomenes, moreover, believes that "Socrates" deserves worse than the worst punishment for his one act of adultery (1.8). The lubricious *Metamorphoses* begins on a moralistic note. One wonders whether there is a connection between this severity and Lucius's credulity. Is his wish to believe that there is nothing impossible (1.20) the same as moralism? Lucius seems to connect the disbelief in the miraculous with the unpersuasiveness of individual experience: each one of us experiences what everyone else regards as impossible (1.20). Such a notion seems to be connected with "conscience," an arbiter of experience that denies innocence. It arranges that one come to believe that one can never justify oneself before another, who will always hold oneself responsible for everything that happens. Fate in one's own perspective becomes guilt in that of another, and conscience makes one consider one's fate entirely from the other's viewpoint. When Aristomenes sees "Socrates" dead, he at once imagines his own condemnation: "What will happen to me when this corpse appears in the morning? To whom will I seem to be telling the truth in presenting the truth? 'You could have at least called for help if you, manly though you are, could not resist a woman. Under your very eyes a man is slain, and you keep silent? How come such villainy did not kill you? Why did savage cruelty spare a witness to the crime? Well, since you then escaped death, now return there.'" Roman law is strict and one is guilty if one cannot prove one's innocence.[16] Even the doorkeeper recognizes Aristomenes' guilt—he must be wanting to depart in order to escape punishment for having killed "Socrates"—and Aristomenes wants to kill himself as the result of the doorkeeper's remark. The words of the doorkeeper, he says, were such as to open up the earth and let him see Tartarus and Cerberus. Aristomenes says that this vision was not something he imagined, but something he now remembers (cf. 11.23). Indeed, the doorkeeper himself speaks as if he should be found guilty if highwaymen killed Aristomenes.[17] He must immediately imagine that the magistrates would ask him why he allowed Aristomenes to leave so early if he did not far more plausibly kill him himself. The will to believe seems to be grounded in the undisciplined imagination, for which whatever is inexplicable to another is the fate for oneself for which one must pay (see also 3.29). The plausible is the morally intelligible (see also 2.27); the impossible is whatever one cannot convince another of—one's own innocence. Aristomenes ends his story by saying that he left his home and country "as if I knew myself to be guilty of human murder" (1.19). The failure of persuasion is tantamount to the admission of guilt; the triumph of persuasion is to make everything seem possible. Under one of two circumstances, then, there would be a coincidence between the morally plausible and the absence of disbelief: either one cannot but be guilty or one ceases to have experiences that do not square with the logic of morality. The moral miracle is conversion against the grain of one's own experiences to a belief in what the moral law says must be the case. Apuleius sees that the ultimate consequence of the view that truth is not an issue for rhetoric is the obliteration of experience and its entire replacement by opinion. Freedom from fate is surrender to opinion.

The *Phaedrus* goes from the issue of the possibility of monsters in light of Socrates' self-knowledge to the task Lysias set himself as the master-rhetorician: to persuade the beloved to gratify the nonlover. Since such a speech cannot be addressed by anyone to anyone, it is only possible as a written speech; but insofar as it is meant to persuade, it represents the limits of persuasion within which rhetoric must stay as long as it is living speech. That Lucius, therefore, becomes a book is a sign that that limit has been crossed, and that the price paid for extending the boundaries of persuasion is the death of soul. The story of Cupid and Psyche is the fitting memorial to that death. If, however, Lysias's speech is considered solely as a piece of writing, it is obviously the perfect preface for any book in which an unknown author asks an unknown reader to gratify him by reading his book, which, he promises, will benefit the reader without any injury to his reputation and without his suffering any regrets. The reader will undergo a change, and none will be the wiser. Apuleius's *Metamorphoses,* then, is a chronicle of the death of soul, on the one hand, and an account of a conversion of soul, on the other, for which no one is responsible but the convert himself.

Apart from his host, Milo, Lucius meets in Hypata two others who are related to his past life.[18] The first is Pythias, who was his classmate in Athens and is now in charge of the markets. When he learns of the price Lucius paid for a fish, he goes over to the fishmonger, shouts abuse at him for charging so much, and has his attendants trample on Lucius's supper. Lucius begins his adventures by experiencing the pointless strictness of Roman law: it grants its magistrates satisfaction but loses sight of human needs. Lucius goes to bed hungry after having fed on stories alone (1.26), for when he wants to sleep in order to make up for his lack of food, Milo detains him with an oath and forces him to answer all his questions. Lucius has a "virginal bashfulness" (1.23; cf. 2.3) that works against his own interests (2.3, 12). The law works with Lucius's own timidity to make him a reluctant ascetic. He is starved into spirituality by the heedlessness of his friend Pythias and the miserly avarice of his host, Milo. His downfall indeed occurs through his uprightness. He sets out to seduce Fotis in order to get at her mistress's magic so as not to tamper with the sanctity of marriage and guest-friendship (2.6). He betrays the insincerity of his attraction to Fotis by calling her his "dear Fotis" as soon as he conceives his plan (2.7; cf. 7.1). He said nothing about her when she first answered his knock (1.22); only when he puts aside his childish fears does he encourage himself by speaking of her beauty and wit. His purpose is to fill his breast with miraculous fables ("fabulis miris exple tuum pectus") in accordance with a long-standing wish. Carnality is merely the way and the obstacle to what he really wants.

Lucius begins his first full day in Hypata with the refusal to believe that anything he looks at is what it is (2.1). His settled disposition is literally to translate everything and deny self-identity: Apuleius warns us even now that Lucius will prove to be someone else. Lucius is prepared to doubt everything for the sake of belief in a wholly human world: the stones he stumbles against, the birds he hears, the trees and fountains, they are all made from men. Lucius thus on his own extends to everything what art does too. At Byrrhena's house he sees four statues of winged Victory, each one of which is believed to be flying ("etiam volare creduntur"), a statue of Diana with her hounds, "from whose throats of stone you will believe a growl is coming," and grapes, "which art, the rival of nature, displays like to the truth" and if seen reflected in water "you will believe they are hanging in the country and not wanting even the truth of motion" (2.4). Lucius wants the imitation of things to be the truth of things. He wants the belief induced by art that a stone is alive to be shown to be a poor version of the belief that a man became by art a stone.[19] The artful duplication of reality is to be replaced by the artful transformation of reality. Persuasion is to yield to faith. There is behind the scenes no humbug Wizard of Oz; in a sense, there is no "behind the scenes." The rhetorician does not just fall for his own line; his line is true. One merely has to be let into his workshop to see for oneself; one does not have to be won over by illusions. Witchcraft is not a more powerful way to convert the soul; it is a way to dispense with any need to convert the soul. The imperative *crede* ("believe") occurs once, and it is addressed to the reader, "So hear, but believe, what is true" (11.23); and what the reader is to believe is what he necessarily does not know ("quae, quamvis audita, ignores tamen necesse est").

At a banquet in Byrrhena's house, where everything that cannot be is ("quicquid fieri non potest ibi est"; 2.19), Lucius, who has just expressed his fear of witchcraft employed against the dead, hears a story from Thelyphron the truth of which is hard to make out. Byrrhena's allusion to the misadventure of Thelyphron provokes the mirth of the other guests, and after Thelyphron retells it for Lucius's benefit, everyone laughs (2.20–31). On the one hand, Thelyphron's wax nose and ears, which duplicate exactly ("examussim") the real, are in themselves halfway between imitation and magic; on the other hand, the resurrected corpse Thelyphron was supposed to guard and which denounces the wife confirms the reality of witchcraft without confirming his own truthfulness, for the wife is effective enough a rhetorician to convince half the crowd that the corpse is lying, and what should decide the matter but obviously could not—Thelyphron's wax ears and nose—cannot be tested since hair now covers his ears and a bandage his nose (2.30).[20] Since Byrrhena tells Lucius that tomorrow the festival of Laughter (Risus) begins, we are left in the dark as to whether or not Thelyphron's tale was a preliminary offering to the god, especially since Byrrhena warns Lucius that he himself is to be the butt of the solemnities: "The solemn day, founded from the first beginning of this city, comes tomorrow, on which day we alone of mortals propitiate the most holy god Risus with a joyous and enjoyable rite. By your presence you will make him more gracious to us. I only wish that you could devise and invent something happy from your own wit in order that we may all the better appease so great a deity" (2.31).

The evidence on the basis of which we have to decide how to take

Lucius's adventure is briefly this. Fotis warns Lucius that a gang of noble youths menaces the town at night and the civil guard can do nothing; Lucius assures her that they cannot harm him if he wears his usual sword (2.18). After Byrrhena's party, Lucius and his servant return home in the dark after a puff of wind extinguishes their torch. Near Milo's house they run across three huge youths and Lucius immediately attacks them and deflates them, perforated with many wounds (2.32). Lucius, however, on waking, immediately imagines his trial and sentence, convinced that no matter how kindly disposed the judge may be, he will never be declared innocent (3.1). Lucius's trial is held in the theater, where to his dismay he finds everyone laughing. After the prosecutor's speech, Lucius is called to defend himself, finds he has no capacity to do anything but weep, "looking not so much at the fierce accusation as at my own wretched conscience," but finally makes a speech that corresponds to nothing we have been told. He thus fulfills inadvertently Byrrhena's wish that he contrive something in honor of Risus: Byrrhena might have guessed that in the circumstances he would lie. His speech makes everyone burst out laughing and particularly Milo. He reflects: "So this is loyalty! This is conscience! I, on behalf of my host, am a homicide and guilty of murder, while he, not satisfied that he did not console me by standing by me, cackles over my death" (3.7). Even when Lucius talks to himself, he speaks in light of the false account he gave the court. When Lucius is brought finally to uncover the cadavers and finds they are wineskins pierced in exactly the same places he remembers having stabbed the robbers, Lucius becomes as rigid as the stone statues in the theater, and though Milo leads him gently away as he emerges from hell ("ab inferis emersi"), he cannot soothe the indignation that has lodged deep in Lucius's heart (3.10).

After his return to Milo's house, the chief magistrates come and urge him to be gay, "for this festival which we annually celebrate to the most gracious god Risus always flourishes by the novelty of invention." Lucius, however, only feigns cheerfulness and does not recover his spirits until he hears Fotis's side of the story. Fotis comes to him with a whip and asks to be beaten or even to suffer worse for her unwitting part in his misfortune. She wants her blood to expiate Lucius's injury: "id omne protinus meo luatur sanguine." Her mistress, Pamphile, had told her to gather the hair-clippings of a certain young man with whom she had fallen desperately in love; but when the barber stopped Fotis, she had collected instead the hair from goatskins, which Pamphile had then mixed in with her concoction to form the three seeing, hearing, and walking men Lucius had assaulted.

There is no easy way to put together these accounts.[21] Either the townspeople dressed up three men in goatskins, or three goatskins were charmed into resembling men. Epicharmus had called men nothing but inflated goatskins.[22] Fotis, moreover, seems to play a double role. Either she set him up for the elaborate joke by warning him of the gang (the magistrate says nothing about any such menace), or everything happened as she says, and the townspeople ascribe to Risus what is due to Pamphile and are the dupes of their own make-believe (though how they could have staged the trial if they had not arranged for the crime cannot be made out). There is, then, either stagecraft or witchcraft. Either the city and its laws are held up to ridicule by comic poetry, or we are confronted by the reality behind such poetry. We are never given the evidence for determining the truth of either version; but Lucius's own story requires that the witchcraft version be true. He slips into magic through a flaw in narration.[23] His initiation into magic depends on his getting the upper hand over Fotis by forgiving her for a crime she did not commit but for which she believes she deserves to be beaten. Her guilty conscience helps him to get over his own humiliation. Lucius spares her in order to force her total surrender. She now generously offers herself for sodomy after he reveals to her that he had always before rejected with contempt female embraces (3.19–20; see also 2.17). A bashful homosexual, who needs wine to dispel his shame (2.11) and believes that hair is woman's greatest glory because it proves that the nakedness women indulge in to show their charms is contradicted by a covering that vindicates the naturalness of shame (2.8–9; cf. 17 and 11.4),[24] falls from the Homeric religion into its precursor and successor through accepting Fotis's version rather than the publicly accepted one. His humiliation at being made a laughingstock is stronger than his relief at not being punished for a crime he did not commit. He prefers to have killed in self-defense three young men and thus proved his Herculean mettle than to be cheated of the imaginary hangman (2.32, 3.1). Lucius himself takes his seduction of Fotis as having resulted in his own enslavement to a slave (3.19, 22; cf. 11.15); and so when she offers him a way to escape, he jumps at the chance. He forgives her by speaking the language of the law: "Uncertain or even hostile chance cannot assign guilt to harmless intentions" (3.14). Hypata, however, makes a mockery of the law; it preserves within the Roman Empire a vestige of the freedom of old Attic comedy (cf. 2.19). Despite the magistrates' offer to compensate him for his anxiety with a public statue (3.11), Lucius prefers to recover his pride by believing Fotis and becoming a bird. That he first has to become an ass before he can be fully free from shame by shaving his head and losing his tail (11.13, 30)—the ambiguity of tail ("cauda") need not be stressed—ought not to conceal the fact that the ass, in symbolizing Set, represents the original of which the horse is an image in pursuit of the beautiful Olympian gods.[25]

Just prior to his transformation Lucius speaks twice of magic in a metaphorical way. He tells Fotis that though he is a keen lover ("cupitor") of knowing magic face to face, she seems to him not unskilled in it, for otherwise he would not now be subject to her (3.19); and after he has seen Pamphile change into an owl and fly away, he remarks: "She indeed by her magical arts voluntarily got transformed, but I enchanted by no incantation, struck with amazement at so manifest a deed, I seemed to be anything whatsoever rather than Lucius, so outside my mind I was, in mindless astonishment I was dreaming while awake" (3.22). Love against his own inclination and sight of a miracle duplicate experientially the effects of magic. Magic itself, however, does not induce in Lucius any magical experiences. He sees that he is an ass but keeps his human sense (3.26; see also 4.2, 6). The ass for him is no more than a costume whose zipper got stuck (see also 4.15). He does not at first think like an ass and share with us the nature of asininity.[26] To be an ass is not to be a cousin to the Houyhnhnms. Indeed, he finds there is no silent and natural obligation among the dumb animals, and his own horse gangs up with another ass to kill him (3.26). Whatever experiences, then, are Lucius's because he is an ass come wholly from the outside. He becomes an ass through his being seen and treated as an ass. He is formed through and through by opinion.

Lucius's first adjustment to his new state takes place through terror (4.6). The robbers whose booty he is carrying mutilate and hurl over a precipice a worn-out ass which, Lucius believes, was faking tiredness, for he ascribes to the ass the plan he himself had in mind and thus betrays the ground of the anger men vent against domesticated animals. Men believe that inside the outer covering of a beast of burden there lies the malignity of man. Lucius then is the proof of anger. Magic has finally supplied the evidence for what anger is already fully certain of, that the stubbornness of things is the willfulness of man (see also 6.29, 8.25, 9.3–4). The stones he stumbled against were Lucius's first example of his belief that in Hypata magic had transformed men into everything (2.1). When Lucius the ass had earlier tried to nibble at a crown of roses gracing an image of the goddess Epona, his own groom had driven him away, calling him sacrilegious and an enemy to the images of the gods (3.27). Lucius now resolves "without malice aforethought or willful guile" to show himself to be a good and loyal ass to his masters. The expression he uses ("bonae frugi") refers primarily to the virtue of slaves (cf. 6.10, 8.24). Lucius complies sincerely. He contemplates escape only when the robbers, angered at his unwilled faltering, decide to kill him too (6.26).

Between his first and second plans of escape comes the story of Cupid and Psyche. The story implies that the relation between love and soul underwent four phases. In the first there was soul without love; in the second love was with soul but soul did not know it; in the third soul knew that it was without love; and in the last soul knowingly is with love forever.[27] We are not told the name of Psyche until the fame of her beauty has so grown that she has provoked the true Venus, whose cult has been abandoned (4.29). Psyche is no more than a moving statue of Venus: "Supplication is made to the girl, and in a human face the power of so great a goddess is appeased." What she first suffers is not due to Venus but to man; no one comes forward to ask for her hand in marriage: "They admire of course her divine appearance [*species*], but everyone wonders at her as if she were an artfully polished image" (4.32; cf.11.4). Venus's own proposal for Psyche's punishment reveals her complete ignorance of her son: "Let this virgin be gripped by the most burning love of the lowest of the low, whom Fortune has condemned in point of dignity, inheritance, and soundness itself, so that throughout the entire globe he may find no equal to his own wretchedness" (4.31). Venus unwittingly describes her son as he really is, or eros, a state, as Diotima says, of the greatest conscious neediness.[28] Venus understands her son pre-Platonically, the way in which the poet Agathon does, as if his kinship with the beautiful guaranteed his own beauty.[29] The belief that love is beautiful testifies to the self-ignorance of love and therefore to the element of self-love in love. Apuleius indicates this by playing on the difference between proper and common nouns, on the one hand, and, on the other, the difference between Greek and Latin. Psyche says to Cupid while she is still in the dark about him: "I love you to distraction, whoever you are, and cherish you the same as my own spirit, nor do I match Cupid himself against you. . . . My honey, my husband, sweet soul of your Psyche" (5.6; see also 5.13, 6.2). Psyche is and is not soul, for the heart of soul is eros, and soul does not know what it is (see also 5.15–16).[30] "You will not see my face," Cupid warns Psyche, "if you will see it" (5.11).[31] It is the story of Cupid and Psyche that reveals finally why Apuleius implied at the beginning that he was incapable of translating into Latin all that he thought in Greek.

After Psyche does see Cupid, "falls voluntarily in love with love" (5.23), and tries to kill herself when Cupid flies away, she meets Pan, who is embracing Echo (5.25). Psyche meets an image of herself and Love. Pan, who pretends not to know anything about her, guesses that she is in love. His guess, he says, is based on much experience and, should it be a correct conjecture, would be that which "prudent men call divination" (5.25). A god, whose name means "everything," is not omniscient. The ending of the *Phaedrus* suggests that Pan is Socrates (279b8–c3).[32] In any case, Pan urges Psyche to set aside her grief and beseech Cupid with prayers. Psyche does not answer Pan; instead, she goes to one of her sisters and tells her that Cupid has divorced her and plans to marry the sister. The sister then arranges to leap off a cliff in the blind hope that Zephyr will come and waft her away to Cupid; but she is crushed and scattered on the rocks below, "bringing food to the beasts and birds" (5.27). Psyche then tells the same lie to her other sister, with the same result. She forgets that the loss of Cupid was due to her own curiosity, against which he had warned her. Soul deprived of love turns to punishment and revenge. The malicious spitefulness of Psyche's sisters is now incorporated into soul. Psyche becomes even more Venus's lookalike, for Venus was born to avenge the castration of Uranus. The basis, then, for the reconciliation of Psyche and Venus consists in the desire to punish.[33] Soon after Psyche's revenge, Ceres and Juno pun on the adverb *amarē* ("bitterly") and the infinitive *amare* (5.31).[34]

Psyche begins to become the human soul not only when the spirit of revenge enters her but when she begins to philosophize. In her wanderings, she sees a temple on top of a high mountain (6.1). She wonders whether her master lives there; but when she climbs to it, she finds scythes and "all the equipment [*mundus*] of harvesting, but everything was lying around at random and carelessly mixed up, tossed aside by laborers as they usually do in the summer heat." Psyche, however, "divides strictly by kinds and once set discretely apart collects them" ("curiose dividit et discretim remota rite componit"). A human being as such, Socrates says, "must understand [literally "put together"] what is spoken of by kind [*eidos*], gathering into one by collection what comes from many perceptions."[35] Psyche while apart from Cupid practices dialectics (cf. 6.10–11). Apuleius thus alludes to the difference between the Olympian gods, whom human souls follow, and the hyperuranian beings, which human souls get to see by following the Olympian gods. The soul's impulse upward diverts the soul away from that which nourishes it. It is lured beyond the visible by the visible gods, who, unlike human beings, however, do not need the hyperuranian beings to be what they are. Hestia is a god and yet has never seen those beings,[36] but it is while Psyche is homeless that she separates and brings together things according to their kind.

At the beginning of the story we are told that Cupid, "with his bad character, in contempt of public order, runs at night through houses not his own, corrupts the marriages of everyone, commits with impunity great crimes, and does nothing good" (4.30). But at the end of the story, after Jupiter, "by whom the laws of the elements are arranged," repeats the charge "You acted against the laws, the Julian law itself, and public order" (6.22), he decrees that Cupid "by the chains of marriage" is to be made law-abiding: "I shall now make a marriage not unequal but lawful and in conformity with civil law" (6.23).[37] The union of love and soul makes the individual soul immortal—every soul is now a proper name—and antinomian eros is no more. Satisfaction replaces longing: the child of Cupid and Psyche is Pleasure (6.24); before the birth of Pleasure, Psyche had guessed that she was going to marry him "who was born for the destruction of the whole world" (4.34), and her sisters had conjectured that Psyche's child would be Cupid (5.14).

The consequences for Apuleius's story of this novel association of law and love are immediate. Everyone connected with the story of Cupid and Psyche dies a violent death: the old woman who tells it, the young girl who hears it, and her husband.[38] Indignation becomes the dominant passion, cruelty more ingenious, and Lucius obsessed with adultery (cf. 7.11).[39] Aristomenes' perspective becomes Lucius's own. The one wholly detachable story Lucius tells concerns a slave who, though his master allowed him a family, "was inflamed with the love of some free woman"; and when his wife killed their son and herself, the master, because the slave had been responsible for his wife's crime, smeared his body with honey so that ants would torture him slowly as they nibbled away at him alive (8.22; cf. 9.4). It follows the last metamorphosis in the book: a dragon, which appeared as an old shepherd, is reported to be eating a corpse (8.21). Apuleius seems to suggest that the ahistorical, magical transformation of man into beast is now the bestialization of man himself through inhuman forms of punishment. The inner corruption of man dispenses with the need for magic.

Perhaps, however, the most striking sign of the change in the *Metamorphoses* is the use of *conscius* and *conscientia*. Before the story of Cupid and Psyche, they are found altogether six times, during the story once, but after it fourteen times; and "bad conscience" only occurs after it (7.3, 9; 10.26; see also 7.27).[40] At the beginning of the seventh book, Lucius learns that it is universally believed that he was responsible for the robbery of Milo's house, and he had by "false loves crept into the affection of the slave Fotis" (7.1). Lucius now realizes that Fortune is truly sightless, as the old and primeval teaching stated, for she always confers her benefits on the bad and undeserving and never chooses anyone rationally. Lucius now thinks of Milo as his dearest host, and the robbery he is accused of "everyone would more rightly call parricide." In his present state he cannot say a single word in his defense, but, "lest present at so wicked a charge I might seem by a bad conscience to agree silently," he brays, "Non Non" (7.3; see also3.29). The pure conscience becomes known not despite but because of the dumbness of the beast.

Even after Lucius gets rescued from the robbers he fares no better. The very gratitude he earned for helping to rescue Charite seemingly induces everyone to treat him morally (cf. 7.27). Stallions look upon him as a base adulterer (7.16). A boy treats him cruelly and claims among other shameful accusations that he attacks every pretty woman on the road (7.22). The stubborn ass has become the lustful ass; desire and bestiality are now one. The peasants want to kill him, "a public husband," "a universal adulterer," "a sacrificial victim wholly worthy of these monstrous marriages"; but someone suggests castration; he calls it a *detestatio* (7.23), which in legal language is a formal renunciation under oath of one's family *(sacra)* prior to adoption. This pun prepares the way for not only Lucius's conversion but also his asceticism: he puns on eating and being, and in renouncing the eating of any animal renounces being anything ensouled ("ullum animal essem"; 11.23).[41]

The only cheerful story in the last third of the book has as its setting a village of a once wealthy city, founded among half-toppled ruins (9.4). The previous digression had no setting and was not called a story but a deed (8.22). Apuleius seems to suggest that the deed is contemporary and the tale is not. It belongs, I suggest, to pre–Cupid and Psyche times, when the cuckold was a figure of fun and the wife's crime treated, in accordance with Aristotle's suggestion, as involuntary.[42] Lucius's obsession with adultery reaches its peak while he is serving in a mill. There, where he goes round during the day in a circle blindfolded, "by unwavering wandering" ("errore certo"), and discovers that the slaves who work there are no better than beasts ("homunculi"), whose half-naked bodies are covered with scars, their foreheads tattooed, their feet chained, and their eyelids eaten away, Lucius does not side with them but with his master: "Celestial providence looked down upon me tortured by the indignity my master suffered" (9.27). For the first time Lucius does something that does not involve his own advantage or disadvantage (see also 8.29): he crushes the hand of the wife's concealed lover in order to expose him. His curiosity now serves the law, and though still angry at Fotis, he now feels grateful for his one solace—the long ears with which he can detect what is said at great distances (9.15).[43] The advantage of long ears was not something Phaedrus the rhetorician knew anything about. Not to be wise ("prudens") like Odysseus but to be as knowing ("multiscius") as he was earns Lucius's gratitude for being an ass (9.13).[44] Somewhere between his curiosity about the mill and his curiosity about what people say and do in his presence as if he were not there (9.12–13), Lucius makes his peace with the moral order and becomes its agent (9.23). Lucius now calls himself a *man* of curiosity with the appearance of a beast (9.30; see also "somnum humanum quievi"; 9.2). Whereas before the Cupid and Psyche story he uttered "O" in vain (in trying to appeal to Caesar), the second time he utters it, he does so in horror at observing sodomy and succeeds, albeit accidentally, in bringing the perpetrators to justice (3.29, 8.29). Lucius thus finds his vocation.

During the time that the spirit of revenge takes over Lucius (cf. 7.26), Lucius becomes more and more a writer. At the end of the story of Cupid and Psyche, Lucius regrets that he did not have pen and tablet (6.25; cf. 6.29, 8.1), and there is no reference to a reader before 9.30;[45] but by the beginning of the tenth book, Lucius is speaking of his own book, in which we can read of a terrible crime (10.2; cf. 7),[46] and we are told we are reading not a tale but a tragedy and are ascending from "sock to buskin." That love is to speech as vindictiveness is to writing seems to be Apuleius's formula.[47] At the end of the ninth book, Lucius says that the expression "the shadow of an ass" became a proverb through his inadvertent betrayal of his master (9.42).[48] The proverb occurs in the *Phaedrus* (260c7); it occurs just after Socrates has shown the absurdity of a rhetorician not knowing the difference between an ass and a horse; and Socrates contrasts that trivial issue—"the shadow of an ass"—with the importance of distinguishing between good and bad. The almost certain execution of his master, whose crime began with his not knowing Latin (9.39), is treated as a joke by Lucius. The funny manner in which his master gets caught spills over into the unfunny consequence and infects it. The shadow of an ass is not trivial, it seems, if the difference between knowledge and opinion is trivial. By claiming to be the original, of which the occurrence in the *Phaedrus* is but one copy, Lucius implies that something always brings to light anyone who tries to hide from the law. Lucius's curiosity, even when not informed by the law, supports the law (9.42). His address to the reader is immediately preceded by a description of himself as an ass armed with helmet, shield, and spear (10.1). The spear, he says, was placed carefully on top of the baggage for the sake of terror.

All the various strands of Lucius's story meet at the arena where a multiple murderess is condemned to have intercourse with Lucius before she is torn apart by wild beasts (10.28).[49] We are far from the mock trial of Lucius at Hypata.[50] He is now an instrument of judicial and theatrical cruelty. Corinth is about to witness in deed everything the reader has read about. A tableau of the judgment of Paris opens the proceedings. A boy simulates a shepherd, one girl is like in appearance to Juno, another "you would believe Minerva," a third represents Venus, "as Venus was when she was a virgin"; they were all "believed goddesses," but Juno's attendants, Castor and Pollux, were after all just boy actors ("isti Castores erant scaenici pueri"). Lucius begins to distance himself from classical paganism; he sees through the imitation to the reality beneath: "*You* would say they were real Cupids who had just flown in from sky or sea" (10.32).[51] Lucius then angrily denounces all judges and connects the present-day corruption of the judiciary with that first of all trials, soon confirmed by the condemnation of Palamedes and Ajax, and culminating in the trial of Socrates (10.33). Lucius implies that wisdom and beauty do not go together, and that he is renouncing the beautiful for both its injustice and its illusoriness. He calls his outburst a digression—the only one he admits to—and reverts to the story lest we will have to put up with an ass philosophizing. Since Lucius appeals so explicitly to Plato's *Apology of Socrates* in defending Socrates,[52] "an old man of divine prudence," against the charge of corrupting the young, inasmuch as he tried rather to restrain them, the very juxtaposition of this digression with the tableau of the Olympian gods implies that the charge of impiety was true and consisted precisely in Socrates' denial of the gods' reality. In the procession that precedes Isis's, there are still impersonations but not of gods (11.8). Only the private imagination now knows the gods, but it suffices (11.25, 30).

The *Metamorphoses* can now be seen as having the following structure. In the *Phaedrus,* Socrates' first speech seems to belong together with Lysias's speech, and the two of them to stand over against Socrates' second speech; but Socrates claims that his first and second speech are one speech and apart from Lysias's speech.[53] Apuleius's book 11, which is preceded by the literal bestialization of sex (cf. *Phaedrus* 250e4) and an indictment of Eros in the choice of Paris (10.33), presents Lucius the lawyer and Lucius the convert together. Apuleius follows appearances and puts together once more Lysias and Socrates' first speech, while he isolates Socrates' second speech from his first in the supposedly detachable Cupid and Psyche story. That story explains how the reattachment of law and religion occurred: the Phaedrus of the first speech is no longer an invention of Socrates but fully independent in a book. A dream informs Lucius that his slave White (Candidus) has survived, and in the morning his own white horse is restored to him (11.20).[54] After his rebirth Lucius no longer has a black horse (11.6; cf. 11.22); perhaps he never did. In Socrates' myth it looked like Socrates.[55]

Notes

1. Cf. W. S. Smith, "The Narrative Voice in Ap. *Met.*" *Transactions of the American Philological Association* 103 (1972): 513–34; C. S. Wright, "No Art at All: A Note on the Proemium of Ap. *Met.*," *Classical Philology* 68 (1973): 217–19; K. Downden, "Ap. and the Art of Narration," *Classical Quarterly,* 1982, 427–28.

2. Cf. R. Thibau, "Les *Métamorphoses* d'Apulée et la théorie Platonicienne de l'Erôs," *Studia Philosophica Candensia* 3 (1965): 89–144.

3. See David Daube, "Greek and Roman Reflections on Impossible Laws," *Natural Law Forum* 12 (1967): 1–84, esp. 5–8.

4. In pseudo-Lucian, *Asinus,* the sexual encounter is put in terms of wrestling and not war (5, 8–10), for the name of the slave girl is Palaestra.

5. This prediction is coupled with the promise that Lucius will be a great *historia* and an unbelievable *fabula. Fabula* occurs thirty-two times in the *Met.,* twelve in the first book alone, but *fabulor* only once (11.6): "omnes in me fabulabantur."

6. Cf. W. R. Nethercut, "Apuleius's Literary Art: Resonance and Depth in the *Met.*," *Classical Journal* 64 (1968): 117–19.

7. Cf. R. Burger, *Plato's Phaedrus: A Defense of a Philosophic Art of Writing* (Birmingham: University of Alabama Press, 1980).

8. *Digest* 28.7.1.15.

9. The clearest sign of this transformation is Lucius's misuse of a Roman republican formula when he first plans to seduce Fotis—"quod bonum felix et faustum itaque, licet salutare non erit, Photis illa temptetur" (2.6)—and its reoccurrence at the end as the conclusion of a dream image's promise: "quod felix itaque ac faustum salutareque tibi sit" (11.29); for the full formula see Varro, *De lingua latina* 6.86.

10. The difference in the two lists recalls a passage in the tenth book of Plato's *Republic,* where Socrates speaks of a craftsman with the capacity to make all implements, all the things that grow from the earth, all animals, including himself, earth, sky, gods, and everything in heaven and under the earth (596c4–9); but when Glaucon expresses astonishment at such a sophist, Socrates speaks of a mirror, by the revolution of which Glaucon could himself make the sun, the things in heaven and earth, including himself and all the animals, implements, plants, "and everything that was just now mentioned" (596e1–3).

11. Cf. Thibau, "Les *Métamorphoses* d'Apulée," 114.

12. Cf. Plato, *Republic* 472d4–8.

13. *Theogony* 820–35. See M. L. West's analysis of the traditions about Typhon in his commentary on *Theogony* 379–81.

14. Cf. *Philebus* 17b6–d2.

15. If Lucius the ass cannot utter anything but the vowel *o* (3.29), and the ass is the silent determinative in the name for the god Seṭ *(śtš)* as well as for "turmoil" *(hnnw)* and "rage" *(hšni)* (compare Typhon) and is incapable of consonantal sounds except *non* (7.4), it is striking that the Egyptian for "not" is *n* or *nn.* One wonders whether Lucius represents the nonvocalic Egyptian hieroglyphs: he is in principle a writing and not a speaking (cf. 10.17, last sentence). Mercury is called in the Cupid and Psyche story "deus vocalis": Venus needs him to proclaim her "libellus" (6.7). Lucius's proof that he is human consists in his ἔκφρασις of the robbers' hideout (4.6), that is, a picture in words. The Latin for ἔκφρασις is *de-scriptio.* Lucius's attribution of humanity to himself through *descriptio* occurs between his own attribution of human sense to an ass (4.5) and a story about the criminal Thrasyleon ("Rash-lion"), who becomes a beast ("bestiam factum"; 4.15) by putting on a bearskin

and dies a beast as if he were in the arena; the execution of the guilty by means of beasts, Apuleius implies, assumes that the guilty are beasts. Thrasyleon is called a bear at the very moment he is killed and a beast when he is dead and cut up (4.21).

16. The danger of false confession is acknowledged in the rescript of Aurelius and Verus cited by Ulpian (*Digest* 48.18.1.27).

17. Leo (apud Helm, note on 1.15, line 4) thought that Apuleius erred at this point and that the remark ought to have been attributed to the servant of Aristomenes.

18. H. van Thiel, *Der Eselroman,* Zetemeta 54/1 (1971), 1:65–67, counts the Pythias episode as in all probability Apuleius's addition to the original Greek version, of which pseudo-Lucian is the epitome.

19. Cf. *Apologia* 63. The intermediate stage between the artifacts at Byrrhena's and magic is found at Cupid's palace: "mirus prorsus homo, immo deus vel certe semideus qui magnae artis suptilitate tantum efferavit argentum" (5.1). See N. Fick, "Du palais d'Erôs à la robe Olympienne de Lucius," *Revue des Etudes Latines* 47 (1969): 378–96; A. Wlosok, "Zu Einheit det *Met.* des Ap.," *Philologos* 113 (1969): 68–84.

20. Cf. H. G. Ingenkamp, "Thelyphron," *Rheinisches Museum für Philologie,* n. s., 115 (1972): 337–42.

21. Cf. H. van Thiel, *Der Eselroman,* 1:90–95.

22. Frag. 246 K; cf. Petronius, 42.4.

23. It is possible that Fotis, aware of the humiliation Lucius experienced but unaware of his curiosity about magic, devised the story in order to make him believe he was not deliberately set up to be the universal object of ridicule but the accidental victim of witchcraft.

24. Cf. K. Alpers, "Innere Beziehungen und Kontraste als 'hermeneutischen Zeichen' in den *Met.* des Ap.," *Würzburger Jahbücher für die Altertumswissenschaft* 6a (1980): 197–207.

25. In a book of laughter, Lucius never smiles and does not laugh after 1.21; *[ad]risi* at 3.19 is a conjecture.

26. Contrast Lucian 13: ἠβουλόμην γὰρ πείρᾳ μαθεῖν εἰ μεταμορφωθεὶς ἐκ τοῦ ἀνθρώπου καὶ τὴν ψυχὴν ὄρνις ἔσομαι. Cf. Augustine, *De civitate dei* 18.18: "nec tamen in eis mentem fieri bestialem, sed rationalem humanamque servari, sicut Apuleius in libris, quos asini aurei titulo inscripsit, sibi ipsi accidisse, ut accepto veneno humano animo permanente asinus fieret, aut indicavit aut finxit."

27. Tentatively, one can say that this sequence corresponds to Lucius's experiences: (1) Lucius as innocent; (2) Lucius after the fall but without knowledge of evil, i.e., Lucius bewitched by Fotis and magic before the Cupid and Psyche story; (3) Lucius after the fall but with knowledge of evil, i.e., Lucius after the story; and (4) Lucius restored (book 11).

28. Plato, *Symposium* 203c6–e5. The double account Psyche gives of Cupid, which so outrages her sisters (5.16), that he is young and old, recalls the end of this passage. They are wicked; they are not stupid.

29. The suggestion of Psyche's sisters that her lover is a snake (5.17–18) recalls Agathon's description of Eros (*Symposium* 196a1–4).

30. That Psyche is soul is shown by her animating inanimate things while she is aware that she is apart from Cupid (6.17; cf. 11.7), but since she does not know that she is responsible for the animation, she is to that extent not soul.

31. Cupid means that he can only be seen by artificial light (i.e., the light of poetry) but that in truth he is not to be seen at night, when there is union, and cannot be seen at all in the daytime, when there is the distance of longing.

32. Cf. Plato, *Lysis* 204b5–c2.

33. "To punish" *(punio)* and "punishment" *(poena)* first occur in the Cupid and Psyche story; the substantive appears for the first time at 4.34 (cf. 4.30), and afterward sixteen times; the verb occurs six times. A curious confirmation of the importance of this is that *impune* and cognates, mostly negated, occur earlier (1.12, 25; 3.3, 6); *cruciatus* and cognates occur nine times before the Cupid and Psyche story and twenty-nine times after it; likewise, *clades* occurs twice before the story and fourteen times after it; *vindicta* occurs four times before and twelve after; *flagitium* occurs four times before, thrice within, and twelve times after; *crimen* occurs six times before, twice within, and thirteen times after; *scelus* and cognates occur six times before and twenty-one times after; *ira* and cognates occur twice before, seven times within, and possibly thrice after; *pessimus* occurs twice before, four times within, and fourteen times after; *noxius* occurs thrice before, five times within, and fifteen times after; and finally, *indignatio* and cognates occur five times before, five times within, and sixteen times after. As no one loses his life, except for "Socrates," before the Cupid and Psyche story, so books 6–10 all end with an imminent execution, either of Lucius (books 6–8) or of others (books 9–10). Sorrow too increases in a way comparable to punishment: *luctus* occurs twice before the Cupid and Psyche story, four times within it, and twelve times after; *aerumna* occurs five times before, twice within, and fifteen times after.

34. The basis for Venus's persecution of Psyche, after Cupid is wounded, is that Psyche has become her slave because she is now "a slave to love." The story translates the metaphor back into "reality," where it has to be understood in light of the Roman law of fugitive slaves (6.4). Psyche herself had prepared for this transformation by deciding to propitiate Cupid, "if not by the wheedlings of a wife, then at least by the prayers of a slave" (6.1).

35. *Phaedrus* 249b6–c1. The reading is not entirely certain.

36. *Phaedrus* 247a1–2.

37. Despite its fairy-tale opening ("erat in civitate quadam rex et regina"), the allusion to the Julian laws makes the story of Cupid and Psyche post-Augustan: Venus, to whom divus Caesar traced his origin, takes vengeance on a mortal who usurped her worship.

38. Cf. F. Dornseiff, "Lukios' und Apuleius' *Metamorphosen*," *Hermes* 67 (1938): 226. Perhaps the most conspicuous sign of the change that the story brings about is that *detestabilis* occurs ten times after the story, beginning at 7.19, and not once before.

39. There are three mentions of *adulter* and *adulterium* prior to the Psyche story (2.27, 29; 4.16), two in the story (6.22, 23), and 23 afterward: *adulterina Venus* occurs at 7. 3. *Stuprum* and cognates occur only at 9.14, 15, 26. *Turpis* first occurs at 6.22 ("turpibus adulteriis") and four times afterward.

40. In all the other works of Apuleius combined, *conscientia* occurs four times; and whereas *sapiens* and *sapientia* occur altogether in the rest of Apuleius seventy times, *sapientia* occurs only once in the *Metamorphoses* (10.33; it refers to Socrates) and *sapiens* never.

41. This pun occurs immediately after the priest Mithras has brought out of the inner sanctum books "partim figuris cuiuscemodi animalium concepti sermonis compendiosa verba suggerentes" (11.22). Shortly afterward (11.24), Lucius himself puts on a cloak covered with animals and, adorned as if he were the Sun ("in instar Solis"), stands in place of an image ("in vicem simulacri"). A few days later Lucius enjoys the delight of a divine image ("inexplicabili voluptate simulacri divini perfruebar").

42. *Nicomachean Ethics* 1131a6.

43. Lucius's original consolation had been the size of his *natura* (3.24). His first proof to us that he had retained his *humanus sensus* was his long deliberation as to whether he should kill the *nequissima facinerosissimaque* Fotis (3.26).

44. Neither *prudens* nor *prudentia* occurs in book 11.

45. Cf. A. Mazzarino, *La Milesia e Apuleio* (Torino: Chiantore, 1950), 16, 123.

46. In the very next sentence, Lucius asserts that a young man, who is "probe littera-tus," is for that very reason ("atque ob id consequenter") endowed with "pietas" and "modestia."

47. A sign that the division between speaking and writing centers on the Cupid and Psyche story is that *inquam* occurs fifty-three times before the story, twice in the story, and once afterward (10.9). Likewise, *inquit* occurs seventy-one times before, twenty-two times within, and forty-four times after the story. *Ait* occurs eleven times in the first three books, once in the story, and seven after it; *aio* occurs six times in the first two books and once in the last (11.24); and *infit* occurs six times before the story, thrice in it, and thrice afterward. Likewise, *dicere* occurs twenty-nine times before the Cupid and Psyche story and eleven times after it. Only once does Lucius use *conversus* to mean transformation (1.1; cf. 2.22); elsewhere (seven times) *conversus* occurs in the sense of turning to face another for speech. Could conversion involve a failure to understand dialogue? The self-absorbed self loses the voice of the other and takes itself as the other. (I cannot say whether the elevenfold occur-rence of *alter* in the "Socrates"-Aristomenes episode, i.e., from 1.2 to 1.19, is connected with this or not; but in all the rest of the *Metamorphoses* combined *alter* occurs just twenty-three times.) It is striking that the first written story concerns a Phaedra, and that Euripides' Phaedra differs from the Potiphar's wife motif by her use of writing in order to punish Hippolytus. Phaedra's nurse appeals to the writings of the ancients for her knowledge of Aphrodite (451).

48. In pseudo-Lucian, the proverb is "from the prying of an ass" (45); on this and *curiositas*, see H. J. Mette, *Festschrift Bruno Snell* (Munich: Beck, 1956), 227–35; A. Labhardt, *Museum Helveticum* 17 (1960): 206–24. The detection of Lucius and his master confirms the power of the law, for the soldiers appeal to the *fidem Caesaris,* while their adversary calls to witness the *deum numen* (9.42).

49. Since the punishment for those who engage in magic *(magicae artis conscii)* is to be thrown to the beasts or crucified (Paulus, *Sententiae* 5.23.17), Lucius finally meets the fate the law prescribes. Despite his own silence, Isis hints at this consideration: "nec . . . figuram tuam repente mutatam sequius interpretatus aliquis maligne criminabitur" (11.6). Lucius must have been terrified throughout that should he revert to his original shape he would be arrested; only religion can save him from the law. Note Isis's use of *vadata* (11.6). There is a curious coincidence between Lucius's silence about the risk of being charged with magic and his silence about what his defense would be were he charged after his transformation with the robbery of Milo's house (7.1). One point in the latter charge is true, that he had insinuated himself into Fotis's affections *falsis amoribus.*

50. H. Rieferstahl (*Der Roman des Apuleius* [Frankfurt: V. Klostermann, 1938], 69) points out that at 3.8 Lucius's slave is to be tortured at the mock trial and at 7.2 is tortured. The word *lex* occurs once before book 6 (3.8), at the beginning of the mock trial; *lex* and *legitimus* occur eighteen times thereafter.

51. Perhaps the first sign of Lucius's withdrawal from paganism occurs at 8.16, where, following Socrates, he rationalizes away the wings of Pegasus (cf. 6.30).

52. Cf. C. Schlam, "Platonica in the *Met.* of Ap.," *Transactions of the American Philologi-cal Association* 101 (1970): 485–86.

53. For how this is to be understood, see Seth Benardete, *The Rhetoric of Morality and Philosophy* (Chicago: University of Chicago Press, 1991), 175–81.

54. Cf. G. J. Drake, "Candidus: A Unifying Theme in Ap. *Met.,*" *Classical Journal* 64

(1968): 102–9. The last time *cupido* occurs (11.21), it refers to Lucius's growing desire for admission into the mysteries *(sacra);* it occurs just after his horse has been restored; see also "desiderium religiosum" (11.23), used of the reader.

55. *Phaedrus* 253e2. *Libido* occurs twenty-three times, seven times before the Cupid and Psyche story (six times of Lucius and Fotis) and twice in that story (5.27, 6.22); and it is from that point forward that *libido* is called *vesana* (5.27, 10.19), *illicita* (7.21 [cf. 6.22], 8.29), *furiosa* (8.3), and *probrosa* (10.5). The last reference to *libido* is to Paris's selling his judgment for it (10.33).

Against Entertainment: Plato and the Poets Revisited

NORMA THOMPSON

Some years ago at the University of Chicago, David Grene opened a seminar meeting on Herodotus by speaking of the space in which history and poetry belong together. He appealed to Enobarbus[1] as a parallel instance of the step outside history of the Solon and Croesus encounter, and then to Demodocus, that enigma whose singing made one believe that "he had been there himself, or heard it from one who was." These references were illuminating, and yet one could observe thereafter a few hurried plunges into Shakespeare and Homer on the side; after a single class, students faced the prospect, not of one impenetrable author, but three. The following week in seminar generated characters from Aeschylus, Tolstoy, and Joyce. Light began to dawn: at the Committee on Social Thought, old literary friends not only had a seat at the table but pride of place; their presence was more unyielding—and perceptive—than that of the newcomers. Educating oneself indeed became a matter of understanding character. (For myself, I was to become David Grene's student through Enobarbus.)

In his evening seminars, in the Friday afternoon Greek tutorials in his office, in the legendary gin and plastic cup parties in his tiny Hyde Park apartment, David Grene would transfix the company with his breathtaking literary circuits through the ages. Characters intruded, and intruded fiercely. Certain favorites from ancient Greek history to twentieth-century Irish drama were called upon often to orient, ennoble, and instruct. Because he was drawn to such interlocutors, it is small wonder that David's occasional inquiries into the critical literature of the day could leave him sputtering about a minginess of imagination in the academy.

The inquiries were never prolonged. Fortunately for generations of devotees, David bypassed the schools and adhered to his select assemblage of characters as vehicles for his thinking. It scarcely needs saying how stimulating David's example has been to his students, who themselves may have only a single trait in common of being refreshingly out of step with the times.

To honor this example, I offer reflections on Iris Murdoch, an author who to my mind outsizes and vexes the professorate with a like-minded exuberance. She was the author of twenty-six novels in addition to dozens of critical and philosophical essays, including her culminating work, *Metaphysics as a Guide to Morals*.[2] That work of philosophy shows her in the expansive mode characterized above; David Tracy notes the "brief and telling reflections with favored Murdochian conversation partners who seem to keep returning like characters in a novel."[3] The most favored conversation partner in *MGM* is Plato, whom Murdoch transforms into a literary character, in a bow toward Plato's extraordinary rearing of *his* brainchild, Socrates. Mikhail Bakhtin's well-known argument that characters create their own "zone" around them takes on particular force with a "figure of good": "[a character always has] a zone of his own, his own sphere of influence on the authorial context surrounding him, a sphere that extends—and often quite far—beyond the boundaries of the direct discourse allotted to him."[4] Murdoch's "strange and attractive book," "meditative and meandering,"[5] is worth further study for its commentary on the space in which history, poetry, and philosophy belong together. For the moment, though, I will focus more strictly on her achievements in the novel in order to evoke the closest parallels with the literary imagination of David Grene.

Character Deficiencies

In Murdoch's novels, the early signals are so agreeable that one eases into the story—only to be startled out of place. Characters emerge to reprove overly compliant readers, disconcerting us and then drifting away. "There have always been readers who hate Iris Murdoch's novels,"[6] Elizabeth Dipple observes gamely. Harold Bloom, for instance, admits to being caught up momentarily but finally pronounces the work forgettable: "Her novels rush by us, each a successful entertainment, but none perhaps fully distinct from the others in our memories."[7] Richard Poirier detects in her the illusion that "[her work exists] not in time but in space, like a painting," and adds: "Life in literature is exhibited by the acts of performance that make it interesting, not by the acts of rendition that make it 'real.'"[8] And Edward Said elaborates: "greatness in literature or any of the other arts is to be found wherever there is a continued need for performance."[9] But these accusations against Murdoch are odd to those aware of her Platonic commitments, for it can be shown that Plato's antiperformance, antientertainment themes profoundly inform her novels.

Consider the distinctions among interlocutors in a typical Platonic dialogue, where inconsequential figures serve to heighten the dramatic exchange between Socrates and his adversary of the moment. Socrates' effect on that adversary is predictably minimal (one thinks of Alcibiades), and his example is of questionable benefit to the larger company (at the least, the charge against him of "corrupting youth" was tenable), but it is undeniable that the glimpse of Socratic virtue that lingers on in the dialogues has riveted the Western world. It would be strange to fault Plato for not making the general run of his characters "better" than he did.

Over time, the novels of Murdoch seem to fit more and more neatly into some such Platonic configuration: an elusive virtuous character, his sharply drawn rival, and the remaining bourgeois set, who are differentiated but still commonplace. In *The Green Knight,* for instance, the ordinary, complacent characters who undergo their various trials and mismatches fade on the completion of the story; when the novel is put down, their names and identities are forgotten. So long as we are immersed in the story and the conventional characters seem to be gravitating toward the good man,[10] they appear to have solidity. In the end, though, we readers have to recognize our intrusion; the characters are not sustainable. Murdoch's evil character in *The Green Knight,* Lucas, who *is* memorable ("I have killed you every day in my thoughts. Please don't scratch the desk."[11]), is neutralized, finally, in contact with the good character; in this case, he vanishes in America. The good and evil characters know each other, and in those contacts, the mischief is countered through a rendition of Socrates' "stingray" effect (*Meno* 80a). Even so, no permanent transformation is effected; Lucas is removed from the immediate scene, numbed, perhaps, but only for the moment; the overtones are ominous. Lucas remains the single most distinct character in our memory. Without identifying with him, we are uncomfortably marked by him. Finally, the extraordinarily good character (Peter Mir) maintains our undivided attention only so long as his amnesia holds and he is *out* of character; in that state, he seeks to extract retribution from the malefic Lucas ("If I may emulate the ruthless frankness of the Professor, I want his death."[12]). But

Mir regains his hold on himself and reestablishes his benevolent posture—whereupon he dies. The truly good do not subsist in this world; Mir is glimpsed as a shade only.

The evanescent quality of Murdoch's good characters is a topic of sustained and, I think, highly productive critical interest. As a first word on this topic, I suggest that even when her withdrawing, almost invisible hero is counterposed to Plato's most visible and active hero—Socrates as "gadfly" (*Apology* 30e)—Murdoch remains interestingly Platonic in her conception of the good character. She compels us to think about the fact that our age may not have the metaphysical underpinnings to support a Socrates.[13] The good man, the only self-defined, self- subsisting character with a well-ordered soul, will not announce himself in our time. The typical characters, who require an anchoring lest they slip away, fail in the end to recognize what is most needed. And slip away they do, even to Murdoch's own dismay[14]—hence the Murdochian predicament of indistinct characters. Where the earlier criticism is surely off course, though, is in attributing an entertainment factor to this phenomenon or in decrying the need for performance.[15] The prospect of entertainment in Murdoch's novels is ever present and always illusory.

The Old Quarrel

In her philosophical writings, Murdoch does not countenance the severe prescriptions set out by Plato ("Plato never did justice to the unique truth-conveying capacities of art"),[16] but her novels tell a different story. There Murdoch acts upon her distrust of the consoling powers of the artist and the poetic magic that encourages an inattention to the world. The form of her novels has been described variously as one that illustrates the "paradox of formlessness within form"[17] and the "aesthetic of imperfection,"[18] as the novelist seeks "a self-exorcism [to purge] the artist's own self-assertiveness."[19] Her novels illustrate the continuing relevance of Plato's thinking about the literary form of philosophic expression; she pays tribute by following his example in a way that makes possible a deepened reading of Platonic dialogues.

The old Socratic issue traditionally described in terms of the "quarrel between the philosopher and the poet" has always been a question of political philosophy, if a subsidiary one. Aristotle's rehabilitation of "pity" in his explanation of catharsis in the *Poetics* did much to alleviate the sting of the philosopher's attack on the poets, but it must be acknowledged that to a great many readers, Plato comes across as off the mark and strangely overagitated on the issue of poetry. To be sure, Plato *has* had his serious commentators who subject his argument to careful and respectful analysis. Yet the response to the best of these commentators (from E. N. Tigerstedt to Stanley Rosen to G. R. F. Ferrari) has been either subdued or disbelieving, even hostile (Allan Bloom). Nothing that Bloom ever wrote so charged his reading public as did his resurrection of Socrates to demonstrate in a contemporary version of Plato's attack the effects of rock music on the souls of the young: "But as long as [students] have the Walkman on, they cannot hear what the great tradition has to say. And, after its prolonged use, when they take it off, they find they are deaf."[20] The perceived irrelevancy of Plato on this subject has not been affected by scholarly treatments of the topic, even best-selling ones. This itself is full warrant for yet another attempt to elucidate the position.

There is particular reason for us today to be clear about the quarrel that so concerned Plato, and that is the political ascendancy of the poets of his description. His term "poet" is, of course, intended to be widely applied. What it assuredly does *not* apply to is our own romantic image of alienated poets, ahead of their time and therefore apart from it, speaking a recondite language to a small number of initiates. Plato's poet is discernibly public and speaks to our ordinary preoccupations like love and death, good and evil. This poetry is essentially educative in function and might take any number of forms. "To grasp the role of poetry in ancient Greece," Elizabeth Asmis suggests, "one might think of Hindu religious drama—in which gods confront the audience directly in terrifying struggles between good and evil—and gospel meetings, along with rock concerts, opera, and television."[21] Plato's interest extends beyond the single poet, ποιητής, the one who makes the poem, to the social effects of this enterprise; accordingly, it will be my practice to refer to Plato's more general notion of μουσική, which includes any art under the purview of the Muses. In Dipple's concise terms, this art includes "all of culture that has to do with image-spawning."[22] This should enliven contemporary interest in Plato's subject, for whereas we have difficulty imagining how the poet of our time could be seen as a threat to anyone, this is far from the case if we consider the effects on the young of our own image-spawning arts. Our era is substantially marked, if not dominated, by the culture of μουσική—arts and entertainment—and at least since the Vietnam War era, this culture has been recognizably a political force. This was doubtlessly so in the Woodstock generation and remains so today, as evidenced, for example, when performers are the wealthiest group of people in the society; when politicians and students alike couch their references in terms of media events, films, and rock lyrics; when stars are valued not only for performance but for their views on politics; and when relations between the White House and Hollywood are a matter of concern as a matter of course.

At the same time, our current political vocabulary is inadequate to the task of describing this quarrel in ways that make clear what is at issue. Artists are thought to be particularly immune from responsibilities; as the refrain goes, they have the right to express themselves. If their creativity is a gift, who are we (ordinary people) to judge? Plato considered such a combination of power and unaccountability on the part of the poet conducive to a degradation of human beings more generally; he believed that the unchecked authority of an individual's creative inspiration carried implications of despotism. Thus the harsh measures taken against the poets in the *Republic* when Socrates, Glaucon, and Adeimantus seek to elucidate the most just regime ("[We must] send [poetry] away from the city on account of its character"; *Republic* 607b)[23] should be evaluated in the context of the full accusation. Plato's attack on the poets is his assertion that a respectable human life requires that there be a personal stake in truth-telling, and that to promote such responsibility a political community must treat its citizens singly and not in a mass. But the culture of μουσική tends toward a mass.

In her novels it can be shown that Iris Murdoch has heeded the full Platonic message, which contained Socrates' qualifying clause that the founders of *kallipolis* "shall listen benevolently" if the poetry "should turn out to be not only pleasant but also beneficial" (607de). In other words, Plato has Socrates concede that there are poets and there are poets. In terms derived from the *Ion* and *Republic,* poets may be "bardic" or "philosophic." The bardic category—headed by Homer and, we shall see, implicating rhapsodes and audiences alike—is powerfully alluring and requires a philosophic countercharm: "we'll chant this argument we are making to ourselves as a countercharm, taking care against falling back again into this love, which is childish and belongs to the many" (608a). The second kind, philosophic poetry, which is not fully articulated by Socrates and perhaps not wholly appreciated by him, has as its most palpable manifestation the Platonic dialogues themselves. The difference between these categories might be simply stated: the first signifies an elevation of the performance; the second, an invitation to private reflection on the part of the reader.

The only consoling outcome of a Murdoch novel is the unflappable Murdoch herself. That this is not a simple matter I hope to show by further exploring the Platonic heritage of this pattern. To anticipate, Murdoch's act of preventing her audience from identifying too closely with any of her characters is the identifying mark of a philosophic poet. It is the recognition that the responsible poet must create space for her audience to think about the creation itself—to reflect on it intellectually and morally. "She is really writing the metaphysical novel," Suguna Ramanathan concludes, "and by manipulating her characters against the artist's usual manipulations, suggests the breakdown of structural narrative codes."[24] Poetic expression has implied duties, Plato and Murdoch remind us, no less than other human activities. Creativity may be a gift, but it is a gift that calls forth judgment from ordinary people if they are not to forfeit their autonomous selves. The philosophic poet allows for no bardic complacency.

The Platonic Model

BARDIC POETS

The Platonic model reveals how philosophic poets leave room for themselves in their created product and thus prevent the wholesale appropriation of their work by the audience. The contrast is to the bardic poets, who really do vanish in their inspired state, thereby setting the stage for an indoctrinated community that relinquishes its ability to judge. Plato sets out this bardic phenomenon most succinctly in *Ion,* where Ion attempts to explain to Socrates the art of his award-winning rhapsody. What he actually succeeds in doing is to give us a glimpse behind the magic of Homeric poetry.

Plato's *Ion* has always struck many readers as a relatively inconsequential work. No less a luminary than Goethe concluded that *Ion* had "nothing at all to do with poetry," and that if Ion had "had only a glimmer of knowledge about poetry, he would have had a ready answer to Socrates' teasing question."[25] Socrates' question concerns the art (τέχνη) of the rhapsode: is it by a particular skill or special expertise that Ion excels at reciting Homeric poetry? The ready answer that Goethe proposes is that "the judicious rhapsodist knows if he speaks appropriately."[26] Ion is not a man of penetrating intelligence, but he does, in fact, produce a version of this answer: "[The rhapsode] will know what it's fitting for a man or a woman to say—or for a slave or a freeman, or for a follower or a leader" (540b).[27] However, the hapless Ion is unable to elaborate. It is with supreme exasperation that Goethe and others wish for an interlocutor more knowledgeable about poetry and poetic inspiration. But this wish is ill-founded. Attempts to fill in the poet who could have held his own with

Socrates always come back to plain dissatisfaction with the rhapsode who could not, and in this circumstance *Ion* is written off as lighthearted and irrelevant. An alternative is to face squarely the ordinary being who is the namesake of this dialogue: a very dull reasoner and a very great rhapsodist. What does *Ion* have to do with poetry, and in what way might Homer be responsible for his rhapsode?

In answer, Socrates introduces the image of the Heraclea stone, a magnetic force that connects Muse, poet, rhapsode, and audience. This is the prototypical image for the bardic model and contains within it the pointers for elaborating on the two major components of Plato's attack on the poets, inspiration (ἐνθουσιασμός) and imitation (μίμησις). In keeping with his general procedure, Plato does not explicitly treat these two subjects at the same time; here, imitation is only implicitly a subject. But that it is of the utmost relevance we gather by the punch line of the work: Ion, twisted in knots over his inability to name the subject on which the rhapsode is supremely competent to speak, declares himself to know the business (τέχνη) of the general. "Are you also a general, Ion?" Socrates asks. "Are you the best in Greece?" The answer: "Certainly, Socrates. That, too, I learned from Homer's poetry" (541b). Homer has rendered *his* hero so plainly and unmistakably, it seems, that Ion literally appropriates him.

Though Ion's susceptibility to Homer's creation is surely meant to alarm the reader, Socrates' explicit topic is inspiration. In the most laudatory terms, he attributes to the poet divine inspiration, all the while managing to associate this inspiration with fantasy, magic, and emotional excess. He introduces the Heraclea stone in order to explain a puzzle: the rhapsode Ion is unparalleled in reciting Homer but fails even to find interest in the work of other poets. How can this be, when there are many subjects about which the poets say the same things (531a)? Socrates concludes that Ion's recitations are not self-generated but inspired and therefore reflective of the divine power of Homer's original connection with the Muse. This divine power, Socrates explains to Ion, "moves you like that in the stone which Euripides named a magnet, but most people call 'Heraclea stone.' For this stone not only attracts iron rings, but also imparts to them a power whereby they in turn are able to do the very same thing as the stone and attract other rings" (533e). The Muse, Homer, Ion, and Ion's audience of 20,000 are all linked, then, in a magnetic chain of "bits of iron and rings."

Each component of the chain has in common the characteristic of having relinquished control over its individual narrative; each is unprepared for any kind of discursive self-justification. In the case of Ion, this is the upshot of Socrates' search for the τέχνη of the rhapsode. Ion is supremely confident that he could earn the acclaim of Socrates if given the chance to perform (531a, 536e), but Socrates insists on keeping separate Ion's act of performance, on the one hand, and his ability to understand and account for his own activity, on the other. As Ferrari writes, "[We] have a tendency in our estimation of poetry to confound the values of performance with the values of understanding, and not to see how the former undermine the latter."[28] Ion readily admits that he is no critic of poetry, but he does presume to interpret Homer adequately ("that's the part of my τέχνη that took the most work"; 530c), even if the work of other poets invariably makes him doze. Socrates introduces the relevant contrasts: the diviners are those who judge well in matters of prophecy; the masters of arithmetic, matters of arithmetic; doctors, matters of nutrition. What subject matter is it over which Ion can claim a comparable mastery? There appears to be none; for every subject matter there can be found an expert who speaks with more authority than he. Ion's lack of judgment about poetry in general is proof that he requires neither art (τέχνη) nor knowledge (ἐπιστήμη) for his success. Contrary to appearances, he has no personal investment in his activity; he is a captive of the force that applauds him.

In the case of the original poet Homer, his place on the magnetic chain signifies his assumption of the power to entrance—a dubious foundation indeed for what amounts to his construction of a theogony. "It is [Homer and Hesiod] who created for the Greeks their theogony," Herodotus observes; "it is they who gave to the gods the special names for their descent from their ancestors and divided among them their honors, their arts, and their shapes."[29] The bardic poets put forth their compelling depictions of the gods (making the audience complicit in the portraits) without indicating the means for any possible corroborations of these depictions. "The poets are the authentic, the only, teachers about the gods," writes Bloom. "The great mystery is how they find out about them, how they are able to present them to men."[30] This poet leaves behind questions of truth for the exhilaration of beauty; Socrates pauses to ask—in the service of what good? "Creative power by itself," Rosamond Kent Sprague remarks, "is nothing without knowledge of purpose and function."[31] In a world of competing narratives, Socrates demands from the bardic poet a fair fight.

From Plato's criticism of the invisible source of the poet's inspiration follows directly his criticism of the visible act of poetic imitation, μίμησις. The problem with inspiration is that the poet invents a reality too fantastic to be verified. The problem with imitation is that the poet reproduces a reality too familiar to be criticized. Ion accepts without any grounds that the highest human type in Homer is the highest human type simply, just as he accepted unquestioningly that Homer was the greatest poet. It appears that the more that Homer can make his audience identify with his imitations, the more irrelevant to them he becomes; the author recedes as his creation takes on its own life. Ion does not wish to *be* Homer; rather, he is drawn to identify himself with Homer's realistic figures who embody the heroic characteristics of the age. This is the consequence of the bardic poet dominating his depicted reality so completely: it is wrested from his control by the likes of Ion.

Socrates thus puts Homer's imitative wisdom in the same category as Ion's ("Surely you are the wise men [σοφοί], you rhapsodes and actors, you and the poets whose work you sing"; 532de), since both eradicate any space for reflection. Socrates contrasts this wisdom with his own, which comes from his separation from the crowd. "As for me, I say nothing but the truth, as you'd expect from a [private] [ἰδιώτης] man" (532e). The alternative—the creation of human masses such as the 20,000 that applaud Ion—signifies the removal of the realm for individual excellence (or virtue, ἀρετή); this is the relinquishing of accountability.

The allure of the bardic poet is, however, not to be underestimated; Adeimantus reminds the interlocutors in the *Republic* that virtue "is a long road, rough and steep" (364d). The culture of μουσική offers continuous diversions, for it is a pleasant exercise to give oneself over to the fantasy of the moment. Ion is never more fulsome in his exchange with Socrates than when he is asked whether his soul, "in its enthusiasm," actually believes that it is present at the actions he recounts: "What a vivid example you've given me, Socrates! I won't keep secrets from *you*. Listen, when *I* tell a sad story, my eyes are full of tears; and when I tell a story that's frightening or awful, my hair stands on end with fear and my heart jumps" (535c). Just so does the poet capture the reader, stirring our hearts into enthusiastic ecstasy, as Floyer Sydenham points out in his eighteenth-century translation of *Ion:* "Plato intends here to hint to us by what means poetry operates so strongly on the soul, that is, by touching some inward string the most ready to vibrate, awakening those sentiments, and stirring up those passions, to which the soul is most prompt."[32] And Plato simultaneously hints that as this effect is achieved without thought, it is a phenomenon that requires a thoughtful monitoring. On reflection, the image of the magnet is a chilling one, for it records the loss of integrity of everyone involved, precisely as the despot would wish.

Plato's countermodel to the bardic poet is revealed in condensed form in book 1 of the *Republic*. Instructors of this work scarcely need reminding of how much pain the reading of this aporetic book causes students coming to it for the first time. This is instructive pain, to be sure; the unsatisfactory attempts to identify justice fall back on frustrated readers and may prompt them to try their hand at resolving the confusion. But perhaps more important than the substantive issues of defining justice in book 1 are the formal points of philosophical interest: Plato prevents our identification with his characters, discomposing us with his renderings of Polemarchus, Thrasymachus, and Socrates while retaining his own composure in anonymity. A deceptively simple pattern may be identified, as the most conventional characters ebb away, the most aggressive is "tamed," while the goodness of the good character is given to us only in bare outline, with his death intimated all the while. Through this modest configuration, Plato interweaves the common man, ordinary language, and a philosophical attachment to the good. "It is the height of art to be able to show what is nearest," Murdoch writes, "what is deeply and obviously true but usually invisible."[33]

Polemarchus, identified as "heir of the argument" about justice when his father Cephalus retreats to the sacrifices, is after a brief exchange with Socrates a presence no more. He loses substance; the reader cannot identify. Plato achieves this effect by conflating the voice of Polemarchus with so many others that it can no longer be singled out, and this because from the start, Polemarchus shields himself from challenges to his opinions. He knows, for instance, that he does not subscribe to Socrates' conclusion that justice is a kind of theft, yet he cannot move beyond his opening statement, introduced by way of Simonides: "However, it is still my opinion that justice is helping friends and harming enemies" (334b). Polemarchus seems unaware of any significant *human* presence behind the argument; it is imagined as a thing in its own right, inherited and therefore straightforward. "The argument seems to be bad," Polemarchus opines (334d), and later: "Said in that way it would be fine" (335b).

The original argument "handed down" to Polemarchus by Cephalus disappeared on the instant, as Socrates transformed its terms from "weapons" to "whatsoever something was deposited" (331e). Before long, Socrates gets Polemarchus to agree that Simonides, the alleged proponent of the view they are discussing, had "made a riddle, after the fashion of poets, when he said what the just is" (332c). Must not the authorship, then, revert to Homer? "The just man, then, as it seems, has come to light as a kind of robber, and I'm afraid you learned this from Homer, for he admires Autolycus" (335e). Following this conclusion, Socrates obscures matters still further by bringing in an unnamed other: "Then if someone asserts that it's just to give what is owed to each man—and he understands by this that harm is owed to enemies by the just man and help to friends—the man who said it was not wise. For he wasn't telling the truth" (335e). Polemarchus does not object. Simonides, Homer, and "someone" are all the same to him, for he has no investment in this argument. In the final twist, Socrates lists no fewer than seven specific figures who might represent these false truth-tellers ("Simonides, or Bias, or Pittacus . . . [or] Periander, or Perdiccas, or Xerxes, or Ismenias the Theban"; 335e, 336a) and then expands the list exponentially to include "any other wise and blessed man" or "some other rich man who has a high opinion of what he can do" (335e, 336a). It is difficult now to attach to Polemarchus any view in particular.

In contrast, Thrasymachus reveals a vigorous personality and hence earns our initial approval. This is to say no more than that the reader has not yet found a character sufficiently sympathetic with whom to identify: Cephalus and Polemarchus both come across as pleasant enough but ineffective; Socrates is effective but vaguely unpleasant. Our sympathy with Thrasymachus does not last, however. He gratuitously introduces the notion of punishing Socrates if it turns out that he, Thrasymachus, is able to prevail in the argument; this is an uncomfortable remark coming on the heels of Socrates' "forced" participation in this discussion (327a–328b). Thrasymachus goes on to accuse Socrates of being a sycophant (340d) and a nonentity (341c) who is in need of a wet nurse (343a). Soon his purely emotional attachment to his argument becomes evident, for Socrates' interrogation makes him sweat profusely and finally blush (350d). We are not unhappy after all to see Thrasymachus in this distress, for his petulance in clinging to his argument seems incompatible with his commitment to the truth.

Socrates' rebuke of Thrasymachus focuses on the importance of the enterprise in which they are all engaged; he is urged to bring into line the content of his arguments with the way he actually lives his life. Significantly, it is to Thrasymachus that Socrates first insists that the definition of justice that they are discussing requires sincerity on the part of the interlocutor ("And don't answer contrary to your opinion, you blessed man, so that we can reach a conclusion"; 346a; see also 350e), since the discussion has the most serious ramifications for how they all choose to live their lives ("Nevertheless, this must still be considered better: for the argument is not about just any question, but about the way one should live"; 352d).

As it is, Thrasymachus's arguments have clearly affected the lives of others. He is stymied by Socrates, then, but his impact continues beyond this encounter. It is noteworthy that when Glaucon takes over the argument from Thrasymachus (who "has been charmed more quickly than he should have been"; 358b), he, too, distances himself from the argument he relates ("don't suppose it is I who speak, Socrates, but rather those who praise injustice ahead of justice"; 361e). Adeimantus attributes his contribution to Thrasymachus and "possibly someone else" (367a). It is as if the discovery of a good argument would be something external, not involving a person's whole being. Socrates seeks to persuade them that arguments are not an indifferent matter, taken up and put down at will, but entail bringing one's self into the search for the truth and attaining a distinctive voice.

At this early stage, Socrates himself is far from an agreeable presence. Or, to make this consonant with our earlier terms: Socrates is widely resented, even hated, by many readers of this work. Plato does not let us see his goodness until we have come and gone a few times; he does not give Socrates to us whole. In book 1, Socrates tends toward bluntness and unkindness, he seems only to react to others without acting or speaking in his own right, and he appears to be drawn to trivial, random argumentation and tendentious proofs. But even if these personality traits are prominent, they do not represent the full story. When Socrates moves from Polemarchus's assertion that it is just to benefit friends and harm enemies to the statement that justice is the art of theft, it seems condescending, but Polemarchus takes no offense. Socrates well understands that Polemarchus holds himself apart from the turns of the argument, that they are mere objects of curiosity to him and do not involve him in any self-scrutiny whatsoever: he is immune from the slight. And Socrates does him the kindness of reinstating an acceptable moral lesson: "For it has become apparent to us that it is never just to harm anyone" (335e). With Thrasymachus, who is contemptuous of such platitudes and has the potential of causing real harm through his teachings, Socrates is more resolute. He temporarily debilitates him. These are benevolent deeds, as becomes evident with Glaucon's sudden interjections (347a), especially at the start of book 2.

Only in retrospect can we appreciate the humane motives of Socrates. First-time readers of book 1 will not notice how attentive Socrates is to Glaucon (347e), or that Socrates himself introduces the notion of the "city of good men" coming into existence (347d). They are still viewing Socrates through the eyes of other characters, such that when Socrates asks Thrasymachus if he supposes that he is "plotting to do harm to [him] in the argument" (341a), the reader may well answer with Thrasymachus: "I don't suppose, I know it well." Such is the plight of the truly good character, "doing no injustice . . . [yet having] the greatest reputation for injustice" (361c). Time and distance are required for us to evaluate the interlocutors in a Platonic dialogue. This may be disorienting, but it also offers the audience the highest tribute of being invited to corroborate Plato's truth. No halfhearted attempts will suffice. "Do you suppose you are trying to determine a small matter," Socrates asks, "and not a course of life?" (344de).

The Murdochian Model

Early reactions to the novels of Iris Murdoch are often similar to the undergraduate reaction to book 1 of the *Republic*. In the case of Murdoch, the realization is "that one is not having as much fun as one had thought in this free-floating world with high comedic moments and rich detail."[34] Readers of *The Book and the Brotherhood,* for instance, may be chastened at the eventual realization that they have cast off all of the characters they had been identifying with throughout the tale, whereas the good character perished before anyone fathomed his presence. His "adversary" lives on, but unremarkably; his part in orchestrating the death of the good character silences him. As usual, the general run of characters evaporates and the author moves on. "In the literary text," Wolfgang Iser notes, "we have the strange situation that the reader cannot know what his participation actually entails."[35] Peter Conradi eloquently refers to this style as Murdoch's way of composing "wounded" novels whose meanings "leak back into life" instead of creating a hermetically sealed world: "The style deliberately defaults on the demand that it be narcissistically 'perfect' and austere, in the interests of the human truths to which it points."[36] This is a distinctively late-twentieth-century realism, with no illusions about the author's ability to contain the world through her representations and no reluctance to seek human meaning on those terms.

Of the ordinary characters in *The Book and the Brotherhood* who vie for the reader's attention only to disappear in the end, we shall examine three (Tamar, Rose, and Gerard) as examples of Murdoch's varying strategies for accomplishing these character withdrawals. Rose and Gerard, the most familiar of voices in the novel, seem to promise smooth endings and a comfortable existence for everyone; Tamar is a hard-luck case who seems to be within reach of a happy ending, not least because of the efforts of Rose and Gerard. So successful is Murdoch in causing the reader to identify with each of these characters that we have the unmistakable urge to rewrite their parts when events take a turn for the unexpected and our approbation begins to falter.

The Oxford ball that is the opening scene of *The Book and the Brotherhood* introduces Tamar (and all of the characters) in a purposeful way. This is the summer dance in which Oxford graduates, including "the brotherhood," come together in reunion to celebrate an enchanted evening of music and champagne. The first line of the novel—an exclamation that "David Crimond is here in a kilt"—hints at the turmoil that this character will cause in due time; Tamar's appearance at the ball, however, looks auspicious enough. A youthful twenty-year-old, Tamar is paired with the handsome Conrad Lomas, and she is "poised ready to fall in love."[37] That moment does not arrive, for when Conrad is temporarily distracted by the appearance of Crimond, he sets into motion events that will make up the most miserable night of Tamar's existence. After a protracted series of near-misses in her search for him and him for her, she finally spots him in the early morning hours, dancing with the slightly disreputable Lily, whom Tamar had earlier avoided ("Lily had taken off one of her sandals and was examining it, now smelling it. Tamar, who did not want to talk to Lily, hoped that Lily would not notice her"; 4). Such is the fortune of Tamar, whose own mother chides her: "And you lost your partner, can't you get anything right?" (104).

In large part, Tamar's life is frightful because of her mother, the third and most inappropriately named of the "flower ladies"—Violet. Violet has spent her life resenting the existence of Tamar, who was conceived accidentally and survived only because Violet could not afford to terminate the pregnancy. This is Violet's malediction: in a better world, Tamar would have been aborted. Under these circumstances, Tamar makes what Murdoch terms an "angelic gamble": "She saw that her safety lay, not in calculated hostility or intelligent self-regarding warfare, but in some genuine surrender of self" (108). Tamar's angelic nature is tested, and passes the most difficult ordeal her mother could possibly conceive. In a scene that brings the reader's indignity to a peak, Tamar is forced to give up her academic training just prior to its culminating moment. It would seem that such a character could never lose our sympathy or goodwill.

In details that are too many and hellish to recount here, Murdoch finds a vulnerable spot and wrenches Tamar away from the reader. Tamar becomes pregnant, and the reader begins to finish the story in all sorts of hopeful ways: marry the father, have the baby, love the child, end the cycle of abuse. Murdoch extends Tamar's deliberations to involve Lily as wise advisor, before concluding the event in the most excruciating way: Tamar has an abortion, nearly dies of remorse and madness, and then is "nursed" back to life by a priest. In the process, Tamar renounces that surrender of self that had earlier won our admiration, and she becomes a truly liberated self. It is an appalling transformation. In the end, the priest is aghast at what he has taken part in: "Tamar had spoken so coldly, and now looked . . . so ruthless, that a strange idea came into Father McAlister's head. Supposing it were all somehow false . . . ?" (509). It is an authorial triumph, as Murdoch forces readers back upon their own happy expectations.

Unlike Tamar, Rose is not personally at the center of trauma in this work; she is there to comfort those who are, and hence has the automatic appeal of a kindly aunt. In the defining opening scene, she is the first to respond to what is surely the appearance of trouble: "How *dare* [David Crimond] come here!" Ever after, her reactions of outrage tend to be our own. Crimond's appearance is an affront to Rose and her group because he had in earlier times caused the scandalous breakup of the marriage between Jean and Duncan. Jean had since returned to Duncan and the scarred marriage continued. Now Crimond was back, dancing with Jean ("He's like Shiva," an observer comments; 34) and mortifying Duncan beyond recovery. Offstage, the humiliation worsens when Crimond encounters Duncan and pushes him into a river. Duncan returns to the rooms of his friends, dripping wet, muddy, and disgraced. He purports to have fallen in accidentally ("I fell in the Cher. Idiotic old drunk!" 44). Rose comes forward in her paradigmatic stance of trying to minimize the fuss and clean up after the messes of other people: "Rose, tucking up her green dress, on her knees, began an artful operation with little doses of water and careful use of the towel, blending the muddy stain into the fortunately dark and ancient carpet" (45).

From the start, we can discern that Rose's self-surrender is not as complete as Tamar's (early) version and indeed that it borders on the hubristic—and therefore is blind to the depths of human suffering. After Jean has left Duncan for the second time, Duncan's torment is sustained and agonizing: "Blackness, that was what he experienced, a feeling of blackness over everything, a black veil over the lamp, black dust upon the furniture, black stains upon his hands, and a black cancerous lump in his stomach" (176). Rose's acts of kindness toward a man in this state are unmerciful: "Rose rang at carefully timed intervals and asked if she could drop in . . . she talked to him about indifferent matters . . . and looked at him with her gentle persuasive loving blue eyes in a way which made him want to scream" (176–77). It is not ill-will that prompts her acts of solicitude, but an inattentiveness and false sense of mission. Jenkin, the unnoticed presence of good, knows better: "Jenkin did not come. He sent one letter in which he sent his love and said that, as Duncan knew, he would be *very* glad to see Duncan, if Duncan ever wished . . ." (177).

Rose is too long-suffering herself, however, for these occasional instances of smothering attention to alienate her readers completely. She carries around her own grief of being in unrequited love with Gerard, and this accounts for much of our lingering sympathy for her. Admittedly, in a Murdoch novel, unrequited love is not a distinguishing mark; here alone, there are seven futile declarations of love: Tamar to Duncan, Duncan to Jean, Jean to Crimond, Lily to Crimond, Crimond to Rose, Rose to Gerard, Gerard to Jenkin. But Rose's love for Gerard is a languishing, impossible one which she recognizes as such and accepts as her life's burden. Never is she more appealing to us as a character than in her flat response to Gerard's declaration of (brotherly) love for her:

"Rose, don't be so exasperating, you know I love you."
"I *don't* know, I know *nothing,* I live on the edge of *blackness* . . ."
". . . you're my closest friend. I love you. What more can I say?"
Rose released him. "Indeed. What more can you say." (568)

All of this would seem to add up to a perfectly decent character to lead the reader through the lives and times of the brotherhood. Murdoch upsets this picture with a single episode, an episode so disturbing because it is both believable and shocking. David Crimond, true to his self-absorbed nature, discards Jean after a time, and a shaky status quo of the Jean-Duncan marriage is reestablished. At this point, Crimond asks for an audience with Rose, which, when granted, he uses to declare his love for her. Rose's eloquent put-down of him is fitting; she is fierce and unforgiving as she has every cause to be. Then—the afterthought. "Oh I shall regret this so much, it will cause me so much pain later, that I behaved so stupidly, so badly. . . . Was it possible that somehow, within a period of minutes, she had *fallen in love* with Crimond?" (411–12). This the reader will not forgive, though Rose regains her composure. The rewrite we wish for is for her never to have thought those thoughts. As she did, we did, and we are once again thrown back on our own sentimental expectations.

Gerard, the last of the apparent pillars in *The Book and the Brotherhood,* is in many respects the most interesting, since there is more distance between our immediate and our considered view of him than there is for any of the other ordinary characters. Our first view of Jenkin is similarly off; he is the good man we cannot recognize, and we cannot recognize him because we are drawn to identify with Gerard. Only slowly does Gerard emerge as flawed, and this despite the fact that these flaws are perceived by the good character as well as his rival. Jenkin muses about his sudden urge to escape the comfortable world led by Gerard: "Gerard was like a perfect older brother, a protector and a guide, an exemplar, a completely reliable, completely loving, resource, he had been, and had uniquely been, for Jenkin, pure gold. Perhaps these were precisely the reasons why he wanted to get up and run?" (133). Crimond's attack fills out this picture: "You value yourselves because you're English. You live on books and conversation and mutual admiration and drink—you're all alcoholics—and sentimental ideas of virtue" (336). Murdoch's skills are extraordinary in bringing this particular "Englishness" to light in a way that comes only with reflection.

The most unmistakable Murdochian clue that Gerard is destined to dissatisfy us occurs in one of those episodes that we wish fervently to rewrite. The story begins as a memory Gerard has of himself as an eleven-year-old. He became the owner of a parrot when friends of his father had to move away suddenly. "Gerard loved the bird instantly, passionately. Its sudden presence in the house, its exalted winged bird presence, was a miracle to which he awakened with daily joy" (56–57). Gerard, "divining" the true name of the parrot, called him "Grey" in resistance to the ill-suited "Polly" that the women of the house preferred, and under Gerard's tutelage, the parrot was soon articulating the "interesting sentence, 'Grey is grey.'" If the parrot was not the source of joy to his sister or mother that it was to him, Gerard cherished him all the more for it: "The parrot was a world in which the child was graciously allowed to live, he was a vehicle which connected Gerard with the whole sentient creation, he was an avatar, an incarnation of love" (58). When the time came for Gerard to go to boarding school, he entrusted the bird to his father's care, sensing no doubt the ill-will toward the bird of his sister and mother. The ending was then assured: "At the longed-for half-term . . . he rushed joyfully into the house and into the study. Grey was not there" (59). Grey, and Grey's disappearance, have everything to do with Gerard's relations with every member of his family thereafter, particularly his father ("who knew how terribly, how unforgivably, he had failed his son"; 60), and Gerard regrets that at his father's deathbed, he had not told him that all was forgiven.

Murdoch has so poignantly described this childhood episode that we carry the wound with Gerard as an adult, and when he happens upon a parrot "very like Grey" that stares "intently at Gerard . . . purposively, as if to keep his attention and preserve their telepathic communion" (217), we know there is only one possible outcome. Gerard must take this bird home; the scene has to be replayed; its ending is now assured. This outcome Murdoch does not give us. "It was impossible" (218). The wound will not be allowed to heal, and we recognize that Gerard's character will not, after all, be one with whom we identify. Once again, Murdoch thwarts our inclination for easy identification with her characters; the entire entourage in *The Book and the Brotherhood* will be discarded as we prepare to think again. "[Murdoch's] prolific novelistic output is her way of not being complacent," Ramanathan comments, "of releasing a frozen and petrified 'Good,' and of remaining close to the 'truth.'"[38] This is to say that Murdoch spurns the solace of the bardic poet.

Only after we have discarded the ordinary characters do we realize that all along the center of the brotherhood has been in Jenkin Riderhood. His character haunts us as it haunts the characters in the novel, for we, too, are certain to neglect the good man before our eyes. Murdoch has sure Platonic instincts in her effort to embody the idea of the good; she brings to mind Socrates' description in the *Phaedrus* of how our souls strain and fail like a winged charioteer to see what we most want to see (248b). Our wings "all broken," we miss the sight we longed for: the truthful and loving exemplar of good. Jenkin for his part does not assert himself; he is the exquisitely rare Murdochian character who holds back from expressing his love for another (Rose). When called upon to act, however, his steps are sure and decisive, even when there is nothing positive to be achieved, as when Tamar arrives at his door, "in hell" and inconsolable: "In the few minutes she had been with him Jenkin had seen into the hell she spoke of, and although he spoke of helping her he did not see any way in which it would be possible. . . . 'Tamar, try to hold onto yourself, I'm going to help you, just *hold on*'" (365–66).

Despite his quiet presence, Jenkin possesses the magnetic quality that Murdoch associates elsewhere with the idea of the good. This is brought out most unmistakably in Gerard's bumbling declaration of love for Jenkin, a declaration that produces uncharitable laughter on the part of Jenkin. Most revealing is Gerard's afterthought: "He felt a separate and sharp pain simply at having had to leave Jenkin's presence. He tried . . . to drive away his sudden forebodings and hold onto Jenkin's laughter as onto something good" (364). We are reminded of another declaration of love that provokes laughter: Alcibiades' for Socrates in the *Symposium*. Alcibiades, like Gerard, is according to common opinion the dominant personality and natural leader, beholden to no one. But Alcibiades reveals that Socrates shames him: "And even now, I know in my heart that if I would open my ears, I wouldn't be able to resist, but would be affected the same way. He forces me to agree that though I have many faults I neglect my own needs."[39] Alcibiades famously describes Socrates as similar to the Sileni "that sit in the statue-maker's shops . . . which when pulled apart are found to have statues of gods inside" (215b). This is to say the goodness of the good character is not on the surface; the idea of good itself, in Adriaan Peperzak's formulation, is "an astonishing secret": "The idea is neither a thing above the phenomena nor simply given to our spontaneity. It is not a look, but rather an astonishing secret, which urges us to discover and admire its genuine but hidden presence."[40] And so with Jenkin Riderhood, the middle-aged schoolteacher who goes his own way and minds his own business. "Where he is, he *is*" (119).[41] As he contemplates a future in South America or India, "to be on the frontiers of human suffering," Jenkin muses about the heroes of our time: "The heroes of our time are dissidents, protesters, people alone in cells, anonymous helpers, unknown truth-tellers" (133). This truth-teller is unknown even to himself: "He knew he would not be one of these."

The promises of happy endings in Murdoch's novels are not only not delivered, they turn out not to have been promised. Her novels appear at first glance to be bardic, to encourage a passive, emotional response, as if we were watching a soap opera of unusual quality. "Television, the dictator's best friend, already erodes our ability to read," she comments,[42] and we realize on second thought that her novels are an extended lesson in relearning the skills of the thinking reader. She repudiates the nonknowledge of the bardic poem for the more difficult attainment of the philosophic poet, and in this it is clear that her paragon is Plato.

Neither Murdoch nor Plato allows their audiences an easy read, for they demand of them something higher. As authors, they do us the honor of keeping themselves anonymous, thereby inviting our active engagement with their creations. Of Murdochian anonymity, Conradi writes that "it is because she is generously unattached, even to her own dearest positions within the work, that the reader experiences so much freedom."[43] Of Platonic anonymity, Paul Plass writes that it is "the recognition that man lives for a truth that dwarfs him, and the means by which he approaches truth . . . must not detract from their end."[44] It is truth, not fantasy, that must do the dwarfing if freedom is to be kept in sight. Murdoch and Plato and other rare teachers share the interest in rejecting the consolations of the culture of μουσική, the culture that spawns images and treats the audience as an undifferentiated mass. The kind of poetic knowledge most worth having is essentially active.

I have used Plato to elaborate on the richness of Murdoch's world, but it is true also that my version of Murdoch gives us a fresh and compelling reading of Plato's world. Their aims are equally fundamental and pertinent to our time: to reclaim *the* political unit—the individual—from the consoling world of arts and entertainment, with the exhortation, do not lose sight of the good.

Notes

1. Marc Antony's sardonic aide-de-camp Enobarbus "is wholly Shakespeare's own, with nothing owed to Plutarch but the incident of the restored treasure and the (altered) name" (Harley Granville-Barker, *Prefaces to Shakespeare* [Princeton: Princeton University Press, 1946], 1:451 n. 44).

2. Iris Murdoch, *Metaphysics as a Guide to Morals* (New York: Viking Penguin, 1992); hereafter, *MGM*.

3. David Tracy, "The Many Faces of Platonism," in *Iris Murdoch and the Search for Human Goodness,* ed. Maria Antonaccio and William Schweiker (Chicago: University of Chicago Press, 1996), 67.

4. M. M. Bakhtin, *The Dialogic Imagination: Four Essays,* ed. Michael Holquist, trans. Caryl Emerson and Michael Holquist (Austin: University of Texas Press, 1983), 320. Ramanathan and others have drawn attention to the significant *marginal* presence of "figures of good" in Murdoch's novels: "Good can be sovereign only by being a 'powerless,' nonintervening source." This powerlessness does not diminish, but enhances, the "zone" to which Bakhtin refers. See Suguna Ramanathan, *Iris Murdoch: Figures of Good* (London: Macmillan Press, 1990), 226.

5. Tracy, "Many Faces of Platonism," 66.

6. Elizabeth Dipple, *The Unresolvable Plot: Reading Contemporary Fiction* (New York: Routledge, 1988), 85.

7. Harold Bloom, introduction to *Iris Murdoch,* ed. Harold Bloom (New York: Chelsea House Publishers, 1986), 1.

8. Richard Poirier, *The Performing Self,* with a foreword by Edward W. Said (New Brunswick, N.J.: Rutgers University Press, 1992), 32, 33.

9. Said, foreword to ibid., x.

10. Murdoch returns time and again to the magnetism of the good in her philosophic writings. See, e.g., *MGM,* 122, 461, 478, 479, 492, 496.

11. Iris Murdoch, *The Green Knight* (New York: Penguin Books, 1995), 198.

12. Ibid., 172.

13. Nor, for that matter, did the age of Plato have such underpinnings. Socrates' self-description as a gadfly occurs just before he is sentenced to death by his fellow Athenians. His success as a good man is a *literary* one; that is, it is possible only in death, as Nietzsche understood: "*The dying Socrates* became the new ideal" (Friedrich Nietzsche, "*The Birth of Tragedy*" and "*The Case of Wagner,*" trans. Walter Kaufmann [New York: Vintage Books, 1967], 89).

14. "One isn't good enough at creating character," Murdoch remarked in 1963 (Frank Kermode, "The House of Fiction," *Partisan Review* 30 [spring 1963]: 63). Then again in 1977: "The creation of character is a difficult thing. I'm not yet particularly good

at it" (Michael O. Bellamy, "An Interview with Iris Murdoch," *Contemporary Literature* 18, no. 2 [spring 1977]: 139). Gordon asks why she "continues to berate herself for a limitation largely imposed by historical circumstance"; I would push the point somewhat further and defend the distancing practice of the philosophic poet. Enobarbus, "a tragedy of loyalty to something other than the best one knows," probably cannot be re-created in our world. See David J. Gordon, *Iris Murdoch's Fables of Unselfing* (Columbia: University of Missouri Press, 1995), 77; and Granville-Barker, *Prefaces to Shakespeare,* 452.

15. Murdoch fans tend to cite Bloom indignantly (most recently, see Barbara Stevens Heusel in *Patterned Aimlessness: Iris Murdoch's Novels of the 1970s and 1980s* [Athens: University of Georgia Press, 1995], 268 n. 1), whereas I agree with his description but attribute philosophic interest to the phenomenon. The issue of performance will be treated separately.

16. Iris Murdoch, *The Fire and the Sun: Why Plato Banished the Artists* (Oxford: Oxford University Press, 1977), 85.

17. Elizabeth Dipple, *Iris Murdoch: Work for the Spirit* (Chicago: University of Chicago Press, 1982), 39.

18. Lorna Sage, "The Pursuit of Imperfection," *Critical Quarterly* 19 (1977): 68.

19. Gordon, *Murdoch's Fables,* 73.

20. Allan Bloom, *The Closing of the American Mind: How Higher Education Has Failed Democracy and Impoverished the Souls of Today's Students* (New York: Simon and Schuster, 1987), 81.

21. Elizabeth Asmis, "Plato on Poetic Creativity," in *The Cambridge Companion to Plato,* ed. Richard Kraut (Cambridge: Cambridge University Press, 1993), 339.

22. Dipple, *Iris Murdoch,* 99.

23. Plato, *The Republic,* trans. with notes and essay by Allan Bloom (New York: Basic Books, 1968).

24. Ramanathan, *Iris Murdoch,* 226.

25. Johann Wolfgang von Goethe, "Plato as Party to a Christian Revelation," in *Essays on Art and Literature,* ed. John Gearey, trans. Ellen von Nardroff and Ernest H. von Nardroff (Princeton: Princeton University Press, 1994), 201.

26. Ibid.

27. Plato, *Two Comic Dialogues: "Ion" and "Hippias Major,"* trans. Paul Woodruff (Indianapolis: Hackett Publishing Co., 1983). Woodruff acknowledges that he renders "certain words in unconventional ways" (17); I will restore the Greek word where appropriate.

28. G. R. F. Ferrari, "Plato and Poetry," in *The Cambridge History of Literary Criticism,* vol. 1, *Classical Criticism,* ed. George A. Kennedy (Cambridge: Cambridge University Press, 1989), 95.

29. Herodotus, *The History,* trans. David Grene (Chicago: University of Chicago Press, 1987), 2.53.

30. Allan Bloom, "Interpretive Essay," in Plato, *The Republic,* 428.

31. Rosamond Kent Sprague, *Plato's Philosopher-King: A Study of the Theoretical Background* (Columbia: University of South Carolina Press, 1976), 97.

32. Floyer Sydenham, *"Ion": A Dialogue of Plato concerning Poetry* (London: H. Woodfall, 1759), 48.

33. *MGM,* 90.

34. Dipple, *Iris Murdoch,* 46.

35. Wolfgang Iser, *The Implied Reader: Patterns of Communication in Prose Fiction from Bunyan to Beckett* (Baltimore: Johns Hopkins University Press, 1974), 290.

·

36. Peter J. Conradi, *Iris Murdoch: The Saint and the Artist* (London: Macmillan Press, 1986), 261.

37. Iris Murdoch, *The Book and the Brotherhood* (London: Chatto and Windus, 1987), 15.

38. Ramanathan, *Iris Murdoch,* 227.

39. Plato, *The Symposium,* in *Plato's Erotic Dialogues,* trans. William S. Cobb (Albany: State University of New York Press, 1993), 216a.

40. Adriaan T. Peperzak, "Heidegger and Plato's Idea of the Good," in *Reading Heidegger,* ed. John Sallis (Bloomington: Indiana University Press, 1993), 272.

41. "I think people who are good . . . make a sort of space around them, and you feel you are safe with them," said Murdoch in an interview. Quoted by Dipple, *Plot,* 204.

42. *MGM,* 210.

43. Conradi, *Iris Murdoch,* 264.

44. Paul Plass, "Philosophical Anonymity and Irony in the Platonic Dialogues," *American Journal of Philology* 85 (1964): 278.

Interlude

〜⋄〜

"The Photographer": An Essay by Soseki

TRANSLATED BY EDWIN MCCLELLAN

Prefatory Remarks by the Translator

This very short essay by Soseki (1867–1916) that I have translated for David Grene comes from a collection of essays Soseki published in 1915 under the title *From Behind the Sliding Glass Door.* The essays vary greatly in tone and subject matter—a maid's kindness when he was a lonely child, the death of a pet dog, the visit of an old college friend who had buried himself in an obscure provincial high school after graduating, a persistent autograph-seeker in a small provincial town who kept pestering Soseki by mail (Soseki lived in Tokyo), a suicidal female reader who visited him in his study behind the glass door and after having told him of her sad plight asked what he would have done with her if she had been a character in a novel he was writing—and predictably I find Soseki as he reveals himself in some more appealing than I find him in others. I have chosen this particular essay, which is probably the most modest one in the collection, because I have always been fond of it, though some readers may find it too insubstantial for their taste. I suppose I like it partly because he shows his vulnerable, superstitious side in his fear of photographs of himself (a fear which I too have not quite overcome); and partly because he is so helpless in his minor skirmish with one of the many encroaching vulgarities of his time: the photographic smile. But perhaps what I like most in the essay is the way Soseki draws the photographer, a modern ghost if ever there was one.

I think it was in 1956 that I first showed my translation of Soseki's novel *Kokoro* (1914) to David Grene and F. A. Hayek, who were my main mentors on the Committee on Social Thought. I did so with trepidation, for I had never done any serious translation before, Soseki was a Japanese writer unknown in this country, and I had no idea what someone like David or Friedrich Hayek would think of what was after all an early example of the modern Japanese novel (whatever that may mean)—a simply told tale about a friendship between a young college student and an older man, the older man's suicide to atone for his betrayal years before of his closest college friend, the passing of an era (the Meiji era, so much like the Victorian era in its longevity and in the way people felt left behind when the monarch died), and the testament he leaves for his young friend to read, that testament being in a way an attempt to make himself understood by someone he had tried to reach out to in life. At the time I showed my translation to my two teachers, modern Japanese novels were just becoming fashionable, but they were all smart, contemporary or near-contemporary novels, nothing so Victorian as Soseki's despairing work. I have never forgotten and shall never forget the generosity of feeling of those two men, the Irish classicist and the Austrian economist, when without any reserve they told me how moved they had been by the novel. The translation was published soon afterward by Henry Regnery and has remained in print ever since. David Grene, then, is inseparable in my mind from that novel, which I still love, and I cannot think of anything more appropriate to dedicate to David than a translation of something else by Soseki, albeit a very slight piece.

"The Photographer"

SOSEKI

Somebody wanted to speak to me on the telephone, I was told, so I got up and left my study to see who it was. It turned out to be someone from a magazine who wanted to come and take a picture of me. When would be a convenient time for me, he asked. I didn't think I wanted a picture of myself taken, I answered.

I had had no dealings with the magazine whatsoever. I did vaguely remember, however, that I had glanced through an issue or two of it in the past three or four years. It had left no lasting impression on me, except that its main interest seemed to be to print innumerable pictures of smiling people. And I did remember thinking at the time how unpleasant it was to see so many faces fixed in that same unnatural smile. So now I tried to be as discouraging to the man as I could.

But it was for the New Year issue, he said, and because it was the year of the hare, he wanted pictures of those people born in the year of the hare. I had to admit that I was indeed one of them. But not yet ready to relent I said:

"But for a picture in your magazine, I would be required to smile, wouldn't I?"

"Not at all," he promptly replied, in a tone suggesting, I thought, that I had all along misjudged his magazine.

"Well, if it's all right for me to have a picture taken with my normal expression, I suppose there's no harm in your coming."

So having agreed to be at home at a specified hour the day after next, I put down the receiver.

He duly appeared at my study door at the promised time, wearing a neat European-style suit and carrying his photographic equipment. For a while we talked about the magazine he was working for, then he took two pictures of me: one was of me sitting in my usual fashion at my desk, and the other was of me standing in my customary stance in the cold, frost-covered garden. Because there wasn't much daylight coming into the study he had to bring out his magnesium flashpan after he had set up the camera. Just before firing it he poked half of his face out from behind the camera and said, "I know I said you didn't have to, but could you, sir, perhaps smile just a little?" For an instant I thought him almost funny. Then immediately I found myself thinking, "What an idiot." And I said dismissively, "You'll have to take me as I am." When next he stood me in front of a clump of trees in the garden and aiming his camera at me said again with half his face showing and the same elaborate deference, "I know I promised, sir, but perhaps . . . ," I felt even less inclined than before to offer him a smile.

About four days later the pictures arrived by mail. They were exactly as he had wanted them: I was shown smiling. Nonplussed I stared at them for a while; surely, I kept thinking, the smile had to have been put there by hand?

Seeking reassurance I showed the pictures to four or five friends who happened to drop in. They were all of the opinion that the smile was not of my own making but another's.

In the course of my life I have on numerous occasions smiled in front of other people when I really had no wish to. Perhaps the photographer had come as an agent of revenge for all those acts of deception I had committed.

The photographer, then, did indeed send me, as he had promised, those pictures of myself smiling that eery, forced smile; but he never did send me a copy of the issue of the magazine in which he said they would appear.

Part Two

"I Know Thee Not, Old Man": The Renunciation of Falstaff

AMIRTHANAYAGAM P. DAVID

The actor in history is David Grene's text; his text and method are the histrionic moment. The extraordinary power of his teaching surely stems from acting. Like great acting, it has to be witnessed to be felt; and while the sense of its greatness, of what it did to you, remains, its living magnetism fades, and one slips back unaccountably and traitorously into the stone and iron of conceptual formulation: the riveting grip of its corrective lesson loosened in time by the infuriating half-grasp of memory. David is no actor. He is a formidable classical scholar, a great translator, a decent farmer. He is a horseman. The stock of his memoirs, from Wicklow to Trinity, from farming in Illinois to Belturbet, County Cavan, from Vienna in the thirties to Hutchins's Chicago to the Committee on Social Thought, is a thing of wonder in itself. Yet David is able to dramatize these realities in the classroom so that somehow they form an entry point for the dramatization of literature, philosophy, history—the distinction becomes moot—and one begins to feel the presence of an author as a protagonist, mortal, historical, and ever present. Even the philology seems to come alive and starts to count in a new way. One becomes self-conscious, about one's accent as much as one's ideas; one feels intimidated, and yet challenged to speak. It is a rare critical formulation that can survive this experience. But they do come nagging in the aftermath.

When essaying a work, David tells us to look back when we're done with it and pursue the meaning of the moments which stick out in the memory. In the case of *Henry IV,* the scene of the renunciation of Falstaff rather eclipses all its antecedents—even as it is their fulfillment. This was my first public lecture, for the University of Chicago's Basic Program. When I prepared the piece, I had not read David's *The Actor in History;* yet the lecture reads at times like a footnote or appendix to that book. David cannot be saddled with the content. But he must own that I have been listening; he must acknowledge the issue; and I hope it shall "study deserving."

When one anatomizes the division of one's feelings in the course of the extraordinary last scene of *2 Henry IV,* the rejection of Falstaff, to try to understand the meaning and scope of the rejection, one is desperate for parallels. A long expected judgement comes to fruition; but its dramatic presence catches us by surprise, moves us in an uncomfortable and unexpected way; and characters we have grown used to suddenly take on dimensions that approach the tragic.

From the beginning of *2 Henry IV,* Falstaff is on the way out. His great body has become a decaying hulk. When he enters the play asking about the results of his urine test, his physicality becomes something a little less engaging than it had been. He has surfeited, and is on the wane; the actor's body, a globe of sinful continents, becomes the most obvious physical expression of the images of national disease and corruption that are thematic in the play. We are used to his changing colors and humors, to the marvelous inventiveness with which he works his way through a scene. But at the end of act 1, scene 2, he stretches our indulgence:

A pox of this gout or a gout of this pox, for the one or the other plays the rogue with my great toe. 'Tis no matter if I do halt: I have wars for my colour, and my pension shall seem the more reasonable. A good wit will make use of anything: I will turn diseases to commodity. (Lines 246–51)

Falstaff now has a distinctive stage walk, as valiant Hotspur did, but war for him is just a profitable color. The limp is a parting gift from the gout or a venereal disease; it will seem a sympathetic war wound in the gait of a con man making the rounds. Most disconcerting is this opportunism of Falstaff's. His first lines in part 1 are "Now, Hal, what time of day is it, lad?" And the prince's response:

Thou art so fat-witted with drinking of old sack, and unbuttoning thee after supper, and sleeping upon benches after noon, that thou hast forgotten to demand that truly which thou wouldst truly know. What a devil hast thou to do with the time of the day? Unless hours were cups of sack, and minutes capons, and clocks the tongues of bawds, and dials the signs of leaping houses, and the blessed sun himself a fair hot wench in flame-coloured taffeta, I see no reason why thou shouldst be so superfluous to demand the time of the day. (Act 1, sc. 2, lines 1–12)

"Indeed, you come near me now, Hal. . . ." says Falstaff. This fat man was one who shared none of our timely anxieties, a great Bacchus in whose presence our own pressing time was thankfully suspended. He stole time under the moon. But in part 2, the unsettled times have become his color and his daylight advantage. More than once he is saved from prosecution by the circumstances of the wars. Says the Lord Chief Justice:

. . . your day's service at Shrewsbury hath a little gilded over your night's exploit on Gad's Hill. You may thank th' unquiet time for your quiet o'er-posting that action. (Act 1, sc. 2, lines 150–53)

And he is saved from his debts by the new call to arms. "You speak as having the power to do wrong," says the judge. Who can deny a twinge of disavowal when Falstaff later takes bribes from his conscripts and abuses the good services of Justice Shallow? Consider his justifications:

If the young dace be a bait for the old pike, I see no reason in the law of nature but I may snap at him. Let time shape, and there an end. (Act 3, sc. 2, lines 335–37)

This sort of thing belongs in the world of Edmund and Iago; it is a sour humor in our Falstaff.

The jokes between Hal and Falstaff have also started to turn a little sour—on both sides, funnily enough. In act 2, scene 1, Mistress Quickly reminds Falstaff of a time when "the Prince broke thy head for liking his father to a singing-man of Windsor"; she goes on, and this is more to her point, "thou didst swear to me then, as I was washing thy wound, to marry me, and make me my lady thy wife." Apparently, the subject of marriage came up as the good Hostess was helping Sir John recuperate from his head wound. And at the beginning of act 2, scene 4 (lines 1–9), we overhear two drawers tell of another incident:

FRANCIS: What the devil has thou brought there? Applejohns? Thou knowest Sir John cannot endure an applejohn.
SECOND DRAWER: Mass, thou sayst true. The Prince once set a dish of applejohns before him, and told him there were five more Sir Johns, and, putting off his hat, said, "I will now take my leave of these six dry, round, old, withered knights." It angered him to the heart. But he hath forgot that.

Falstaff angered to the heart? A line of good humor has clearly been crossed.

The final act is Falstaff's all too timely attempt to capitalize on the death of Henry IV and the accession of Hal. In this exploit there is all haste—no time even to change clothes. And here is something truly novel: Falstaff interrupts his gormandizing and leaves in the middle of a feast at Justice Shallow's happy table. What time of day is it? At two o'clock sharp—Shakespeare marks the hour—there they are in London, Falstaff and his friends, ready to greet the new-crowned king's procession.

We have already begun to judge him. Falstaff is simply not the man we thought we knew. Besides that, one has long since known, in the back of one's mind somewhere, that Hal was planning to deny him. And yet, when the moment arrives, and the new king's verses cut across the theater, we shudder. "My King! My Jove! I speak to thee my heart," says Old Jack. "I know thee not, old man. Fall to thy prayers." Does Falstaff kneel? An audience must be affected, if it has a heart that can be spoken to. The scene's action is no surprise, yet its pathos surely is. We had no idea how it would feel, yet we did not expect to be so disarmed. It is an astonishing moment in drama. "I know thee not" resounds somewhere in our hollowest parts, and finds no bottom. How does this happen? What has really been rejected here, and by whom?

I do not myself find an allusion to the Gospel in this denial of Hal's. The strewing of rushes does presage, perhaps, an entry into Jerusalem; but to call Hal Peter and Falstaff Christ is to go too far. What *is* going on here is the dénouement of a morality play. The clues to this interpretation are often pointed out by editors. From the figure of Rumour, painted full of tongues, who opens part 2, to the names of policemen and country conscripts and justices (e.g., Shallow, Silence, Mouldy, Shadow, Wart, Fang, Snare), we are apparently dressed in the habits of the old morality plays. Falstaff is himself called "Reverend Vice" by Hal in part 1 (act 2, sc. 4, line 458). The theme is stock: a prodigal son turns out well, resisting the wiles of an aged tempter. The crucial figure of the Lord Chief Justice, Hal's final choice in a succession of fathers (act 5, sc. 2, line 118), is wholly explained on these terms. It is he who is interposed between the new king and Falstaff, he whom Falstaff tries to talk past in the procession, and he whom Henry V finally upholds. The sick realm is revived and Justice restored to her rightful seat, as the boy, whose heart, it turns out, is gold as his crown, sloughs off the tutor and feeder of his riots.

The genuineness of the character of the Lord Chief Justice argues in favor of this reading. Unlike practically everyone else in the play, his is no humor or color, conceit or something-seeming. He is an honest man doing an honest job. Hal cannot both uphold this character, and the virtue he stands for, and still find Falstaff funny. Recall that Falstaff's choice new jokes, with which he hopes to keep Hal laughing through all the periods of the judicial year (act 5, sc. 1, lines 66–80), are concerned precisely with the workings of justice, whose true operations he has seen through, in the model of Justice Shallow:

It is a wonderful thing to see the semblable coherence of his men's spirits and his: they by observing of him do bear themselves like foolish justices; he by convers- ing with them is turned into a justice-like servingman. Their spirits are so married in conjunction, with the participation of society, that they flock together in con- sent like so many wild geese. If I had a suit to Master Shallow, I would humour his men with the imputation of being near their master; if to his men, I would curry with Master Shallow, that no man could better command his servants. It is certain that either wise bearing or ignorant carriage is caught, as men take dis- eases, one of another.

He then adds, in words that redound upon himself:

Therefore let men take heed of their company.

This, however, is a decisive instance where the parody scenes, which are the comical mirror of the historical action in these plays, must not be allowed to reflect on their serious counterparts. Falstaff's wit at the expense of Justice Shallow must not be allowed to show up the office of the Lord Chief Justice. This means that Hal must become immune to the joker's jokes. Falstaff boasts of his comic technique and its success with Hal:

O, it is much that a lie with a slight oath and a jest with a sad brow will do with a fellow that never had the ache in his shoulders! O, you shall see him laugh till his face be like a wet cloak ill laid up. (Act 5, sc. 1, lines 84–88)

Yet when they next meet, it is Falstaff's face, his comic instrument, that is finally seen through. This, I think, is the sense of Hal's line in the rejection speech:

How ill white hairs becomes a fool and jester! (Act 5, sc. 5, line 48)

The parody of justice is shown up as soon as the parodist; his comic pow- ers are cut short, before they can work their charms, and his company is forsworn.

Reply not to me with a fool-born jest,
Presume not that I am the thing I was,
For God doth know—so shall the world perceive—
That I have turned away my former self;
So will I those that kept me company. (Act 5, sc. 5, lines 55–59)

Clearly, however, the morality play is subverted. Falstaff is something far more subtle and complex in feeling than Vice personified, or even the Jester, else his renunciation could never have achieved its jarring effect. We must look to the source and nature of this theatrical phenomenon, this rotund hill of flesh, that he can weigh so far against our better judgment.

This is, after all, a very strange world in which to stage a morality play. The lesson of Gaultree is hardly one that upholds justice or honorable dealing. Political efficacy seems to define the only successful virtue. So why does such a political realist as Shakespeare come to cast his history in the brazenly naive form of a morality play? What is the germ of this experiment?

At the end of *Richard II,* after a play in which history has taken shape dramatically as tragedy, we come to the remarkable soliloquy in prison, where Richard's meditations on his condition merge into Shakespeare's meditations on the dramatization of history:

I have been studying how I may compare
This prison where I live unto the world;
And, for because the world is populous,
And here is not a creature but myself,
I cannot do it. Yet I'll hammer it out.
My brain I'll prove the female to my soul,
My soul the father, and these two beget
A generation of still-breeding thoughts;
And these same thoughts people this little world,
In humors like the people of this world,
For no thought is contented. The better sort,
As thoughts of things divine, are intermixed
With scruples and do set the word itself
Against the word, as thus, "Come, little ones,"
And then again,
"It is as hard to come as for a camel
To thread the postern of a small needle's eye."
Thoughts tending to ambition, they do plot

Unlikely wonders—how these vain weak nails
May tear a passage through the flinty ribs
Of this hard world, my ragged prison walls,
And, for they cannot, die in their own pride.
Thoughts tending to content flatter themselves
That they are not the first of fortune's slaves,
Nor shall not be the last—like seely beggars
Who, sitting in the stocks, refuge their shame
That many have and others must sit there;
And in this thought they find a kind of ease,
Bearing their own misfortunes on the back
Of such as have before endured the like.
Thus play I in one person many people,
And none contented. (Act 5, sc. 5, lines 1–32)

The notion of personified thought that is sketched here belongs peculiarly to the essential mimetic structure of the morality play. Yet in Shakespeare's construction it is already gone a step beyond, for his thoughts, his proto-characters, are never static emblems of vice and virtue but are instead inherently at variance with themselves. Perhaps Shakespeare recognized in this notion of a morality play with three-dimensional characters the germ of a new and more flexible and perhaps truer way of giving dramatic form to history than in the tragedy he had just written. I am therefore tempted to suggest that both the morality structure of the later plays and its subversion can be traced to these meditations of Richard's.

Shakespeare's interest in the morality play is not such as to draw a moral out of history. The very Gospels cannot yield this man an unambiguous directive—even Richard's "better sort" of thoughts "do set the word itself / Against the word." Shakespeare is rather drawn to the morality play's mimetic structure, the notion or "technique" of personified thoughts. This mimetic structure is the means by which Richard, Shakespeare's actor, may compare the stage where he lives, transformed into a prison, with the world of historical reality from which he is now permanently exiled.

Such a comparison has two connotations for the Henry plays; one we might call "historical," the other "histrionic." In the first case, Richard's meditation on history produces a philosophy of considerable subtlety. It is a philosophical view of history because it sees the processes of history as rooted in the processes of thought, or the relation of thoughts. But the relations between thoughts are not here deductive or logical; they are, rather, dramatic. Shakespeare's thoughts are in conflict, with each other

216 AMIRTHANAYAGAM P. DAVID

and within themselves. They are also fertile, in Richard's conception, the offspring of his brain and soul, and still breeding as they make their way in the world. The trick of the shrewd observer of history—a trick learned too late for Richard, and perhaps in general—is to tell the historical wind-eggs from the viable thoughts. Skill in this art would be prophetic. But beyond such a midwife's prognostication, as to which thoughts may give birth to the future, Shakespeare's sense of the theatricality of human reason will not allow for anything so sterile as a science of history and fate. In tracing the forms of action and character to their originals in thought, Shakespeare is no reductionist. It is not ideology, for example, that moves history. Shakespeare conceives of thought—scrupulous, ambitious, or content—as at variance with itself. This inner conflict of thoughts is all one with their fertility. Only such an irreducibly dramatic conception of thought can accord with the sorts of characters we have, and the sort of history we make.

The historical connotation of Richard's speech gets played out in the purely deliberative scenes of *2 Henry IV,* scenes which are almost antidramatic in nature, whose protagonists usually have counties and titles for names. In act 3, scene 1, after King Henry soliloquizes on sleep, he exclaims to his courtiers, "O God that one might read the book of fate"; he is at a loss to understand how fortune could have turned the English scene and its alliances upside down in a scant ten years, and how King Richard was able to prophesy these workings of necessity (that Necessity which "so bowed the state / That I and greatness were compelled to kiss") despite the fact that Henry's avowed thought ("I had no such intent") was opposite. Warwick responds to this conundrum in Richard's vein:

There is a history in all men's lives,
Figuring the nature of the times deceased,
The which observed, a man may prophesy,
With a near aim, of the main chance of things
As yet not come to life, who in their seeds
And weak beginnings lie intreasured.
Such things become the hatch and brood of time,
And by the necessary form of this
King Richard might create a perfect guess
That great Northumberland, then false to him,
Would of that seed grow to a greater falseness,
Which should not find a ground to root upon
Unless on you. (Lines 80–92)

Here is history read as the key to a kind of reproductive process, whose "necessary form" can allow for prophetic insight into the future's "hatch and brood" and is, perhaps, the very form of Necessity herself. This genetic theory of historical necessity need make no apologies as philosophy, when compared, say, with the triadic fantasies of a Hegel. Yet there is no pedantry in Shakespeare; he shares with the Greek dramatists, and perhaps with the philosopher Plato as well, a sense of the dramatic life of thought. It is a king who cannot come to terms with fate, it is a king who listens to Warwick's teaching, and it is a king's doubtful question that finally lends the theory a certain sublimity:

> Are these things then necessities?
> Then let us meet them like necessities;
> And that same word even now cries out on us. (Lines 92–94)

Despite the determinacy of these generative processes, it would seem that they still do not produce necessities, until they are *treated* as necessities, in the mind of a trapped protagonist. For Necessity is perhaps first of all a word and a thought; only as such may she enter into deliberation and action, and so become something real.

The scene at Gaultree (act 4) is also purely deliberative. Shakespeare appears to delight in playing one reading of history against another, or one prognostication against another, on the part of the rebels and the loyal Westmorland, among the rebels themselves, or between them and Prince John. The atmosphere could hardly be called suspenseful. It is almost dialectical. The debate between Mowbray and Westmorland, as to what would have happened if Mowbray's father could have actually fought the duel that King Richard put a stop to, is a debate—with due allowance for Mowbray's chivalric flourishes—between rival history professors ("You speak, Lord Mowbray, now you know not what," says Westmorland, in fine academic style). These stage rivals are also rival historical figures who are also rival historians. Shakespeare is evidently interested in the relation between thought and action, or in this case thoughts on history and history, entirely for its own sake, even at the expense of dramatic movement. The germ of this interest lies in Richard's prison speech. Echoes of its genetic metaphor recur in Hastings's lines to John:

> And though we here fall down,
> We have supplies to second our attempt;
> If they miscarry, theirs shall second them,

And so success of mischief shall be born
And heir from heir shall hold this quarrel up
Whiles England shall have generation. (Act 4, sc. 2, lines 44–49)

John's response, however, intimates a new point of departure:

You are too shallow, Hastings, much too shallow,
To sound the bottom of the aftertimes. (Lines 50–51)

This is the contempt of a man who has seen through the historians and the prophets and has learned to stage history from behind the scenes. The treachery at Gaultree is his first play. Richard also learns to stage his history, but he must stage it as a tragedy, with himself as the tragic hero. John is more like God *ex machina*.

I spoke also of a histrionic connotation in Richard's prison soliloquy. Richard's notion of generative thoughts is both a theory of history *and* a theory of drama. To reduce drama to a skeleton of personified thoughts might seem too gross an intellectualism, especially as a response to Shakespeare, but I believe what Shakespeare found in the mimetic structure of the morality play is an idea so familiar as to be innocuous to modern theatergoers and actors, if it is couched in slightly different terms. If Richard's "thoughts" are called "premises," for example, we have the notion that characters and situations begin as thoughts in the sense of dramatic premises, which take flesh and become fully realized on the stage. (The realization is not like a deduction; it can discover a pathos unforeseen in the premises, as I have suggested.) The difference between the historical and histrionic implications of Richard's theme stems from the difference between historical and dramatic premises. A successful history play would perhaps be one that harmonized these two kinds of thought and ways of thinking in such a way as to tell the truth about history as well as to realize a dramatic catharsis. Neither comic nor tragic premises will do for this history of the wastrel prince. But perhaps in the pattern of the morality play, there are promising possibilities for the story and its staging. The unique power of the scene of the renunciation of Falstaff is somehow a creature of these kinds of ultimate premises.

On the level of the individual characters and actors, Shakespeare's staging is also best conceived as the realization of his thoughts or premises, precisely in the terms of Richard's prison fantasy. Consider an example like that of Hotspur. Here is a fiery and delectable thought indeed, a thought tending to ambition, perhaps to plot unlikely wonders. As he is fleshed out onstage, he inspires the dramatist to concrete speech, and he grows in the telling, so that speeches and thoughts give birth to each other, until the character achieves a distinct imaginative life of its own. And within the imaginative world of the Henry plays, Hotspur can grow larger even than his stage presence, as he lives on in part 2 in the memory of his wife:

> He was indeed the glass
> Wherein the noble youth did dress themselves.
> He had no legs that practised not his gait;
> And speaking thick, which Nature made his blemish,
> Became the accents of the valiant,
> For those that could speak low and tardily
> Would turn their own perfection to abuse
> To seem like him. So that in speech, in gait,
> In diet, in affections of delight,
> In military rules, humours of blood,
> He was the mark and glass, copy and book,
> That fashioned others. (Act 2, sc. 3, lines 21–32)

Even after death, a character can be an inspiration, a still breeding thought.

Shakespeare's mature command of the physical machinery of the stage is also a grand ally in the realization of his fancy. Consider the development in his use of props, for example. Where the mirror in Richard's abdication scene is effectively used, if perhaps a bit heavy-handedly, the unbounded ingenuity of Shakespeare's devices in the Henry plays is totally unforced. I think for example of Northumberland's crutch and nightcap, the pathetic accoutrements of his feigned illness. He must cut a very sad figure as he appears onstage in the first scene of *2 Henry IV*, this policy'd old man who always seems to let his side down. But as he rises to the pitch of the news of his son's death, the crutch and cap are flung away, and on his own two feet, he finds a voice of genuine power:

> Hence therefore thou nice crutch!
> A scaly gauntlet now with joints of steel
> Must glove this hand. And hence thou sickly coif,
> Thou art a guard too wanton for the head
> Which princes fleshed with conquest aim to hit.
> Now bind my brows with iron, and approach
> The ragged'st hour that Time and Spite dare bring
> To frown upon th' enraged Northumberland!
> Let heaven kiss earth! Now let not Nature's hand
> Keep the wild flood confined, let Order die

And let this world no longer be a stage
To feed contention in a lingering act;
But let one spirit of the first-born Cain
Reign in all bosoms, that each heart being set
On bloody courses, the rude scene may end,
And darkness be the burier of the dead. (Act 1, sc. 1, lines 145–60)

It is as though in discarding his props the actor removes his mimetic mask and thereby opens a window to expression that is larger than his premises, one that is conscious of history taking shape as drama—albeit in a rude scene and a lingering act, fed only by the thoughts of Cain.

Other effective examples abound, such as Falstaff's sheathed bottle of sack at Shrewsbury in part 1 or Rumour's anatomized costume or Doll Tearsheet's hidden pillow in the scene of her arrest (act 5, sc. 4). The crown of all these props is the crown itself, which, lifeless piece of stage fakery that it is, becomes larger than life, more golden than gold, through the generative investiture of Hal's and his father's thought. The ultimate "prop," however, must be the actor's own body, and no one is blessed with more resources in this area than Falstaff himself. (One might consider not just the use of his own body but his imaginative use of Hotspur's corpse at the end of *1 Henry IV*.)

Now it might seem that I stretch the case too far in applying Richard's speech to the case of Falstaff. How could one profitably treat so vivid a dramatic presence as though he were a mere thought? The comic parts of the history plays are surely a very theatrical kind of theater and not some kind of extended meditation. Yet consider Falstaff's first lines in part 2, where he tells us exactly what kind of thought and begetter of thoughts he is, inside his author's head:

Men of all sorts take a pride to gird at me: the brain of this foolish compounded clay-man is not able to invent anything that intends to laughter more than I invent, or is invented on me; I am not only witty in myself, but the cause that wit is in other men. (Act 1, sc. 2, lines 6–10)

Are not the history plays completely both, drama and thought, an exploration of the generative relation between imagination and action, as it plays out in history?

As Falstaff is fleshed out, we come to know him uniquely and individually. This is why the morality play is subverted. It is easy enough to condemn a vice, or a vice in someone—even here, God help the wicked—but to deny a man whom we know, that is too much. It is vicious in itself. Falstaff and Doll are as true a couple as Shakespeare ever drew, alongside Hotspur and Lady Percy. When he says, "Peace, good Doll, do not speak like a death's-head, do not bid me remember mine end"—we know him. When he hears, at the very end, of Doll's incarceration, and he says, "I will deliver her"—we know him. And when he tries to explain, this man of colors, his Hal's rejection of him as "but a colour," and Shallow replies, "A colour that I fear you will die in, Sir John"—we know him feelingly. It is intolerable that Hal should say, "I know thee not."

But Falstaff, like Hotspur, grows into something more expansive than our ken. His speech on sherry is of a different order altogether. Here playwright, actor, and character aspire together to a higher level of mimetic representation, where the thought fleshed out in the body of the actor becomes thought and imagination's stuff once more and achieves an allegorical, even an anagogical significance. The only thing like it in the other plays is, again, Richard's speech in prison. "I wasted time, and now doth time waste me," Richard says, in the fullness of his condition. Time has made of him a "numbering clock," fleshed out thus:

My thoughts are minutes, and with sighs they jar
Their watches on unto mine eyes, the outward watch,
Whereto my finger, like a dial's point,
Is pointing still, in cleansing them from tears.
Now sir, the sound that tells what hour it is
Are clamorous groans which strike upon my heart,
Which is the bell. So sighs and tears and groans
Show minutes, times, and hours. But my time
Runs posting on in Bolingbroke's proud joy,
While I stand fooling here, his jack of the clock. (Act 5, sc. 5, lines 51–60)

It is a strange conceit, a man turning into a clock; but presumably quite effective when rendered on the stage.

Again, what may be a bit unwieldy in Richard's embodiment becomes fluid and natural in Falstaff.

A good sherris-sack hath a twofold operation in it: it ascends me into the brain, dries me there all the foolish and dull and crudy vapours which environ it, makes it apprehensive, quick, forgetive, full of nimble, fiery and delectable shapes, which delivered o'er to the voice, the tongue, which is the birth, becomes excellent wit. (Act 4, sc. 3, lines 96–102)

Note again, behind the fertility of sound and style, the dramatist's concern with the production of thought, conceived as a kind of pregnancy brought to birth. (In Richard, it was "My brain I'll prove the female to my soul, / My soul the father . . .") Shakespeare discovers in this thought called Falstaff, witty in himself and the cause of wit in other men—including in the author himself—the generation of wit from the actor's tongue, at the very moment he delivers this excellent wit onstage. It is a supreme moment of histrionic fulfillment. Falstaff *was* Shakespeare—Shakespeare after a good sherris-sack. At the very least, a drink or two helped rouse this spirit Falstaff out of our author's teeming mind.

The second property of your excellent sherris is the warming of the blood, which before, cold and settled, left the liver white and pale, which is the badge of pusillanimity and cowardice; but the sherris warms it and makes it course from the inwards to the parts' extremes: it illuminateth the face which, as a beacon, gives warning to all the rest of this little kingdom—man—to arm; and then the vital commoners and inland petty spirits muster me all to their captain, the heart, who great and puffed up with this retinue, doth any deed of courage: and this valour comes of sherris. (Lines 103–114)

Falstaff, through his body, his gesture, his tongue, becomes an army, a Leviathan, a commonwealth, a blessed plot, a little cosmos. Now at last we get some sense of the scope of the renunciation: "banish plump Jack, and banish all the world."

A sense of the magnitude of this loss can lead to two critical maneuvers, neither of them profitable. The first is to take Hal's side—or rather, the side of the morality Justice—and say that Falstaff had it coming to him. It might be added that what was good about Falstaff has been incorporated in the new king. This is simply to deny the theatrical reality. "Presume not that I am the thing I was," says Hal. The rejection is a schism; however inevitable and foreshadowed, it is nevertheless a shocker, which will shiver Falstaff's heart. The second way is to minimize the climactic significance of the denial: the plot is just a scaffolding in any case; we have come to the theater to be entertained by its resident genie, who in his inimitable way has got through scrapes before and will probably come back jollier and funnier than ever. (His return is advertised before we leave the theater.) But this is seriously to misunderstand the organic movement of the play. "I know thee not, old man" is not just one line, a carrot, to be mixed in with the other ingredients of some dramatic stew. To be sure, the spirit of Falstaff has animated the whole sequence of events, and his are the tastiest parts; yet the rejection is decisive—it is a resolution. The line has as crucial and fixed a place in time and space as a cadence in music. "I know thee not" is a resolving chord that resonates backward through the plays and jogs some lovely moments loose: "Come thou must not be in this humour with me, dost not know me?" says old Jack to his Hostess (act 2, sc. 1); or this memorable exchange from part 1:

FALSTAFF: I would Your Grace would take me with you. Whom means Your Grace?
PRINCE: That villainous abominable misleader of youth, Falstaff, that old white-bearded Satan.
FALSTAFF: My lord, the man I know.
PRINCE: I know thou dost. (Act 2, sc. 4, lines 465–70)

"I would Your Grace would take me with you" seems almost to have a theological connotation. It is the intimacy of their knowledge of each other in this role-playing which makes the lines of banishment so disturbing—an intimacy which makes damnation as fierce as it would render forgiveness gracious.

FALSTAFF: But to say I know more harm in him than in myself were to say more than I know. That he is old, the more the pity, his white hairs do witness it; but that he is, saving your reverence, a whoremaster, that I utterly deny. If sack and sugar be a fault, God help the wicked! If to be old and merry be a sin, then many an old host that I know is damned. If to be fat be to be hated, then Pharaoh's lean kine are to be loved. No, my good lord, banish Peto, banish Bardolph, banish Poins; but for sweet Jack Falstaff, kind Jack Falstaff, true Jack Falstaff, valiant Jack Falstaff, and therefore more valiant being as he is old Jack Falstaff, banish not him thy Harry's company, banish not him thy Harry's company—banish plump Jack, and banish all the world. (Lines 471–85)

Says Hal: "I do, I will." Is this a betrothal? To a divorce? The consummation is come. And finally, what of Hal's first soliloquy: "I know you all and will awhile uphold / The unyok'd humour of your idleness." Is not the journey from "I know you all" to "I know thee not" Hal's journey in these plays?

Criticism cannot fathom this conflict. Falstaff is the redeeming spirit of this drama; for all that, this drama is his renunciation.

Who is this upstart Hal, this imp of fame, who casts out our demigod of the stage? What sort of thought is he? Not a very savory one, to my mind. Volumes can be written about the decline of Falstaff in part 2, but has anyone looked at Hal lately? He enters the play in act 2 a world-weary cynical snob. Can anyone sympathize with these lines he addresses to Poins:

But indeed these humble considerations make me out of love with my greatness. What a disgrace is it to me to remember thy name—or to know thy face tomorrow—or to take note how many pairs of silk stockings thou hast with these, and those that were the peach-coloured ones—or to bear the inventory of thy shirts, as: one for superfluity, and another for use. (Act 2, sc. 2, lines 11–18)

The lines seem intended to bait the audience. It was supposed to be something that won our trust in Hal, this fellow who never had the ache in his shoulders, that led him to mingle with the common folk. If our company has now grown tiresome to him, by all means, let him find new friends—but to take it out on *us,* to insult *us* who must count our shirts—that is less than winning.

Hal confesses in this scene that he has developed a taste for "small beer." The significance of this admission only comes home in Falstaff's sherris-sack speech. He there points up the emasculating effect of thin drink, as he parts company with Hal's sober brother John—the conniving victor at Gaultree, a man, Falstaff complains, he cannot make laugh. Once he has praised strong sack, he singles out the Hal that he thinks he knows, to distinguish him from his brother:

Hereof comes it that Prince Harry is valiant, for the cold blood he did naturally inherit of his father he hath, like lean, sterile and bare land, manured, husbanded and tilled, with excellent endeavour of drinking good and good store of fertile sherris, that he is become very hot and valiant. If I had a thousand sons, the first human principle I would teach them should be to forswear thin potations, and to addict themselves to sack. (Act 4, sc. 3, lines 117–25)

Those who persuade themselves that Henry V has incorporated the lessons he learnt under the tutelage of fertile sherris and plump Jack must reckon with the almost unnatural transformations in his capacities and humor. Hal is on the way to becoming something new—"Presume not that I am the thing I was"—and education by sherris-sack must be purged to admit the taste of small beer. Hal's future is plain to see in sober John, the model of political efficacy in the new order of the world. By play's end, Falstaff cannot make Hal laugh either.

One aspect of Hal in act 2, scene 2, at first seems promising: we are led to understand that he cannot show grief in public for his father's illness, because the world would call him hypocrite. We are moved for a second by the fact that this comparative cipher, in dramatic terms, may feel some genuine anguish at the thought that he cannot express his sadness. But the fact is, Hal *is* a hypocrite. Nowhere is this made more clear than in the famous crown scene. When an actor speaks in soliloquy, we can expect to hear his honest thoughts. When Hal first takes his father's crown, he calls it his due. But when he comes back to explain himself, he tells his father, tearfully, that he had spoken to the crown as an enemy and a murderer. This is after the king's sermon on the decline of England—"When that my care could not withhold thy riots, What wilt thou do when riot is thy care?"—time enough for Hal to prepare his own text. Where else did he learn to extemporize like this but from Falstaff? Yet there is a crucial difference between the two: while Falstaff counterfeits with a wink in our direction, Hal would fool us if he could. Certainly the king is won over.

Finally what wisdom is there in Hal's cruel rebukes? For instance,

Leave gormandising, know the grave doth gape
For thee thrice wider than for other men. (Act 5, sc. 5, lines 53–54)

I understood the conceit when Hal eulogized Hotspur: how could so small a grave contain so great a spirit? King Harry can hardly now be saying, how great a grave for so tiny a sprite. We know Falstaff better than that, and we know ourselves better than that. What does it matter the size? The grave gapes for all of us, and none gets half a grave.

So the tables are turned. The morality play is squarely at variance with itself. The prodigal son is a thorough hypocrite; and the aged tempter Vice is a teacher and a great spirit. There is another dimension to this inversion. The significance and novelty of Machiavelli's immoralism in political theory have long been overstated, but it seems to me one cannot overstate the influence of this beardless Italian upon the theater. The emergence of the figure of the Machiavel onto the Italian and then the English stage represents in itself a rethinking of the morality play. In sober John, we see the final piece in the puzzle of Shakespeare's ambivalent construction. The rejection of the white-bearded Satan is not in this case, as in the morality play, a renunciation of the world—such a renunciation cannot be the theme, or the prerogative, of a man who would be king— but rather a banishment of one "worldly world" for the sake of another. The hero's choice in this morality play is not between virtue and vice but between two different kinds of stage villain and their domains: it is a choice between the Tempter and the Machiavel. Hal rejects the corpulent wit of his pseudofather, the drunken sponger Jack, for the backstage whispers of his real brother, the sober manipulator John. This is, in a sense, to renounce the indulgent fertility of a histrionic world, and imagination's time, for the legal hours and policy'd courses of the world of history.

Someone has been had. Who or what is really being renounced here, and by whom? I think we can get an answer if we look at Hal's opening soliloquy in part 1. Consider the address of this psychic Machiavellian:

I know you all, and will awhile uphold
The unyok'd humour of your idleness. (Act 1, sc. 2, lines 192–93)

It is a fool of an actor who does not implicate the audience with these lines. It is *we* who sustain the fantasies of a Hotspur and a Falstaff with our imaginative sympathy; it is we who indulge and expand the reality of our comic hero. It is also we, *our* hero, *our* theater, that must be renounced. Thoughts tending to policy will still interest King Harry—those thoughts that originate in our sober minds, which, given voice, compete and collide until they find their place in the emerging pattern of fate. His father's latest counsel was for foreign wars, and the advice of brother John, who has the last word in this play, will continue to be a bird song in Harry's ear. But as for that fat man o' th' castle and his excellent wit—

I have long dreamt of such a kind of man,
So surfeit-swelled, so old and so profane,
But being awaked, I do despise my dream. (Act 5, sc. 5, lines 49–51)

This awakening must be what Hal had meant when, in his opening soliloquy in part 1, he spoke of

Redeeming time when men think least I will. (Act 1, sc. 2, line 214)

The redemption of Hal's time is a renunciation of Falstaff's time; and Falstaff's time is nothing but that of the theater itself.

The morality play is in part a conceit, but evidently Shakespeare was very serious about its native themes of renunciation and redemption. He seems to have been impressed by this figure of Harry; and as long as there is no lack of bright young actors with faces just blank enough to keep us guessing, it will remain a popular role. We are faced with a conundrum: here is Shakespeare at variance with himself. On the one hand, his fertile brain discovers for us our Falstaffs, our most addictive theatrical pleasures; on the other, a part of him despises our indulgence. Fall-Staff, his theater, his audience, are a mock Shake-Speare, a spent, sold-out dream from which our playwright would prefer to wake, before he must dance for a return engagement. Yet I would suggest to you, and to Shakespeare, that *our* time is not Hal's time. In Falstaff's corpulent frame, be all our sins remembered; but in his excellent wit, nimble and forgetive, in its transformative histrionic power, which can make a delectable world out of a sinful globe, our time is redeemed. We for whom the grave doth gape, we who must count our shirts—we have found some redemption in the theater. And if you can hear me, in your own measureless grave—you whose countenance once shook a spear—so did you.

Transforming Conventions: The Trope of Decorum and Thomas Sheridan's Captain O'Blunder

SANDRA F. SIEGEL

By the turn of the seventeenth century the prevailing English perception of the Irish—whoever in that seventeenth-century English view the Irish were construed to be—was of a wild, barbaric, and savage people. Although this view commanded and continued thereafter to command attention, it had receded from circulation by the second decade of the eighteenth century. A competing English perception of a domesticated, cowardly, and foolish people increasingly claimed greater attention. Two views so contrary, the one of Ireland as a place inhabited by wild savages and the other of Ireland as a place inhabited by comic blunderers, nevertheless relied on the same prevailing notions of national character, temperament, or, simply, "blood." Claims were made intermittently that behavior was a result of situational causes and, hence, that the Irish were educable; but such claims were generally regarded with skepticism.[1]

Whether the behavior of the Irish was regarded as situational or un-

An earlier version of this paper was presented in Galway at the Eighteenth Century Ireland Society in March 1994. I am especially grateful to Kevin Barry, who invited my contribution and who, with Thomas Bartlett, presided over the meeting. Another version was presented in Minnesota at the American Society for Eighteenth Century Studies in October 1994. Christopher Wheatley shared his wide knowledge of Thomas Shadwell and the early Irish drama. I wish to thank David Hayton and Maureen Waters for their thoughtful reflections. I dedicate this essay to David Grene: wise teacher, generous friend.

avoidable, their Irish-English speech marked them as inclined to ridiculous behavior. I know of no argument in the eighteenth century or after that explains this. Jonathan Swift drew attention to and criticized the view that was commonly held:

How is it possible that a gentleman, who lives in those parts, where the Townlands (as they call them) of his estate produce such odious sounds from the mouth, the throat, and the nose, can be able to repeat the words without dislocating every muscle that is used in speaking, and without applying the same tone to all other words, in every language he understands? As it is plainly to be observed, not only in those people, of the better sort, who live in Gallway and the Western parts. . . . It is true, that in the city-part of London, the trading people have an affected manner of pronouncing. . . . It is likewise true, that there is an odd provincial cant in most counties of England, sometimes not very pleasing to the ear: and the Scotch cadence, as well as expression, are offensive enough. But none of these defects derive contempt to the speakers; whereas, what we call the Irish Brogue is no sooner discovered, than it makes the deliverer, in the last degree, ridiculous and despised; and, from such a mouth, an Englishman expects nothing but bulls, blunders, and follies.[2]

These observations about the sound of speech in the Townlands or other parts, or the pronunciation and cadences of the Scots, and so forth, interest Swift because they enable him to compare English responsiveness to some sounds that are odd with their indifference to other sounds that are equally odd.

It is important to bear in mind that Swift is not of the opinion that "bulls, blunders, and follies" are necessarily forthcoming from such a mouth: they are what an Englishman expects will be forthcoming. Swift would have his readers shift their attention from the viewed (the Irish) to the viewers (the English). Why do Englishmen laugh when they hear an "Irish Brogue"? Why are they indifferent when they hear the speech of others that is no less strange? When Englishmen might have responded differently upon hearing the "Irish Brogue," why did that particular sound elicit laughter? If I seem to bring a little too much pressure to bear on this passage, that is because otherwise strong readings of Swift are indifferent to this passage, while those that are mindful invariably misread it.

Swift, of course, occupied an intermediate position between those who regarded themselves as English and those who regarded themselves as Irish. He affiliated himself, as circumstances inspired him, with one or another side of that acrimonious divide. But he never affiliated himself with the English who expected from the mouth of an Irishman nothing but "bulls, blunders, and follies." In this respect, Swift was an exception. By the end of the eighteenth century, the figure of the Irish "blunderer" and the belief in the propensity of the Irish to commit "bulls" commanded sufficient attention that Richard Lovell Edgeworth and his daughter Maria devoted a book to the subject. The countless editions of this essay that were produced upon publication and, subsequently, throughout the nineteenth century indicate the measure of interest the subject enjoyed.

I

In their *Essay on Irish Bulls* the Edgeworths insist that no "race" or "national character" has a greater proclivity than any other to commit "bulls and blunders."[3] Although they offer no explanation for why the words "blunders" and "bulls" came to be associated with Ireland, the cumulative effect of the examples they marshal from across centuries and from across geographical boundaries is designed to persuade their readers that there is nothing unique about the position that the Irish famously occupied. In other words, rather than deny the propensity of the Irish to commit "bulls, blunders, and follies," they confirm that the propensity is equally distributed and universally shared.

We should bear in mind that the Edgeworths make no effort to explain the commission of "bulls, blunders, and follies," nor do they seek to explain why, despite the universality of the phenomena they describe, Ireland and the Irish have been singled out. Their *Essay on Irish Bulls* might be regarded as an exercise in pointing: neither does it have nor does it claim to have explanatory force. That is its weakness. Its interest lies in the persuasiveness with which it confirms the conspicuous presence of English laughter at Irish blunders. Moreover, their *Essay* carried forward Swift's incipient conceptualization of the notion of "the blunder," facilitating its introduction into social discourse. Yet, although the *Essay on Irish Bulls* confirms the acuity of Swift's observations in "On Barbarous Denominations," it nevertheless fails to pursue the question Swift raises: why did the English laugh at the Irish? To answer that question we need to turn to Tudor and Stuart jestbooks.

II

Until the turn of the seventeenth century, jestbooks, or "jokebooks," which they came to be called, and which enjoyed hundreds of variants, dwelled upon the ineptitude and indecorous behavior of Englishmen whose propensity to commit verbal and behavioral blunders was a commonplace. After the 1690s these collections increasingly depict "Irishmen" who, in these fictional anecdotes, are imagined to behave in characteristically blundering ways.[4] The epithets that attached themselves to the Irish and to Ireland adhered so tenaciously thereafter that their appropriateness was seldom questioned (although Thomas Sheridan attends to them in his farce *The Brave Irishman*). The remarkable history of these editions belongs to another subject. It is enough to point out here that anecdotal versions of the commission by Englishmen of verbal and practical blunders receded proportionately to the prominent appearance of Irish blunderers in the same popular genre of jestbooks. This is more suggestive when we recall another commonplace that circulated during and after the 1690s. "The English pronunciation of Latin was . . . notoriously difficult for other Latinists to understand." John Evelyn, for example, "confirmed the justice of the complaint" frequently lodged against English speakers when "he commented on the 'odd pronouncing of Latin' by his fellow country-men," "'so that out of England no nation were able to understand or endure it.'" And in the dedication to his new translation of Castiglione's *Courtier,* Robert Samber wrote in 1729: "I have been told by several learned Foreigners in the most polite parts of Europe, that they are in pain when we speak Latin."[5]

There is, then, a curious resemblance between the view held of English speakers of Latin in "the most polite parts of Europe" and the view of English men toward speakers of Irish English who, in the proliferation of popular literature during and after the eighteenth century, come to occupy the place that English speakers had occupied. Ridicule appears to have shifted from English laughter at their own blunders to laughter at those committed by distinctly Irish figures. The anecdotes that competed for attention in *Bog-Witticisms, Teagueland Jests, The Irish Miscellany,* and *The Comical Sayings of Paddy from Cork* are indicative of the drift away from those that were typically contained in, for example, *A Hundred Merry Tales* and *Joe Miller's Jests.*

Thomas Sheridan's *The Brave Irishman: A Farce* is written against the prevailing current of opinion. He composed the play probably while a student at Trinity, a play he would soon produce as manager of the Smock-Alley Theatre in Dublin. His farce anticipated by fifty years the argument that the Edgeworths propose in their *Essay on Irish Bulls.* The history of that play, which I will sketch briefly here, is remarkable.

III

During the years when Sheridan's farce enjoyed popularity, particularly in Dublin, no printed version was published. When, however, the first printed version appeared, in 1754, bearing a title different from that inscribed on the only extant manuscript in Sheridan's hand, Sheridan disclaimed authorship.[6] This did not prevent the publication, under his name, either during or after his lifetime, of the play he disclaimed. For this reason alone the play might claim our interest. There is at least one other reason. Sheridan's farce marks a moment as interesting as it is odd: although Sheridan repudiated his authorship of all of the printed versions of the one play he wrote, he is best known for this play (although his repudiation of the printed versions has been ignored).

For thirteen years, between 1745 and 1758, during which Sheridan managed the Smock-Alley Theatre and acted in some of the plays he produced, *The Brave Irishman: A Farce* enjoyed such popularity that Isaac Sparks, an actor who was frequently cast in the leading role, came to be called, endearingly, according to the part he played, "Captain O'Blunder." It is likely that Sheridan relied on his own manuscript when he produced the play. It is also likely that at least one other manuscript evolved as a result of productions by other managers and actors, and that this script departed from the original play that Sheridan wrote. This manuscript, upon which the printed versions are based, displeased him. The two extant manuscripts, the one in Sheridan's hand and the second inscribed in a hand that is not Sheridan's, incline one to suppose that this farce, which was so successful on the eighteenth-century Dublin stage, endured for reasons that were historical and political rather than literary or theatrical.[7] Neither was the claim made in the past nor do I wish now to make the claim that Sheridan's farce was richly conceived or deeply original. The changes that emerged, of which I will single out only one, illuminate Sheridan's repudiation of subsequent versions and the appeal of those versions to his contemporaries.[8]

In Sheridan's manuscript Captain O'Blunder, who comes to London from Ireland, is not the symbolic embodiment, as the name suggests, of the blunderer of whom the "Irish," in a certain English view, were the characteristic paradigm: on the contrary, Sheridan's manuscript version of the play clarifies that the name serves to describe the way in which others view the man who bears the name "O'Blunder." Like Swift before him, Sheridan's interest is in how the Captain is viewed by others rather than in the character of the Captain himself. Like Swift, he turns attention from the viewed to the viewer. Preconceptions incline one to see only what one expects to find. He explores what some viewers are likely to find who bring with them certain preconceptions about Ireland.

An eighteenth-century Dublin or London audience need not have read or seen the play to have found the protagonist, Captain O'Blunder, farcical. The mere joining of the rank of captain with the name O'Blunder would have aroused amusement for at least two reasons. Proper names are not typically descriptive of the objects they identify. The Captain's proper name is. One expects that he is called O'Blunder because he blunders, that O'Blunder's behavior will enact the significance of his name as his life will illuminate its meaning. An eighteenth-century audience would have had at least one other expectation. By placing an "O" before the proper name, Sheridan further identifies Blunder as an Irish captain. Captains, however, were understood to be "Gentlemen," and "Gentlemen" were understood to be decorous. Gentlemen do not blunder. For this reason, too, then, the name Sheridan attached to his protagonist would have alerted his audience to their own preconceptions. Although Sheridan set the play in the sixteenth or seventeenth century rather than in the eighteenth, social relations in the latter century precluded the possibility that one might be "a blunderer" and "a Gentleman" at the same time. If a stereotype is a walking cliché, "Captain O'Blunder" is a walking oxymoron. In order for him to be the embodiment of the blunderer his audience imagined and properly belong to the realm of the cultural imaginary, either Sheridan would have had to have revealed his blunderer as a counterfeit captain or he would have had to have revealed his Captain as a counterfeit blunderer. Instead his play is devoted to unraveling the conventions that inform social relations. Captain O'Blunder proves to be an admirable "Gentleman" (in contrast to the putative London and French "Gentlemen" who surround him). The versions Sheridan disclaimed differ. There can be no doubt that the unpublished manuscript inscribed in his hand supports this reading. Here is a passage from Sheridan's manuscript that all of the printed versions delete. It is a passage in which Lucy is driven by her servant, Betty, to see more clearly:

BETTY: Pray tell me Madam how can you have such an aversion to a Man whom
    you never saw?
LUCY: O hideous! is he not an Irishman?
BETTY: And pray what then Madam?
LUCY: Why I am told they are meer Beasts
and have Horns in that Country.
BETTY: I believe not more than their Neighbours [. . .]
It is time to lay aside these popular Prejudices. . . .

These Beasts with Horns are of course the same Bulls that are playfully reproduced in the etchings in the first edition of the Edgeworths' *Essay on Irish Bulls*. In contrast to Sheridan's manuscript version of the play, in the unauthorized printed versions of the play, Irishmen have Wings, like angels, and the line about "prejudice" drops away. Having been schooled as an Irish boy in London to an awareness of the harm some inflict on others because of their "prejudice" and having been pursued by scandals nearly from the time of his having completed his studies at Trinity, this is not likely to be a passage that Sheridan would be inclined to delete. A few facts about his life and a few moments that he found to be memorable are worth recalling.

IV

Sheridan, the son of Reverend Dr. Thomas Sheridan, was born in 1719 in Dublin, where he spent most of his boyhood in a house frequented by guests, among whom was Jonathan Swift. His father's house was attached to the school over which he presided and which was reputed to be the finest in Europe. That meant, above all, that "Gentlemen" sent their children there to be properly "polished"—a word Dr. Johnson would have approved of. The Reverend Dr. Sheridan followed the English custom, not common in Dublin then, of orchestrating school performances in his Schoolhouse. In addition to Shakespeare, as part of their education his pupils performed Aeschylus, Sophocles, and Euripides in Greek and Terence, Lucan, and Horace in Latin. It was said that when Dr. Sheridan's pupils performed, attendance at theaters in Dublin diminished considerably.[9] This was not young Thomas's only contact with the theater: at age fourteen he was sent across to London to the Westminster School where, his frame then small, as it was to remain, he was "draped in the distinctive clothes of a Westminster King's scholar, an outfit which included a long double-breasted jacket with knee breeches and a trencher cap."[10] He spent several evenings each week for two years as a spectator at the Drury Lane, Goodman's Fields, the Haymarket, or Covent Garden. Although the fourteen-year-old Thomas was a spectacle in London theaters, the stage that transfixed him continued to be a verbal rather than a visual art: to perform was conceived primarily as a verbal act. To act meant above all to be a master of speaking. Acting, rhetoric, and oratory were as necessary as education was to a "Gentleman," although education alone was not assurance that one had any claim to that rank.

In the autumn of 1735, when Thomas returned to Dublin from London, Swift, Thomas's godfather, then in his seventies, devoted two or three hours each day to hearing Thomas read aloud and presumably to guiding his delivery. Swift wrote to Dr. Sheridan: "Did I tell you, that I much esteem your younger son, but thought him a little too much on the *qui vive* which I would have you reform in him. I know no other fault in him. He is an English boy, and learned it there."[11]

Shortly after he returned to Dublin, Thomas, aged sixteen, entered Trinity College. In recording his memory of his conversations with Swift he reported a decade later: "When I told him the course of Reading I was put into, he asked me, Do they teach you English? No. Do they teach you how to speak? No. Then, said he, they teach you Nothing."[12] Whether Sheridan's memory of what Swift said is accurate matters less than his own confirmation of this belief, which he presented in *An Oration* "before a numerous Body of nobility and Gentry, Assembled near the Theatre." On that occasion in 1752 he proposed to form "the Hibernian Society for the Improvement of Education." He argued that too many Irish youths were being sent to England, where they become Anglicized and estranged from Ireland: the result is "the decay of all noble improvements in Ireland. If in Ireland there were proper schools the inclination to study elsewhere would subside." Therefore, he called for the establishment of an Academy in Ireland where oratory, the arts, and the sciences could be learned and "the Nation saved from impending Ruin."[13]

This he learned as much from his father and perhaps from Swift as he did from his education at Trinity, where "playgoing was a popular recreation with most Trinitarians."[14] If at age sixteen young Thomas, after two years in London, had become "an English boy" appearing to Swift to be "a little too much on the *qui vive*," a little too much on the lookout, too sophisticated for his years, a fault Swift lamented, then, beginning in 1745, when Sheridan assumed the management of the Smock-Alley Theatre in Dublin, he was, perhaps, too innocent, less on the *qui vive* than his own interests required.

V

Several years after Sheridan composed *The Brave Irishman: A Farce,* a succession of scandals surrounded his performances as well as his management of the Smock-Alley Theatre, nearly all of which turned on two issues: whether he had any claim to being a gentleman and the "Hibernian" theme. Whatever the causes might have been that entangled Sheridan in slander, rumor, suspicion, and ill-will, his play, retrospectively, could be viewed as having anticipated in certain important respects the predicament in which Sheridan repeatedly found himself. To some it undoubtedly must have appeared as though there were uncanny correspondences between Sheridan and O'Blunder. One scandal, for example, that began in February 1747, when riots forced the closing of the theater, inspired pamphlets that pronounced "DUBLIN IN UPROAR" and culminated in a trial whose jury acquitted Sheridan. Rather than elaborate this and other scandals, I will isolate two incidents that occurred during the "uproar." The first occurred in the theater; the second in the courtroom.

Vanbrugh's *Aesop* was being performed. Sheridan had cast himself in the leading role of Aesop. A young man in "a military dress and sword" caused a disturbance in the dressing rooms. After a short interval, the disturbance was audible throughout the house. Sheridan interrupted the play, drove away the gentleman, and resumed his role as Aesop. Within minutes, the gentleman approached the stage and threw an orange that struck Aesop's nose. The nose tumbled from Sheridan's face. The gentleman crossed the stage and walked toward the dressing rooms. Again, Sheridan interrupted his performance, and on this occasion, when words failed to dissuade the gentleman, Sheridan attempted to strike him with Aesop's stick. When the gentleman refused to be subdued, Sheridan reportedly said to him (speaking in the garments of the character of Aesop to his adversary in military dress and sword): "I am as good a gentleman as you are," a remark which soon circulated inaccurately as "I am as good a gentleman as any in the House"—a remark much quoted in the papers and for which Sheridan eventually apologized. The press and pamphlets that circulated so widely during and after the courtroom drama which followed appear to have transfixed Dublin.[15]

The defense for "the Gentleman from Galway in Connought," as the Dublin and London press referred to the soldier named Kelly, argued that Sheridan "hindered the Gentleman to ravish Actresses, and defend himself and his honor against Outrages from Players." At the culmination of the trial the gentleman's defense attorney arose and said he wanted to see a curiosity: "I have often seen a Gentleman Soldier, and a Gentleman Taylor but I have never seen a Gentleman player." Sheridan stepped forward, bowed modestly, and said: "Sir, I hope you see one now."[16] Whether an actor could be a gentleman was a variant of a more inclusive question that was posed frequently and pervasively. To some in London the question appeared to have become a "national hobby."[17]

VI

It is worth pausing over the effect of the irresolvable question that vexed social relations in Dublin as well as in London: who was to be regarded as a "Gentleman"? Was being a gentleman a matter of blood? Or was becoming one a matter of behavior? Tocqueville was not alone in observing the differences between English and European social relations. "An illustrious name," he observed, "is a great advantage and cause of much pride to him who bears it, but in general one can say that the aristocracy is founded on wealth—a thing which may be acquired, and not on birth. . . . the nobility and middle classes of England followed the same business, embraced the same professions, and what is far more significant, intermarried with one another." An equally acute observer of the high incidence of intermarriage remarked upon how easy was the mingling of orders and yet "how decided was the propensity for distinctions of rank."[18]

Although in Dublin and London during and after the eighteenth century there were those who regarded the recognition of a "Gentleman" to be determinate and unproblematic, to understand the complexity of social relations one must bear in mind the irresolvability of the question: on whichever side one found oneself inclining, whether one thought "blood" or "behavior" defined a "Gentleman," such crossings of rank through intermarriage would make the recognition of rank increasingly difficult, yet precisely that difficulty would itself exaggerate the propensity for distinctions. Where the mingling of rank occurs, all ranks are uneasy: those of high rank are vulnerable to the suspicion of being counterfeit and are fearful of discovery, while those of low rank are vulnerable to suspicion of being counterfeit and are hopeful of discovery. It is not surprising, then, that between 1700 and 1900—these are approximate dates—books on the subject of "the Gentleman" that were designed to enable readers to detect the signs of rank and to conform to the requirements inscribed in print enjoyed unbounded popularity. It could be said that during these years there were countless books on numerous other subjects. Yet no other subject appeared to have become "a national hobby," as to some did the subject of defining and recognizing "the Gentleman."[19]

Among such behavior manuals, etiquette books, and instructional guides, the letters Chesterfield wrote to his infant son that were published posthumously by his wife were destined to become a book more famous than any other. Such books attempted the impossible task of specifying adornment of every variety: how to clothe thoughts and how to deliver them; how to comport oneself; how to adorn one's body for every conceivable occasion. Manuals of behavior encouraged specularity: moreover, the performative behavior on view sustained the spectacle in the court and in the marketplace. Readers of guides to decorum sought confirmation that their own behavior was decorous (even if their blood was mixed) or sought the discovery that others were counterfeit whose behavior betrayed the claims of their lineage.

VII

The half-dozen or so scandals that pursued Sheridan—of which I have briefly cited one—occurred as part of this preoccupation with rank. We must keep in mind what is often forgotten in accounts of social life on both sides of the Irish Sea: the complication of identifying rank in London was at least trebled in Dublin by a far more complex linguistic predicament, and by, as Nicholas Canny so clearly points out in "Identity Formation in Ireland," intermarriage, which occurred readily in Dublin between the New English, the Old English, and the Gaelic Irish when it was economically expedient. It is likely that intermarriage occurred for other reasons as well. One indication of the complex and volatile social relations that characterized Dublin by the eighteenth century is the permeable image of the Irish that English depictions convey.[20] David Hayton proposes that around the eighteenth century English perceptions of the Irish shifted: earlier, the inhabitants of Ireland were viewed as courageous; subsequently, they were viewed as cowardly. David Hayton's observations call for fuller elaboration than the scope of this essay allows: for my present purpose I wish only to add to his observations that in the eighteenth century this virtue—"bravery"—is, of course, a telling sign of whether one is or is not a "Gentleman." For instance, "A Narrative of the Affair between Mr. Brown and the Inspector Wherein all the Facts are Got in their True Light" was published in London in 1752. (Mr. Brown was implicated, as Sheridan's father was, in the preparation and circulation of Swift's *Drapier's Letters*.) "The Inspector took it into his Head to attack the character of Mr. Brown, in his Paper of April 30, without the least Offence given, or indeed without any Causes whatsoever. For this Purpose he laid hold on a private Affair, which happened between Mr. Brown and another Gentleman, related to circumstances of the Story, but added many others to throw on him an *Imputation of Cowardice* [my emphasis], than which nothing can be more odious, more defamatory amongst Gentlemen."[21]

When Thomas Sheridan, as a young student about to be graduated from Trinity College, began to compose *The Brave Irishman: A Farce,* it is likely that, as the son of the Reverend Dr. Thomas Sheridan, in whose prestigious position in Dublin Thomas took pride, he thought his own rank as a gentleman was secure. And yet, his association with the theater aroused doubt. Moreover, English preconceptions of Irishmen or of Anglo-Irishmen or men simply born and schooled in Ireland (in Dublin as well as in the Pale) were, as Swift understood, firmly in place. Sheridan most certainly knew of the frequently performed farces and comedies and the various popular jestbooks that depicted Irish figures derisively. The plays as well as the jestbooks confirmed the fear and contempt for the sometimes barbaric and other times comic but in these versions always blundering "Irish"—whoever that word "Irish" was construed by readers to be. It is likely from the surprise he registers in the theater during the *Aesop* episode that it did not occur to Sheridan that those preconceptions with which he was so familiar applied to him. Despite this supposed innocence with respect to his own position, his earliest written work and his only play, the unpublished version of *The Brave Irishman: A Farce,* nevertheless, as we have seen, attends to those preconceptions. While his play anticipated the predicament he would himself encounter, he pursued with equal devotion after he left the theater various projects that were designed to reform the English language. His play had as its instructional purpose to unsettle conventions in order to arouse more thoughtfulness; in his later work, he undertook to eliminate the problems that arise from the circulation in one kingdom of different sounds that nevertheless are intended to convey the same meaning. He devoted himself to stabilizing the meanings of words and to developing a method that would eliminate among speakers of the same kingdom the differences in speech that set them apart from one another.

VIII

In 1762, about eighteen years after he composed *The Brave Irishman: A Farce,* Sheridan presented a plan to the Earl of Northumberland in which he proposed "to put an end to the odious distinction kept up between subjects of the same king."[22] He had in mind the differences in speech that separated inhabitants of the same kingdom from one another because of variations among speakers of the same language. In Sheridan's view, such variants were falsely perceived by some as differences that justified inequities. He proposed to eliminate these inequities by eliminating variations in speech. His ambitions led him beyond the boundaries of the king's subjects: he proposed to eliminate all human misunderstanding—the sometimes calamitous repercussions verbal and practical blunders produced.[23] He devoted himself to persuading the Crown and the state to assign one, and only one, meaning to each word. After having assigned the meanings, the Crown and the state would then develop a system of education that would impart to schoolchildren each word's precise meaning. Other subjects of importance would occupy an equally prominent place in the curriculum: instruction on how to pronounce and deliver, in cadences perfected through practice, sounds that would be transmitted to auditors who in turn would be equally well instructed to receive precisely those same meanings with perfect understanding. To promote this project, Sheridan produced a dictionary of English pronunciation.

If Sheridan's efforts to standardize English were in part a defense against the expectation that Swift, his attentive godfather, understood so well, that from the mouth of an Irishman an Englishman expects nothing but "bulls, blunders, and follies," then Dr. Johnson's remarks about him were, from a certain point of view, from the point of view of what Englishmen commonly expected to hear, understandable. Of Sheridan, Johnson is reported to have said: "Dull, naturally; but it must have taken him a great deal of pains to become what we now see him; such an excess of stupidity, sir, is not in nature." Johnson was also known to have said of Sheridan to an acquaintance that he had "the misfortune to be an Irishman."[24]

Now it is not necessarily the case that Dr. Johnson regarded all who had the misfortune to be Irish to have such an excess of stupidity. One sign of Sheridan's stupidity, however, in Johnson's view, was that Sheridan, having been born in Dublin, committed the audacious act of having produced the text—his *Dictionary of English Pronunciation*—upon which his educational "Plan" to eliminate those "odious distinctions of subjects under the same king" would rely and upon which he thought the greatness of the kingdom depended. What Dr. Johnson failed to see in Sheridan's "excess of stupidity" is the telling sign of Sheridan's parodic resistance to his countrymen on the other side of the Irish Sea who expected from such a mouth nothing but "bulls, blunders, and follies." The failure of his "Plan" would have obliged Englishmen to acknowledge the force of their attachment to their expectations, while its success on both shores of the kingdom would have obliged them to abandon the folly of these same expectations. Moreover, while Dr. Johnson regarded Sheridan's effort as ridiculous, he did not consider his own broad Staffordshire English to be an obstacle to preparing his own *Dictionary of English Pronunciation*. He is, indeed, the kind of Englishman Swift describes in the long passage I cited earlier. Which is surprising. We are accustomed to hold Dr. Johnson in high regard for his contribution to shaping, rather than to following, opinion. With respect to Thomas Sheridan and the question of Irish bulls, Dr. Johnson, who was not alone, blundered.

Notes

1. See D. W. Hayton, "From Barbarian to Burlesque: English Images of the Irish c.1660–1750," *Irish Economic and Social History* 15 (1988): 5–31.

2. Jonathan Swift, "On Barbarous Denominations in Ireland," in *The Prose Works of Jonathan Swift*, ed. Herbert Davis, 14 vols. (Oxford: Basil Blackwell, 1957), 4:281.

3. Maria Edgeworth and Richard Lovell Edgeworth, *Essay on Irish Bulls* (London, 1802).

4. Detailed readings of these texts are the subject of a book in progress of which this essay forms one part.

5. Peter Burke, *The Art of Conversation* (Ithaca: Cornell University Press, 1993), 57–58.

6. Esther K. Sheldon, *Thomas Sheridan of Smock-Alley* (Princeton: Princeton University Press, 1967), 20–26. Sheldon's meticulous pioneering study of Sheridan establishes the essential material for carrying forward studies of his life and work. There are, as Sheldon points out, two manuscripts of *The Brave Irishman*, one that is inscribed in Sheridan's hand and one that is not.

7. Ibid. Although I agree with Esther Sheldon that the manuscript in Sheridan's hand and the Larpent Manuscript are close, Sheridan's manuscript differs from the Larpent and from all printed versions of the play in one important respect, which I address in this essay.

8. I owe special thanks to Jacky Cox at the Modern Archive Center, King's College, Cambridge, for her generous assistance. I am grateful to William Lefanu for answering my queries and for permission to publish the manuscript of *The Brave Irishman* that is in Sheridan's hand, which is among the Lefanu Papers, box II, 9, at the Modern Archive Center. The transcriptions, which conform strictly to this manuscript, are my own.

9. Sheldon, *Thomas Sheridan,* 9–17.

10. Ibid., 11. For a description of Sheridan's dress, see Frederic H. Forshall, *Westminster School, Past and Present* (London, 1884), 59, as cited by Sheldon, *Thomas Sheridan,* 11.

11. ALS, Swift to Dr. Sheridan, 2 Mar. 1735, Lefanu Papers, Modern Archive Center, King's College, Cambridge.

12. Thomas Sheridan, *An Oration, Pronounced before a Numerous Body of the Nobility and Gentry, Assembled at the Musick-Hall in Fishamble-street, On Tuesday the 6th of this instant December, And now first Published at their unanimous Desire. By Thomas Sheridan, A. M. The Second Edition* (Dublin: printed for M. Williamson, 1757), 19–20, as quoted by Sheldon, *Thomas Sheridan,* 16. See also John Watkins, *Memoirs of the Public and Private Life of the Right Honorable Richard Brinsley Sheridan, with a Particular Account of his Family and Connexions* (London, 1817).

13. Thomas Sheridan, *An Oration on Elocution* (1752).

14. Sheldon, *Thomas Sheridan,* 14. For the influence that the theater and the college

exerted on each other in the seventeenth and eighteenth centuries, see William Smith Clark, *The Early Irish Stage, The Beginnings to 1720* (Oxford: Clarendon Press, 1955), chaps. 1–2.

15. For an account of this riot, see Sheldon, *Thomas Sheridan,* 81–88; Watkins, *Memoirs,* 56–65; and W. J. Lawrence, "The Famous Kelly Riots," *Irish Times,* 2 Sept. 1922.

16. See Watkins, *Memoirs,* for an account of the courtroom scene.

17. Shirley Robin Letwin, *The Gentleman in Trollope: Individuality and Moral Conduct* (Cambridge: Harvard University Press, 1982), 11. I am indebted to Letwin for her discussion of the importance of the question of the gentleman, although I do not always agree with her conclusions.

18. Alexis de Tocqueville, *On the State of Society in France Before the Revolution of 1789* (London, 1856), 151–53, 179–81. Madame de Stael-Holstein, *Letters on England* (London: Treuttel and Wurtz, Treuttel, jun., and Richter, 1830), 124–37, as cited by Letwin, *Gentleman in Trollope,* 9.

19. Letwin, *Gentleman in Trollope,* 11.

20. Nicholas Canny, "Identity Formation in Ireland: The Emergence of the Anglo-Irish," in *Colonial Identity in the Atlantic World,* ed. Nicholas Canny and Anthony Pagden (Princeton: Princeton University Press, 1987). I rely here on the language and argument that Nicholas Canny presents.

21. *British Library Tract* 641 d. 31, 10.

22. "Heads of a Plan for the Improvement of Elocution; and for Promoting the Study of the English Language; In Order to the Refining, Ascertaining, and Reducing it to a Standard: Together with Some Arguments, to Enforce the Necessity of Carrying Such a Plan into Execution," in Thomas Sheridan, *A Course of Lectures on Elocution: Together with Two Dissertations on Language; and some other Tracts relative to those Subjects. By Thomas Sheridan, A.M.* (London: printed by W. Strahan, for A. Millar, R. and J. Dodsley, T. Davies, C. Henderson, J. Wilkie, and E. Dilly, 1762).

23. Sheridan, *A Course of Lectures on Elocution.*

24. See Burke, *Art of Conversation,* 56; and Hayton, "From Barbarian to Burlesque," 15.

Synge: Reality and the Imagination of Place

NICHOLAS GRENE

"When I was writing *The Shadow of the Glen,* some years ago, I got more aid than any learning could have given me, from a chink in the floor of the old Wicklow house where I was staying, that let me hear what was being said by the servant girls in the kitchen" (Synge, 4.53).[1] This was the passage of Synge's 1907 preface to *The Playboy of the Western World* that, in trying to establish the authenticity of his language of the people, served only to confirm the worst suspicions of his nationalist critics. He was not of the people, he could not truly express their lives: his dialogue was faked up from the eavesdroppings of the gentleman. Such was the literal and politically hostile reading of the passage. What we may plausibly conjecture Synge meant here was that, as he sat in that house in Tomrilands in his tiny bedroom above the kitchen, trying to imagine the voices of his characters Nora and Dan Burke, Michael Dara and the Tramp, the actual voices of the women talking in the kitchen below served to verify his written dialogue. The sound of the speeches in the play was, you might say, tuned to the real.

For me the story begins some fifty years later in another old Wicklow house, with my father reading aloud *The Shadow of the Glen*. His marvelously dramatic voice brought to life one after another the visiting tramp, the weary melancholy of the "widowed" woman of the house, the venomous old man emerging from his pretend death under the sheet, the limp lover making love, Irish country style, to the supposed dowry left behind. And set into the story extraordinarily for me—aged seven? eight? nine?—were the names of the places I knew. Michael Dara's sheep were being driven past our own house in Clash from the fair in Aughrim just six miles away, and on along the road by which I went to school each day in Ballinatone up to the glen that gave the play its title, Glenmalure. This was a play, one of the first that I had ever heard, but it was a play sited amid the actual places of my life. There seemed some extraordinary mixture of categories in a story—a made-up play printed in a book read to me by my father—and the real, everyday places that surrounded me. Even today, some forty years further on, living still in the same Wicklow house, I continue to wonder about the character of reality and place in Synge's drama. How is reality constructed in the plays, and what place does place have in that construction? For whom is this reality real, and what relation does it bear to the reality of an actual known topography? Such are the questions I want to explore in this essay.

Synge had, it appears, a very precise imagination of his plays' interiors. When asked by a director some question about the set, he knew exactly where everything should go as if the set were a quite real place that he could see in his mind.[2] At first it seems as though his offstage topographies are just as accurately, precisely, literally rendered. The Wicklow plays use place-names all within a convincingly limited distance of the valley of the Avonbeg, where all three plays are set (see map 1): Aughrim, Glenmalure, Glen Imaal, Seven Churches (= Glendalough), Lough Nahanagan *(The Shadow of the Glen);* Clash (= Ballinaclash), Arklow *(The Tinker's Wedding);* Ballinatone, Grianan, Laragh *(The Well of the Saints).* Similarly *The Playboy,* set in an area of North Mayo which Synge visited in 1904, and again in 1905 on his commissioned tour of the so-called Congested Districts, has a verisimilitude of local naming (see map 2). The action is imagined as taking place on the Belmullet peninsula, the most remote northwestern corner of Ireland. Pegeen Mike orders her trousseau from Castlebar, the nearest major town; Shawn Keogh will call a piper from Crossmolina or from Ballina, some twenty-five or thirty miles west of Belmullet; Christy imagines honeymoon outings with Pegeen Mike on Neifin, the mountain to the southeast, or in Erris to the north; when settled with her he will spend his nights poaching salmon in the Owen (= Owenmore river) or in Carrowmore Lake. Only the minimalist *Riders to the Sea,* though obviously set on Inishmaan, Synge's favorite of the Aran Islands, hardly names names. For Synge, one of the problems of the mythological setting of *Deirdre of the Sorrows* was that "these saga people . . . seem very remote; one does not know what they thought or what they are or where they went to sleep, so one is apt to fall into rhetoric" (4.xxvi). Against such a tendency to a spurious mouthing of language in mythological drama is the felt need in Synge for an embeddedness in the real, the reality of which is partly guaranteed by the reference to real places.

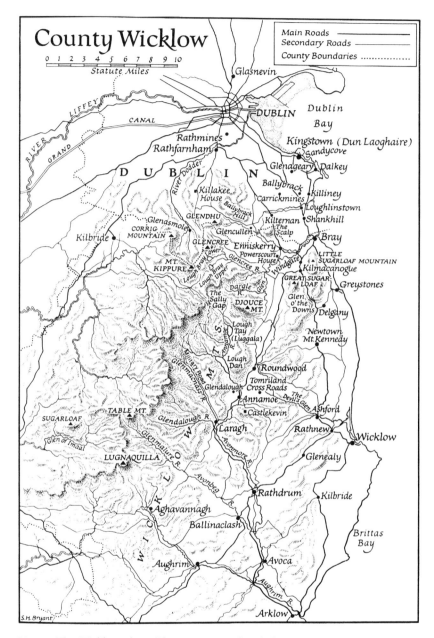

Map 1. The Wicklow plays. (Photo courtesy of Nicholas Grene and the Photographic Centre, Trinity College, Dublin. First published in *Letters to Molly: John Millinton Synge to Maire O'Neill*, ed. Ann Saddlemyer [Cambridge: Harvard University Press, 1971])

Map 2. The Playboy country. (Photo courtesy of Nicholas Grene and the Photographic Centre, Trinity College, Dublin.)

Yet they don't have to be real. Two of the Wicklow place-names most frequently mentioned in the plays are fabricated. Rathvanna, referred to repeatedly in *The Shadow of the Glen, The Tinker's Wedding,* and *The Well of the Saints,* does not exist on any Wicklow map and never did; no more does Ballinacree, which returns insistently in *The Tinker's Wedding.* In the process of writing *The Shadow of the Glen* Synge struck out the perfectly real and plausible Aughavannah, just over the mountain from Glenmalure, and replaced it with the invented Rathvanna.[3] He may have wanted a word that was a shade less polysyllabic, or he may have thought Augha-vannah ugly or hard to pronounce; whatever his reasons, they had to do with the sound of the name in his fictional dialogue, which took precedence over the literal authenticity of the real place-name. It was similar with Ballinacree. Sarah Casey in *The Tinker's Wedding* takes pride in her title of "Beauty of Ballinacree," citing it as evidence of her local fame (in spite of Michael Byrne's deflating comment, "It's the like of that name they do be putting on the horses they have below racing in Arklow"; 4.11). But the likely local place-name here is Ballinacor.[4] The change is slight, again maybe made for greater euphony, or for the more romantic associations of "cree" (= Irish *croí*, "heart"). The point is that for a local listener, Rathvanna and Ballinacree would strike the ear as false notes—though I am bound to say I didn't hear them as such forty-odd years ago. Where are Rathvanna and Ballinacree? Were these forms of Aughavannah and Ballinacor current in Synge's time? Why would Nora Burke and Michael Dara in *The Shadow* and Sarah Casey and Michael Byrne in *The Tinker's Wedding* refer to places that don't exist? The plays do not provoke such questions because it was not presupposed that they would have audiences of local listeners. The Wicklow plays were not directed specifically toward Wicklow people, any more than *Riders to the Sea* was written for the Aran islanders, or *The Playboy* for the men and women of Belmullet. What, then, is the nature of the only intermittently real places in texts designed for audiences too distant from their settings to appreciate (or deprecate) their localization?

One of the objects of Synge's imagination of place in the plays is to render the sense of what it is to live in a local community. A peculiarity of Ireland is the so-called country townland: not a town, not even a village, but an area of land which may have in it several farms, several houses, without any specific center of population. In areas where many people are called by the same name, it helps to identify them by the townland where they live. For instance, in *The Playboy*, there might well be three or four Shawn Keoghs in the neighborhood, so the one engaged to Pegeen Mike, and waiting for a papal dispensation to marry her (they are cousins), is "Shawn Keogh of Killakeen." Killakeen is not a real townland in the Belmullet peninsula or indeed anywhere else in Ireland,[5] but Shawn Keogh as a character in the play is made more real by being given this local habitation and name. And it makes possible the magnificent scorn of Pegeen's rejection of him in act 3:

I'm thinking you're too fine for the like of me, Shawn Keogh of Killakeen, and let you go off till you'd find a radiant lady with droves of bullocks on the plains of Meath, and herself bedizened in the diamond jewelleries of Pharaoh's ma. (4.155)

I want to come back to the "radiant lady"; but the snorting irony here is in the contrast between the diminutively local and real title, "Shawn Keogh of Killakeen," and the sardonically rich expanses imagined beyond.

Synge's plays tend to have one fixed setting: the cottage rooms of *The Shadow* or *Riders,* the shebeen of *The Playboy,* the side of one road or another in *The Well of the Saints* or *The Tinker's Wedding.* The infant Abbey Theatre, for which these plays were written, could not afford anything more elaborate by way of mise-en-scène. The characters create the spaces in which they live by reference and allusion. The Tramp and Michael Dara in *The Shadow* on the day of the play's action have both traveled the same road up to the head of Glenmalure from the Aughrim fair, and the Tramp has scathing things to say about Michael Dara's herding skills: "it's a poor herd does be running back and forward after a little handful of ewes the way I seen yourself running this day, young fellow, and you coming from the fair" (3.47). In fairness to Michael Dara it might be said that he is trying to drive ewes that have just been separated from their lambs—sold in the fair—which is not the easiest of jobs. But Michael Dara is not a "mountain" man; he is "a kind of a farmer has come up from the sea to live in a cottage beyond" (2.41), and for Nora Burke his poor herding is a mark of his difference:

There's no one can drive a mountain ewe but the men do be reared in the Glen Malure, I've heard them say, and above by Rathvanna, and the Glen Imaal, men the like of Patch Darcy, God spare his soul, who would walk through five hundred sheep and miss one of them, and he not reckoning them at all. (3.47)

It is not so much the geography as the social psychology of place that is sketched in here: the remote mountain glens as a community apart, strange and semimythologized.

We are encouraged throughout Synge's plays to imagine the places in which his characters live, to go the roads they travel by their routes. In the opening scene of *The Playboy* the publican Michael James is off to Kate Cassidy's wake. Against the protests of Pegeen Mike, who is afraid of being left alone all night in the house, he argues that he couldn't possibly be expected to make his way back: "it's a queer daughter you are if you'd have me crossing backward through the Stooks of the Dead Women, with a drop taken" (4.63). The "Stooks of the Dead Women" is in fact the name of a sandy head down in Dingle in Kerry, a totally different part of the country from where *The Playboy* is set; Synge recorded the folklore attached to the place in his "In West Kerry" travel essays (2.264). Here, though, it is displaced to Mayo to make a convincingly spooky-sounding locality which Michael James might well be afraid to cross at night. And then there are the "bona fide" travelers. A splendidly solemn licensing law (which survived in Ireland up to the early 1960s) restricted drinking in public houses outside permitted hours to "bona fide" travelers, the definition of such a traveler being someone at least four miles from home. It is to this that Michael James refers in *The Playboy* when he reassures Christy that his pub is free from police visits: "what would the polis want spying on me, and not a decent house within four miles, the way every living Christian is a bona fide saving one widow alone?" (4.67). In other words, everyone (except for Widow Quin) in the neighborhood lives sufficiently far from the pub that they can drink freely there at any hour of the day or night. Christy, however, draws the wrong conclusions from this when he assumes that the girls who visit him in the second act have traveled four miles to meet him:

PEGEEN *(turning round astonished)*: Four miles!
CHRISTY *(apologetically)*: Didn't himself say there were only bona fides living in the place?
PEGEEN: It's bona fides by the road they are, but that lot come over the river lepping the stones. It's not three perches when you go like that. (4.107)

To live in a place is to know it as an actual inhabited location, shortcuts and all, not as the space mapped by roads and licensing laws.

Beyond the intimately known locality are places further off which are known only by hearsay report. To the people of Wicklow in *The Well of the Saints,* Aran and the holy well of the play's title are the stuff of distant description (see map 3):

TIMMY: Did ever you hear tell of a place across a bit of the sea, where there is an island, and the grave of the four beautiful saints?
MARY DOUL: I've heard people have walked round from the west and they speaking of that. (3.79)

Similarly for the Aran girls in *Riders to the Sea,* the coast of Donegal where their brother's drowned body has been found is unimaginably far away. "There was a man in here a while ago—the man sold us that knife—and he said if you set off walking from the rocks beyond [Connemara on the mainland], it would be in seven days you would be in Donegal" (3.15). Such witnesses are needed to authenticate the otherwise apparently incredible stories of the peculiarities of unseen places, as in the exchange between the credulous Jimmy Farrell and the skeptical Philly O'Cullen in act 3 of *The Playboy:*

Map of Ireland

Map 3. Ireland. (Photo courtesy of Nicholas Grene and the Photographic Centre, Trinity College, Dublin.)

JIMMY: . . . Did you never hear tell of the skulls they have in the city of Dublin, ranged out like blue jugs in a cabin of Connaught?

PHILLY: And you believe that?

JIMMY (*pugnaciously*): Didn't a lad see them and he after coming from harvesting in the Liverpool boat? (4.133).

Those who travel, peddlers, seasonal laborers who work in England, act as authority for the creation of a world outside the reach of local knowledge.

To the extent that we are taken into the mental landscape of the characters in Synge, are encouraged to imagine the places in which they live and the way in which they imagine the places beyond where they live, the effect is one of dramatic realization, supporting the illusion of the actual. But other things are going on as well in the references to space and place in the plays. As the allusions move out beyond the immediate locales that the people know intimately and take in larger regions, the topography becomes vaguer and more confused. Of just what "western world" is Christy Mahon playboy, for instance? The western world seems through much of the play to refer to the western seaboard of Ireland, presumably stretching from Kerry in the southwest—which is where Christy comes from—up to Mayo in the northwest. But there is also the reference to the "Western States," that is, America, to which Shawn Keogh offers Christy a ticket and where, he says, Christy will be happier: "isn't beyond the best place for you where you'll have golden chains and shiny coats and you riding upon hunters with the ladies of the land?" (4.115). The only idea of the grand life Shawn has is derived from impressions of the Anglo-Irish landowning class hunting to hounds, so it is this image that he projects out to a (for him) purely notional "Western States." The title "playboy of the western world" has a gestural largeness that defies precise definition, taking in the literal reference to the West of Ireland and overlapping with the awareness of the western continent beyond the ocean.

North, south, east, and west swim beyond the consciousness of Synge's characters as regions of the mind created from hearsay knowledge, fantasy, and folklore. The "east" is a counter for certain sorts of remote or exotic activities regardless of actual geography. The "eastern world," *an domhan thoir,* in Irish folklore is traditionally the place of adventure and wonder.[6] So, in the guessing-game as to Christy's crime in the early scenes of *The Playboy,* it is conjectured that he had joined other nationalists to fight against England in the Boer War: "Were you off east, young fellow, fighting bloody wars for Kruger and the freedom of the Boers?" (4.71). Pegeen is disappointed at the tameness of what Christy tells her of his former life: "And I thinking you should have been living the like of a king of Norway or the Eastern world?" (4.83). In the line which (literally) brought the house down on the night of the first production of *The Playboy,* Christy refuses Widow Quin's offer of his choice of sweethearts "from Binghamstown [= An Geata Mor] unto the plain of Meath." "It's Pegeen I'm seeking only, and what'd I care if you brought me a drift of chosen females, standing in their shifts itself maybe, from this place to the Eastern World" (4.167).

Similarly with the south. In *The Well of the Saints* Martin Doul, for so many years blind but now disillusioned with his regained sight, dreams of a land elsewhere in the distant counties of Cork and Kerry: "I've heard tell there are lands beyond in Cahir Iveraghig and the Reeks of Cork with warm sun in them, and fine light in the sky" (3.115). It is to this southern erotic haven that he invites the beautiful young Molly Byrne to elope with him: "Let you come on now, I'm saying, to the lands of Iveragh and the Reeks of Cork, where you won't set down the width of your two feet and not be crushing fine flowers, and making sweet smells in the air" (3.117). Molly rejects him scornfully, he goes blind again, but it is to a modified version of this imagined south that he goes out with his wife, Mary, in defiance of the persecution of the people: "we're going on the two of us to the towns of the south, where the people will have kind voices maybe, and we won't know their bad looks or their villainy at all" (3.149). The brutal dismissal with which Timmy the Smith greets their exit is comparably vague: "There's a power of deep rivers with floods in them where you do have to be lepping the stones and you going to the south, so I'm thinking the two of them will be drowned together in a short while, surely" (3.151). Real roads, specific rivers, and actual destinations hardly come into this on either side; the aspiration toward a putative south and the ill-will of the imagined deaths are both figurative and felt to be figurative.

The real, the local, and the immediate live in unselfconscious proximity to the imagined and the mythic in Synge's characters' sense of place. Look back at Pegeen's "radiant lady with droves of bullocks on the plains of Meath, and herself bedizened in the diamond jewelleries of Pharaoh's ma" (4.155). The "droves of bullocks" are there as ironic counterpart to the "drift of heifers" which Shawn has just reminded them he has to offer as dowry. The plains of Meath, the rich grazing county on the opposite, eastern side of Ireland from the desperately poor land of Mayo, are appropriately antithetical. But the grandeur of the diamond jewelleries and the wild exoticism of "Pharaoh's ma" (the Scriptures? Nefertiti?) are flights way beyond anything conceivably real. Time/space categories are collapsed or elided in the characters' speech. Christy, thinking that Pegeen has turned against him in act 2, resolves that "it'd be best, maybe, I went on wandering like Esau or Cain and Abel on the sides of Neifin or the Erris plain" (4.109). We can see what brings Esau to mind, deprived of his birthright, and Cain, doomed to banishment east of Eden; but Cain *and* Abel? Unless the ghost of Abel tags along with Cain, they must presumably come in together as a fixed unit, CainandAbel, from Christy's aural memory of sermons, which would have been his main source of scriptural knowledge. The construction of the simile leaves these figures of the Pentateuch wandering around the actual North Mayo countryside with the desolate Christy Mahon.

The mental mapping of Synge's characters goes beyond sublunar geography toward an imagination of Heaven and Hell. Christy fervently implores Widow Quin to help him win Pegeen at the end of act 2, with promises of prayers in recompense: "I'll be asking God to stretch a hand to you in the hour of death, and lead you short cuts through the Meadows of Ease, and up the floor of Heaven to the Footstool of the Virgin's Son" (4.131). Such baroque phrasing no doubt derives plausibly enough from the florid language of Catholic prayer. But the "short cuts" represent the domesticating countryman's touch. Even in Heaven, Christy is sure, if you know someone well-disposed who is a native of the place, you can be shown a shortcut. Christy's most elaborate imagination of Heaven comes in his famous image of Helen of Troy in act 3 of the play. In the love duet with Pegeen, Christy pictures her in an assured future of their love together: "If the mitred bishops seen you that time, they'd be the like of the holy prophets, I'm thinking, do be straining the bars of Paradise to lay eyes on the Lady Helen of Troy, and she abroad pacing back and forward with a nosegay in her golden shawl" (4.149). In Synge, sexual attractiveness is often measured in terms of the desires of celibate male frustration; here the envy of an imagined bench of bishops contemplating the beauty of Pegeen is projected up to the holy prophets in Paradise. But notice that in this afterlife, the Christian heaven is next door to the Elysian fields, in which the Lady Helen of Troy walks; and the ascetic denizens of Heaven are imprisoned there, raging for the sensual liberty which Helen enjoys. Through the wild indecorum of Christy's vernacular geography of Heaven, Synge exposes and subverts the traditional opposition of classical Hellenism to the revealed religion of Judeo-Christianity.

What audience is implied in Synge's plays and from what vantage point do they watch? It is not an audience of local people, as I said earlier. For such people it would be bewildering that the characters of the Wicklow plays should refer to unreal places, Rathvanna and Ballinacree, as well as real ones, or that Michael James should refer to the Kerry Stooks of the Dead Women as a landmark of the Belmullet peninsula. Synge needed an imagination of place and setting, and quite a precise one, as the starting point for his drama, but he did not have to make it correspond in detail to an actual location. Many of the references to place in the plays are designed to render the convincing sense of characters inhabiting a small, known, and limited area. An audience is encouraged to believe in the imagined glen of *The Shadow,* the island of *Riders,* the remote coastland of *The Playboy* as real places. These places, though, both are and are not Glenmalure, Inishmaan, Belmullet. They call up the realities of these real areas as the supporting signs for the fictive spaces they actually are.

In the Aran Islands of *Riders* the world of the island is distinguished from the "big world." The implied audience of Synge's plays is of the big world looking in at the otherness of the staged lives. The characters of the plays imagine outward, from what is known and familiar in their immediate surroundings, through the middle distances of hearsay report, to the more purely fantastic spaces of eastern and western worlds, Heaven and Hell. The audience perspective on this is necessarily an outside one, based on a wider and more orthodox geography or cosmology. We cannot enjoy the wild imagination of the "radiant lady on the plains of Meath" unless we have some sense of the unlikelihood of her being "bedizened with the diamond jewelleries of Pharaoh's ma." If we had no awareness of the heterodoxy of Helen's classical Elysium bordering the prophets' Paradise, the subversive power of the image would be lost on us. The imagination of the people in Synge's plays is freed up to construct the world differently, overriding normal distinctions of space and time so that Esau, Cain, *and* Abel may seem to people Neifin and the Erris plain. The experience of that freedom as freedom is only available to those who ordinarily observe such distinctions as normal, for whom this is a different construction of the world from their own.

There is a difficulty here, and it is a difficulty related to the problems caused by Synge's remarks about the chink in the floor. Is the world of Synge's plays not overlooked, just as his dialogue in this eavesdropping vignette seemed to be merely overheard? Is there not a patronizing inauthenticity in a folk drama which postulates a sophisticated audience looking in on the folk it dramatizes? I think that is the risk Synge's work runs, the reason why not only the original hypersensitive Abbey audiences reacted so violently against what they thought of as a travesty of Irish life, but why, down the years, many intelligent and discriminating Irish people have remained uneasy with Synge. Synge's plays *are* imagined from the outside rather than the inside of the communities he represents. And yet the success of the plays, for those of us who feel their success, rests on the way their creation of reality can impose itself upon us in reading or in the theater. This is not, finally, a realist art; its aim is not to reproduce the actualities of life in Wicklow or Mayo or the Aran Islands. But life in those places did give rise to the experience of the plays and gives them much of their realized specificity. Beyond that, Synge's characters exist within situations vivified by their (and his) imagination of the world, a world all the more imaginatively vivid for its unlikeness to that occupied by the audiences addressed.

Notes

1. This, and all other quotations from Synge, are taken from J. M. Synge, *Collected Works,* ed. Robin Skelton (Oxford: Oxford University Press, 1962–68): vol. 1, *Poems,* ed. Robin Skelton; vol. 2, *Prose,* ed. Alan Price; vols. 3 and 4, *Plays,* books 1 and 2, ed. Ann Saddlemyer. References are given parenthetically in the text.

2. See W. G. Fay and Catherine Carswell, *The Fays of the Abbey Theatre* (London: Rich and Cowan, 1935), 139.

3. See my essay "Synge and Wicklow," in *Wicklow: History and Society,* ed. Ken Hannigan and William Nolan (Dublin: Geography Publications, 1994), 713.

4. There are places called Ballynacree in Counties Antrim, Meath, Tipperary, and Wexford, but none in Wicklow: see *Townlands Index* (Dublin: H. M. Stationery Office, 1904).

5. There is a Killakee in County Dublin, but no Killakeen listed in the *Townlands Index.*

6. I am very grateful to Dr. Angela Bourke of the Department of Irish, University College, Dublin, for this and other related information.

Mallarmé and English

FRANÇOISE MELTZER

Until the 1950s, most French textbook anthologies of literature introduced the "Symbolist" poet Stéphane Mallarmé as a writer who had failed. The main reason for such a judgment is Mallarmé himself: the poet had always promised to produce his famous "le Livre," in which poetry, poetics, literary genres, and language were to be radically rethought. In fact, he imagined his Book as a rethinking of thought itself. Even the typography and the book as a material object were to be reinvented (it was to open, for example, in four different ways). Le Livre was to be the culmination of Mallarmé's art; indeed, everything else was merely a preface, a type of prelude to the great symphony the Livre was to comprise. As early as 1867, Mallarmé conceived the notion of this great Work (as he initially called it). To his friend Eugène Lefébure he wrote, "Yesterday I finished my first outline of the Work, clearly delineated and totally endurable, if I myself endure. I contemplated it quite calmly and without any horror, and, closing my eyes, *I saw that it existed*."[1] What Mallarmé wanted to produce was, as his biographer Gordon Millan puts it, "something modern which could stand comparison with the masterpieces of the Classical Age and the Renaissance."[2] Basing himself on an article he had read in the *Revue des Deux Mondes,* Mallarmé believed that two great masterpieces had been produced in Western civilization: the Venus de Milo, which he saw as classical or pre-Christian, and the Mona Lisa, which was Christian. His own work, both "modern" and post-Christian, was to be the third.

For David Grene, who may believe, with Mallarmé, that the only language in which to write great modern poetry is English.

Mallarmé was twenty-five when he wrote these courageous (and pretentious) words to Lefébure; they clearly demonstrate the belief the young man had in his own gifts. The Work is "totally endurable" and will exist so long as he himself endures long enough to produce it. The Work's "existence" here, then, depends upon that of Mallarmé; it is in him.

Nearly twenty years later, the poet Paul Verlaine asked Mallarmé to write an autobiographical entry for his series *Les hommes d'aujourd'hui*. In his self-portrait, Mallarmé speaks for the first time publicly about the Work (he writes constantly about it in his correspondence throughout his career), which has now become "le Livre." The Book's "existence," however, has changed in nature, as has the poet's self-confidence (although the latter is not evident in this carefully construed public self-image):

What am I talking about? It is very hard to explain. A book, quite simply, in many volumes, a book which is truly a book, structured and premeditated, and not a mere collection of random acts of inspiration, even if they were marvelous. . . . I will go further, I will say: the Book, persuaded as I am that there is only one, which has been attempted whether they knew it or not by anybody who has ever written, including men of genius.[3]

In other words, every poet is trying somehow to capture what is already there, what *already* exists. Indeed, "The Orphic explanation of the Earth . . . is the sole task of the poet and the supreme literary game."[4] Like Orpheus, then, the poet is doomed to an impossible mission, unable to look directly at what he must uncover although he is always somehow in its realm and haunted by its presence. A few months later, writing to Vittorio Pica, Mallarmé is even clearer about the pervasive existence and yet hermetically coded aspect of the Book:

A Book which is an explanation of Man able to satisfy our greatest dreams. I believe that all of this is written in Nature in such a way that only those who are not interested in looking at things cannot see it. This work exists. Everyone has attempted it without realizing it. There is no genius or fool who has not discovered some part of it, albeit unknowingly. To demonstrate this and thus lift a corner of the veil of what just such a poem can be is, in my isolation, my joy and my torture.[5]

The Book's "existence" is now permanent, transcending time and the individual poet, since it is written in nature. In Mallarmé's verse, the Book is often elided with the absolute. Like the blue sky (in the famous poem "L'azur"), the Book seems to mock the poet by making its presence, and its inaccessibility, constantly evident. Hence, for example, the window is a predominant image in Mallarmé's work: as in looking through a pane of glass, the poet's vision can glimpse what is beyond but is simultaneously confronted with a transparent but ineluctable obstacle.

Mallarmé's view of the elusive but ever-present nature of the absolute is somewhat reminiscent of Proust's belief in the Celtic notion: that souls are captured in nature, and it is up to chance whether or not we are able to recover them. But if for Proust such a recovery is based on random events (the famous involuntary memory), for Mallarmé such a recapturing of the Book involves intense mental effort, even torture. The randomness is based, not on sensory events as in Proust, but rather on the mysterious and cruel workings of fate, on what he was later to call a throw of the dice.

We have come a long way from Mallarmé's initial conviction, twenty years before, that he would produce the Book if he could "endure"; that it was all there in his mind waiting to be written. Now the Book, every-where and yet as elusive as Eurydice, has been sensed and even partially captured by every writer of every talent and capacity. Mallarmé himself will be satisfied if he can lift merely "a corner of the veil."

Although there are still "men of genius" for him, Mallarmé has shifted from seeing himself as a genius to hoping that his erratic genius will visit him. In a move directly opposite to the change in the meaning of the word "genius" between the sixteenth and nineteenth centuries, Mallarmé sees himself as having genius, rather than being one.

Clearly, he set himself up for failure. The nature of the project is so vast, so abstract, not to mention impossible, that he is unable even to articulate it except by constant recourse to metaphor. Indeed, among other ideas at stake in the Book is the very origin of literature: "I believe," he writes in the same letter to Pica, "that Literature, rediscovering its origins which are a combination of Art and Science, will provide us with a Theater whose performances will be the truly modern religious celebra-tion." It is worth remembering here that Descartes had nearly identical views on literature, based on the third of his famous dreams. In that dream, as Descartes's obsequious biographer Adrien Baillet tells us (1691), the philosopher sees a dictionary on the table and then an anthology of poems entitled *Corpus Poetarum*. Two poems by Ausonius are involved, one is "Quod Vitae Sectabor Iter?" and the other, "Est et Non." Baillet tells us how Descartes interprets his own dream:

He judged that the dictionary represented all the sciences gathered together; and that the anthology of poems ... indicated ... Philosophy and Wisdom joined together. For he believed one shouldn't be much surprised to see that the poets, even those who fool their time away, have many maxims that are deeper, more sensible, and better expressed than those found in the writings of philosophers. He attributed this wonder to the divinity of Enthusiasm and the force of Imagination, which emitted the seeds of Wisdom (found in the minds of all men, like the sparks of fire in flintstones) with much more ease and brilliance than even Reason can do among the philosophers.[6]

Ausonius's poem on which way of life to choose is, Descartes decides, the wise path of "Moral Theology," and the "Est et Non" are the "Truth and Falsehood in human knowledge and the secular sciences"—the yes and no of Pythagoras. These must be combined to achieve an "admirable science."

My point in going into the Descartes text is threefold. The first purpose is simply to note how strangely close Mallarmé's project is in tenor and vision to that of the famous philosopher. Descartes's interpretation of his dream could have been penned by Mallarmé: he, too, believed that poets could seize truth and profundity more fully than philosophers and scientists armed with "Reason." He, too, believed that poetry and reason could join to form an "admirable science." Finally, Mallarmé (precisely one of those poets "who fool their time away") was equally convinced that the poet's secret is "Enthusiasm" (which Mallarmé, basing himself on the works of Poe, calls "sensation," whereas Descartes is using the term in a sense closer to that of Socrates). Descartes's metaphor would strike a chord in Mallarmé as well: enthusiasm and the imagination emit the seeds of wisdom, which are found in the minds of all men "like the sparks of fire in flintstones." The organic vocabulary (seeds, flintstones, fire) emphasizes the ubiquity and potential development of wisdom. The poet has the tools to uncover it, but frequently, as Descartes suggests, he is unable to explain the means of his own discovery. Once again, we return to Orpheus, who can only find what he is seeking by never looking at it directly. Orpheus, then, becomes the metaphor for metaphor itself—and for modern poetry (in Mallarmé's sense).

The second purpose I have in mentioning Descartes is to point out that when language such as that used by both writers (which is, as I have said, very similar in tone, vocabulary and tenor) comes from a great philosopher, rather than a poet, there is a curious tendency to see it as less pretentious, less ambitious, even less ridiculous. Descartes is arguably a greater philosopher than Mallarmé was a poet, and he did produce the Method based on his visions. Mallarmé never produced the Book he envisaged; but his poetry is motivated in every line by the conception he had of his larger project. The cause of this inequity of evaluation has,

I think, to do with a third point, and that is the valence of the term "reason."

Descartes thinks that the poet frequently has more wisdom precisely because he is motivated by enthusiasm rather than reason. This pre-Pascalian moment is echoed by Mallarmé. In between, of course, comes the Enlightenment, which makes reason into the intellectual raison d'être of all thought. In a move that makes him more postmodern than modern, Mallarmé is trying to imagine a modernity freed from the shackles of empiricism and positivism (which permeated, after all, his age). If we see, as David Tracy has argued, modernity as the repression of the discoveries of the sixteenth and seventeenth centuries, Mallarmé's "modernity," as distinct even from that of Baudelaire (we will return to this point), can be seen as a return to the more radical modernity of Descartes. Indeed, Mallarmé's insistence that language is inadequate to express what he so passionately felt was "*poésie pure*" and his determination to depict "not the thing, but the effect it produces" (partially inspired by Poe), are what Descartes intuitively understood to be the gift of the real poet. It is, I would argue, the legacy of the Enlightenment that makes us judge such language as almost pathetic in a poet such as Mallarmé and as provocative and profound in Descartes. Tied as we are (still) to the *product,* Mallarmé is seen as one who did not deliver; determined as we are (still) by reason, philosophers are somehow less suspect than poets, especially when a seminal work follows—even if it is based on a dream.

My point here is not to pass judgment on one or the other of these writers, or to hierarchize them, but rather to indicate the kind of thinking in which we almost unwittingly engage when confronted with a poetics as against a "method." Until the late fifties, as I noted earlier, Mallarmé was seen as a failure because he did not produce what he promised, and his abstract prose describing the indescribable (to echo the German Romantics) was seen as obscure and confused. As Millan points out, at the time of Mallarmé's death, "Outside the literary and artistic circles of Paris many of his countrymen had never heard of him, and few had ever read a line of his poetry." Even today, he is seen by most people as "the epitome of the obscure" and as an "unnecessarily difficult writer."[7]

At the end of the fifties, however, and culminating in the sixties and seventies, Mallarmé was seized upon by some major writers who were later to be dubbed "postmodern." Blanchot, Derrida, De Man, Kristeva, to name the most obvious, all began working on Mallarmé *because* his work is unfinished, fragmented, and obsessed with writing about writing. Derrida, for example, will analyze Mallarmé's notion of mimesis and show that it is identical to that of Plato (but not "platonic"). These traits in the poet resonated with the attempt to free thought from the Enlightenment, to demonstrate how close and indeed blurred the line between poetry and philosophy has always been, to show how what has been viewed as marginal (correspondence, notes, unpublished material) is often as significant as what passes for central—indeed, as in the case of Mallarmé, sometimes more central. Mallarmé for these writers becomes postmodernity par excellence, the writer who always writes about the impossibility of writing, who is more concerned with process than product, whose writing is uncontained by any notion of textual sovereignty, and whose wisdom does not look to reason as equivalent to understanding.

The problem here is that these writers necessarily concentrate on Mallarmé's theory of poetry rather than on his poems (except for the late, highly experimental, and unfinished ones, especially "Un coup de dès" and "Igitur"). Millan notes that this bias has in turn generated another view of Mallarmé as a failure: "This excessive emphasis upon the unfinished works, or at any rate on those which he himself felt unable to publish, has in turn meant that in most people's minds Mallarmé is now clearly identified with the notion of failure."[8] Mallarmé's idea of the "modern," then, is appropriated by postmodernism as an early version of its own agenda. As such, Mallarmé's "failure" is celebrated as a demonstration of the crisis in language, the limits of a poetry robbed of transcendence—the inevitable consequences of a post-Kantian age.[9] But for "most people" (to return to Millan's phrase) it is still a failure.

Mallarmé, too, saw himself as something of a failure, and this for two reasons. The first is personal: he judged himself to be hopelessly indolent, depressed, paralyzed by the overwhelming possibilities of the infamous "white page." Writing itself was torture; indeed, the only thing more painful for him than writing was not writing. He once complained, to his friend Henri Cazalis, that as a schoolboy he used to write reams of pages at the least provocation. Increasingly, however, writing became painful and daunting. Over and over again Mallarmé writes to his friends about his depression, his inability to work. Here is one of hundreds of such examples:

I am in a cruel position. The mundane things of this life seem too vague to me to take any pleasure in them and I only feel alive when I am writing poetry. Therefore I am bored because I am not working. On the other hand, I am not working because I am bored. How can I escape from all this?[10]

Despite occasional years of great productivity, the agony of writing was never to abate in him. Mallarmé becomes the poet who writes of the horror of not being able to create, who fills pages with descriptions of the blankness and whiteness of his paralysis. Small wonder, then, that contemporary critics, fascinated as they are with the liminal edge between thought and writing, should turn with increasing interest to Mallarmé.

Added to his chronic depression (which was not helped by his admiration for Poe) were Mallarmé's continual financial problems. It is well known that he chose to become a teacher of English because it offered him time off for writing. It is equally established that his spoken English was terrible and that he was never interested in teaching the high-school classes he was assigned or in living in the provinces where the schools to which he was posted happened to be located. Unlike many writers who were also teachers (Simone Weil, for example), Mallarmé rarely, if ever, writes of a brilliant student. On the other hand, once he returned to Paris (1871), he had many disciples (such as Paul Valéry) whose work he read scrupulously and whom he taught and helped. But the towns of Tournon, Avignon, and Besançon, where he worked (in "exile," as he saw it, from Paris) from 1863 until 1871 filled him with horror. In all of Mallarmé's verse, autumn is a time of deep sadness—not only because of the obvious hints of winter but more significantly because autumn signals a return to the classroom. Teaching, the necessary evil of earning a living, was an obstacle to writing.

Nevertheless it is important to remember that Mallarmé chose to teach English. His entire life was caught up in what he considered to be the great wealth and history of that language. Although his greatest influences came from Baudelaire and Poe (the latter because of the former), he loved, among others, Shakespeare, Milton, Byron, Shelley, Whitman, and Keats. He was equally in admiration of earlier English literature: Chaucer and *Piers Plowman* are frequently cited with great admiration. He knew and studied Wyclif's Bible.

Mallarmé often translated English works to make money, but not only for that reason. His love of Poe was such that he translated a good portion of his work even though Baudelaire had already done so. He produced an edition of "The Raven" (a poem that obsessed him, as much for its poetics as explained by Poe in "The Philosophy of Composition" as for its verses) with illustrations by his great friend Edouard Manet. Mallarmé's work *Les dieux antiques* is a loose translation of George Cox's *Mythology*. He spent time in London and befriended many contemporary writers and essayists, lectured at Oxford and Cambridge, and wrote of the British scene for French journals and of the Parisian scene for British ones (in particular, the "Gossips" for Arthur O'Shaughnessy's *The Athenaeum*). He wrote a long article defending Manet and Impressionism in general to the British, which remains one of the best essays on the subject. He also undertook the writing of a philological textbook on the history of the English language, which resulted in the small volume *Les mots anglais* (published by Truchy in 1877).

Mallarmé agreed to this last project because he needed money. He did not consider *Les mots anglais* part of his oeuvre; indeed, in the auto-biographical entry he wrote for Verlaine, he specifically asked that it be omitted from his list of publications (along with the Cox translation). He only published it, he insists, to assuage his financial difficulties.[11]

Previously (before the recent interest in Mallarmé already men-tioned), this work was duly regarded as being of little import to Mallarmé scholars; they agreed with Mallarmé himself that a philological textbook on the English language was of no great concern to Mallarmé studies. As early as 1927, however, two critics argued that the source of the entire Mallarméan aesthetic was to be found in *Les mots anglais* (Monda and Montel). While I do not subscribe to such an extreme view, I do think that this work has a lot to tell us, not only about Mallarmé's ideas on poetry, but specifically on the role that English played in his notion of "*poésie pure.*"

The major point argued in *Les mots anglais* is that English, unlike French, has retained all of the etymologies of the languages that have fashioned it. It contains the "seeds of barbarism" and the "legacy of antiq-uity"—that is, English is both "gothic" and classical because it is the com-bination of Anglo-Saxon and *langue d'oïl* (itself the melding of Latin and Greek). French, on the other hand, underwent a kind of forced cleansing, with the sixteenth-century Pléiade. The Pléiade's insistence on a standard-ized orthography and on the use only of words with Latinate etymologies was a mixed blessing, since it stripped the French language of the cross-breeding which characterizes English. (Mallarmé also mentions the pres-ence in English of Hebrew, Arabic, Ethiopian, Syrian, Chaldean, Asiatic languages, Germanic, and so on.)

Perhaps because it is an island, muses Mallarmé, England has a lan-guage which has progressed by amalgamation rather than exclusion. It has then, by virtue of its history, a doubled lexical wealth to draw upon. As a result, he continues, contemporary English in turn reflects the double aspect of the era (which for Mallarmé is modernity): it is both retrospec-tive and future oriented, and this is its genius. It is also what makes a Shakespeare possible, and a Chaucer (whom, it should be noted, Mal-larmé sees as "moderns"). Unlike French, the Anglo-French duality at the heart of the English language allows for a linguistic trait which Mallarmé considers fundamental to extraordinary writing: the ability to state the same thought with two synonyms which do not share a common root. "Example," writes Mallarmé: "Act and deed, head and chief, mirth and jollity, steedes [sic] and palfreys."[12]

This doubled texture of English, he adds, has produced "one of the most exquisite forms of style in modern English poetry." It comes from "placing a noun between two adjectives," so that the noun is surrounded by this dual aspect of the language. His example, which is one of his most beloved sentences in all of literature, comes from Chaucer: "I see the woeful day fatal come."

"Fatal" verges on the adverbial here, but the point is well taken: here is a richness of expression impossible in French. Here is a language actually "othering" itself, as the two synonyms both mirror their meaning and, by virtue of their divergent etymological histories, are in contrast to each other as well, thus strengthening both the power of the sentence and its resonance. This "double treasure" is one from which all great English writers have benefited, writes Mallarmé, citing Milton, Shelley, and Byron as examples and, above all, Shakespeare. Unlike the French, none of these authors was "tempted by a misguided patriotism to separate the barbaric element from the classical, that is to say, French."[13] Rather, the English have cultivated "two plants which have produced, without hesitation, a fraternal and magnificent vegetation on the same stalk."[14] And although most European languages carry the vestiges of Greek and, more recently, German, Italian, and Spanish as well, for Mallarmé there is no other language thus double-stalked as is English; no other language that can reinforce and twin its meaning through the intimate juxtaposition of two contrasting linguistic histories.

Thus, English allows for a type of defamiliarization, almost in Freud's sense of the uncanny: that which is most familiar and yet long hidden or repressed. *Les mots anglais* shares another trait with Freud's essay on the uncanny: it too is rife with etymological "demonstrations" which are frequently tenuous and sometimes simply wrong. But as with Freud's essay, despite its questionable philology, *Les mots anglais* contains a wealth of information frequently unrelated to the apparent thrust of the text.

In any case, it is clear, as I have tried to show, that the way in which English is enriched by a double heritage allows (at least in Mallarmé's eyes) for a kind of "othering" in its expression. This was precisely what Mallarmé wanted to do in French but, because of the nature of that language, was unable to accomplish. Mallarmé's constant laments about the inadequacy of language as a whole to convey the subtlety of the poet's thought is perhaps less a condemnation of language itself (although it is certainly partly that) than it is a complaint against the French language, impoverished as it has been by its sixteenth-century scouring.

It was partly in an attempt to emulate English, I think, that Mallarmé willfully made use of neologisms, syntactic abnormalities, and archaisms. He wanted language to be defamiliarized in order to emphasize its limits. Mallarmé agreed with Poe that music was the greatest art because it moves us to "glories beyond the grave"—that is, music, unlike language, does not have the baggage of material referents to be passed through in order to get at the idea. A language that can repeat an idea by recourse to a different etymology allows for emphasis on the idea rather than the thing. This, it will be recalled, is what Mallarmé meant by "*poésie pure,*" and this is what English does naturally. Moreover, English is consequently much richer in abstract nouns; and abstraction is what Mallarmé is all about.

Those who accuse Mallarmé of being willfully obscure are right. The reason, however, is not merely a penchant for hermeticism to be decoded only by the "happy few," as Stendhal put it. Mallarmé is also trying to render the French language strange, to make it foreign. He is attempting, in other words, to imitate what lurks in the English language, what its native speakers themselves do not recognize as strange: its otherness to itself. Since French does not enjoy a dual etymology, and since it is impoverished in synonyms for abstractions, Mallarmé can only perform the strangeness through syntactical gymnastics, archaic words, and neologisms.

Let us take an example from his particularly difficult poem "Hérodiade." Part of one line reads "*la Rougeur de ce Temps prophétique.*" What happens here is that the subject of the phrase, redness, already an abstraction unconnected to any form or object, is modified by an even less concrete notion, time. The noun "time" in turn is modified by the abstract adjective, "prophetic." The result is that while the syntax promises specification, it produces metaphors of increasingly conceptual tenor. In fact, "time" is sandwiched between "redness" (Latin) and "prophetic" (Greek), not unlike "woeful" and "fatal" encasing "day" in Chaucer's "I see the woeful day fatal come." The difference, of course, is that "*rougeur*" and "*prophétique*" do not suggest the same meaning, because French cannot do that. Poetically, however, the effect is similar: the noun is modified by contrasting but resonating notions which empower the idea—here, of gathering doom. The whole of the phrase then accumulates (almost in Longinus's sense) a redness which suffuses the entire image. Thus it is not surprising that Mallarmé turns to color words as abstract nouns with such frequency. To give another example: his famous "whiteness of the page" insists upon an abstract referent in which the initially more concrete "page" dissolves. The "whiteness" is as much a performance of Mallarmé's poetics, then, as the obsession with the impossibility of writing (as it is usually read).

Another reason that Mallarmé's poetry has such recourse to color is linked to the issue of sixteenth-century cleansing. The strict controls exerted over the language extended to *bienséance* in linguistic as well as social decorum. Bald color words were largely barred from the lexicon (with some exceptions). Thus, when Mallarmé repeats the word "*l'Azur*" in the poem by the same name, he is also creating a shock effect for the French reader. Since color words were never restricted in English poetry, the effect cannot be the same for the reader of that language. Here is one of the reasons, then, for Mallarmé's legendary nontranslatability: what rings new and even radical to the French ear simply falls flat to the English one.

So, too, Mallarmé plays with the French reader by combining a distinctly Corneillian tone with "modern" poetic disjunctions. The nurse says to Hérodiade, for example: "*Pardon! L'âge effaçait, reine, votre défense / de mon esprit pâli comme un vieux livre ou noir.*" The first part of the line could be Corneille. The second, with its "paled mind" compared to an old or black book, not only throws the reader off guard but also, with its simile of the book, echoes Chaucer again: "*vieux*" and "*noir*" are both from Latin, but their odd placement (again, encasing the noun) simultaneously emphasizes their contrasting meanings and allows for an overall cumulative effect of the catachresis. The paled mind is like an old, black book. Although "paled" also means "faded" here, the effect is nevertheless a contrast of white and black forced into a conceptual alliance. Moreover, the nurse, portrayed by these few words as old, narrow, and darkened, is in further contrast to Hérodiade, who describes herself consistently in words having to do with sterility, ice, virginity, and whiteness. She becomes the horror of the pure white page—all consciousness—against which the nurse is the lesser, and therefore blackened (unburdened by hyperconsciousness), page of the traditional poet.

Hérodiade's description of herself reads like Mallarmé's experience of writing: "*Oui, c'est pour moi, pour moi, que je fleuris, déserte!*" Or, in a line which alludes to Baudelaire but goes much farther, "*J'aime l'horreur d'être vierge et je veux / Vivre parmi l'effroi que me font mes cheveux / . . . Nuit blanche de glaçons et de neige cruelle!*" ("*Nuit blanche*" repeats the black/white catachresis of the pale, black book. The phrase also means, in French, a sleepless night, thus underlining incapacity and frustration.) This paralysis, as if the poet were caught in ice, will become explicit in the famous swan sonnet, "*Le vierge, le vivace et le bel aujourd'hui,*" which, again echoing Baudelaire, goes farther: the swan *dreams* of dreaming of a voyage. Baudelaire's voyages are enjoyable fantasies; Mallarmé is much less sanguine about the outcome. If Baudelaire's albatross is unable to walk because of his huge wings, at least it can soar. Mallarmé's birds cannot even fly.

Even in an early poem such as "Brise marine" (1865), which is usually viewed as overly derivative of Baudelaire, the poet sings of a voyage of escape ("Anywhere out of the world," as Baudelaire puts it) but he is already aware of the futility of the undertaking. Unlike Baudelaire, with his chimeric boats heavy with the exotic goods of the Orient, Mallarmé fears that his vessel will end up mastless, adrift, even shipwrecked. Nevertheless, with the complete knowledge of the hopelessness of the journey, he hears the song of the sailors: "*Mais, ô mon coeur, entends le chant des matelots!*" Again, catachresis: with Mallarmé, the sailors become the sirens. But if the poem is suffused with Baudelairean "*ennui,*" it is specific to writing: "*ni la clarté déserte de ma lampe / sur le vide papier que la blancheur défend.*" It is an ennui, moreover, which still believes in "*l'adieu suprème des mouchoirs.*" As with Kafka (with whom he shares not a little), it is always already too late with Mallarmé.

English haunts the poems of Mallarmé much like the watermark of which he writes lurks in the page, creating a white on white that emphasizes the futility and yet necessity of writing for him. That is, English becomes the possibility of escape, of fresh air ("*brise marine*"); simultaneously, it is a forlorn hope that comes (like Mallarmé's English itself) too late.

One of the manuscripts found after the poet's death was a notebook called "Les thèmes anglais." It consisted of two hundred pages of English idioms, parables, quotations, and so on. Clearly, Mallarmé acquired through tremendous effort a reading and writing knowledge of English. He knew its philological history, its linguistic roots, its syntactical configurations, its grammar. But he could never speak it—indeed, he was incomprehensible. In a way, English is like an analogue of Mallarmé's Book because, like that notion, it is his constant, tireless project and yet unfinished and a failure. As such, English is Mallarmé's proof of the existence of pure poetry and of thc hopelessness of attaining it because of the limits of the mind. Quite aware that he was consumed by that which nourished him, Mallarmé needed both to know English, in order to imagine and believe in a better linguistic habitat for the poet; and not to know it, in order to make of defamiliarization a tool for a new, modern poetry.

Notes

1. 27 May 1867, Bibliothèque Doucet, Mondor Bequest MNR Ma 558. In deference to David Grene, notes will be kept at a minimum.

2. Gordon Millan, *A Throw of the Dice: The Life of Stéphane Mallarmé* (New York: Farrar, Strauss, Giroux, 1994), 158.

3. Stéphane Mallarmé, *Oeuvres completes,* ed. Henri Mondor and G. Jean-Aubry (Paris: Gallimard, 1961), 662–63.

4. Ibid., 252–53.

5. Ibid.

6. Adrien Baillet, *La vie de Monsieur Descartes,* 2 vols. (Paris, 1691), 1:80.

7. Millan, *A Throw of the Dice,* 1.

8. Ibid., 2.

9. I am thinking here specifically of the first *Critique of Pure Reason,* which created waves of angst in Europe that are hard for us to imagine today (e.g., Kleist's famous "*Kantkrise*," which was not in the least unusual at the time).

10. To Frederic Mistral, 30 Dec. 1864, *Mallarmé correspondance: Lettres sur la poésie,* ed. Bertrand Marchal (Paris: Gallimard, 1995), 217.

11. *Oeuvres completes,* 1643.

12. Ibid., 913.

13. Ibid., 914.

14. Ibid., 915.

T. S. Eliot as Religious Thinker: *Four Quartets*

DAVID TRACY

Introduction: The Conflict of Interpretation on Eliot

The conflict of interpretations on T. S. Eliot has reached an impasse. The first reception of Eliot as poet, critic, and thinker during his lifetime was one kind of exaggeration. Practically everything he then said (no matter how confused or foolish) was either explained away or placed on tablets of stone for further "New Critical" reflection. The present widespread rejection of Eliot is just as exaggerated: every foolish act, every obnoxious opinion (even if later repudiated), is taken as the signal clue to his person and his work. What is lost in all this conflict is the poetry itself, that is, the one reality that should concentrate any reader's attention, the one phenomenon that made Eliot one of the greatest poets of our century. The poetry, not the criticism, not the private person, is what most needs new modes of reflection, new openness, new readings. Otherwise it will be lost in the contemporary conflict of ideological interpretations, from which there can seem no honorable exit for any thinker or poet, like Eliot, who believed in and tried to show another dimension to reality (sometimes called a religious or spiritual dimension). That dimension is, to be sure, implied in but never reducible to the ideologies affecting it.

Eliot's critical writings, however uninteresting and sometimes wrong-headed, are not the key to the one great mystery of Eliot: the greatness

This paper, originally delivered at Northwestern University, is the result of a course I had the honor to teach with David Grene.

of his poetry—its range from *Prufrock* through the *Quartets;* its multiple voices; its auditory genius; its effortless ability to reach beyond all one's views about T. S. Eliot the man and the former opinion-maker. In my judgment anyone with an ear for the peculiar, plural rhythms of the English language cannot reject that poetry. Anyone with any taste at all for a poetics of the spirit in the twentieth century, a century so tentative and restless, senses the integrity of the spiritual and philosophical aspects of Eliot's poetry. His best thinking is not in his criticism at all (although some small part of that remains very good indeed). Eliot's best thinking is in his poetry. It *is* the poetry.

It is impossible to understand Lucretius as the great poet-philosopher he is without knowing how to unite his full-fledged materialism to the journey of the Epicurean way. It is impossible to understand Dante without sensing something of the highly rational and formal spirituality of his version of medieval Christianity. It is equally impossible to understand T. S. Eliot without some sense of how his spiritual vision (at once Christian and Buddhist) does not close in upon itself at all into a narrow dogmatic view of religion and culture (as do some of his essays). Rather, Eliot's poetry opens up into a grounded spiritual vision of great multiplicity, subtlety, and tentativeness. Not to understand how materialism can be an integral view of all reality is not to understand either the poetry or the thought (more exactly, the poetry as thought) of Lucretius (whom Eliot, it should be recalled, greatly admired). To understand only materialism as a view of life is to hinder one's understanding of Dante, Eliot, and many others. In any case we impoverish our experience foolishly under some rubric of what constitutes the really real—the one word, as Nabokov insisted, that should always be used in quotation marks. Eliot came to fruition as a poet and thinker in *Four Quartets*. There we find how twentieth-century poetics of the spirit informed—indeed, transformed—by an enormous range of Western and non-Western religious and philosophical ideas can be rendered plausible for any honest and open mind. In the poetry is Eliot's integrity.

There is need, therefore, to reconsider what kind of religious thinker T. S. Eliot actually was. This need can be pressing, since so many of Eliot's interpreters and, more unfortunately, some of his own more doctrinal essays have contributed to a reading of him as a conservative Christian apologist—more complex and subtle in his strategies and thoughts than C. S. Lewis, to be sure, but in the same kind of Christian doctrinal and apologetic tradition. No matter that Lewis and Eliot both resisted this reading of their common Christian stance: it has become a commonplace both of Eliot's critics and of some of Lewis's admirers.[1] Within the negative, Eliot has also been read as a finer, more subtle, less comically paradoxical Christian apologetic thinker than G. K. Chesterton, with his aggressive version of Christian thought. Eliot strongly resisted Chesterton's traditional and joyful reading of Christianity, just as Chesterton always maintained a wide distance from Eliot's far too modernist and too bleak version.

My own belief, which I share with other readers, is that in Eliot's greatest poetry, *Four Quartets,* his position as a religious thinker was not a version of Christian apologetics at all but something quite other. Indeed the *Quartets,* although as deeply Christian in sensibility as they are exceptionally musical even for Eliot's often praised auditory imagination, render a version of religious thought that is often closer to ancient Neoplatonism, at times even to Buddhism, than it is to Christian orthodoxy. The final vision of the *Quartets*—the vision of annunciation and incarnation—is profoundly Christian. But if we go outside the poetic framework, the form of that Christian thought, in its amazing Platonic vision of God as the impersonal God, bears more resemblance to that other great and troubling Christian thinker contemporary to Eliot—Simone Weil—than it does to either Chesterton or Lewis. More puzzling still is its dissimilarity to the arbitrarily other T. S. Eliot of some of the early, pointedly polemical essays—especially the often reprehensible and exclusionary *After Strange Gods* (1934) or even the more inclusive but too apologetic visions of *The Idea of a Christian Society* (1939), or *Thoughts after Lambeth* (1931).

We have then, no small puzzle: the most famous explicitly Christian poet in Anglo-American literature since Gerard Manley Hopkins is not what many critics or admirers or, perhaps, Eliot himself believed that he was. In my judgment, Eliot (in the *Quartets* specifically, but not in the essays and not even in that other lesser great poem *Ash Wednesday*) presents something richer, stronger, indeed altogether more unsettling for any thoughtful reader than most interpretations of his religious thought suggest.

To call the poet Eliot a thinker is not to deny his insistence that his mentor Dante taught him to find spatial forms for time and to make words "sensuous embodiments" of ideas.[2] The *Quartets,* more than any other of his poems or plays, realize this poetically. Dante also taught Eliot how to see poetry not as a replacement for intellection (including doctrines as abstract summaries of thought) but as an aid for any reader or listener. In other words, Eliot, through Dante's example, could lead his audience to feel and even realize what believing some doctrine or abstract thought is like within the mind and/or spirit. This almost tactile, experiential knowledge is indeed pure Eliot—and, to be sure, an all-important aspect of

Dante himself. There are, however, certain other realities to be understood if one is to sense how Eliot in the *Quartets,* without ever breaking Dante's basic rubrics, freed both himself and his readers not only to *feel* thought but to think *through* his poetry.

The first reality is from both Dante and Donne: meditative poetry (as distinct from such devotional poetry as that of George Herbert) helps the poet to render and the reader/listener to sense how poetry can evoke abstract thought once it finds an appropriate poetic form (as in Dante's pictorial form; as in the *Quartets'* musical form). For Eliot, Dante had the good fortune to write before the modern dissociation of sensibility, that is, before the split between feeling and thought, with which Eliot (here joining many countermoderns and postmoderns alike) charged modernity.[3]

The second rubric for understanding Eliot's poetry as religious thought is his reading of what a poet can do once the modern split had occurred. Recall his recovery of a poetics of detachment and impersonality, his affirmation of the metaphysical poets and the French symbolists and modernists (his two principal modern poetic models, just as Dante was his great premodern mentor). For Eliot, metaphysical poetry famously "elevates sense for a moment to regions ordinarily attainable only by abstract thought." That is exactly what devotional poetry never does for Eliot but what the *Quartets* enact for any alert reader. To be sure, Eliot learned from Mallarmé that poetry could never replace the absence of mystical experience nor the thought attendant to that experience. However, by evoking a feeling of that absence and by provoking the feelings that abstract religious thought allows (including the abstractions of the fourteenth-century English mystics) Eliot, as both poet and religious thinker, went as far as any twentieth-century poet in the English-speaking world has ever done to evoke and provoke both ancient and new, both Eastern and Western religious spiritual thinking.

Ash Wednesday is the great poem of traditional Christian imagery and thought. However, the *Quartets* are something else again. No little of their power lies not only in their wondrously musical rhythms and leitmotivs and their brilliant Dantesque use of words and images as sensuous embodiments of often highly abstract thoughts on time, history, and eternity but in their odd, puzzling, unsettling, often untraditional but eminently thoughtful religious vision. To understand Eliot's thought as religious thought more fully I propose the following strategy. First, I shall recall how, in "Burnt Norton," notes of religious thinking enter which, although not unfamiliar to Christian orthodoxy, are marginal—even destabilizing—toward orthodox belief. In the final section, I shall try to articulate more directly the form Eliot's thought takes.

The moment in the rose garden of Burnt Norton is the first and perhaps the central of the many "unattended moments" (as Eliot will name them in "The Dry Salvages") in the *Quartets*. These moments of intuition of another dimension to time happen in and out of time: timeless intuitions of temporal reality which can be recollected only in time.

It is striking that the central imagery of the entire passage in the rose garden is, through and through, Buddhist, not Christian. One cannot but recall that Eliot, as a young man, almost became Buddhist save, as he later recalled "for reasons practical and sentimental." In terms of an explicit religious way Eliot became a deeply committed Anglican Christian but without ever losing this sense of the genius and importance of Buddhism for any serious contemporary spiritual way. The subtle undertow of a kind of Buddhist transformation of consciousness that often pervades Eliot's poetry, although rarely his critical prose, is present in the marvelous imagery of the rose-garden scene in "Burnt Norton": the lotus, the clouds, the emptiness of the pool. These images function not as direct Buddhist source or influence (like the Fire Sermon in *The Waste Land*) but as something far more important: a central vision, in keeping with Mahayana Buddhist teaching on formlessness and form—the heart of reality as transience. Buddhism, after all, is the only religion or philosophy in which what is construed as the central problem for humankind (the transience of all reality) is also understood to be the central religious solution for all those who will cease clinging and let go into the emptiness-fullness-transience of reality. Most of us cannot. "Humankind cannot bear very much reality." But there are always such moments as those in the rose garden of Burnt Norton, as well as many other unattended moments, to help us recall this other spiritual dimension of reality.

As Cleo McNelly Kearns persuasively argues,[4] Buddhism, for Eliot, was less a set of teachings than an extremely subtle method of transformation of consciousness which shifted all perception by its highly refined sense of how consciousness is transfigured by proper attention to the particulars of all experience—especially all unexpected, initially unattended experiences like that in the rose garden with the cloud and the full/empty pool. The imagery and the words, I suggest, are worthy of a fine Zen Buddhist haiku and help one to sense through close attention, awareness, awakeness, how the clarifying, dissolving forms in the poem display the thought that reality is emptiness *(sunyata)*. Eliot's nice use of Buddhist ways not only of dissolving images but even language can be seen in the syntactic difficulty a reader has in asserting whether the pool is empty or full, the unclarity in the exact subject-verb-object structure of the sequence, the indefiniteness of all fixed identities ("they") in the scene. The startling power of Buddhist practices, its suspicion of all false consolations (including any ordinary Christian understanding of God) as illusions to which we compulsively cling: all this is rendered through the fine imagery of the first full manifestation of nonbeing in the rose garden in "Burnt Norton." The rose may be the rose of Dante's *Paradiso,* the children in the trees may be the dead/alive children of Kipling's lovely story "They"— but the voice here is the voice of the Buddha.

This Buddhist teaching of the spiritual practice of attention to "this here now," rather than particular Buddhist teachings on nonbeing or suchness, I am convinced, is what most attracted Eliot to Buddhist practices and doctrines. Moreover, Eliot found very precise images to entice any attentive reader to this awareness. Eliot's "still point of the turning world" passage in "Burnt Norton" is in harmony with Buddhist teaching on nonbeing but suggestive through its new imagery of a different philosophical-spiritual vision of reality: the Heraclitean "coincidence of opposites" disclosed in the quotations from Heraclitus that introduce "Burnt Norton," as well as Eliot's nice transformation of the Mallarmé image ("Garlic and sapphires in the mud") to begin the next movement after the "still point" passage. Indeed, only in this long movement of the poem does one reach the central image of "Burnt Norton" and perhaps of the entire *Quartets:* the still point of the turning world.[5]

Eliot's imagery here cannot but alert the reader to new thought when philosophically and theologically construed through the careful imagery. The image strictly speaking bears neither Buddhist nor Christian overtones, although it could cohere with some versions of both. Eliot's still point is not here strictly Buddhist (as the earlier imagery of emptiness suggests to some commentators). In fact there is a clear non-Buddhist insistence in Eliot (as in classical Platonism) on an ordered determinateness: order, balance, the ordered reconciliation of opposites. This Heraclitean-Platonic image still holds but now in a more explicitly ordered whole far more reminiscent of the role of form in Neoplatonism than of a Buddhist sense of radical indeterminacy, nonbeing, emptiness.

Another reader—especially one aware of the explicitly Christian language of *Ash Wednesday,* the doctrinal orthodoxy of Eliot's essays, and, within the *Quartets* themselves, the pervasive Christian sensibility and imagery culminating in the explicit language of "the hint half guessed, the gift half understood, is Incarnation"—would surely not be foolish to read the image of the still point in Christian theological terms. Not foolish, but not quite right either. Here, the impersonality of the image itself makes one hesitate to interpret the still point in explicitly Christian terms. Indeed the still point—this abstract spiritual center outside the self and history—seems to be a strictly impersonal reality, one from which emanates all movement and pattern. The still point is, to be sure, the source of all energy, pattern, and movement, where opposites are reconciled (as in Heraclitus and most Neoplatonism). What the image is not is personal—like the Jewish, Christian, or Islamic personal God.

I do not claim, of course, that this impersonal center, this still point of Eliot, cannot be reconciled with some understanding of the Christian God. (The Christian Neoplatonists, in their various ways, attempted exactly that.) But in "Burnt Norton" no such reconciliation occurs. As do Iris Murdoch in her Platonized Buddhism and Simone Weil in her Platonized Christianity,[6] Eliot in "Burnt Norton" distances himself from all conventional concepts of personal deity and, perhaps, from orthodox Christianity's personal categories for ultimate reality. Thus does Eliot of the *Quartets* leave the Eliot of the controversial essays on Christianity far behind to join himself to the tradition of marginal Christian Platonist thinkers from Dionysius through Eckhart. This Platonic legacy is intensified rather than lessened when Eliot turns to the more explicitly Christian images of the later *Quartets,* for all the *Quartets* are pervaded by moments displaying an Eliotic religion of manifestation and meditation. Even history—the religiously empowered heart of prophetic Judaism and Christianity—becomes, for Eliot, a manifestation of "a pattern of timeless moments." In the later *Quartets* ("Little Gidding" V) Eliot's religious thought, in its now explicitly Christian form, sometimes transforms itself into some vision just as puzzling and radical as that pervading the central images of "Burnt Norton" (the Buddhist imagery of the lotus and the pool and the Heraclitean-Platonist imagery of the still point).

Eliot's Religious Imagination: Manifestation and Meditation

There are various ways to make useful distinctions among the most basic forms of religious expression.[7] When one is attempting to highlight the reality of the participation of human beings in the cosmos and, in Jewish and Christian faith, in relationship to God and history, the most basic distinction is that between religion as manifestation and religion as proclamation.

Religion as manifestation signifies the sense of radical participation of any person in the cosmos and in whatever is construed as the divine reality.

A sense of God's radical immanence in both cosmos and self is as strong as, indeed, the sense of the felt relationship of self, nature, and the divine. This sense of religion as manifestation is in sharp contrast to religion as proclamation. In the latter case (and the three great prophetic and monotheistic traditions of Judaism, Christianity, and Islam are all proclamation traditions at their religious heart) a sense of God's transcendent power is also a source of the divine disclosure as principally in history, not nature. Indeed, the proclamation traditions introduced a new sense of distance between God and human beings and a strong sense of an interruption of the once powerful, indeed fundamental sense of belonging to or radical participation in the cosmos.

In my judgment, the most intriguing aspect of Eliot's Christian view (in his poetry far more than in his prose) is how Eliot's "religion as manifestation" instincts affect even his Christian view of history. In some of his best prose Eliot displays a characteristically prophetic (i.e., proclamation) view of history—as in his fine essay on Joyce where, prophetlike, he denounces contemporary history as "the immense panorama of futility and anarchy."[8] Moreover, throughout the *Quartets*—especially but not solely in the third movement of each quartet (except "Little Gidding")— Eliot continues the imagery of *The Waste Land* on history as chaotic, anarchic, and possibly futile. And yet the *Quartets* as a whole (which, after all, clearly bear the marks of the cataclysmic events of World War II, including Eliot's own activities as a warden during the London Blitz) show a more manifestation-oriented understanding of religion, and even of history. It is not merely that the Western, indeed Eurasian cultural tradition becomes more unified and ordered for Eliot in the *Quartets;* neither the fragmented vision of *The Waste Land* nor the narrow orthodoxy of such essays as *After Strange Gods,* which displays a shameful, exclusionary, even anti- Semitic view of history, prevails.[9] Rather, in the *Quartets,* history (now seen in the context of the still point) becomes manifestation, that is, history as a pattern of timeless moments.

This is clearly the case in the powerful Dantesque history-as-manifestation imagery of "Little Gidding" (especially the familiar compound-ghost of the fourth movement of "Little Gidding," which brilliantly unites Dante's *Purgatorio,* the London Blitz, and a great deal of English literary history). History is manifestation in both "East Coker" and "The Dry Salvages." In "East Coker," Eliot's personal time of a visit to this "sacred" place becomes the manifestation time of both solar time (the cycle of the seasons) and the biological time of a single human life. Time also becomes historical time, in which all cultures and movements rise and decay, the centuries pass, and, in memory *sub specie aeternitatis,* all historical actors and actions unite in a new sense of history. Charles I and Milton, the experiment of Little Coker, Eliot's own English ancestors, and Eliot himself in his pilgrimage to East Coker: all now yield, at the last, not to the conflicts of their own historical moment but to the rhythm and stillness of history as a pattern of timeless moments in time. Moreover, in "The Dry Salvages," the archaic religious imagery displays another form of religion as manifestation, as well as Eliot's personal American history: the river as "within" the Mississippi of his St. Louis childhood, the sea all "around" us, and the sea of the New England summers of his youth. All these realities—indeed all history—in the *Quartets* is not finally Jewish-Christian prophetic proclamation (although that is real in *The Waste Land* and remains real at times even in the *Quartets,* especially in the third movements of the first three *Quartets*). In the *Quartets,* history becomes manifestations of timeless moments in time. In our beginning is our end. In our end is our beginning.

Of course the sense of participation in nature does not die in prophetic traditions, as the Jewish liturgical year, the Christian sacraments, and Islamic ritual make clear. However, the prophetic traditions, with their strong sense of God's transcendence allied to the powerful prophetic sense of an ethical responsibility to resist evil and face historical suffering, have their own ways of responding to evil, suffering, and hope (including straightforwardly ethical-political ways), as Eliot's essays *The Idea of a Christian Society* (1939) and *Notes Towards the Definition of Culture* (1948) argued in largely prophetic, not meditative, terms.

Many indigenous traditions, however, have never lost the earlier religious sense of radical participation in nature and the cosmos. Those traditions—once named "pagan" by Jews, Christian, and Muslims—return to haunt the conscience, the always ethical conscience of the prophetic, proclamation-oriented traditions, as they so brilliantly do in Eliot's imagery of the peasants "dancing around the bonfire" in the first movement of "East Coker" or the wondrous archaic image of the river as "a strong brown god—sullen, untamed and intractable" of the first movement of "The Dry Salvages."

Indeed it is difficult to overemphasize the importance of such a sense of what I can only name a felt synthesis of the human, cosmic, and divine realms for most ancients and medieval thinkers and, seemingly, for the Eliot of the *Quartets.* I agree fully with Louis Dupré in *Passage to Modernity*[10] that the most important and widely overlooked consequence of modernity (which he persuasively dates as beginning as early as the nominalist

crisis of the fourteenth century and the humanist developments of the
fifteenth century) is the breakup of both the ancient and the medieval
senses of a synthesis of God, self, and cosmos.

Clearly all ancient and even most Jewish, Christian, and Islamic un-
derstandings of what I here call a felt synthesis of God, cosmos, and self
are principally religious expressions of participatory manifestation, not
disruptive proclamation. The ancients may indeed have had a sense of
cosmos that encompassed an understanding of the divine realm (the gods,
even Zeus and Jupiter) as well as the human realm now understood as
microcosmos and of human reason as a *logos* participating in both the cosmic
and the divine realms. The ancient syntheses (notice again how the *Quartets* begin with Heraclitus) were, one and all, felt syntheses of the intrinsic
relationality of the cosmos, the divine, and the self. Those syntheses were
grounded in various forms of religion as manifestation, that is, in a sense
of our radical participation in the cosmos.

Eliot saw clearly that the monotheistic traditions changed but never
broke this ancient "pagan" sense of felt synthesis and intrinsic relationality
among God, self, and cosmos and radical participation of the self in the
cosmos and in God. The Christian doctrine of redemption and its focus
on evil, suffering, and transformation do not prevail in the *Quartets* (as
they do in *The Waste Land*). Here again following his principal mentor,
Dante, Eliot sees both the patristic and medieval periods (even aspects of
Augustine) as being dominated by reflection not on redemption but on
creation. How could any radically monotheistic tradition with its doctrine
of a Creator God assume the continuance, in a new, transformed configuration, of a synthesis of God, self, and cosmos? Here was the great challenge of patristic and medieval thinkers. On the whole, they never lost a
sense of radical participation and ordered relationship—the sense I called
above a sense of the felt synthesis of God, self, and cosmos.

Especially through Platonic resources, the medievals (even the cham-
pions of Aristotle like Aquinas) managed to maintain God's radical immanence in nature and humanity without loss of God's transcendence. Recall, for example, the subtlety of medieval discussions not only of efficient
causes but of formal and final causes as well. Recall, above all, how reason
(logos) for the Christian thinkers like Anselm or Aquinas—and Augustine
before them—was never equivalent to modern rationality. Reason for the
ancients and medievals was ordinarily understood (and, it seems clear,
experienced) as radically participatory in the cosmic and divine (note Eliot's brilliant use of Heraclitus on the common *logos* of all humanity at the
very beginning of the *Quartets*). For most patristic and medieval theologians human being—including human reason as participatory *logos*—was

still *microcosmos* (as for the ancients) and now also *imago dei* for the Christian. Reason was a profoundly participatory reality related to God, cosmos, and self. This patristic and medieval sense was kept alive in Eliot's Anglo-Catholic tradition, a Christian tradition centered on manifestation and meditation, sacrament, liturgy, and high culture.

Modernity changed all this. No synthesis—neither ancient nor medieval—any longer held. As modernity advanced in its more scientific seventeenth-century form and, even more so, its more reified eighteenth-century form, the sense of any radical participation of humanity in an increasingly mechanized cosmos failed. Ancient *logos* and medieval *ratio* became modern rationality. According to Eliot, in one of his most famous formulations, the late-seventeenth-century "dissociation of sensibility" (i.e., the separation of feeling and thought) set in. The medieval synthesis, of course, could not hold. Each element was split away and forced to function increasingly on its own. Cosmos became nature, and science adopted a dominating attitude toward it (Eliot, even in his period under the influence of Bertrand Russell, always distrusted scientism). God withdrew from the synthesis into ever greater transcendence and hiddenness. The self was divested of its former state as *microcosmos* and possessed increasingly vague memories of its reality as *imago dei*. The self became ever more purely autonomous and isolated from any sense of radical participation in the cosmos or a radical felt relationship to God as creator. Ancient and medieval reason-as-*logos* was cut off from any participatory sense with the cosmos and the divine and was relegated to a narrower and narrower range of what would count as rational and thereby real.

Consider, for example, the relative narrowness of most modern debates on rational approaches to God (i.e., what becomes the conflict of the "isms"): deism, modern theism and atheism, modern pantheism, and panentheism. Whoever had the best set of rationally endorsed abstract propositions backed by a modern form of argument could be taken seriously—and no one else. It is no surprise that modernity's first major innovation here was the explicitly nonparticipatory notion of the God-self-world relationship named deism. It is not that modernity was simply a disaster on this crucial issue of reason as participatory in the cosmos and the divine. But consider the difficulties. First, thought now lived by understanding itself, as not merely distinguished from but separate from feeling and experience (again, Eliot's "dissociation of sensibility"). Theological rationality often separated itself from religious sentiment and communal religious experience,[11] hence the import for Eliot of those forms of early modern religion which resisted this separation: the communal experiment of East Coker or Donne's metaphysical poetry. Second, the only form considered appropriate to developing a modern theology was the form of modern theory: analytical definitions, rigorous argument, and, as the theologian-philosopher Bernard Lonergan said of some of the modern neo-Scholastic manualists, clear and distinct ideas and very few of them. No other forms—certainly not the laments, the songs, the narratives of suffering peoples, premodern forms uniting spirituality and theology, the experiment with form of the great modernists, or scriptural forms themselves—were adequate, on this reading, for a genuine theology. Neither Dostoyevsky nor Dante, neither the biblical Ruth nor Job, need apply. They possessed the wrong form for modern thought. Third, explicitly spiritual exercises—especially those developed by, for example, Irenaeus or Augustine to help transform the mind and cleanse the vision in order to understand suffering, evil, hope, and God—no longer found a place in the functioning of modern philosophical and theological rationality. At its worst, modernity bequeathed us a mechanistic notion of the cosmos, a dominating attitude toward nature, and an ever more narrow notion of rationality, culminating in positivism, an increasingly autonomous self become a possessive individualism, and a deistic God: a warm kind of deism, perhaps, but deism all the same. The prospects for any kind of modern theology that agreed with these aspects of modernity were not promising. For T. S. Eliot, unlike many "modern" Christian liberal apologists, the once emancipatory hopes of modernity were now clearly spent.

For Eliot, modern thought at its best (e.g., that of F. H. Bradley) made us realize that there is no turning back, in hopeless and intellectually helpless nostalgia, to a simple retrieval of any of the syntheses of the ancients or the medievals. Eliot was never, for example, a neo-Thomist philosophically. The achievements of modernity—in science and technology, in democratic politics and cultural pluralism—should not be denied and should be defended. And Eliot did defend them: not always, to be sure, but at his most lucid and best moments. Eliot knew that any response that religious thought today may achieve can only be sought by moving through, not around, modernity. Eliot always remained a literary modernist. He never joined C. S. Lewis or G. K. Chesterton but continued with the great modernists (Joyce, Woolf, Proust) as they attempted to articulate some new hope: Joyce's "epiphany," Woolf's "luminous moments," Proust's "involuntary memories," and Eliot's own splendid "unattended moments." These moments, he shows, evoke attentiveness and offer some alternative to the fired remains of modernity, even if that alternative proves merely some "fragments to shore up against our ruin."

Philosophy and Theology as Ways of Vision and Ways of Life

The most fragmented of the many fragments Eliot found to shore against his own ruin was the modern self. For modern culture the self serves, at one and the same time, as the most privileged and the most fragmented of realities. The modern self's privilege also becomes its cul-de-sac; after the collapse of the ancient and medieval syntheses, all culture for Eliot suffered a dissociation of sensibility whose chief victim was the fragmented self of the modern sensibility. Not only was feeling separated from thought but so, too, was form from content, and practice from theory. Eliot's Harvard professors William James and Josiah Royce were exceptions on the separation of practice and theory, just as Eliot's dissertation subject, F. H. Bradley, with his holistic Hegelianism and stylistic philosophy, was an exception to the separations of feeling from thought and form from philosophical content.[12] Indeed, as some critics have surmised, it may well have been that Eliot's own philosophical position was what today would be named hermeneutical pragmatism.

I do not believe that, as a religious philosopher, Eliot would have been helped much by contemporary hermeneutics and a revisionary pragmatism. Eliot's problem with philosophy lies deeper: like Kierkegaard or Nietzsche, everything in him resisted the professionalization of philosophy in the modern academy. He had no hesitation in embracing the professionalization of banking without ever abandoning his multifaceted sociopolitical critique of the cultural leveling imposed by modern capitalism. Like most of us, Eliot acknowledged that banking must be professionalized to function well. He was, from all reports, a good banker. And yet Eliot resisted, with all the considerable cultural power he possessed in his lifetime, the professionalization of modern philosophy. He never resisted a philosophical insistence on precision, care, and conceptual clarity in either modern analytical philosophy (he greatly admired that side of Bertrand Russell's logical atomism) or Aristotle, Aquinas, and all good forms of modern Scholasticism, like Jacques Maritain's. Eliot believed, as the ancients did, that philosophy was as much a way of life as a way of thought. The professionalization of philosophy enforced the latter as a modern academic discipline and let the former live at best an underground life occasionally surfacing as a new modern "ism," as in the existentialism contemporary to Eliot.

Eliot wanted a philosophy as a vision of life that could unite feeling and thought again (Bradley) but render that union in realized ideas as poetry (Dante, the metaphysicals, the "objective correlative"). He wanted all this, moreover, in a manner that also reunited theory and practice, including such specific practices as the kinds of "spiritual exercises" that had become so central a part of his personal life. Instinctively he turned to Plato, Lucretius, Dante, Donne. Expansively, Eliot turned quite naturally to the "whole" Eurasian cultural context, ancient and modern, as he recalled his earlier scholarly immersion in Buddhism and Hinduism and his more recent study of archaic traditions by means of anthropology and history of religions, as well his acquaintance with the Christian mystics from John of the Cross to Julian of Norwich.

If Eliot were working now he would surely have discovered such work as that of Pierre Hadot on ancient philosophy as a way of life.[13] Like Michel Foucault, who also insisted that the modern self is at once privileged and fragmented by the modern cultural regime, Eliot would have welcomed Hadot's erudite studies of how all ancient philosophers (Stoic, Epicurean, Aristotelian, Platonist, Skeptic, Cynic) practiced spiritual exercises[14] in direct and correlative relationship to their theories. Not until modernity did Western philosophy split theory from such spiritual practices. Only in Western modernity did philosophy help reinforce the fragmentation of the modern self allied to the related split of form from content (the systematic treatise replaced the philosophical dialogue) and feeling from thought (feeling became merely private and emotivist).

This detour into Hadot's work is worth recalling, I believe, if we care to understand Eliot's philosophical and theological achievement in the *Quartets*. It is not just that he shows one, as his mentor Dante did, how it feels to believe a particular religious doctrine. He also incorporates in the *Quartets* very diverse traditions of spiritual exercises (Buddhist, Hindu, Christian, archaic, secular) to reunite spiritual practice and philosophical, theological thought and, thereby, help his reader realize ideas by showing how philosophy-theology is both a vision of life and a way of life. Each spiritual and philosophical way demands rigorous and constant awareness, self-vigilance, and self-discipline (exercises particularly encouraged by both ancient Stoicism and Eliot's own Puritan and Unitarian heritage). Classical Christian doctrines (like "annunciation" and "incarnation") are present in the *Quartets* not for apologetic reasons but to suggest how the Christian incarnational-sacramental vision is experienced as both a felt idea and a disciplined way of life. Eliot insisted throughout the *Quartets* on a center outside the self: in everyday glimpses of another dimension to reality; in unattended moments; in the still point; in the deeply impersonal imagery of Eliot's Buddhist, Hindu, Platonist, and even Christian mystical resources. Indeed, every one of the central images from "Burnt Norton" through "Little Gidding" frees the attentive reader/listener to see and feel many different forms of philosophy-theology as both a plausible vision of life and a way of life. The "still point of the turning world" and "the hint half guessed, the gift half understood, is Incarnation" are, in the *Quartets,* not one but, as Buddhists say, perhaps not two either. Multiplicity of the religious vision, not exclusivity, reigns.

The central and pervasive exercise of the *Quartets,* however, is not to be found even in such crucial spiritual exercises as Buddhist detachment or Christian *caritas.* Eliot displays both detachment and *caritas* as visions of life and ways of life through all the marvelous musical, visual, and verbal means at his disposal. He tries to manifest the final vision of "Little Gidding"where the Fire and the Rose are one, just as Dante tried to suggest the Christian vision and way of love in the *Paradiso* or just as a classic Japanese Zen haiku displays detachment. And yet the *Quartets* teach yet another lesson: to hope that any of us might experience love and detachment here and now would be "to hope for the wrong thing" ("East Coker" III). Rather, "The only wisdom we can hope to acquire is the wisdom of humility; humility is endless." And humility, for Eliot, in his greatest poetry, as distinct from many of his own rather oracular essays, was the most important spiritual exercise we late arrivals can learn to practice if we too would understand and experience classical philosophies and religions at all, that is, a spiritual dimension to life.

In the *Quartets,* and there alone, Eliot forged a meditative poetry worthy of his beloved Dante. But he achieved it not in the premodern terms of Dante but in the modernist forms of Eliot's own century, at once so frightening and so luminous. After the *Quartets,* Eliot wrote no further major religious and philosophical poetry. For my part, I wish he had also not written any further essays on religion, philosophy, and modern society. Even at their best, the later social-political essays distract and disperse Eliot's best religious thought—his amazing Anglican inclusivity, his moving religious, philosophically expansive, pluralistic range in the *Quartets.* The *Quartets* concentrate one's attention upon the only kind of religious thought that can make some sense to many of us: great artistry evocative of some genuine experience of a spiritual dimension to life united to some philosophy which helps one reflect critically upon and find plausible— however momentarily—the actuality of that other dimension. Heraclitus and the Buddha, Plato and Dante, communicate all this. So too does T. S. Eliot in the wondrous power of *Four Quartets.*

Notes

1. Inter alia, see Alzina Stone Dale, *T. S. Eliot, The Philosopher Poet* (Wheaton: Harold Shaw Publishers, 1988).

2. "Dante" (1929), in T. S. Eliot, *Selected Essays: New Edition* (New York: Harcourt, Brace, and World), 199–241.

3. "The Metaphysical Poets," in ibid., 247–48.

4. See Cleo McNelly Kearns, *T. S. Eliot and Indic Traditions: A Study in Poetry and Belief* (Cambridge: Cambridge University Press, 1987); Cleo McNelly Kearns, "Religion, Literature, and Society in the Work of T. S. Eliot," in *The Cambridge Companion to T. S. Eliot,* ed. A. David Moody (Cambridge: Cambridge University Press, 1994), 77–94. Here, as throughout these reflections, I am indebted to Kearns as well as to several other commentators, especially the sensitive and erudite commentary of Derek Traversi, *T. S. Eliot: The Longer Poems* (New York: Harcourt Brace, 1976), 85–215; A. David Moody, *Thomas Stearns Eliot, Poet* (Cambridge: Cambridge University Press, 1979), 203–64; Helen Gardner, *The Art of T. S. Eliot* (New York: Dutton, 1959); Helen Gardner, *The Composition of "Four Quartets"* (New York: Oxford University Press, 1978).

5. Besides Traversi, *T. S. Eliot: The Longer Poems,* see also Ethel F. Cornwell, *The "Still Point"* (New Brunswick: Rutgers University Press, 1962), 17–64.

6. Iris Murdoch, *Metaphysics as a Guide to Morals* (London: Penguin, 1993), esp. 80–90, 461–92; Miklos Veto, *The Religious Metaphysics of Simone Weil* (Albany: State University of New York Press, 1994). A study is needed of the possible influence of Weil on Eliot here.

7. I have clarified and defended these distinctions in writing elsewhere, especially David Tracy, *The Analogical Imagination* (New York: Crossroad, 1985), and *Dialogue with the Other* (Louvain: Peeters Press, 1990).

8. T. S. Eliot, "Ulysses, Order and Myth" (1923), in *Selected Prose of T. S. Eliot,* ed. Frank Kermode (New York: Farrar, Straus and Giroux, 1975), 177.

9. It is true that Eliot never allowed *After Strange Gods* to be republished. It remains, nonetheless, a disgraceful performance—especially because of what can only be called its anti-Semitism. I agree fully with Cynthia Ozick's melancholy conclusion that "it is now our unsparing obligation to disdain the reactionary Eliot," in "T. S. Eliot at 101," *New Yorker,* 10 Nov. 1989, 154. On the debate on this troubling issue, see also Christopher Ricks, *T. S. Eliot and Prejudice* (London: Faber, 1988); Peter Dale Scott, "The Social Critic and His Discontents," in *Cambridge Companion to T. S. Eliot,* 60–77.

10. Louis Dupré, *Passage to Modernity* (New Haven: Yale University Press, 1994). I should note that the interpretations of modernity in this section of the text are my own interpretations of contemporary, post-Eliot debates on modernity, especially but not solely Dupré's. I believe this reading of the problematic of modernity to be in harmony with Eliot's reflections but it is not his own. I have also noted in the text those places where I am explicitly interpreting Eliot himself on modernity.

11. Michael Buckley, *At the Origins of Modern Atheism* (New Haven: Yale University Press, 1990).

12. On Eliot's philosophy, see the helpful study by Jeffrey Peal, *Skepticism and Modern Enmity* (Baltimore: Johns Hopkins University Press, 1989); see also Richard Shusterman, "Eliot as Philosopher," in *Cambridge Companion to T. S. Eliot,* 31–48.

13. Pierre Hadot, *Philosophy as Way of Life,* ed. and with an introduction by Arnold Davidson (Oxford: Blackwell, 1995).

14. Ibid., 79–145.

Rousseau on Providence

VICTOR GOUREVITCH

Kant held that Newton and Rousseau revealed the ways of Providence: "After Newton and Rousseau, God is justified, and Pope's thesis is henceforth true."[1]

Rousseau discussed Providence and Pope's thesis that "Whatever is, is right" most fully in a long letter that he wrote to Voltaire in 1756, about a year after the publication of the *Second Discourse* (1755) and at a time when he is likely also to have done work on the *Essay on the Origin of Languages.* These three writings, together with the Replies that he drafted to the criticisms of the *Discourse,* are also closely related in theme: in them Rousseau explores the natural order and man's place in it.[2] The *Discourse* is the only one of these writings the publication of which Rousseau himself initiated. The *Letter to Voltaire* differs from the other writings in this group by discussing man's place in the natural world in theological terms. Indeed, it is the only record we have of a theological discussion which Rousseau freely initiated with a near-equal, "a friend of the truth speaking to a Philosopher" [2]. Still, he clearly did not think of it as an entirely private discussion. He allowed a few copies of the letter he sent to Voltaire to circulate, and its unauthorized publication, some years later, cannot have taken him completely by surprise.[3] None of his numerous other discussions of religious issues are addressed to a near-equal or to a philosopher; most of them are public; some are frankly apologetic; others are carried on by characters of his invention, and, as he repeatedly points out, the reader is therefore not free to attribute to him the views which they express; in his last writing, he goes so far as to embed what little he says

For David Grene, the man, the teacher, the thinker, in lasting affection and gratitude.

about his religious views in a discussion of lying, and even in that context he says of them only that they are "more or less" the same as those which he had Emile's tutor attribute to the Savoyard Vicar.[4]

The immediate occasion for the *Letter to Voltaire* was a small booklet Rousseau received in early 1756, made up of two didactic poems by Voltaire, a *Poem on Natural Law*, written in 1751/1752, and a *Poem about the Lisbon Disaster*, written just a few months after the devastating earthquake which struck Lisbon on Saturday, 1 November, All Saints' Day, 1755. The quake was followed by tidal waves and extensive fires, causing the death of thousands of people and destroying much of the city. The disaster made a deep impression throughout Europe. Even Voltaire writes about it in impassioned tones, and with none of his usual detachment and irony. His *Poem* is a sustained attack on "optimism" or, as its subtitle announces, "the axiom 'All is Well' [or: Good]," Leibniz's thesis that this is the best of all possible worlds, and the thesis of Pope's *Essay on Man* (1733/1734) that "Whatever is, is right."[5] In 1737, the French Jesuit *Journal de Trévoux* had coined the term "optimism" to mock Leibniz's "best [*optimum*] world possible." It mocked "optimism" because, as Voltaire points out in the Preface to his *Poem,* the theologians very correctly saw that the optimists' argument, that this is the best world possible, relegates the Fall, redemption, and salvation to a strictly subordinate role in men's lives. Initially, then, "optimism" referred to a philosophical position, and not, as it does now, to a mood or an attitude; and the context in which it was introduced illustrates how entangled the permanent problem of the origin of evil had become with Christian theology. The discussion of "optimism" revolved around what Locke had called the Reasonableness of Christianity and around the relation between nature and grace. It most prominently engaged Bayle and Leibniz, Fénélon and Bossuet, Malebranche, and Arnault, in addition to innumerable lesser divines and literati. The point at issue between the optimists and their critics was not whether the world is free of evils—no one claimed that it was—but whether it ever could be or have been free of them. The optimists held that it had not been and could not have been. Their critics held that it had or could have been.[6] In 1753 the Royal Academy of Berlin announced as the topic for its 1755 Prize competition a thorough discussion of Pope's thesis, of the relation between it and Leibniz's teaching, and of whether it is tenable or not. The competition was widely perceived as an invitation to write that it is not tenable, for the Academy's president, Pierre Moreau de Maupertuis, had recently published an *Essai de philosophie morale* in which he had claimed to prove that the evils of men's lives outweigh the goods. Bayle had reviewed a number of earlier comparisons between the goods and evils in our lives, especially in his *Dictionnaire* articles "Manichéens" and "Xenophanes"; Leibniz had reviewed some in his *Théodicée* (I, §§12–19; III, §§251–53); and Rousseau had spoken to the issue and alluded to Maupertuis's argument in the *Second Discourse* (I [34] and Note IX [1]); Kant considered entering the competition; Lessing and Mendelssohn wrote— but did not submit—a highly critical analysis of Pope's *Essay* under the ironic title *Pope a Metaphysician!;* and now Voltaire, writing under the impact of the earthquake, makes essentially the same claim Maupertuis had made: life's evils exceed its goods.

Voltaire's *Poem* is not particularly long, no longer than the first of the four Epistles that make up Pope's *Essay.* In form as well as in content, it proceeds on two levels: in form, it is divided into the *Poem* proper, preceded by a prose Preface and followed by occasionally rather extensive Notes; in content, the *Poem* proper is an essentially theologico-moral meditation on divine Providence, while the prose Preface, and especially some of the longer Notes, summarize philosophical-scientific objections to the view that this is the best of all possible worlds. Voltaire leaves it to the reader to establish the connection between the feelings he expresses in the *Poem* proper and the prose arguments he presents in the Preface and the Notes. He does not, himself, integrate them into a clear, coherent whole.

He claims not to want to take issue with Pope ("whom I have always admired and loved") or with the views of Shaftesbury and Bolingbroke and the thought of Leibniz, which, he rightly notes, Pope wove together into the *Essay on Man.* Rather, he claims to want to take issue with the defining tenet of "optimism," "All is well [or: good]," on the grounds that it might encourage "fatalism" and complacency in the face of imperfection and evil, that "*All is well* [or: *good*], taken in an absolute sense and without hope for a future, is simply an insult to the suffering in our life" [8]. His ostensible aim is, then, to reclaim a place for hope. Hope, in this debate, is traditionally understood as hope for personal immortality.[7] He further claims to challenge the optimists' "All is well (or: good)" on the grounds that evil is incompatible with God's being all-good and all-powerful. He thus appears to side with the theologians.

The *Poem* opens with a description of devastation and an outcry at the horror and the injustice of it. How, in the face of such destruction, can the philosophers maintain that "all is well [or good]"? (*Préface* [1], *Poem*, lines 4–5, 122–24). The Lisbon disaster is not a unique occurrence. The threat of death and destruction is a constant refrain throughout the *Poem:*

Eléments, animaux, humains, tout est en guerre.
Il le faut avouer, le mal *est sur la terre.* (Lines 125–26)

Evil(s) *(mal, maux),* in this debate, refers primarily to what was called "physical evil(s)," the evils men suffer rather than the evils they might inflict, foremost among them, death, but also such often great and to all appearances undeserved losses as those of Job, or of the victims of the Lisbon earthquake. Voltaire therefore adds to the traditional list of evils the fact that we find ourselves forced to try to understand what apparently we simply cannot understand.[8] The quest for the origin of evil, in this debate, is the quest for the general, overarching cause(s) of such evil(s).

Voltaire weaves into his *Poem* a brief review of the possible alternatives regarding the origin of evil: Manicheanism, the view that the whole is subject to two principles, one good, the other evil (lines 129–30, 138), which had recently been given renewed currency by Bayle (*Dictionnaire,* especially "Manichéens," "Marcionites," "Pauliciens," "Zoroastre," and the Appendix: "Eclaircissemens sur certaines choses répandues dans ce Dictionnaire" II; cf. Leibniz, *Théodicée* II, §136); the view that evil is divine punishment, either collective, for original sin (line 149), or particular, for the sufferers' individual sins (lines 17–23); the view that evil is a divine trial to determine whether and how much eternal bliss any individual deserves (lines 155–58); the view that evil is the inevitable by-product of the workings of nature's inexorable laws, either because God is indifferent to their workings (lines 150–52, 15–16, 42–44) or because evil is inevitable even in the best of all possible worlds and may therefore be said to contribute to the general good (lines 179, 66–68); and, finally, the view that evil is the by-product of strictly material necessity that is not subject to divine control (lines 153–54).

In this Lisbon *Poem,* Voltaire summarily rejects the first alternative, Manicheanism: "God alone is master" (line 138). The remaining four alternatives naturally form two classes: evils due to human failure or sin, what at the time was called moral evil(s); and evils due to the constraints on the parts of wholes because they are *parts,* what Newton's spokesman Samuel Clarke referred to by the traditional name of "evil(s) of imperfection," and Leibniz called "metaphysical evil(s)."[9]

For all intents and purposes, Voltaire ignores "moral evil." His criticism of "optimism" deals exclusively with what the philosophers called "evil of imperfection" or "metaphysical evil": whether—and in what sense—evil is the necessary consequence of the nature of things. He lists two versions of this alternative: that evil is a necessary consequence of inherent limitations matter imposes on intelligence and will (lines 153–

54); and that evil is the necessary consequence of God's initial decrees and that He lets them run their course:

Sans courroux, sans pitié, tranquille, indifférent. (Line 151)

In the *Poem about the Lisbon Disaster* Voltaire says nothing about the first version of this alternative. He discusses only the second version of the view that evil is the necessary consequence of the nature of things or of necessary laws, namely, that in an order made up of different parts or kinds, each kind must necessarily accommodate to the whole of which it is a part, and that such accommodation manifests itself as physical evil. Each thrives at the partial expense of the others, and the evils that each suffers redound to the others' benefit.[10] For all intents and purposes, this is the only argument Voltaire seriously considers.

He objects to this "metaphysical evil" argument on what might be called moral-theological grounds, and on what might be called philosophical-scientific grounds. He spells out his moral-theological objections in the body of the *Poem,* and he relegates his philosophical-scientific objections to the Notes.

He finds the optimists' necessary laws argument morally and theologically repugnant because it entails that we, as well as the rest of the world, would be less well off if there were no evils.

"Tout est bien, et tout est nécessaire."
Quoi! l'univers entier sans ce gouffre infernal,
Sans engloutir Lisbonne eut-il été plus mal? (Lines 42–44)

It is, further, morally and theologically repugnant because a necessity that visits evils on innocent and guilty alike is unjust and therefore reflects ill on an omnipotent God (lines 173–74).

He also finds the optimists' necessary laws argument ineffectual: necessity is not a consolation, even if our evils do prove to be others' goods.[11] It does not help to be told that the world was not made for us or that to complain is to display pride, or to have Paul rebuke the pot that would ask its potter, "Why hast thou made me thus?" (Romans 9:20–21). This pot is sentient and so, surely, has a right to complain (lines 61, 83–96); and pity for our fellows is, surely, not pride but simply the just claim to be recognized in the eyes of God as worth more than sticks and stones.

C'est l'orgueil, dites vous, l'orgueil séditieux,
Qui prétend qu'étant mal, nous pouvions être mieux. (Lines 35–36)

Quand l'homme ose gémir d'un fléau si terrible,
Il n'est point orgeuilleux, hélas! il est sensible. (Lines 57–58)

In the *Poem* proper, Voltaire maintains that an omnipotent God is not bound by natural or rational necessity and hence could dispose things differently.

Non, ne présentez plus à mon coeur agité
Ces immuables loix de la nécessité,
Cette chaîne des corps, des esprits et des mondes.
O rêves des savants! ô chimères profondes!
Dieu tient en main la chaîne, et n'est point enchaîné;
Par son choix bienfaisant tout est déterminé: (Lines 71–76)

In the lengthy note he appended to this passage, he states his objection in philosophical-scientific, rather than in moral-theological, terms: evils cannot be due to the workings of general laws because, in the realm of nature as well as in the realm of human affairs, the phenomena do not conform to strict laws. In both realms there are "indifferent" phenomena: not all bodies are necessary to the order and preservation of the universe, and not all events make a difference.[12] What is more, even if the phenomena did conform to strict laws, we could not know that they do, because, speaking philosophically, we have no access to first principles (Note to line 210); or, speaking theologically, the unaided human reason cannot fathom God's ways:

La nature est muette, on l'interroge en vain;
On a besoin d'un Dieu qui parle au genre humain. (Lines 162–63)

In short, the world does not conform to the principle of sufficient reason.[13]

Voltaire claims that his review of the alternative accounts of Providence leaves him unable to choose between them and that he therefore follows Bayle, who, scales in hand, teaches doubt but, he adds in a Note, never denies Providence or the immortality of the soul (*Poem*, Preface [10], lines 191–96, and Note to line 192). Neither does Voltaire explicitly deny them. Although the argument of his *Poem* is not particularly rigorous, its ostensible aim is clear enough: to combine a cosmology that allows for some indeterminacy in nature and in conduct with a theology that appears orthodox because it allows for divine intervention in the course of nature.[14] Newton's cosmology appears to allow for such a combination, whereas the optimist Leibniz's cosmology does not.[15] Newton may be a respectable ally against Leibniz, but Voltaire's true model is, as he acknowledges, Bayle. His case against optimism closely parallels Bayle's case for Manicheanism: both argue that the evils which we experience are proof—or at least very strong evidence—that evil is constitutive of the very nature of things; and both do so with intense antiorthodox animus. The *Poem*'s clearly intended effect is the very opposite of its ostensible aim: it leaves the reader under the impression that this is a poem *against* Providence, and Voltaire's protestation to the contrary—"I do not rise up against Providence" (line 222)—only reinforces this impression. For by arguing *both* that there are no theoretical reasons why God cannot intervene in the course of nature *and* that there are strong moral reasons why He should intervene in it at least to the point of sparing the innocent, Voltaire leaves his reader under the impression that God is indifferent, arbitrary, even malicious. In his tragedy *Oedipus,* he attributes to his hero the sentiment Shakespeare attributes to Lear at the nadir of his fortunes: "As flies to wanton boys, are we to the gods; They kill us for their sport." It is the sentiment to which he gives expression throughout the Lisbon poem. He expressed it even more bluntly to Pastor Jacob Vernet: *"de cette affaire* [i.e., *le tremblement de terre de Lisbonne*] *la Providence en a dans le cul."*[16] As for the immortality of the individual soul, the poem that ostensibly sets out to restore the hope for it ends by bitterly and defiantly questioning it.[17] It would seem that the only hope Voltaire holds out is hope for a better, "future," "new order of things" (Preface [8], [10]) in *this* life. He attacks what was then called optimism—the reasoned trust that this is the best world possible—in the name of what is now called optimism—the belief that the evils of this world can be reduced or even eliminated altogether. In the process he comes close to replacing Providence and the immortality of the soul with a project for a progressive history.[18]

By contrast, Rousseau, in the *Letter* he wrote to Voltaire in response to his Lisbon poem, defends optimism in the original sense of the term. The trust that this is the best world possible is perfectly consistent with what, in a text he had drafted just a short time before but never published, he described as his "sad . . . system" (*Preface of a Second Letter to Bordes* [6]). Most immediately, his defense of optimism in this *Letter* consists in once more showing that most of the evils we suffer are of our own making ([7], [8])[19] and in vindicating our commonsense trust in "the ordinary course of things" ([10], [12], cf. [25]) and our belief or hope in the conformity between the order of things and our moral lives. The debate between the two is framed by the question of whose view of Providence is the least cruel and the most consoling (Voltaire, *Poem,* lines 31, 59, 70, 102, 141–45, 155; Rousseau, *Letter* [4], [6], [10], [23], [28], [29], [30]).

Rousseau begins by briefly praising Voltaire's earlier *Poem on Natural Law* and noting that the views he defends in it are sharply at odds with the views he expresses in the accompanying *Poem about the Lisbon Disaster.* He is perfectly right. In the earlier poem Voltaire upholds the view that this is the best order possible and that the evils that attend it are the inevitable but modest price we pay for its goods—in short, the "optimism" which he so systematically criticizes in the later poem.[20] Rousseau rather pointedly remarks that since Voltaire does not hesitate to contradict himself, then neither need he, Rousseau, hesitate to contradict him, and he devotes the longest part of his *Letter* ([6]–[22]) to a detailed criticism of the Lisbon poem. He goes on briefly to discuss the distinction between general and particular Providence ([23]–[26]) and the premises of any belief in Providence ([27]–[31]), and he ends the *Letter* with a brief invitation to Voltaire to expand the argument of the *Poem on Natural Law*—which Rousseau describes as the "catechism of man"—into what here he calls a "kind of civil profession of faith" or the "catechism of the citizen" [35], and what in the *Social Contract* he will call a "purely civil profession of faith" (IV 8 [32]).

Rousseau does not deny that the Lisbon earthquake was a great calamity, or that our lives are beset by innumerable evils. He does object to Voltaire's treating all evils as if there were no differences between them, and putting mortality and great cataclysms on the same footing as evils that are wholly or largely due either to a lack of prudence ([8], [9]) or to an excess of pride [21]. He therefore rejects Voltaire's attributing responsibility for all the evils that beset us to an omnipotent God. Voltaire's *Poem* leaves us questioning God's goodness and justice, and feeling forsaken and dejected. What is more, by couching his distressing message in verse, Voltaire makes it more accessible and insidious. "Thus I could not approve of reasoning about such subjects in public in popular language [*langage vulgaire*] and, if I may say so, still less in verse" ([31] "ms. 2," cf. [10]). He urges Voltaire instead to write a Catechism of the Citizen in verse "so that, with everyone able to learn it easily from childhood on, it might instill in all hearts those sentiments of gentleness and humanity which shine in your writings" [35]. Voltaire was fully aware of the issue. In the Exordium to the *Poem on Natural Law* he had written:

L'art quelquefois frivole et quelquefois divin,
L'art des vers est, dans Pope, utile au genre humain. (Lines 20–21)

In contrast to Voltaire, Rousseau sets out to show that the evils that beset us are either unavoidable but minor, or of our own making and hence at least partly avoidable, and so to console us ([4]–[8]). He sides with Leibniz and Pope, who leave us feeling reconciled and even hopeful because they have God combining the most good(s) with the fewest evils possible; "or (to say the same thing even more bluntly, if need be), if he did not do better, it is that he could not do better" [5]. Faced with the alternative between divine beneficence and divine omnipotence Rousseau publicly opts for the first ([6], cf. [27]).[21] In short, he defends the traditional, rigorously rational "necessary laws" argument against Voltaire's criticism of it.

They disagree not only about the highest objects, the attributes of God or the nature of things, but also about what is closest to hand and our day-to-day existence. Voltaire claims that nobody would be prepared to live his life over again (line 220 and Note). Rousseau allows that that may be how swaggerers feel who make a show of scorning death by setting too low a stock by the goods of life, or the malcontent rich, or melancholy men of letters ([11], [12]). But such people who, like Voltaire himself, enjoy life and cling to it all the while they claim that we suffer more evils than we enjoy goods are manifestly in bad faith ([11], [36]). They fail to acknowledge "the sweet sentiment of existence" [11].[22] If Voltaire had consulted, instead, ordinary folk—tradesmen, artisans, or the peasants of the Valais—whose attitudes carry weight if for no other reason than that they make up the greater part of mankind, he would have had to acknowledge that in the full context of our lives the goods we enjoy outweigh the unavoidable general evils we suffer [12].[23] Rousseau levels at Voltaire's account of our lives the same charge he levels at Hobbes's account of the state of nature as a war of all against all: if life were as burdensome as Voltaire makes it out to be—or as permanently threatened as Hobbes makes it out to be—the species could not long have endured [11].[24] The fact that it has endured clearly shows that we would rather be than not be, and this alone suffices to justify our existence "even if we should have no compensation to expect for the evils we have to suffer, and even if these evils were as great as you depict them" [11]. He allows that in some cases evils do outweigh goods, and that the wise may then choose suicide [12].

Just as the idle rich and sedentary men of letters are not the people to consult about the balance of goods and evils, scientists may not be the most reliable guides in showing us how to orient ourselves in the workaday world. Voltaire had invoked the "learned geometer" Crouzas and Newton's cosmology as proving that in the realm of nature as well as in the realm of human affairs there are "indifferent" phenomena, that some things or events could just as well be one way as another, that the dust a carriage raises makes no more difference in the scheme of things than it does whether Caesar spat to the left or to the right on his way to the Senate the day he was assassinated [17]. Rousseau mocks him for being categorical about the nature of mathematics and claiming "demonstrated" knowledge about the movements of the heavenly bodies while professing to follow Bayle and to suspend judgment about Providence. "How likely is one to be believed when one boasts of knowing nothing while asserting so many things?" [19]. He agrees with Leibniz against Voltaire and Samuel Clarke in rejecting "indifferent" phenomena. Even imperceptible causes acting constantly for long periods of time have sometimes significant physical or moral effects [17].[25] As for Crouzas's criticism of Pope, he had read and discussed it at length some fifteen years earlier (to François de Conzié, 17 January 1742, CC I:132–39). However, in the context of his present discussion of Providence he chooses to cast himself in the role of the common man who has not read him and may well not be able to understand him [14], and who refuses to accept on authority scientific claims which fly in the face of common experience and about which he says that he can anyway not make sense [18]. He had assumed this role of a man who knows nothing and esteems himself none the less for it as early as in the First Discourse ([4], [60]–[61]), and a few years later he has the heroine of Nouvelle Héloïse also say about herself that she may not have understood Crouzas and then proceed to censure his criticism of Pope for the very same reasons as those for which Rousseau censures Voltaire's Poem: reading it leaves one discouraged, whereas reading Pope's Essay buoys one's spirits (Nouvelle Héloïse II 18, OC II:261). Clearly, the issue, for him, is less whether Voltaire's or Crouzas's science is in some ultimate sense true than what might be its effect on our moral life.

The premise of the Letter to Voltaire, the starting point of all of Rousseau's thought, is that we find our bearings in our day-to-day existence by what twice in this Letter he calls "the ordinary course of things" ([10], [12]) and once "the order of human things" [25], the familiar, shared, comparatively regular and stable world of common experience.[26] We trust and are attached to the "ordinary course of things" as to nothing else.[27] The ordinary course of things may not be the necessary laws of things, but we trust that it exhibits them. All conduct and all inquiry rest on this trust and attachment. Voltaire rejects the necessary laws argument because it purportedly fails to reconcile us to the order of things. Rousseau adopts it because, in his view, it alone succeeds in reconciling us to the common or ordinary course of things, and in freeing us from dependence on the capricious will of others.[28]

Our trust and attachment to "the ordinary course of things" manifests itself perhaps most conspicuously in our trust that all things somehow cohere and constitute a whole, and indeed the best of possible wholes or worlds, or that whatever is, is right. Rousseau fully recognizes that in a whole made up of parts—or kinds or species—the good of one part inevitably differs from the good of another, and hence from the good of the whole ([21], [22]).[29] The goods of the various kinds or species are not compossible; nor even are the goods of all the members of our species.[30] There are, then, "evils" inherent in the very "system" or "constitution" of the universe ([8], [21], [22], [5], [23]). Gains necessarily entail losses.[31] Evils cannot cease.

All of Voltaire's examples of physical evil involve death and the fear of death. Death, the fear of it and the hope or the fear of immortality, is perhaps the most constant theme in reflections on Providence. Rousseau insists, perhaps more radically than anyone before him ever had, that in itself—in the ordinary course of things—death is not frightful and that it becomes so primarily in the anticipation and the elaborate religious and social rites that have come to attend it ([10]; cf. [8] and *Discourse on Inequality* I [19]).

More generally, his claim that most of the evils we suffer are of our own making is frequently said to have radically altered the debate about the origin of evil by shifting the responsibility for it from necessary laws and from man's natural wickedness or original sin to society and, more specifically, to political society.[32] However, this claim only raises the further question as to how Rousseau accounts for political society. His answer is unequivocal: political society is an inevitable and irreversible consequence of nature's necessary laws.[33] The further frequent contention that his teaching substitutes social for original sin[34] is particularly misleading, if only because sin has no place in his teaching.

The claim that Rousseau shifted the responsibility for evil to political society is frequently coupled—explicitly or implicitly—with the claim that in his view a political order can be devised that would rid the human condition of all or virtually all evils; that if we made the evils we suffer, we can also unmake them.[35] Now, while it certainly is true that Rousseau explores ways of reducing the evils attendant on political society, he nowhere envisages the possibility of eliminating them altogether. On the contrary: "Everything that is not in nature has its inconveniences, and

civil society more than all the rest" (*Social Contract* III 15 [10]). Tensions—
"inconveniences"—between the good of the whole and the good of its
parts are inevitable, and even the best possible balance between their competing claims is precarious.

The "inconveniences" that inevitably attend on civil society are so-
called metaphysical evils. Rousseau does not use the expression. He is
reluctant to call even inevitable inconveniences "evils." The optimist denies "general evil" [23]. The formula "Whatever is, is right" is but another
way of saying "Providence is general." It is emphatically not a formula of
uncritical acquiescence to whatever may happen to be the case.[36] There
is no particular Providence [25]. The optimist does not deny particular
evils. No philosopher ever has [23].

The traditional distinction between general and particular evil and
the corresponding traditional distinction between general and particular
Providence permits Rousseau to criticize Voltaire for wrongly concluding
on the evidence of particular evils that evil is general and as a consequence
in effect denying Providence; and it permits him to criticize the priests
and the devout for attributing purely natural events to Providence and in
effect denying particular evils [24].[37] Voltaire's mistake—Rousseau calls it
the philosophers' mistake—is formally the same as the mistake of the
priests and the devout who attribute to divine Providence particular goods
and evils instead of recognizing that

in the order of human things . . . everything depends on the common law, and
there is no exception for anyone. It would seem that in the eyes of the Lord of
the universe, particular events here below are nothing, that his Providence is
exclusively universal, that he leaves it at preserving the genera and species, and at
presiding over the whole, without worrying about how each individual spends
this short life. ([25]; cf. *Replies to Charles-George Le Roy* in *Discourses &c,* p. 230,
OC III:237, and *Essay on the Origin of Languages* 9 [32])

Rousseau's "particular evils" in large measure overlap with the tradition's "moral evils": evils due to our doing badly what it is within our
control to do well or badly, evils of omission or commission that may
properly be said to be of our own making; or, in the traditional formula
which Rousseau at one point uses, the source of moral evil is "man, free,
perfected, hence corrupted" ([8]; consider *Social Contract* I 6 [1]–[3], I 8
[1]). Indeed, one of his primary aims in drawing the distinction between
general and particular evil as he does is to disentangle the permanent problem of evil from the theological, but primarily from the Christian theolog-

ical accounts of it, and to reclaim a commonsense middle ground for the exercise of what might be called human or personal Providence or prudence, the judgment, habits, and skills required to strike and maintain the best balance possible between competing goods. The need to set up civil society arose as a result of the inexorable workings of the laws of nature; how we structure civil society and arrange our lives is, within limits, up to us.[38] The Lisbon earthquake occurred as a result of the inexorable workings of the laws of nature, just as earthquakes frequently occur in remote wildernesses [9]; it was an evil because countless innocents suffered and died; but they suffered and died for want of human—not divine—Providence or prudence. Divine Providence—Rousseau says "nature"—does not guide men to build cities or to build them in one place rather than another ([8]; cf. *Second Discourse,* N. XVII). To protest, as Voltaire does, that the earthquake should not have struck Lisbon is to demand that the laws of nature accommodate to man. Rousseau, by contrast, holds that man must accommodate to the laws of nature [9].

This is, precisely, Voltaire's main objection to "optimism": a whole in which all its parts are subject to the same laws, in which beings endowed with sense, and in particular human beings, do not enjoy a privileged place, in which their only consolation for death is that their mortal remains serve as food for worms, is not a well-ordered whole (*Poem,* lines 99–100). Rousseau indicates, discreetly but clearly, how petty such complaints are,[39] and that for earthlings to assume they are worth more in the eyes of God than are the inhabitants of Saturn is an act of thoughtless self-importance ([21]; cf. *To Philopolis* [12]). But he also tries to meet Voltaire's objection head-on: if we are parts of a whole, and hence necessarily subject to evils, the question is not "whether each one of us suffers or not; but whether it was good that the universe be, and our evils were inevitable in the constitution of the universe" [23]; in other words, the question is not "why man is not perfectly happy, but why he exists" [8]. Having stated the question in minimal terms, Rousseau answers it in minimal terms:

the greatest idea of Providence I can conceive is that each material being be arranged in the best way possible in relation to the whole, and each intelligent and sentient being in the best way possible in relation to itself; which means, in other words, that for a being that senses its existence, it is preferable to exist than not to exist. [26]

The "sweet sentiment of existence" [11] decisively tips the balance in favor of the goods of human life. It thus establishes a presumption in favor of what Voltaire demands of a well-ordered whole, or of general Providence. Rousseau goes so far as to claim that it also establishes a presumption in favor of immortality: the "rule" that for a being that senses its existence it is preferable to exist than not to exist

has to be applied to each sentient being's total duration, and not to some particular instants of its duration, such as human life; which shows how closely related the question of Providence is to that of the immortality of the soul. [26]

In other words, the presumption in favor of immortality is a presumption in favor of the immortality of the individual soul. It is striking that immediately after denying particular Providence [25], Rousseau appears to qualify this denial with a "rule" that leaves open the possibility of particular Providence. The evidence for this rule would seem to be the well-nigh universal hope for immortality. Rousseau himself frequently speaks of his own hope for it, and he ends this *Letter* by telling Voltaire that the case he has been making for Providence and, in particular, for the immortality of the soul is the only case he has ever made in which he has taken his own interests into account. The remark echoes a similar remark by Socrates as he sets out to inquire into the immortality of the soul on the day on which he was to drink the hemlock (*Phaedo* 70C 1–2). The well-nigh universal hope for immortality is closely tied to our feeling that justice calls for happiness—or misery—in proportion to deserts.[40] No natural sanctions back up this feeling.[41] Yet our moral life rests on the trust that what is conforms to what should be. We may therefore be moved to hope that merit unrewarded here and now might be rewarded hereafter and to hope or to fear that wickedness unpunished here and now might be punished hereafter—but not to the point of eternal punishment "which neither you nor I, nor any man who thinks well of God, will ever believe" [26]—and hence to hope or to fear that the individual soul is immortal. Such hope may encourage the righteous, and such fear deter the wicked.[42] Rousseau therefore proposes as one of the three or four positive dogmas of the civil religion in the *Social Contract* "the life to come, the happiness of the just, the punishment of the wicked" (IV 8 [33]); and he therefore also holds that publicly to proclaim that the soul is mortal is subversive of sound citizenship (*Social Contract* IV 8 [32]⋆). His "rule" takes up Glaucon's and Adeimantos's challenge to Socrates: in the absence of natural sanctions and of immortality, would not a person acting justly to his detriment be a fool, and only a person acting unjustly to his benefit prove rational?[43] He acknowledges that his "rule" does not meet this challenge.

The immortality of the individual soul is no more than an assumption: "I am not unaware that reason can doubt it" [26].

So is the necessary condition for "optimism" or for general Providence, that all things together constitute a whole and indeed the best ordered whole possible, no more than an assumption:

instead of saying, *All is well* [or: *good*], it might be preferable to say, *The whole is good* or *All is good for the whole*. Then it is quite obvious that no man could give direct proofs pro or con; for these proofs depend on a perfect knowledge of the world's constitution and of its Author's purpose, and this knowledge is indisputably beyond human intelligence. [23][44]

So, finally, is the sufficient condition for Providence, the existence and nature of God, no more than an assumption:

If God exists, he is perfect; if he is perfect, he is wise, powerful, and just; if he is wise and powerful, all is well; if he is just and powerful, my soul is immortal. . . . If I am granted the first proposition, the ones that follow will never be shaken; if it is denied, there is no use arguing about its consequences. [27]

Although he does not deny the first proposition, Rousseau does not think it proved:

I candidly admit to you that on this point neither the pro nor the con seems to me demonstrated by the lights of reason. . . . What is more, the objections, on either side, are always irrefutable, because they revolve around things about which man has no genuine idea. [29]

In short, the God of the *Letter to Voltaire* is a premise, and the Providence of the *Letter* a "great and consoling dogma" [23]. They are not conclusions.

Yet Rousseau professes to believe in God as firmly as he believes any other truth. The fact that he cannot establish the existence of God by reason does not lead him to deny it or even to suspend judgment regarding it. For, he goes on to tell Voltaire, doubt is too violent a state for his soul to bear. When his reason wavers, his faith or belief *(foi),* incapable of remaining in suspense for any length of time, decides on its own and without involving his reason: "to believe or not to believe are the things in the world that least depend on me" [29]. Reason had left the scale in balance. The weight of hope and of a thousand objects of preference tip the scale in favor of the more consoling alternative [29].[45]

In the copy of the letter that he sent to Voltaire, Rousseau breaks off his discussion of this delicate subject at this point. He has been remarkably bold: he has ignored or rejected outright many of the positive teachings of the Churches; in particular, he has rejected every version of predestination; he has rejected eternal punishments; he has not hesitated to allow for suicide in his own name rather than in the name of one of his characters, as he does in the *Nouvelle Héloise;* he has denied divine omnipotence, and he has denied particular Providence; he well knows that in so doing he has undercut a major justification for prayer and tacitly rejected the possibility of miracles; and, finally, he has said explicitly that the nature and existence of God do not admit of rational proof any more than does the immortality of the individual soul. In the following paragraph, which he omitted from the copy of the letter he sent to Voltaire, he goes even further.[46] In it he details the argument against the existence of God and of general Providence. He tells that what struck him most forcefully in his entire life was Diderot's showing, in the twenty-first of his *Pensées philosophiques,* that the manifest order we behold can be accounted for by matter, motion, and chance, without invoking an ordering intelligence, prime mover, wisdom, or beneficence.[47] It is clear why he would have omitted this paragraph from the letter he sent Voltaire, as well as from the version of it which he allowed to be published: as he says, it convinces, and he knows of no conclusive refutation of it.[48]

Diderot's Epicurean *Pensée* sweeps aside the classical objection to Epicurean cosmology, an objection which both Diderot and Rousseau mention, that it is far less likely that the universe came about by chance than that a poem might be "composed" by sufficiently many throws of the letters of the alphabet.[49] Rousseau recognizes, indeed he stresses, that Diderot's *Pensée* cannot overcome our finding it utterly implausible that order would arise by chance. It radically challenges our trust that all things somehow cohere and constitute a whole; it dramatically illustrates the discontinuity between "the ordinary course of things" and what might be the true account of them. It may convince, it does not persuade [30]. The contrast Rousseau draws, here and many other places, between being convinced and being persuaded[50] corresponds to the contrast that he goes on to draw between demonstration proper and proofs of sentiment, and between physical and moral certainty. To convince and to demonstrate is to establish "physical" certainty; to persuade and to offer proofs of sentiment is to establish "moral" certainty. Rousseau says that in the face of Diderot's *Pensée,* he sets aside the strictly rational proof and yields, instead, to the proof of sentiment. He readily acknowledges that what he calls proof of sentiment could equally well be called prejudice. He claims nevertheless to yield to it because Diderot's *Pensée* is so utterly at odds with ordinary experience and sentiment or prejudice that to live and to act in conformity with it would require a restructuring of our ways and beliefs that is beyond most, if not all, men's power. Rousseau insists that in such cases, ordinary experience must be heeded; and that in most cases it will and ought to prevail. For ordinary experience makes for our obstinate trust in the stability and regularity—the orderliness—of our world. Therefore, to challenge it in the name of alternatives that are not certain and, he pointedly adds, not useful is, as he repeatedly tells Voltaire, simply cruel ([6], [30], [31]).

Rousseau's move from reason to sentiment honeys the cup, masking the wormwood taste that Diderot's—and Voltaire's—views leave.[51] It contributes to the shift from religion to religiosity in which his thought played such an important role.[52] At the same time, the successive reflections by which he moves from reason's inability to prove the existence of God and hence of Providence, to his being unable to remain in doubt about it and finding it cruel to cast doubt on it, to his therefore believing it out of sentiment or prejudice and out of inclination for the more consoling and disinclination for the more cruel alternative, clearly prepare the way for the widespread contemporary rejections of belief in God in the name of "intellectual honesty" or of "the refusal to make the sacrifice of the intellect."

The fact that Rousseau presents these reflections in the first person does not entitle us to attribute to him the views that he attributes to the first person. The first person may here be, as it so often is from the *First Discourse* on, "an honest man who knows nothing and esteems himself none the less for it" (*First Discourse* [4]).[53] More specifically, the suppressed paragraph of the *Letter to Voltaire* raises anew the question of what, precisely, might be his own views, and in particular the question of his materialism or, rather, of his Epicureanism.

Although he returns to the problem of materialism throughout his life, Rousseau does not ever discuss it at any length. He chooses to write from the perspective of the ordinary course of things, and philosophical materialism breaks with the ordinary course of things. It is what he early called one of those metaphysical subtleties that do not directly affect the happiness of mankind (*First Discourse* [1], [57]). When he does speak about it, he does so in terms of the perennial question: is motion of the nature of matter, or is it not? If it is not, then, according to the received argument, a self-moving and immaterial agent—soul or god—must at least initially have imparted motion to it. In that case, strict materialism is untenable. Now, Rousseau's various pronouncements on this question simply cannot be reconciled.[54] It therefore seems safest to conclude that in his view, materialism, strictly and narrowly so called, like the existence of God and the immortality of the soul, is a problem that reason cannot resolve.

However, regardless, now, of whether or how his teaching may be "materialist," his account of human things is best understood as a form of Epicureanism. Its premises are the classical Epicurean premises: rejection of teleology, and in particular of the view that man is a political animal and political life is the human good, in favor of the view that happiness consists in tranquillity of soul and hence in a soul at one with itself (*Second Discourse* II [19]; *Fragments politiques, OC* III:531; cf. *Origin of Languages* 9 [27], [28], [31]). Tranquillity of soul is certainly one major reason he gives for choosing the more consoling alternative regarding immortality.

His Epicureanism is in large measure mediated by Lucretius.[55] It diverges most conspicuously from classical and, in particular, from Lucretius's Epicureanism by attending far more to the many who fail to find "sweet solace" (V 21, 113; VI 4) in its stark teaching. It takes far more seriously than Lucretius would appear to do that

> *haec ratio plerumque videtur*
> *tristior esse quibus non est tractata, retroque*
> *vulgus abhorret ab hac* (I 943–45 = IV 18–20)

This is one reason it adheres so much more closely to "the ordinary course of things," and hence assigns so much more positive a role to political life and, with it, to religion, than do its classical Epicurean models. Yet even in this it remains faithful to Epicurus's teaching:

it would be better to follow the story about the gods than to be a slave to the fate of the natural philosopher; for the former leaves the hope that the gods can be swayed by entreaties, whereas the latter confronts us with inexorable necessity.[56]

For Epicurus, as for the Rousseau of the *Letter to Voltaire,* the issue is less whether his physics is in some ultimate sense true than what might be its effect on our moral life.

Rousseau ends his *Letter* by inviting Voltaire to elaborate the rudiments of the religion of sentiment which he has been sketching into a Catechism of the Citizen [35]. He expects him to have understood and agreed with his brief earlier remark that public debates about the existence of God are not useful [31]. Political society requires religion. But not any religion. He claims only to be following Voltaire's example in holding "that one cannot too forcefully attack the superstition that disturbs society, nor too much respect the Religion that upholds it" [31]. Three short paragraphs later "the superstition that disturbs society" has become "Religions that attack the foundations of society," which, he now says, must first be exterminated if there is to be civil peace [34]. A sound political society requires what, in the *Social Contract,* he will call a "civil religion." It may require beliefs, but it may enforce only conduct. For what matters in civil life is what one does. As he had said all along, believing or not believing in matters where demonstration has no place does not depend on ourselves ([32], cf. [29], [33]).

Notes

1. Immanuel Kant, *Gesammelte Schriften,* herausgegeben von der Deutschen Akademie der Wissenschaften (Berlin: Walter de Gruyter, 1902–), 20:59.

2. For translations of these texts and details about them, see Jean-Jacques Rousseau, *"The Discourses" and Other Early Political Writings,* ed. V. Gourevitch (Cambridge: Cambridge University Press, 1997). I have discussed the *Letter to Voltaire* briefly in the introduction to this volume (pp. xxv–xxxi). All references to the works contained in this volume and in its companion volume, Jean-Jacques Rousseau, *"Social Contract" and Other Later Political Writings,* ed. V. Gourevitch (Cambridge: Cambridge University Press, 1997), are by part or by book and chapter, followed by the paragraph number in square brackets.

Otherwise unidentified references in square brackets throughout the present essay are to the relevant paragraph of the *Letter to Voltaire.*

All references to works by Rousseau not included in the above two volumes are to the five-volume Jean-Jacques Rousseau, *Oeuvres complètes,* ed. B. Gagnebin and M. Raymond (Paris: Pléiade, 1959–95), abbreviated *OC,* followed by a roman numeral indicating the volume and arabic numeral(s) indicating the page(s). References to Rousseau's correspondence are to R. A. Leigh's magisterial edition of Jean-Jacques Rousseau, *Correspondance complète* (Geneva: Institut et Musée Voltaire; Oxford: The Voltaire Foundation at the Taylor Institution, 1965–89), abbreviated *CC,* followed by a roman numeral indicating the volume and arabic numeral(s) indicating the page(s).

3. Rousseau recounts the circumstances surrounding his writing of the *Letter* in *Confessions* IX (*OC* I:429–30), and the circumstances surrounding its eventual publication in *Confessions* X (*OC* I:539–42). For full details, see R. A. Leigh, "Rousseau's Letter to Voltaire on Optimism," *Studies on Voltaire and the Eighteenth Century* 30 (1964): 247–309; summarized in *CC* IV:50–59 and in B. Gagnebin's "Notice bibliographique," *OC* IV:1880–84.

Voltaire acknowledged Rousseau's *Letter* in a brief note (12 Sept. 1756, *CC* IV:102) which simply ignored the issues Rousseau had raised. Rousseau believed that Voltaire wrote *Candide* as his full reply to the *Letter* (*Confessions* IX, *OC* I:430).

Regarding the distinction between private and public discussions of theological issues—or between discussions of theological issues with philosophers, on the one hand, and with authors, on the other—see also *Lettre à d'Alembert, OC* V:10, trans. p. 11.

4. On addressing the public regarding religious issues, see *Social Contract* II 6 [10], II 7 [9]–[11]; on Emile, *"Je l'ai choisi parmi les esprits vulgaires," Emile* IV, *OC* IV:537, Bloom

trans. p. 245; cf. *Emile* I, *OC* IV:266, Bloom trans. p. 52; on the stage setting for the Savoyard Vicar's *Profession of Faith*, *OC* IV:558, 606, and *Lettres de la Montagne* III, *OC* III:749–50; on Franquières, the *Letter* to him, [9], *OC* IV:1137–38; on private, in contrast to public, discussions of religious issues, *Lettre à d'Alembert*, *OC* V:12; on his last writing, *Rêveries* III, *OC* I:1018, cf. the letters to Verne of 18 Feb. and 25 Mar. 1758; on the parallels between the vicar's and Julie's professions of faith, *Confessions* VIII, *OC* I:407.

5. *Tout est bien*, "all is well [or: good]," is how the contemporary French translators rendered Pope's "whatever is, is right": *An Essay on Man*, Epistle I, line 294, Epistle IV, line 394. However, in Voltaire's *Poem*, and especially in Rousseau's *Letter*, *tout est bien* becomes a formula in its own right and with its own meaning. A further reason for preserving an explicit reference to "good" in translating *tout est bien*, is that both Voltaire and Rousseau are concerned not only with Pope's dictum but also with Leibniz's proposition that "this is the best world possible": e.g., *Essais de Théodicée: Sur la bonté de Dieu, la liberté de l'homme, et l'origine du mal* (1710), I, §§8–10 *et passim*.

6. Leslie Stephen surveys much of this literature in *History of English Thought in the Eighteenth Century*, 2 vols. (New York: G. P. Putnam's Sons, 1876). A. O. Lovejoy surveys some of the English and the Continental literature in "The Parallel of Deism and Classicism" (1930), reprinted in *Essays in the History of Ideas* (Baltimore: Johns Hopkins University Press, 1948), 78–98, and in *The Great Chain of Being* (Cambridge: Harvard University Press, 1948), chaps. 7 and 10.

7. Hope humbly then; with trembling pinions soar;
Wait the great teacher Death, and God adore!
What future bliss, he gives not thee to know,
But gives that hope to be thy blessing now.
Hope springs eternal in the human breast:
Man never Is, but always To be blest:
The soul uneasy and confined from home,
Rests and expiates in a life to come. (Pope, *Essay*, Epistle I, lines 91–98)

8. *L'homme, étranger à soi, de l'homme est ignoré.*
Que suis-je, où suis-je, où vais-je, et d'où suis-je tiré?
Atomes tourmentés sur cet amas de boue,
Que la mort engloutit, et dont le sort se joue,
Mais atomes pensants . . .
Au sein de l'infini nous élançons notre être,
Sans pouvoir un moment nous voir et nous connaître. (Voltaire, *Poem about the Lisbon Disaster*, lines 209–16)

9. Samuel Clarke, *A Demonstration of the Being and Attributes of God* (1705), 218–21; cf. Augustine, *Enchiridion* XI, and Thomas Aquinas, *Summa Theologica* I, q. 48, iii, resp.; Leibniz, *Théodicée* I, §21.

10. See dying vegetables life sustain,
See life dissolving vegetate again:
All forms that perish other forms supply. (Pope, *Essay*, Epistle III, lines 15–17)

Ainsi du monde entier tous les membres gémissent;
Nés tous pour les tourments, l'un par l'autre ils périssent:
Et vous composerez dans ce chaos fatal
Des malheurs de chaque être un bonheur général! (Voltaire, *Poem about the Lisbon Disaster*, lines 117–20)

11. *"Ce malheur, dites vous, est le bien d'un autre être."*
    De mon corps tout sanglant mille insectes vont naître;
    Quand la mort met le comble aux maux que j'ai soufferts,
    Le beau soulagement d'être mangé des vers! (Voltaire, *Poem about the Lisbon Disaster*, lines
      97–100)

Consider also the Preface to the *Poem* [3] and lines 67–68.

12. Voltaire supports his mention of "indifferent phenomena" with a brief reference to the "learned geometer" Crouzas and to some "proofs" of Newton's. Jean-Pierre de Crouzaz (1663–1750) published two volumes criticizing Pope's *Essay*. Voltaire is here relying on his *Examen de l'Essai de M. Pope sur l'homme* (Lausanne and Amsterdam, 1737), 87–94. Not surprisingly, Pope reserved a place for Crouzas in the *Dunciad* (IV:198).

Voltaire draws Newton's "proofs" that some phenomena are "indifferent" largely from Newton's spokesman Dr. Samuel Clarke: *A Demonstration of the Being and Attributes of God* (1705), 130–31, 137–38.

13. See esp. *The Leibniz-Clarke Correspondence* (1715/1716, originally published in 1717, French translation 1720; ed. H. G. Alexander, Manchester: Manchester University Press, 1956): Dr. Clarke's Third Reply, no. 2; Mr. Leibniz's Fourth Paper, no. 2; see also no. 3; Voltaire, *Elements de la philosophie de Newton* I, 3, lines 1–15, 63–66.

14. Voltaire succeeded so well in appearing orthodox that the great twentieth-century neo-Thomist scholar Etienne Gilson cites the concluding verses of an intermediary version of the *Poem*,

    Le passé n'est pour nous qu'un triste souvenir:
    Le présent est affreux, s'il n'est point d'avenir,
    Si la nuit du tombeau détruit l'être qui pense.
    Un jour tout sera bien, voilà notre espérance;
    Tout est bien aujourd'hui, voilà l'illusion. (Lines 215–19)

as very close to what he calls "Christian optimism," in contrast to the philosophers' optimism which the *Journal de Trévoux* had mocked: *L'esprit de la philosophie médiévale,* 2d ed. (Paris: Vrin, 1944), 111 n. 1; see n. 17 below.

15. Leibniz charged that according to the doctrine of Sir Isaac Newton and his followers: "God Almighty wants to wind up his watch from time to time; otherwise it would cease to move. He had not, it seems, sufficient foresight to make it a perpetual motion." To which Clarke replies: "The notion of the world's being a great machine, going on without the interposition of God, as a clock continues to go without the assistance of a clockmaker; is the notion of materialism and fate, and tends, (under the pretense of making God a *supra-mundane intelligence,*) to exclude providence and God's government in reality out of the world." *Leibniz-Clarke Correspondence,* Leibniz's First Paper, no. 4; Clarke's First Reply, no. 4.

In Koyré's memorable formulation: "the God of Leibniz is not the Newtonian Overlord who makes the world as he wants it and continues to act upon it as the Biblical God did in the first six days of Creation. He is, if I may continue the simile, the Biblical God on the Sabbath Day, the God who has finished his work and who finds it good, nay the very best of possible worlds, and who, therefore, has no more to act upon it, or in it, but only to preserve it in being. This God is, at the same time—once more in contradistinction to the Newtonian one—the supremely rational Being, the principle of sufficient reason personified." *From the Closed World to the Infinite Universe* (Baltimore: Johns Hopkins University Press, 1957), 240–41.

16. Cited by H. Gouhier, *Rousseau et Voltaire* (Paris: Vrin, 1983), 76. "While always appearing to believe in God, Voltaire really always only believed in the Devil; since his supposed God is nothing but a maleficent being who according to him takes pleasure only in doing harm" (Rousseau, *Confessions* IX, *OC* I:429).

17. The first, unauthorized, publications of the *Poem* ended

> *Le passé n'est pour nous qu'un triste souvenir:*
> *Le présent est affreux, s'il n'est point d'avenir,*
> *Si la nuit du tombeau détruit l'être qui pense.*
> *Mortels, il faut souffrir,*
> *Se soumettre en silence, adorer et mourir.* (Lines 215–19)

Voltaire quickly recognized that the ecclesiastical authorities might find this ending too gloomy. He therefore inserted "hope" between the final "adore" and "die." Even this seemed inadequate, and he reworked the ending massively. He now summarizes his difference with the optimists as follows:

> *Un jour tout sera bien, voilà notre espérance;*
> *Tout est bien aujourd'hui, voilà l'illusion.*

These are the lines which Gilson quotes as coming close to expressing "Christian optimism" (n. 14 above). However, in his own copy of the poem, Voltaire changed these lines to read

> *Un jour tout sera bien, quel frêle espoir!*
> *Tout est bien aujourd'hui, quelle illusion.*

See George R. Havens, "Voltaire's Pessimistic Revision of His Conclusion of His *Poème sur le désastre de Lisbonne*," *Modern Language Notes* 44 (1929): 489–93.

18. Voltaire does not go quite so far as Kant, who replaces the doctrine of the immortality of the soul with the moral imperative to practice progressive politics: *Idee zu einer allgemeinen Geschichte,* 9. Satz, 3. Satz *i. f.,* and 6. Satz, Anm.

19. *Second Discourse* I [9], Note IX [1]; *To Philopolis* [10]. In the *Confessions* Rousseau describes himself as calling out in the *Second Discourse,* "Fools, who constantly complain about nature, learn that all your evils [*maux*] are due to yourselves" (*OC* I:389). This is also the guiding thought of *Emile,* which opens: "Everything is well [or: good] as it leaves the hands of the author of things: everything degenerates in the hands of man" (*OC* IV:245, trans. p. 37); and again: "Our greatest evils come to us from ourselves" (*OC* IV:261, trans. p. 48).

20. *Poème sur la loi naturelle,* part II, lines 37–40, 115–24; cf. Job 38, 39; Thomas Aquinas, *Summa Theologica* I, q. 22, resp. 2; and contrast with *Poem about the Lisbon Disaster,* lines 97–100, 125–26.

21. As he also does in the civil religion: one of its few positive dogmas is the existence of the powerful—*not* the all-powerful—Divinity (*Social Contract* IV 8 [33]); so, too, in the Savoyard Vicar's *Profession of Faith: Emile* IV, *OC* IV:588–89, Bloom trans. pp. 276–77; and in the *Letter to Franquières* [14]). His character M. de Wolmar, in a private conversation, is

more cautious: faced with the choice between accounting for the existence of evil by "lack of intelligence, power, or goodness in the first cause," he refuses to choose (*Nouvelle Héloïse* V 5, *OC* II:595–96 and n. (a) *ad* p. 596).

22. See also *Nouvelle Héloïse* III 22, *OC* II:389; so, too, Leibniz, *Théodicée* I, §§12–13, III, §253.

23. See also Leibniz *Théodicée* I, §13. However, in *Emile* Rousseau holds that the prospect of death accompanied by the hope of a better life hereafter—of immortality— alone makes this life and its burdens bearable: *Emile* II, *OC* IV:306. He attributes the same sentiment to the Savoyard Vicar: *OC* IV:588.

24. *The State of War* [8].

25. See also *Discourse on Inequality* I [53] and Lucretius I 311–28, IV 1286–87. "History is in general defective in that it records only perceptible [*sensible*] and manifest facts which can be fixed by name, place, date; but the slow and progressive causes of these facts, which cannot be specified in the same way, invariably remain unknown" (*Emile* IV, *OC* IV:529).

26. See, e.g., Bacon's "common course of nature" and "common course of the universe" (*Novum Organum,* The Second Book of Aphorisms, esp. no. xvii); Spinoza's "common order of nature" (*Ethics* II xxix, scholium, and II xxx, proof); Locke's "ordinary course of things" (*Essay* IV, 17, §§xiii, xiv); Hume's "ordinary course of events," "course of nature," and "the common and experienced course of nature" (in "Of the Immortality of the Soul," in *Essays Moral, Political, and Literary,* ed. T. H. Green and T. H. Grose [London: Longman's, Green, 1874–75], II:400; and *Human Understanding* XI *passim*).

27. E.g., Plato's *pistis* (*Republic* VI 510A); Lucretius's *fides prima* (*De natura rerum* [Bailey ed.] IV 505); Descartes's "teaching of nature" (*Meditations* VI); Hume's "belief" and "species of instinct" (*Human Understanding* V, esp. part II); Husserl's "Urdoxa" (*Ideen* I, §104); Santayana's "animal faith" *(Scepticism and Animal Faith).*

28. Regarding the moral and political import of "necessary laws" and trust in them, consider *Emile* on the contrast between dependence on men and dependence on things (*OC* IV:311, 320, Bloom trans. pp. 85, 91) and *Social Contract* II 7 [10] on the laws of nature and of the state.

29. "*Ce qui trompe en cette matière, est . . . qu'on se trouve porté à croire que ce qui est le meilleur dans le tout, est le meilleur aussi qui soit possible dans chaque partie.*" "*[L]a partie du meilleur tout n'est pas nécessairement le meilleur qu'on pouvait faire de cette partie.*" Leibniz, *Théodicée* III, §§212, 213.

The problem harks at least as far back as *the* break with pre-Socratic philosophy, Socrates' criticism of Anaxagoras's claiming that reason rules and yet failing to show that what is the case is best both for each thing/being taken by itself and for the common good of all things/beings (*Phaedo* 98B 2–3). Leibniz quotes Socrates' comment in a somewhat free translation on several occasions, most conspicuously in *Discourse on Metaphysics* §20. However, he breaks off the quote just before Socrates acknowledges that neither he himself nor anyone else could do what he charges Anaxagoras failed to do—namely, to show that what is the case is, indeed, best both for each thing/being taken by itself and for the common good of all things/beings (*Phaedo* 99C 8–9). He refers to his own attempt to show what Socrates says he could not show, namely his *Théodicée,* as a popular writing: Leibniz's Second Paper, no. 1 (*Leibniz-Clarke Correspondence,* ed. Alexander, 15).

30. *Second Discourse* II [52]; *Origin of Languages* I [13]; *Social Contract* I 8 [1]; *A Christophe de Beaumont, OC* IV:967; cf. *Nouvelle Héloïse* V 2, *OC* II:538.

31. "The constitution of this universe does not allow for all the sensible beings that

make it up to concur all at once in their mutual happiness[;] but since the well-being of one makes for the other's evil, each, according to the law of nature, gives preference to himself, regardless of whether he is working to his own advantage or to another's prejudice; straightaway peace is disturbed as regards the one who suffers, [and] not only is it natural then to repel the evil that pursues us, but when an intelligent being perceives that this evil is due to another's ill-will, he gets irritated at it and tries to repel it. Whence arise discord, quarrels, sometimes fights" (*On War* [42]). See also *Origin of Languages* 9 [32]* and Editor's Note; *To Philopolis* [11]; *Second Discourse* I [17]; *Political Economy* [50]; *Poland* V [1].

32. E.g., "*Die Gesellschaft hat in ihrer bisherigen Form der Menschheit die tiefsten Wunden geschlagen; aber sie ist es auch, die, durch ihre Umgestaltung und Neugestaltung, diese Wunden heilen kann und heilen soll. Das ist die Lösung die Rousseaus Rechtsphilosophie dem Problem der Theodizee gegeben hat.*" E. Cassirer, *Die Philosophie der Aufklärung* (Tübingen: J. C. B. Mohr, 1932), 210. See also Jean Starobinski, *J.-J. Rousseau: La transparence et l'obstacle* (Paris: Gallimard, 1971), 33–35.

33. Consider the argument of the *Discourse on Inequality;* of the *Origin of Languages,* chap. 9; of *Social Contract* I 6 [1]–[3] and *Discourse on Inequality* II [25]; and "It is easy to see how the establishment of a single Society made the establishment of all the others indispensable, and how, in order to stand up to united forces, it became necessary to unite in turn" (*Discourse on Inequality* II [33]); also "He who willed man to be sociable inclined the globe's axis at an angle to the axis of the universe with a touch of the finger. With this slight motion I see the face of the earth change and the vocation of mankind settled: I hear, far off, the joyous cries of a heedless multitude; I see Palaces and Cities raised; I see the birth of the arts, laws, commerce; I see peoples forming, expanding, dissolving, succeeding one another like the waves of the sea: I see men clustered in a few points of their habitation in order there to devour one another, turning the remainder of the world into a dreadful desert; a worthy monument to social union and the usefulness of the arts" (*Origin of Languages* 9 [23]); and see the important fragment at OC III:529–33.

34. "*Il n'y a donc pas, dans chaque âme humaine, un péché originel, qui s'oppose à son salut individuel, mais il pèse sur l'humanité un péché collectif: le péché social.*" P.-M. Masson, *La religion de Jean-Jacques Rousseau,* 3 vols. (Paris: Hachette, 1916), 2:278.

35. E.g., *Narcissus* [30], and *Social Contract* II 5 [6].

36. When the Genevan naturalist Charles Bonnet, writing under the pseudonym "Philopolis," seemed to maintain that the formula was one of uncritical acceptance, Rousseau replied: "If all is right [or: good] in the way in which you understand it, what is the point of redressing our vices, curing our evils, correcting our errors? Of what use are our Pulpits, our Courts, our Academies? Why call the Doctor when you have a fever? How do you know whether the good of the greater whole, which you do not know, does not require you to be delirious, and whether the health of the inhabitants of Saturn or of Sirius would not suffer because yours was restored? Let everything go as it may, so that everything always go well. If everything is as best it can be, then you must blame any action whatsoever. For since any action, as soon as it occurs, necessarily brings about some change in the state things are in, one cannot touch anything without doing wrong, and the most absolute quietism is the only virtue left to man. Finally, if all is good as it is, then it is good that there be Laplanders, Eskimos, Algonquins, Chickasaws, Caribs, who do without our political order, Hottentots who have no use for it, and a Genevan who approves them. Leibniz himself would grant this" (*To Philopolis* [11]; cf. *Origin of Languages* 9 [32]–[34]; *Social Contract* I 3 [3]).

37. Julie and Saint-Preux, the two main characters of the *Nouvelle Héloise,* discuss the

question of universal and particular providence in terms of the specifically Christian debates about grace and election. Julie writes: "According to you, this act of humility [i.e., prayer] is without benefit to us, and God, having given us everything that can incline us to good by giving us conscience, thereafter abandons us to ourselves and lets our freedom act. That is not, as you know, the doctrine of Saint Paul nor is it that professed in our Church. . . . To listen to you, it would seem that it is a bother for it [i.e., the divine power] to watch over each individual; you fear that a divided and constant attention might tire it, and you find it fairer that it do everything by general laws no doubt because they cost it less care." Saint-Preux replies: "I . . . do not believe that after having provided in every way for man's needs, God grants to one person rather than to another some extraordinary assistance, which the one who abuses the common assistance does not deserve, and the one who uses it well does not need. This acceptance of persons does injury to divine justice. Even if this harsh and discouraging doctrine could be deduced from Scripture itself, is not my first duty to honor God? However much respect I may owe the sacred text, I owe its Author more, and I would rather believe the Bible falsified or unintelligible than God unjust or maleficent" (*Nouvelle Héloise* VI 6, *OC* II:672, and VI 7, *OC* II:684; see also V 5, *OC* II:595–96; and *Lettre à d'Alembert, OC* V:12, trans. p. 13). When the Censor's Office required that Saint-Preux's remark be struck, Rousseau replied "These pages must remain exactly as they are. If Saint-Preux wants to be heretical regarding grace, that is his business. Besides, it is necessary that he defend man's freedom, since elsewhere he makes the abuse of this freedom the cause of moral evil: he absolutely has to be a Molinist if he is not to be a Manichean" (to Malesherbes, Mar. 1761, *CC* VIII:237; cf. p. 120).

38. Regarding these limits, see esp. *Second Discourse* P [6], *Geneva ms.* I 2 [5].

39. "I die, I am eaten by worms; but my children, my brothers will live as I have lived, and by the order of nature I do for all men what Codrus, Curtius, the Decii, the Philaeni, and a thousand others did voluntarily for a small number of men" [22]. Cf. Lucretius, *De natura rerum* III 931–63 and 1024–35.

40. This is how Rousseau has the Savoyard Vicar state this feeling: "God, it is said, owes his creatures nothing; I believe that he owes them everything he promised them by endowing them with being. Now, to give them the idea of a good and to make them feel the need for it, is to promise it to them. The more I turn inward, the more I consult myself, the more do I read the following words inscribed in my soul: *be just and you will be happy*" (*Emile* IV, *OC* IV:587). Contrast Kant, *Kritik der praktischen Vernunft* I 2.2.

41. "Considering things in human terms, the laws of justice are vain among men for want of natural sanctions; they only bring good to the wicked and evil to the just when he observes them toward everyone while no one observes them toward him" (*Social Contract* I, 6 [2]). See also *Emile* II, *OC* IV:334–37, Bloom trans. pp. 100–101; *Nouvelle Héloise* III 18, *OC* II:358–59. Indeed, the Stoics were wrong to hold that virtue secures happiness (*To d'Offreville* [18]).

42. This is how Rousseau has the Savoyard Vicar describe these rewards and punishments: "I could not recall after my death what I was during my life without also recalling what I felt, hence what I did, and I do not doubt that this memory will some day make for the happiness of the good and the torment of the wicked" (*Emile* IV, *OC* IV:590–91, Bloom trans. p. 283). He has Julie make much the same point in much the same terms: *Nouvelle Héloise* VI 11, *OC* II:729 together with note (a).

43. *To Franquières* [22]; *Social Contract* I 6 [2]; *Emile* II, *OC* IV:334–37, trans. pp. 100–101, and IV, *OC* IV:626, trans. p. 307; *Nouvelle Héloise* III 18, *OC* II:358–59; *Fiction, ou morceau allégorique sur la révélation, OC* IV:1053. Cf. Plato, *Republic* II 358e–367e, cf. I

330d–331b, X 608d–621d, and *Phaedo* 63C 6; Spinoza, *Political Treatise* II, §12, I, §5; and "everything you tell me about the advantages of the social law might be fine if, while I scrupulously observed it toward the rest, I were sure that all of them would observe it toward me; but what assurance can you give on this score, and could my situation be any worse than to find myself exposed to all the evils which the stronger might choose to visit upon me, without my daring to make up for it at the expense of the weak? Either give me guarantees against every unjust undertaking, or give up hope of my refraining from them in turn. It makes no difference that you tell me that by repudiating the duties which natural law imposes on me, I deprive myself at the same time of its rights and that my acts of violence will authorize all those one might choose to commit against me. I accept it all the more readily as I do not see how my moderation might guarantee me against them. Besides it will be up to me to get the strong to side with my interests by sharing with them the spoils of the weak; that will do more for my advantage and my security than will justice. The proof that this is how the enlightened and independent man would have reasoned is that this is how every sovereign society accountable for its conduct to itself alone reasons" (Rousseau, *Geneva ms.* I 2 [10]).

44. "the good of the greater whole, which you do not know" (*To Philopolis* [11]).

45. Again, "the prejudices of childhood and the secret wishes of my heart tipped the scale to the side I found most consoling. It is difficult to avoid believing what one so ardently desires, and who can doubt that one's interest in accepting or rejecting the judgments in the other life determines most men's faith as to what they hope or fear" (*Rêveries* III, *OC* I:1017; cf. *Rêveries* II, *OC* I:1010).

46. The omitted paragraph was first published by George Streckeisen-Moultou in his *Oeuvres et correspondance inédites de J.-J. Rousseau* (1861), with a note explaining that it was part of the manuscript of the *Letter* in his possession.

47. Diderot's *Pensées philosophiques* had been publicly condemned a decade earlier and led to their author's imprisonment at Vincennes. Rousseau had included a discreet reference to them in the *First Discourse* [51].

48. Although he repeatedly returns to the argument of this *Pensée*—in a letter to the pastor Jacob Vernes, 18 Feb. 1758, *CC* V:32–33; in the Savoyard Vicard's *Profession of Faith*, *Emile* IV, *OC* IV:579, trans. pp. 275–76; in the *Fiction, ou morceau allégorique sur la révélation*, *OC* IV:1046; and in the *Letter to Franquières* [11]—Rousseau never publicly acknowledged that he found it convincing or that he knows of no refutation to it: "*je n'y sais pas la moindre réponse qui ait le sens commun*" [30].

49. Cf. Lucretius *De natura rerum* (Bailey ed.) I 196–98, 823–27, 906–14, 1021–28, II 688–94, 1013–21, and V 187–94, 416–31, with Cicero, *De natura deorum* II 37; see also, e.g., Plato, *Laws* X 889b–892c; Aristotle, *Physics* II 4.196a24–196b4, II 6.198a5–13, II 8.199b5–7; and Fénélon, *Traité de l'existence et des attributs de Dieu* I 1; Leibniz, *Philosophische Schriften* (Gerhart ed.), VII:273.

50. *Narcissus* [2]; *Origin of Languages* 4 [4], 19 [2]; *Emile* IV, *OC* IV:453; *Nouvelle Héloïse* V 5, *OC* II:594–95; *Social Contract* I 7 [9]; and cf. *Rêveries* III, *OC* I:1016.

51. Lucretius, *De natura rerum* (I 936–42 = IV 11–17). Tasso adopts the metaphor at the beginning of *Jerusalem Delivered* (I 3). Rousseau quotes Tasso's formulation in the Second Preface to the *Nouvelle Héloïse* (*OC* II:17). He translated portions of the first two books of Tasso's poem: *OC* V:1277–95.

52. See, e.g., the cogent comments by Jean Ghénno, *Jean-Jacques, histoire d'une conscience* (Paris: Gallimard, 1962), 2:109–11; or by Karl Barth, *Protestant Thought from Rousseau to Ritschl,* trans. Brian Cozens (New York: Simon and Schuster, 1969), 91–92.

53. And consider: "doubt is as rare among the People as assertion [*l'affirmation*] is among true Philosophers" (*Discourse on Heroic Virtue* [13]).

54. We cannot know whether motion is essential to matter; we can therefore not deny that it is; and hence cannot reject materialism or atheism: *Letter to Voltaire* [30]. It is impossible to conceive of movement as a natural property of matter: *Fiction, ou morceau allégorique sur la révélation, OC* IV:1046. Motion cannot be of the essence of matter if we can conceive of matter at rest: author's note inserted into the Savoyard Vicar's *Profession of Faith, Emile* IV, *OC* IV:574★; *Lettre à Christophe de Beaumont, Archevêque de Paris, OC* IV:955; and the fuller discussion of the difficulties surrounding these problems, ibid., pp. 955–57.

While Rousseau also raises questions about Buffon's "organic molecules" as well as about Lucretius's "soul atoms" (*To Franquières* [13]), there is no reason to believe that he is prepared to reject them out of hand any more than he categorically rejects Locke's suggestion of thinking matter: *Emile* IV, OC IV:575★; *Fiction, ou morceau allégorique sur la révélation, OC* IV:1046. Regarding the parallel between Buffon's "organic molecules" and Lucretius's *primordia rerum*, see Jacques Roger's classic *Les sciences de la vie dans la pensée française du XVIIIè siècle* (Paris: Armand Collin, 1971), 548–51, 581, as well his "Diderot et Buffon en 1749," *Diderot Studies* 4 (1963): 221–36. On the mid-eighteenth-century French debates about thinking matter, see John W. Yolton, *Locke and French Materialism* (Oxford: Clarendon, 1991).

55. The pervasive influence of Lucretius's poem, especially on the *Second Discourse*—the writing of Rousseau's which Diderot most influenced and liked best (*Confessions* VIII, *OC* I:389), and which Rousseau himself several times explicitly describes as about "the nature of things" (P [7], E [6], I [52])—was first noted by J. de Castillon, *Discours sur l'inégalité parmi les hommes. Pour servir de réponse au Discours que M. Rousseau, Citoyen de Génève, a publié sur le même sujet* (Amsterdam, 1756). It is documented in Jean Morel's classic "Recherches sur les sources du Discours de l'inégalité," *Annales de la Société Jean-Jacques Rousseau* 5 (1909): 119–98; see also L. Robin, *La pensée hellénique,* 2d ed. (Paris: PUF, 1967), 550–51 n. 1; L. Strauss, *Natural Right and History* (Chicago: University of Chicago Press, 1953), 271 n. 37; J. H. Nichols Jr., *Epicurean Political Philosophy* (Ithaca: Cornell University Press, 1976), esp. 198–207; J.-J. Rousseau, *Diskurs über die Ungleichheit/Discours sur l'inégalité,* ed. H. Meier (Paderborn: Schöningh, 1984), s. v. Lukrez. Rousseau cites Lucretius directly in his detailed challenge to the theological account of creation (*Lettre à Christophe de Beaumont, Archevêque de Paris, OC* IV:957), and he mentions the *clinamen* (swerve) of Lucretius's atoms (*De natura rerum* II 292) in the *Fiction, ou morceau allégorique sur la révélation, OC* IV:1046. René Hubert sees a parallel between the *clinamen* and the "accidents" in Rousseau's *Second Discourse: Rousseau et l'Encyclopédie* (Paris: Gamber, 1928), 95. For the Lucretian echoes in the *Essay on the Origin of Languages,* see V. Gourevitch, "'The First Times' in Rousseau's *Essay on the Origin of Languages,*" *Graduate Faculty Philosophy Journal* 11 (1986): 139–41, and "The Political Argument of Rousseau's *Essay on the Origin of Languages,*" in *Pursuits of Reason: Essays in Honor of Stanley Cavell,* ed. J. Cohen, P. Guyer, and H. Putnam (Lubbock: Texas Tech University Press, 1993), 21–35.

56. Diogenes Laertius, *Lives* 10 (Epicurus), Letter to Menoeceus, 134. On the relationship between Epicurus's physics and his moral teaching, see, e.g., Bailey's Prolegomena to his edition of Lucretius (vol. I, p. 64).

Dostoyevsky's Trojan Horse: *A Raw Youth*

JOSEPH N. FRANK

A Raw Youth is a curious hybrid of a novel and represents something of an anomaly among the great creations of Dostoyevsky's last period, which began with *Notes from Underground* in 1864. Written between *The Devils* and *The Brothers Karamazov*, *A Raw Youth* is far from attaining the artistic stature of these two great works. To be sure, its severest critics have considerably exaggerated its defects, and a just appreciation of the book has also been hampered by the now superseded and totally errone-ous notion that Dostoyevsky was a hasty and careless writer, capable of throwing anything on a page to meet a deadline. The consensus of critical opinion, however, is surely right in maintaining that here Dostoyevsky sinks below the level of his masterpieces.

A Raw Youth unquestionably contains some extremely effective and moving scenes of childhood in Dostoyevsky's best "philanthropic" man-ner, and his inner portrait of a rebellious adolescent is often quite touching and persuasive. The book is also distinguished by Dostoyevsky's most modulated and sympathetic depiction of a member of the Romantic Ide-alist generation of the 1840s in Russian culture, which rises to a visionary height of lyrical pathos. Nonetheless, all too much of the text relies on a moth-eaten melodramatic plot; and the touches of genuine feeling and

This essay is a reduced version of a chapter in the fifth volume of my books on Dostoyevsky's life and works. I began to work seriously on Dostoyevsky at the University of Chicago, and my doctoral thesis for the Committee on Social Thought was on *Notes from Underground*. I was then taking courses and tutorials with David Grene, and my own work was greatly influenced then, and has remained so, by the inspiring example of his approach to literature and cultural history.

ideological elevation are more or less swamped by a dreary, quasi-criminal intrigue that Dostoyevsky never succeeds in integrating with his deeper theme.

Why should *A Raw Youth* have slumped so markedly when compared with Dostoyevsky's other major novels? Writers, even great ones, do not necessarily produce masterpieces each time they put pen to paper; and perhaps no really satisfactory answer can ever be given to such a question. But so far as an answer is possible, it may perhaps be located in the implicit self-censorship that Dostoyevsky exercised on his creative faculties in this particular instance. He was not working freely here, as he had always done in the past, and following his inspiration wherever it might lead; he was writing under the pressure of a commitment to the *Notes of the Fatherland,* the journal that had contracted to publish his novel. It was also the leading organ of the radical Populists, who were carrying on the social-cultural tradition that Dostoyevsky had fought all through the 1860s. To be sure, for reasons of his own, Dostoyevsky had chosen this commitment quite freely; but since such a choice of venue obviously inclined him to trim his inspiration to the literary and ideological standards of his Populist readers, this may help to explain why he produced a work inferior to his best creative level.

Dostoyevsky himself stated later that he had decided to write only a "first draft" of the novel about fathers and children that had begun to burgeon in his notes. This preliminary version initially seemed to be working toward *The Brothers Karamazov,* but he reduced the theme of parricide to that of parental irresponsibility and substituted a relatively innocent and boyishly illusory romantic rivalry between father and son for the merciless Oedipal clash in *The Brothers Karamazov* that made such a deep impression on Freud. In other words, Dostoyevsky decided to write a social-psychological novel of relatively limited range, giving up any attempt to dramatize the collision of conflicting moral-spiritual absolutes that invariably inspired his best work. He thus devoted himself to writing a book whose theme did not tap the deepest sources of his imagination, and that was, in addition, out of kilter with the literary means he had developed to express his own worldview.

A Raw Youth is a novel combining elements of both the picaresque and the bildungsroman (the novel of education). The protagonist is a young man, the illegitimate son of a Russian nobleman of ancient lineage by a serf mother, who is thrown for the first time into a worldly milieu and, under the impact of his experiences there, acquires maturity and self-knowledge. Dostoyevsky mentions both *Gil Blas* and *David Copperfield* in his notes as guideposts for his own creation, and both are classic examples of these two novelistic genres. Both types, though, require extended stretches of time for their action to be accomplished: the picaresque hero must come into contact with a wide range of adventures up and down the social scale, and a transition to maturity can be completed only over an extended period. What happens here, however, is that Dostoyevsky treats his subject with his usual *roman-feuilleton* technique, which compresses events into a brief span of time, strives for tightly plotted effects of mystery and surprise, and creates a world in which characters exist in a constant state of heightened emotional tension. This supercharged atmosphere is quite appropriate for Dostoyevsky's other major novels, in which his eschatological vision of human life blends with his crime-thriller plotting to create a unity of dramatic suspense, psychological veri-similitude, and moral-philosophical profundity. But when the same treatment is accorded a subject of lesser scope, where the conflicts hardly raise issues of earth-shaking importance, the tragedy becomes melodrama and the sustained fervor is apt to seem exaggeratedly inflated.

Unfortunately, this is what occurs all too often in *A Raw Youth;* and to make matters worse, Dostoyevsky draws liberally on a whole range of effects familiar from his other creations. Numerous incidents and motifs, borrowed from his indigenous artistic repertory, are scarcely changed in their new employment, and they invariably seem incongruous, out of place, and greatly diminished in their effectiveness. Not that we cannot find repetitions and recurrences of character types and motifs in the other novels—but these have always been recast and assimilated to a new artistic context. What strikes one in *A Raw Youth* is precisely this lack of a new artistic fusion, or perhaps, more accurately, the impossibility of such a fusion taking place because of the disparity between Dostoyevsky's purely social-psychological theme and his technique. With a central figure whose life involved some supreme moral-metaphysical ambition, it was relatively easy to invent a plot action (or to employ an already-existing one, as in *The Devils*) that would be both spectacular and true to character. Where the mainspring of the theme, however, is not any such ambition, it is difficult to invent convincing action that both creates extreme dramatic tension and is psychologically plausible. Dostoyevsky, alas, takes the easy way out in *A Raw Youth* and stuffs it with all sorts of hackneyed plot ingredients (concealed letters, lawsuits over disputed heritages, attempts at blackmail, etc.), which allows him to whip up excitement by means that are purely mechanical and remain external to his themes. Moreover, he obviously found it impossible to integrate his main thematic-ideological concerns with such shopworn devices; and instead of these emerging naturally from the plot action as they do elsewhere, they appear as extraneous intrusions in the form of static monologues and inset stories.

It would be unfair, however, to bear down too heavily on the defects of *A Raw Youth,* which is by no means a negligible novel if judged by any standards other than those of the greatest Dostoyevsky. And if some of its defects may be ascribed to having been written for the Populist journal, this place of publication also gives a special interest to many details of the text, in which, as it were, Dostoyevsky plays hide-and-seek with his presumptive readers. *A Raw Youth* is Dostoyevsky's first artistic response to the challenges posed by the new phase of Russian culture inaugurated by the ideology of Russian Populism in the 1870s. What fascinated Dostoyevsky with this new ideology of the left was that it did not reject the Christian moral ideals of love and self-sacrifice, as the Nihilism of the 1860s had done so thoroughly, but it refused to accept such ideals as divinely inspired and hence as the only means through which human life could be transformed. No longer could he (or would he) attack the radicals head-on, as he had done during the previous decade; their Populist ideology evoked too many echoes of that Utopian Socialist past which still continued to vibrate in his own sensibility—a past in which he had sympathized with those who, far from rejecting the divinity of Christ, had wished to give his teachings an earthly realization through the power of example. The Populists were no longer the all-destroying devils whom, in *The Devils,* he had wished to expel from the body of Russian man, and who were fit only to be drowned in the sea; they now cherished the same Christian moral values as Dostoyevsky himself and shared his idealization of the Russian people. What was necessary, from his point of view, was to bring them back to a full acceptance of the faith of the people as well; and we can observe him obliquely advancing this message in his text, which thus becomes a kind of Trojan horse introduced into the very journalistic citadel of the former enemy.

A Raw Youth is written as a first-person confessional memoir by the title character, Arkady Dolgoruky, the natural son of the once-wealthy aristocrat now down on his luck (he has already run through three fortunes) and philosophical seeker after truth Andrey Petrovich Versilov. Arkady sets out, a year after the events have occurred, to recount the circumstances that have brought about a change in his life and transformed his character. While Arkady-as-narrator obviously knows the future of the events he is so laboriously conveying, his naive determination to stick to the facts of his past as he had encountered them *then* allows Dostoyevsky to preserve the sudden peripeties of his intricate plot. At the end of the book, Arkady remarks, "I have suddenly become aware that I have re-educated myself through the process of recalling events and writing them down"; and this process of reeducation takes place as Arkady-as-narrator evaluates the past behavior of Arkady-as-character.

The intrigue of *A Raw Youth* is unusually complex and bewildering, and the fact that Arkady fails to understand much of what is going on around him does not help matters at all. The major plot involves Versilov and the nineteen-year-old Arkady, who has just come to live with his family (his unmarried peasant mother and equally illegitimate sister Liza) for the first time. Arkady carries a letter entrusted to him and sewn into his jacket that compromises Katerina Akhmakova, the beauteous widow of a general and a princess in her own right. The letter asks for legal advice about committing her elderly father, Prince Sokolsky, to an institution for the mentally enfeebled; and she fears that, if he learns of this document, she will be cut out of his will. Both Katerina and Versilov are in search of this letter and suspect that Arkady possesses it or can lead them to its whereabouts. Two other subplots also run through the book, each concerning another child of Versilov's. One centers on his legitimate daughter by his deceased first wife, Anna Andreyevna, who has designs on the warmhearted but addlepated elderly Prince Sokolsky. The enormously wealthy prince is an ardent but, by this time, quite harmless admirer of female pulchritude, and toward the end the helpless prince is kidnapped by the much younger Anna, who plans to marry him and ensure her future. A second subplot focuses on Arkady's sister Liza, who has an affair with a *young* Prince Sokolsky and becomes pregnant by this well-meaning but flighty and spineless aristocratic scion.

All these plots taken together illustrate the moral chaos of Russian society, and especially of the upper class, that Dostoyevsky wished to drive home; each reveals some infraction or violation of the normal family relationship, or of the moral code governing the relations between the sexes. Also, each of the subplots is meant to bring out, as is typical for Dostoyevsky, the significance of the main one by modulation and contrast. Arkady, who has become madly infatuated with the ravishing Katerina, and is troubled by the sexual stirrings appropriate to his age, is tempted to behave like Anna Andreyevna and to blackmail the haughty Katerina into submission with his letter.

At the core of the book is the character of Arkady, on whom Dostoyevsky later commented in his *Diary of a Writer:* "I took an innocent soul, but one already soiled with the dreadful possibility of depravity, with a precocious hatred for his insignificance and 'accidental' nature, tainted also by that breadth of character with which a still chaste soul already consciously allows vice to enter its thoughts, cherishes it, and admires it in shameful but bold and tempestuous dreams—and with all this, left solely to its own devices and its own understanding, yet also, to be sure, with God." The sexual emphasis of these lines might seem to confirm the view, expressed most forcefully by Horst-Jürgen Gerigk, that the key to Arkady's character lies in such a crisis of puberty; but while Arkady is certainly undergoing such a crisis as a raw youth, the important point is contained in the last phrase of Dostoyevsky's text. Arkady's problem is not simply that he has been stirred by sex but that he is left "solely to his own devices" and has nowhere to turn for moral guidance and support; his sexuality is physically but not thematically primary and is only the biological manifestation of life's challenge to his sense of values and moral conscience.

With his mixture of justified exasperation and scarcely suppressed rage, his quasi-comical and self-glorifying aspiration toward dominance and power, Arkady is an adolescent variation of the underground man. He is, however, projected as a touching and sympathetic figure, not at all as a grotesque *persona* who acts out one or another dead end of Russian radical ideology. Determined to live as a self-proclaimed egoist and to isolate himself entirely from society, he hopes to amass a fortune and "to become a Rothschild"; once having scaled such a financial height, he will have gained absolute power over the whole world—or rather, the "consciousness" of such power. But these scarifying intentions, inspired by the influence of Pushkin's *The Covetous Knight* (one of Dostoyevsky's old favorites), are nothing but the pitiful, compensatory daydreams of a poor, neglected schoolboy who has been left to fend for himself emotionally and has suffered constant humiliation because of his irregular parentage. Dostoyevsky thus grounds Arkady's "underground" impulses and behavior in a "philanthropic" social-psychological context that makes them understandable and forgivable. One recalls that, just before writing this novel, he had told an acquaintance, shocked by the "frightening truth" of *Notes from Underground,* that he could now write "more brightly, in a more conciliatory way." And this is exactly what he does in *A Raw Youth,* where Arkady's love-hate dialectic with the world is seen as the twisted expression of an essentially candid and high-minded young personality shamefully thrown back on itself.

Arkady's youthful freshness and innocence are conveyed both by the naively enthusiastic and hyperbolic style of his narrative and, more obviously, by numerous incidents that reveal his "true" nature. Even after making up his mind to become "a Rothschild," he cannot restrain himself from spontaneously using his savings to look after a baby girl left on the doorstep of his home. Moreover, the "ideological" expression of his ego-ism also has a magnanimous aspect that recalls the underground man's phase of Social Romanticism, though here it is not given any satirical edge: Arkady wishes to become a Rothschild not because he values money for its own sake, not because he wishes to wallow in luxury and to indulge his appetites to the fullest, but solely for the sensation of power that his wealth would entail. Once this feeling was attained, the fantasy of the unhappy boy imagines himself donating all this enormous wealth to humanity. "Then, not from ennui, not from aimless weariness, but because I have a boundless desire for what is great, I shall give all my millions away, let society distribute my wealth and I . . . I will mix with nothingness again." Arkady here parallels the underground man in his "sublime and beautiful" phase, when he imagines that "I became a multi-millionaire and at once devoted all my wealth to the improvement of the human race . . . and I'd go off, barefoot and hungry, to preach new ideas and inflict another Waterloo on the reactionaries."

Arkady's character thus contains a large dose of innate youthful ideal-ism and innocence, which impels him toward some sort of "ideal" goal; but this goal has been deflected and distorted by the seething resentments of his ego and by the reigning selfishness of his corrupt society, with its shameless scramble for wealth and position. Arkady is initially infected by such corruption, but Dostoyevsky takes care to indicate that he wishes to obtain his financial goal only by "honorable" means. He would train his body and mind, subsist only on black bread, tea, and a little soup rather than eating his meals, and save half of the little allowance he received from his guardians. In this way he submitted himself to something "like the monastic life and performing feats of monastic self-discipline. It's a feeling, not an idea," he writes. Such self-discipline, even if at first misdirected, can always for Dostoyevsky be turned into a genuine desire for self-sacrifice on behalf of a worthier goal. The same combination of "ideal-ism" and a self-centred egoism can also be seen in Arkady's father, Versi-lov, though these traits manifest themselves differently in the world-weary and highly sophisticated aristocrat than they do in the turbulent ado-lescent.

Versilov is far and away the most interesting character in the book, and after part 1 Dostoyevsky is unable to prevent him from taking the center of the stage away from Arkady despite the latter's function as first-person narrator. Arkady becomes so embroiled in keeping up with the runaway plot that he has little time to focus on his own evolution, while Versilov continues to grow and expand as the enigma of his personality is gradually unraveled. Initially, he is presented as a typical member of the generation of the 1840s, an affluent and high-minded gentleman filled with the "humanitarian" ideas of his time. Despite his "advanced" ideas, however, Versilov did not scruple to seduce a bewildered peasant girl, Sofya, who had been married off with no regard for *her* wishes to a much older husband. Such affairs, of course, were routine for Russian landowners, but Arkady suggests that there was more here than merely a momentary flare-up of passion. Prettier and more compliant girls, with whom Versilov could have amused himself, were readily available but neglected.

Versilov did not abandon Sofya entirely, taking her along as a companion on his European travels so long as she still remained attractive; but this did not prevent him from turning over Arkady's upbringing entirely to strangers, and callously leaving Sofya to fend for herself when he became infatuated with Katerina Akhmakova in Bad Ems. The poor Russian girl, unable to speak a word of any other language, was rescued by "Auntie" Tatyana Pavlovna, who looks after Arkady's welfare as well and turns up in crucial moments of his life to operate as a sharp-tongued, irascible, but unstintedly devoted deus ex machina throughout the plot. Versilov's character always exhibits this same mixture of abstract and lofty high-mindedness with a personal self-centeredness that rides roughshod over all other considerations.

Arkady's attitude to Versilov in part 1 combines a secret admiration and hero worship of his glamorous father with hostile resentment and gnawing envy. He had once caught a glimpse of Versilov performing in some amateur theatricals in a sumptuous Moscow mansion—his one and only momentary admittance to the splendiferous upper-class world from which he had been excluded—and he had never gotten over this impression during all his years of solitary childhood misery. At first he had idealized this radiant image of his father enthroned in another and higher realm; but what he hears of the gossip about Versilov changes his mind entirely. Versilov is rumored to be guilty of the most dishonorable behavior—of once having been in love with Katerina, then of having proposed marriage to her invalid stepdaughter, who subsequently poisoned herself, and finally, of failing to respond with a challenge to a slap in the face given by the young Prince Sokolsky in outrage at this tawdry sequence of events. Arkady is plunged into despair by this destruction of his idol, and while initially having dreamed of coming to Petersburg to help him fight such "calumny" with the aid of the famous letter in his possession, he subsequently abandons all idea of doing so. But the narrator-Arkady also analyzes some of the motives of the character-Arkady at this juncture. "I must confess that the letter sewed in my pocket did not alone arouse in me the passionate desire to rush to Versilov's aid. . . . I had visions of a woman . . . a proud, aristocratic creature . . . whom I should meet face to face. She would laugh at me, despise me, as though I were a mouse; she would not even suspect her future was in my power. . . . Yes, I hated that woman, but already I loved her as my victim." It is through such self-scrutiny that Arkady will finally come to understand and forgive Versilov's similar love-hate relationship with the irresistible Katerina.

What happens in part I is designed to change Arkady's image of his father, who is by no means simply the scoundrelly blackguard that Arkady, in abandoning his hero worship, had now made him out to be. Versilov's conduct, all the same, reveals his inability ever to escape entirely from the insidious coils of a flattering and complacent self-concern. Every deed of Versilov has an ambiguously double aspect and is inwardly undermined by the desire always to be on a "pedestal." Dostoyevsky uses several minor episodes to present the continuously shifting perspective from which Versilov is viewed, and this perspective is simply the objective correlative (to use a useful, if now-forgotten, term of T. S. Eliot) of his own inner uncertainty and moral instability. The strongest sense we get of Versilov's character, however, is not in such carefully contrived incidents but during his lengthy conversations with Arkady. If there is one circumstance in which a Dostoyevsky character comes to life, it is when he or she is given a monologue; and some of the best pages in *A Raw Youth* are those in which the characters express themselves in relative independence of the intrigue. Versilov's conversations with Arkady in part I successfully communicate the mixture of charm, intelligence, and blasé sensibility that make him so appealing a personage; but they also reveal an attitude of disillusionment or despairing frivolity, an ingrained inability to take himself (or anything else) with unqualified seriousness, which indicates his basic lack of moral substance. It is Dostoyevsky's ability to convey both the sensitivity of Versilov's insight and the disengaging twist of his self-reflexive irony that manages to redeem a good many of the scenes of *A Raw Youth*.

The history of Versilov will gradually disclose his hopeless inability to master the passions that lie at the root of his self-debilitating mockery, and that illustrate Dostoyevsky's theme that the noblest and most sincerely held ideals are ultimately futile if not grounded in an emotive source penetrating the entire personality. The discussion in the Socialist group at Dergachev's between Arkady and the unhappy young man Kraft, who commits suicide a few days after their conversation because he has lost faith in Russia, specifically brings out the importance of values being embedded in an "idea-feeling" pervading the personality to its very core, and the impossibility of replacing such an "idea-feeling" by any abstract notion such as a "future unknown people." Dostoyevsky here is obviously transposing, in these particular terms, his perennial theme of humanity's need for an irrational faith (specifically, a faith in Christ as God–Man, and hence a belief in immortality and resurrection) as the only secure buttress of moral values.

The attack on Kraft by other members of the Dergachev circle also inspires Arkady to spring to his defense with a lengthy and impassioned outburst. Just as Kraft is in the grip of an idea-feeling about Russia, so Arkady has his own idea-feeling of becoming a Rothschild; and no abstract argument can touch the resentments of his ego in which this idea-feeling has its root. Arkady is searching for a new ideal, a new faith, that can help him to overcome his smoldering need for revenge and power; but he sees in his Socialist interlocutors only a demand that he surrender his individuality entirely. His tirade at this point has frequently been compared to that of the underground man, as he affirms a similarly passionate, egoistic self-assertion against a Socialist world consisting of "barracks, communistic homes, *stricte nécessaire,* atheism, and communistic wives without children." Just how seriously one is supposed to take this outpouring is difficult to judge: Dostoyevsky knew very well that such doctrines were now entirely out of date, and Arkady's anachronistic attack was probably intended both as another illustration of his callowness and also to evoke a tolerant smile from the up-to-date readers of *Notes of the Fatherland.* It may very well, in addition, have been meant to cushion the much more pertinent challenge to the Populist position that Dostoyevsky also manages to slip in.

In the course of defending his own egoism, Arkady raises the question of what might inspire him to surrender it voluntarily. "Why should I be bound to love my neighbor, or your future humanity," Arkady cries, "which I shall never see, which will never know anything about me, and which will in its turn disappear and leave no trace (time counts as nothing in this) when the earth in its turn will be changed into an iceberg and will fly off into the void with an infinite multitude of other similar icebergs?" A life without the prospect of eternity thus can cripple the will to be "noble and self-sacrificing" in the present—and Arkady (and through him Dostoyevsky) was talking precisely to those who had dedicated themselves to realizing such an ideal *without* any hope of this kind. From where would they derive the idea-feelings necessary to support their beneficent aims if, like Kraft, they became disillusioned with those aims for whatever reason? Dostoyevsky is in effect telling his Populist readers, through Arkady's naively awkward explosion, that altruistic (Christian) values cannot sustain such idea-feelings without the aid of a faith in Christ transcending reason; and this will also be the lesson that he hopes will emerge from the portrayal of Versilov's career as well.

The first section of *A Raw Youth* is largely devoted to depicting Arkady's character in its initial phase of hostility and rancor, and to exhibiting Versilov as a tolerant and all-comprehending observer of his son's unruly turbulence. The encounters between the two are touching and effective because they spring from the basic father-son relationship and are not yet distorted by the complications of the intrigue; the plot only begins to dominate in the second section, which takes place after a lapse of two months. Now the novel turns into a series of picaresque adventures as Arkady—transformed into a fashionable young dandy-about-town—plunges into a whirl of social life with an eagerness fostered by his previous sense of exclusion. "Why those old painful lacerations, my solitary and gloomy childhood, my foolish dreams under my quilt, my vows, my calculations, even my 'idea'?" Arkady asks himself. "I imagined and invented all that, and it turns out that the world's not like that at all." But neither, as it also turns out, is the world as rosy-hued as the bemused Arkady now believes it to be; in fact, he experiences one disillusioning shock after another, and these become so severe that he is seized by the criminal impulse to set the entire world on fire.

All of Arkady's misadventures in this second part may be viewed as an exposure to the effect of what Dostoyevsky calls "the Russian curse." This phrase is used by the young Prince Sokolsky to describe his own character, but in fact it applies to all the others from the upper classes as well; they all exhibit one degree or another of the prince's hopeless moral instability, which disintegrates, under extreme pressure, into a pathological split personality. "No, you don't know my nature," he tells Arkady, "or else there is something I don't know myself, because it seems I have more than one nature." Prince Sergey nourishes the highest conceptions of his obligation to maintain, as a member of one of Russia's oldest aristocratic families, the most rigid standards of personal honor; yet he is guilty of the most contemptible and disloyal conduct and continually violates his own standards. When Arkady, at the height of his euphoria as a man of the world, is accused of dishonesty at a high-toned gambling establishment, his supposed "friend" Prince Sokolsky refuses to acknowledge his existence at all.

The same "Russian curse" casts its shadow over the beauteous Katerina, whom Dostoyevsky fails to characterize in any memorable fashion; she remains a somewhat indistinct figure of a wellborn society woman longing vaguely for a more meaningful life and unhappily trapped in a web of sordid circumstances. One of her major scenes in this part is a rendezvous that she arranges with Arkady that arouses his fervent hopes, and in which he displays all the youthful ardor of his infatuation. He learns later from Versilov, however, that Katerina had arranged to have their interview overheard. This revelation is a crushing blow to his amorous pretensions, but Katerina's betrayal of his confidence does not destroy his faith in her moral integrity. It leads him, rather, to a growing awareness of the complexity of human motivation, a knowledge which he is then honest enough to apply to himself. The upshot is that Arkady feels less and less like judging others harshly and peremptorily as the book proceeds, and the emotional pressure of his resentments gradually ebbs as he becomes conscious of his own fallibility.

None of these disillusionments is as severe as the one that occurs in relation to Versilov, whose elevation of spirit makes his vulnerability to "the Russian curse" all the more disturbing and unsettling. At the beginning of part 2, Versilov is presented as a propounder of the loftiest ideas, as a man deeply and penetratingly preoccupied with the most crucial problems of his time; but his wisdom and insight are always tinged with a feeling of impotence. Haughtily impugning the "materialism" of the modern world, he predicts to Arkady that it will finally collapse in "general bankruptcy" and lead to a class war between "the beggars" and the "bondholders and creditors." But when Arkady inquires anxiously what can be done about this frightening perspective of the future, he only replies that "to do nothing is always best. One's conscience is at rest anyway, knowing that one's had no share in anything." Versilov also advises Arkady "to become a great man" by obeying the Ten Commandments "in spite of all your doubts and questionings," and to have faith in God. But when Arkady retorts irritably to these well-worn pieties that perhaps he does not believe in God, Versilov casually replies that "it is a very good thing" to be a Russian atheist; "our atheists are respectable people and extremely conscientious pillars of the fatherland, in fact" (one suspects that this odd comment was occasioned by the Populist "atheistic" acceptance of Christian morality already referred to). Versilov's words, in any event, are a series of moral perceptions that end either in hopelessness or self-negation; it is small wonder that Arkady, though properly impressed, can find little in them to guide his own life.

Indeed, Arkady's "egoism" is hardly likely to be affected by Versilov's ideas about loving one's neighbor, which anticipate those of Ivan Karamazov. Versilov appears in a much less advantageous light, indeed as mentally unbalanced, as the intrigue of part 2 unfolds; but it cannot be said that Dostoyevsky succeeds in making him as interesting a psychopath as he does when portraying him as an "idealist." Versilov's lack of moral equilibrium is depicted either in terms of trivial capriciousness (such as his senseless act of challenging the young prince to a duel and withdrawing the challenge an hour later) or as a dark intriguer conniving against his own son. He plays a shameful role in relation to the confiding Arkady, who imparts the secret of his bewitchment by Katerina to his father. Leading him to open his heart completely, Versilov encourages Arkady's effusions only in the hope of obtaining information about the letter to use against Katerina. The scene takes place in the same sinister and tawdry atmosphere (a sleazy tavern) that had formerly symbolized the profound moral malaise eating away at Svidrigailov in *Crime and Punishment*. What was appropriate for Svidrigailov, however, seems strained and overdone for Versilov, who hardly has the same degree of crime on his conscience; his flouting of the social code and his love-hate passion for Katerina scarcely seem to require the same type of setting.

Similarly, we can observe Dostoyevsky struggling to inject some deep significance into Arkady's confidences to his father, which, as he approaches the ticklish matter of the letter, bring about a change in Versilov's previously assumed affability. "His eyes began to glow," Arkady notes. "A strange line, a line of deep gloom, was visible on his forehead." Arkady senses the presence of heinous depths in Versilov that he thought had been overcome, and he steps back at the last moment from confessing that the letter is still intact in his possession. To take revenge, Versilov informs Arkady that his passionate words to Katerina had been overheard, by prearranged connivance with Tatyana Pavlovna. "If I were Othello and you Iago," Arkady tells him, "you could not have done better." Versilov is no Iago, though, but rather a species of Othello himself, unable to control the surges of his irresistible fury against the woman who had spurned his love. Using what he learns from Arkady, Versilov writes Katerina an insulting letter asking her not "to seduce" an innocent lad to gain her sordid ends; and Arkady is thus humiliated and betrayed by his father in the eyes of the woman he adores.

Much of part 2 is vitiated by similar attempts of Dostoyevsky, using all the resources of his technical skill, to inflate the rather paltry material of the plot intrigue by various means (such as the Shakespearean allusions). Dostoyevsky only strikes a more successful note when he concludes the section with Arkady's dream of his childhood. Here Arkady's boyhood suddenly emerges as he recalls the one-and-only visit of his peasant mother to the school for young noblemen in which he had been placed by Versilov (as he thought, but actually by Tatyana Pavlovna). Made aware of his lowly social status by brutal mistreatment, the poor, forsaken boy has come to internalize the standards of class snobbishness responsible for his persecution; and when his mother arrives, he receives her coldly, ashamed of her humility, awkwardness, and lower-class dress and comportment. Arkady's "education" had dried up the sources of the most natural and instinctive emotions, and he thus cannot respond to his mother's love out of abasement before his upper-class schoolfellows, who in any case treat him with contempt. It is only six months later that the memory of her visit abruptly floods back, and Arkady's aching loneliness and need for love momentarily triumph over the barrier of class prejudice. Coming across the faded, blue-cotton handkerchief in which his mother had wrapped a few coins to leave with him, he suddenly, overwhelmed with grief and contrition, kisses the memento as he lies sobbing in his bed. All the genuine pathos of his human situation is poured into such a scene, and by placing it close to the end of his second section, Dostoyevsky indicates that Arkady has now opened himself to an involvement with others and to the responsibilities that such involvement entails.

By the end of part 2, Arkady is thus ready for the major transformation of his personality that will be the reward for all his sufferings. An essential factor in this transformation is his encounter at last with the "legal" father whose name he bears—the peasant Makar Ivanovich Dolgoruky. Makar is the only peasant character of any importance in Dostoyevsky's novels (we are not counting the peasant convicts in the semidocumentary *House of the Dead*), and his inclusion can surely be attributed to a desire to make literary capital out of the Populist idealization of the peasantry, as well as, unquestionably, an urge to compete with Tolstoy's Platon Karataev in *War and Peace*. While Versilov's injunctions to Arkady had been that of a man who, at bottom, entertained no belief in his own convictions, Makar is filled with a tranquil certainty that Arkady has never encountered before. The religious "wanderer" is depicted as a person of great dignity and purity of heart. Nothing could contrast more strongly with the motives and machinations of the "educated" characters, who are unable to overcome the various egotistical ambitions that color all their conduct. Moreover, the words of old Makar, waiting to die with a calm and joyous serenity of spirit and an untroubled faith in Christ's promise, provide Arkady with the moral inspiration he had vainly been seeking all his life.

What Arkady finds embodied in Makar is a secure conviction of the ultimate goodness of God's creation and a profound sense of wonder and awe at the transcendent mystery both of human existence and of life after death. Makar's ecstatic celebration of the beauty of life comes, as is usual in Dostoyevsky, from a consciousness haunted by death; but death for

Makar is no longer the stabbing anguish of terror before the mystery of the unknown that Dostoyevsky had depicted in *The Idiot*. It is, rather, the natural fulfillment of a life devoted to God—a life whose termination it would be "sinful" to protest against and which still keeps its contact with the world of the living. "'You may forget me, dear ones,' Makar says, 'but I love you from the tomb.'" It is after this affirmation that the deeply impressed Arkady declares to Makar: "There is no 'seemliness' in them. . . . I won't follow them. I don't know where I'm going, I'll go with you." Both Arkady and Makar are in a feverish and slightly hysterical state during this dialogue, and their weakened condition helps to add psychological plausibility to their rhapsodic words. Although Arkady's resolution "to follow" Makar and presumably to become "a wanderer" like him is obviously not meant to be taken literally, the impression left by Makar will never be forgotten.

Dostoyevsky manages to make Makar a touching and believable fig-ure despite the obvious idealization and despite the manifest aim of illus-trating the indestructible connection, in the soul of the Russian peasant, between Christian faith and the virtues that the Populists admired. This aim comes out most clearly when Arkady, as an up-to-date young man, decides to argue with Makar in favor of the "modern" secular emphasis on "good works" that Dostoyevsky saw as the heart of the Populist moral-ity. "I drew him a picture of the useful activity in the world of the man of science, the doctor, of any friend of humanity, and roused him to real enthusiasm. . . . 'That's so, dear, that's so!' Makar said. 'God bless you, your thoughts are true!'" Makar is thus wholly on the side of working to alleviate the ills of mankind and of human society; but he adds that the life of "the desert," the life of a Christian hermit or ascetic inspired by faith, is also necessary. Without such an ideal, even the friends of human-ity "will forget their great work and will be absorbed in little things." Arkady enthusiastically tells Makar that he is preaching "absolute commu-nism"—a remark that both illustrates Arkady's simplicity and also allows Dostoyevsky to identify his own social ideals (as expressed through Makar) with those of the radical Populists. What continued to separate them, to be sure, was Dostoyevsky's conviction that such ideals could *only* be real-ized if the intelligentsia, in "going to the people," fused with them com-pletely by accepting their Christian faith in a supernatural Christ.

Arkady's conversations with Makar, which run through the first five chapters of the third part, are obviously placed as a parallel to Versilov's discourses at the beginning of the second part and are meant to be taken partly as a commentary on them. Makar's stories about Pyotr Valeriano-vich indicate Dostoyevsky's awareness of the ethical stirrings that had created a new literary type, "the repentant noblemen," who had replaced the "superfluous men" of the 1840s and appeared among the ranks of those "going to the people." Arkady responds: "I like your Pyotr Valerianovich. He's not a man of straw, anyway, but a real person, rather like a man near and well known to us both."

The scenes depicting Makar's stately descent into a dignified death alternate with the unrolling intrigue that presents Arkady with his greatest temptation. Arkady's old schoolfellow Lambert, who has been evoked by him in various recollections, finally makes his appearance on the scene to serve as his Mephistopheles. The figures of Lambert and his French mistress, Alphonsine, are pure caricature. The same is true for Lambert's two accomplices, the scallywags Trishatov and Andreev (the latter nicknamed *le grand dadais),* who are the same type of grotesque as several of the minor characters in *The Idiot* but lack the rueful cynicism that made these latter characters intermittently amusing. Dostoyevsky plays variations on his major themes in this comically absurdist key, and these two latter figures reveal the depths of iniquity and despair to which Arkady might have sunk.

Lambert has always been the epitome of soulless and shameless carnality for Arkady, and his arrival stirs Arkardy's lascivious longings with the plan to blackmail Katerina into sexual submission by means of his letter. Torn between "seemliness" and naked lust for Katerina, Arkady finds himself exposed to the full range of the conflict of opposites that constitutes "the Russian curse." "It always has been a mystery," he writes from his later vantage point as narrator, "and I have marveled a thousand times at that faculty in man (and in the Russian, I believe, more especially) of cherishing in his soul the loftiest ideal side by side with the most abject baseness, and all quite sincerely." The same enigma will soon torment Dimitry Karamazov; but here we are still with Arkady, whose situation at this point is very similar, in its inextricable tangle of love-hate feelings for Katerina as both goddess and temptress, to that of his father. And the recognition of this identity allows him to understand and emotionally to assimilate the events that climax the book in a furious cascade of melodrama.

Of greatest thematic importance in these final pages is a lengthy confession-speech by Versilov, which is uttered just after Makar Ivanovich has passed away. This death temporarily transfigures Versilov's personality, and in a sudden surge of confidence and genuine intimacy he finally divulges to Arkady the "idea" that has given inspiration to his life. To express this "idea," which is not an idea at all but a vision, Dostoyevsky reaches back into his unpublished files and resurrects the myth of the Golden Age, inspired by Claude Lorrain's painting *Acis and Galatea,* originally meant to have been included in Stavrogin's confession in *The Devils.*

Its use in this new context, however, is quite different from its initial significance. Stavrogin's dream of the Golden Age was conceived to show that, despite his rational disbelief in the existence of any distinction between good and evil, he knows the difference very well on the level of subliminal moral feeling. Versilov's version is not moral-psychological but historical-philosophical; it illustrates Dostoyevsky's own ideas about the future of European civilization and its relation to Russia. Moreover, in the ideological structure of *A Raw Youth,* Versilov's fantasy parallels that of Makar and is intended to supplement it by disclosing the essential unity of the Russian spirit even in such widely disparate representatives: Versilov projects in terms of European history what Makar expresses in terms of Russian apocalyptic religiosity.

Just as Makar Ivanovich had been a "wanderer" in Russia as a religious pilgrim, so Versilov says of himself: "I was a solitary wanderer" in Europe. In his own way, like Makar though on a different cultural level, he too was preaching the fulfillment of the reign of love and the advent of the Kingdom of God. "I cannot help respecting my position as a Russian nobleman," Versilov declares. "Among us has been created by the ages a type of the highest culture, never seen before and existing nowhere else in the world—a type of worldwide compassion for all." This type of Russian nobleman is a prototype of "the man of the future," and his role is precisely to transcend destructive national differences. The Russian European thus fulfills the injunctions of Christian love on the level of European history, since the law of his being is to be most himself in total abnegation to others. The Russian peasant-pilgrim Makar and the Russian European Versilov, each inspired by his own form of the Christian promise, are thus united in their service to this vision of a new Christian Golden Age.

But the difference that still continues to exist between them is captured in Versilov's remarkable evocation of an atheistic world deprived of belief in a divine Christ—a world that is the final outcome of the inexorable European process of self-destruction. "The great idea of old has left them, the great source of strength that till then had nourished and warmed them was vanishing like the majestic setting sun in Claude Lorrain's picture. . . . The great idea of immortality would have vanished, and they would have to fill its place, and all the wealth of love lavished of old upon Him who was immortal would be turned upon the whole of nature, on the world, on man, on every blade of grass." The result would be, in its own way, a Golden Age, but one stemming from profane, rather than sacred, love. "Men left forlorn would begin to draw together more closely and more lovingly; they would clutch one another's hands, realizing that they were all that was left for one another." Versilov can intuit both the

beauty and the pathos of this ultimate phase of European civilization because, despite all his other virtues as a Russian European, he has been
infected by the virus of atheism and is incapable of returning to the faith
of the Russian people.

Yet he understands that the profane Golden Age he imagines, a world
without immortality, would be pervaded by an aching sense of sadness
and sorrow. Versilov's character has been depicted as torn by irony, self-
doubt, melancholy, while Makar's is vitalized by a joyous serenity and
childlike gladness even in the face of death. The secret of Makar's tranquillity is of course his belief in the goodness of God—a belief that he expresses in a manner recalling the Christian pantheism of Saint Francis of
Assisi—and in a life beyond the tomb. This accent placed on the "sorrow"
of a world without God—even a world that realizes, in its own way, the
highest aspirations of Christian love—is Dostoyevsky's artistic answer to
the sublimest secular ideals of Socialism, which by this time he had identified with all of Western civilization.

Versilov finally breaks off his speech, acknowledging that "the whole
thing is a fantasy, even one that is quite unbelievable," but "I couldn't have
lived my whole life without it," he adds, "and without thinking about it."
He defines himself as "a deist, a philosophical deist," who presumably
believes in God but not in Christian miracles, but who yet cannot entirely
suppress his longing for a faith closer to that of Makar. "The remarkable
thing," he confides, "is that I always completed what I envisaged [the
Golden Age] with a vision, as did Heine in his 'Christ on the Baltic.' I
could not get by without it, could not fail to imagine Him in the last
resort among the orphaned people. He would come to them and stretch
out his arms to them and say: 'How could you have forgotten Him?' And
there and then the scales would fall from their eyes and there would burst
forth a great exalted hymn to the new and total resurrection. . . ."

This brilliant portrayal of the Golden Age, including a Feuerbachian
world in which humankind, rather than alienating its love to the supernatural, would lavish it on themselves, is one of the high points of Dostoyevsky's work. It equals, in expressive poignancy, Raskolnikov's dream of the
plague in the epilogue of *Crime and Punishment,* and one can hardly find
its match elsewhere until Hans Castorp's famous dream in the snow in
The Magic Mountain, which also begins with classical Greek imagery re-
creating a Golden Age and may well have been influenced by Dostoyevsky. One feels almost embarrassed in descending from such heights to
follow Dostoyevsky as he dutifully cranks up the machinery of his plot to
display the vacillations of Versilov on the level of the intrigue.

The ameliorating effect of Makar's death proves to be very short-lived, and all the most acute symptoms of "the Russian curse" now assail Versilov. Literally, he becomes two people: one who is contrite and remorseful over his eccentric and outrageous behavior, while the other continues to perform the most disgraceful actions under the uncontrollable influence of "a second self." "Do you know that I feel as though I were split in two?" Versilov says. "He looked around at us all with a terribly serious face and with perfectly genuine candor. 'Yes, I am really split in two mentally, and I'm horribly afraid of it.'" Just after these words, moved by the irresistible destructive force of his "second self," he smashes the icon left him as heritage and gage for the future by Makar. The Russian European "wanderer" from the intelligentsia, whatever the elevation of his spirit, is finally unable to take up the burden of the cross that would be the "allegory" of his reunion with the Russian people.

The plot proceeds fast and furiously at this point, like a reel of film turning at an accelerated pace, and it would be tedious to attempt to follow all its twists and turns. Suffice it to say that Arkady, while sitting in a jail cell, overcomes his temptation to blackmail Katerina into sexual submission and resolves not to seek revenge or any sort of personal advantage. "At such moments," he writes as narrator, "a man's future is determined, his final views on life are forged. 'Truth is there and that's where I must pursue it!' he says to himself." Arkady's single night in prison marks his transition to responsible manhood. It is now his passion-racked father who takes up the dastardly plan that Arkady had put behind him, and Versilov's demonic "second self" displays its last convulsions in joining Lambert to carry out the scheme of humiliating and blackmailing Katerina.

At the final moment, though, the gentlemanly Versilov is unable to withstand the sight of Lambert threatening Katerina with a pistol, and he leaps out of concealment to pistol-whip his erstwhile accomplice. Katerina faints dead away when he springs out of hiding, and he carries her in his arms, "the way a nurse holds a baby," as he walks up and down the room before depositing her gently on the bed. With gun in hand, he presumably intends to kill both her and himself in a high-Romantic *Liebestod* that would not have been out of place in his favorite opera, *Lucia di Lammermoor;* but Arkady, another onlooker in hiding, deflects his aim and the bullet only wounds him in the shoulder. The scene ends with Tatyana Pavlovna rushing in "screaming at the top of her voice" (all this takes place in her apartment), and with Versilov and Lambert both lying on the floor in pools of blood.

Arkady ventures some explanation of Versilov's incoherent behavior, remarking on the strange phenomenon of "the double" by which Versilov had been possessed. But Arkady confesses that "I have no explanation" and leaves it to the readers to come to their own conclusions, though he speaks of "the wicked symbolism" embodied in the smashing of the icon that presumably made it more than a "pathological" symptom. In remaining faithful to the callowness of his narrator, however, Dostoyevsky took the considerable risk of turning Versilov *too obviously* into a pathological case, and thus furnishing fuel to the critics who had always charged him with an unhealthy concern with psychic abnormality. Of all his major novels, *A Raw Youth* is the only one in which such a charge seems partly justified by the text. Elsewhere, psychic disorder is always presented as the symptom of a profound moral-spiritual crisis; here the balance tilts disturbingly because Versilov's convictions are too loosely linked to the plot action to allow his behavior to seem anything other than a sign of derangement despite Arkady's feeble speculations.

Versilov is now a helpless semi-invalid, entirely dependent on Sofya and Tatyana Pavlovna, and "as sincere and unaffected as a child. . . . His intelligence and his moral standards have remained unchanged, while his striving for an ideal has become even stronger." Nonetheless, the old, capricious Versilov emerges in a scaled-down replay of the superb death-bed scene of Stepan Trofimovich Verkhovensky in *The Devils*. Versilov first expresses a desire to observe the Lenten fast of the Orthodox Church, but then, two days later, because "something had irritated him unexpectedly, something he described laughingly as 'an amusing incongruity,'" he abandoned his intention. "'I do love God very much, my friends,' he said, 'but I simply have no talent for these things'"; no conversion of "the philosophical deist" to the rites of Orthodoxy takes place.

As for Arkady himself, it appears that he is in correspondence with Katerina, who is living abroad unmarried; there is even a hint that a certain intimacy has developed between them, but Arkady decorously refuses "to divulge the contents of this correspondence or repeat what we said to each other during our last meeting." All this, as with Raskolnikov and Sonya at the end of *Crime and Punishment,* "is a completely *new* story and, indeed, is still located in the future." Other details of the intrigue are also tidied up, but of most importance is Arkady's recasting of his "Rothschild idea," which he insists he has not abandoned at all but merely transformed. "Well, that new life, the new path I have discovered and am now following *is* precisely my 'idea'. . . but in such a completely different form that it is hardly recognizable." Presumably, the rigorous, almost monastic self-discipline he had imposed on himself to become a millionaire will now be employed to succor his family. But the generous Tatyana Pavlovna, his good angel in the guise of scolding taskmistress, promises to continue to support everyone until he completes his studies.

Dostoyevsky did not conclude his epilogue, however, only with the remarks of Arkady as narrator; it also contains extracts from a letter written to Arkady by his former mentor in Moscow, to whom he sent his manuscript for comment. Nikolay Semyonovich is described as a "completely objective and even coldly egotistical man, yet one of undoubted intelligence"; and much of what he says is taken from Dostoyevsky's notes for the preface he had intended to write to answer his critics when the novel, published in installments, appeared as a book. In addition to this external motivation, however, it is likely that, by the time he had reached the last stages of composition, he also felt an internal aesthetic need to shift to an outside observer—an observer who could transcend the necessary limitations of Arkady's still largely intellectually undeveloped point of view. One of the problems of the novel is that no general ideological theme emerges from the purely personal philanderings of Versilov that motivate the plot action; nor does Arkady's evolution from insubordinate adolescent to responsible adulthood provide any larger framework either. Hence the comments of Nikolay Semyonovich allow Dostoyevsky to guide the reader toward a broader social-cultural comprehension of what he had been striving to communicate.

To begin with, Nikolay Semyonovich extends Arkady's experiences so that they become typical of many more members of his generation; they are not only a matter of his individual destiny. "There are a great many boys like you, whose gifts really do always threaten to develop for the worse [into] either subservience or a covert desire to overthrow the status quo. But this desire to overthrow the status quo springs more often than not from a covert yearning for order and 'nobility' (I use your terms). Youth is pure because it is youth." Nikolay Semyonovich then launches into some remarks about the Russian novel that transpose Dostoyevsky's ideas about Tolstoy and his own place in Russian literature.

If he were a novelist, says this judicious gentleman, he would always make sure that his "heroes came from the Russian hereditary nobility, because it is only among that type of cultivated Russian that an appearance of beauty and refinement in living is possible, something so essential to a novel if it is to leave an elegant impression on the reader." Without mentioning Tolstoy, Dostoyevsky's spokesman obviously refers to him when affirming that a novelist aiming to leave such an elegant impression "would only write historical novels, since there are no longer beautiful types in our time. . . . Such a novel, written by a great talent, would belong not so much to Russian literature as to Russian history; it would provide an artistically finished picture of a Russian mirage, but one that really existed so long as no one guessed it was a mirage." The reference to *War and Peace* is unmistakable; and we see that Dostoyevsky had no illusions about the "beauty" of the forms of life of the Russian nobility. Since they were based on the slavery of serfdom, he knew very well that they had only been a "mirage," capable of enduring only if their foundation remained unquestioned. "Yes, Arkady Makarovich," he is told by his counselor, "you are *a member of an accidental family,* in complete contrast to all our recent types of legitimate hero who had boyhoods and youths quite unlike yours"—an obvious allusion to Tolstoy's trilogy, *Childhood, Boyhood, Youth.* As the letter continues, various members of Versilov's two families are also characterized, but we need only cite what is said about Versilov himself, who embodies a chaos of opposites. "He belongs to one of the oldest families of the nobility while at the same time belonging to the Paris commune. He is a genuine poet, loves Russia, and yet completely denies its value. He has no religion, but he is prepared to die for almost anything vague, which he cannot name but in which he can passionately believe, on the example of many, many enlightened Russian Europeanizers of the St. Petersburg period of Russian history." Torn by such contradictions, what traditions and moral-cultural heritage can he transmit to his children? "I confess," confides Nikolay Semyonovich, "I would not want to be a novelist trying to describe a hero from an accidental family! It would be thankless work and one lacking formal beauty. Serious mistakes would be possible, and exaggerations and oversights. . . . But what choice does a writer have who has no wish to write historical novels but is possessed by a longing for the present scene? He has to guess . . . and get it wrong!"

Whether Dostoyevsky actually thought he had "gotten it wrong" can only remain an open question; but here he seems to be speaking in his own voice, and riposting against those who had objected to the scabrous and unsavory aspects of his subject, which for him were essential to his depiction of the moral uncertainty and instability of contemporary Russian reality. And while he was perfectly justified in wishing to be judged by his own artistic aims rather than those of Tolstoy, it is just here that *A Raw Youth* is most vulnerable: it is in comparison with his own other works, not those of Tolstoy, that it falls so sadly short. If the defects of *A Raw Youth* prove anything, it is that Dostoyevsky needed to allow his eschatological imagination its fullest moral-metaphysical scope to do justice to his own talent; and he would take this artistic lesson to heart three years later when he came to write *The Brothers Karamazov.*

Henry James and Modern Moral Life

ROBERT B. PIPPIN

I

I want to discuss James's treatment of modern moral life. That can be a controversial and easily misunderstood topic.[1] To many readers, James seems manifestly hostile to Puritan or New England moralism, suspicious of the hypocrisy and smugness that characterize his morally judgmental characters, and thereby uneasy with the category of morality itself. For others, his commitment to "life" and to the supreme importance of beauty and taste might seem to place his deepest interests simply "beyond good and evil." For still others, the topic itself sounds immediately dreary, unworthy of James and his supreme subtlety, another lessons-for-life, edifying, choosing-up-sides, for the good people–against the bad, anachronistic approach to a work of art, and a modernist, experimental work at that.[2] I do not think I am guilty of any such sins, but as with anything else it all comes down to what one means by moral life and by a literary treatment. I cannot present any grand theory here. I want only to claim that James presents important human conflicts in one way rather than other possible ways, that this has for him historical and broadly social bases, and that "that way" has various implications and presuppositions we would do well to consider. Absent a theory about all of this, at least some preliminary remarks are in order.

Among the many related issues immediately raised by such a topic, one in particular is essential in appreciating both the radicality and the importance of James's views. The very idea of a moral point of view, tied as it is so essentially to the notions of personal accountability, already presupposes some notion of the subjects of such claims and the nature of their experience of one another, how, especially, they might come to appreciate some shared meaning in their interactions, evaluations, and assessments. To understand the simplest elements of any moral evaluation, I have to know something about what another intended, what motivated him or her, even simply just how to describe what it is that person is doing. It could even be said that for James one important aspect of the modern moral framework itself is some sort of entitlement "to be properly understood," some claim on others to an appropriate attempt at understanding. (James suggests this sometimes by identifying a "moral sense" with "great intelligence.")[3]

Very often, both the interpretive and evaluative aspects of such efforts are based on very general assumptions, widely shared in various historical communities, assumptions about human motivation, what it is to be an individual or subject, religion, the nature of social and political conflict, various types and presumed hierarchies among human beings, and so forth. And here James's views on the problem of consciousness (the basic conditions for the possibility of the determinate meaning on which moral assessment depends), its "historicity," let us say, and the nature of human sociality are extreme, brilliant, and underappreciated. Most notably, in the historical communities that he describes, there are very few, if any, such shared, stable assumptions left, at least very few that can be reliably assumed by the participants, and yet attempts at some resolution of the problems of meaning and evaluation must, and largely still do, go on. That historical and psychological issue and its relation to the possibility of moral meaning, and therewith to the moral-life theme, will form the bulk of the discussion in what follows. I shall eventually make some use of James's acknowledged masterpiece, *The Golden Bowl,* to press these latter points.

II

I begin by assuming that it is uncontroversial that James is quite interested in what can be broadly called ethical or normative matters: how one is to live well, better than one had; what makes for a happy or fulfilling life; what costs might be involved in trying to live well; what conflicts, perhaps tragic and irreconcilable ones, necessarily arise among ends and goals in any such aspiration to a higher or better life. The novels are full of characters who begin their lives as quiet passengers on some busy train of life and wake up for one reason or another, insist on a turn at driving, and must then decide where to go (where it is worth going) and how to get there. The values or ends or goals most often at issue in these adventures and pursuits are distinctly modern ones and can be summarized (a bit too simply) as "a free life" (this is shown necessarily to involve an aware, or properly felt, life) and that consummation devoutly wished in the classical novel, enduring human love. But almost always in such cases our heroes and heroines also always experience an indisputably real limitation on such an exploration: something like the experience of the *claims of others* to be, and to be treated as, free, equally independent subjects. It is not long before these awakened characters "collide" with someone (or are "run into" by a reckless driver) and must assess what to make of such collisions. Violating or ignoring such claims might or might not make one's life better or happier (it usually would), but, apart from that, the characters come to experience some unmistakable call of conscience in such cases: ignoring such claims would be wrong. I take this (this claim by others to a kind of acknowledgment) to be a distinctly and somewhat narrowly moral consideration, distinct, that is, from the broadly ethical, "how is one to live well?" themes so prominent in, say, Lambert Strether or Isabel Archer. Recognizing or accepting such a claim to acknowledgment is not just some further component or element of what for us would *be* a flourishing or happy life. Such a claim, understood as a moral claim, is not conditional in this way on such an end and our desire for it. The nature of the claim is not based on such a reason.[4] Since the basis of this moral experience, first described as such by Kant, is entitlement to treatment as a free subject, this will of course also mean an exploration of how James seems to understand the nature of such freedom, in all its relevant senses: independence, absence of constraint, autonomy, authenticity, self-determination, and even political freedom.

For example, this moral dimension is unmistakable in James's confident insistence on the reality of moral evil,[5] an evil motivated often by egoism and enacted often in deceit (the lie being the moral pivot around which so many novels turn), and in his treatment of the problem of sacrifice, especially the sacrifice of one's own happiness or good in recognition of some requirement not directly relevant to one's happiness or good. How to get beyond such generalities and understand the basis for this confidence and for the implications drawn are the relevant questions.

III

Moreover, James treats this link between moral assessment and possible moral meaning (or successful interpretation) in a radically historical way, and that also calls for a brief explanation. The framework or set of questions I want to propose is of course an alternative to standard views of James as either a high-culture, aristocratic aesthete, locating all questions of value in taste, or a psychological realist, uninterested in moral questions except as experienced or felt. But I do not have in mind what is often meant when critics offer interpretations of James's understanding of the nature of moral life and moral categories and moral judgment, whether those interpretations are supposed to help us judge actions or see a better kind of human life.[6] This is because I want especially to emphasize the *modernity* of James's view of moral life. By such a historical emphasis I mean James's keen appreciation of the unique situation within which relatively self-aware Western individuals must begin now to engage and understand each other in some normative way, in the light of what they owe and should expect from each other. This situation is treated as so distinctive in human time as to render inevitably superficial any gloss about the nature of morality or moral experience itself, or a good human life.

The one book where this theme is richly treated, *The American Scene,* would require a separate study. But a general acknowledgment of James's historical consciousness is also a fixture in some sense of the standard or received picture of James. It is obvious enough that James's characterizations, plots, and dilemmas are everywhere informed by an awareness of the specific historical situation faced by these characters, the situation of Western modernization, let us call it, for want of a better term. The famous international theme, with the Americans versus the Europeans, is clearly treated not only typologically and, one might say, anthropologically, but *historically.* "Great changes" are coming, warns the elder Mr. Touchett in *The Portrait of a Lady,* as they all await "the idea of an interesting woman," the American, Isabel Archer, and "not all for the better,"[7] a view of things the "progressive" Lord Warburton quite naively thinks he understands and is prepared for.[8] And this contrast, between the new and the old, is not treated cyclically, as if just another cycle in the eternal rotations of human time. Everything of significance in the basic manners of civilized life known heretofore, in the role of history, hierarchy, expectation, is about to change. The Americans are about to take charge of the planet, and there has never been a people like the Americans. What will they do with it? is the question that animates many of the more reflective Europeans and Europeanized Americans.

Such a general claim is easy enough to establish. That these views about modernity are worth taking much more seriously than previously conceded, that they ought to shape a whole interpretation, is another matter. This is so because the major categories of the international theme

are often treated very much as they appear on the surface of James's narrative, and on the surface they can, again, seem very conventional, very
much representative of what James himself calls "the good conservative
tradition," the one "that walks apart from the extravagant use of money
and the unregulated appeal to 'style'" and that takes as its principle something like the following:

> . . . it takes an endless amount of history to make even a little tradition, and an
> endless amount of tradition to make even a little taste, and an endless amount of
> taste, by the same token, to make even a little tranquillity. Tranquillity results
> largely from taste tactfully applied, taste lighted above all by experience and pos-
> sessed of a clue for its labyrinth.[9]

But no thoughtful reader of James can rest content with any view
of *him* as just, straightforwardly, representative of "the good conservative
tradition," the high-minded critic of "the age of trash triumphant."[10] It is
everywhere clear that James believes that many aspects of traditional (in
essence, largely premodern) European customs, manners, and mores
were, by the late nineteenth century, in some sort of end-game situation
and that they deserved to be. Upper-class and upper-middle-class European life—arranged marriages; rigidly defined, predictable social classes;
convent education; accepted notions of honor and social esteem; conventional constraints on conduct and speech; widely shared intuitions about
the higher and the lower—had all largely become more social theater
than social reality, as James depicts it. Where such forms are observed, or
whenever a character speaks forcefully for them, James is also careful to
conjure up a whiff of decay and death, perhaps even cruelty and obsession,
certainly self-serving egoism, ritualistic formalism, and rigidity, as with
Gilbert Osmond, that greatest of Jamesean villains. James suggests a number of reasons for such exhaustion, the chief of which is quite unsentimen-
tal: money. Europe and the European system simply cannot finance itself
any longer, and the sorts of compromises now necessary with the modern
manufacturing classes make socially impossible the preservation of this
way of life. Certainly the European participants cannot resist the temptation to make some great use of the mountains of money now being created in the greatest period of American capital expansion (that period "of
the new remorseless monopolies that operate as no madness of ancient
personal power thrilling us on the historic page ever operated").[11]

On the other side of this presumed Jamesean historical situation, neither can one rest content with the standard picture of the American

modernity that comes with this new American money: charm, freshness, energy, and, in a way, innocence; and with all that, inevitably and in an inevitably contaminating way, American vulgarity, commercialism, and materialism, historical amnesia, naïveté, simplistic moralism, Puritanism, and self-righteousness. It is enough just to note that none of these categories even begin to be relevant to any fair assessment of where we are left with the greatest American characters, like Isabel Archer and Lambert Strether, who are almost "heroically" beyond any Europeans.

In other words, although James, like many other late-nineteenth-century writers, understands his historical context as undeniably empty of the large moral frameworks and categories and typologies within which intelligible human engagement and understanding were formerly possible, it is still the case that the way his novels and stories work, come to engage and grip us, would not be explicable were he not to have succeeded in establishing something like the necessity, the practical unavoidability, of the moral categories his narratives call forth.[12] While much of this moral dimension involves the importance of the possibility of one's actions being justifiable to those whom such actions affect (James's frequent phrase is "being squared"), the criteria of such acceptance or mutual recognition have nothing to do with natural law, the wisdom of tradition, religious scripture or religious feeling, pure practical reason, the resolution of class conflict, or reliance on some benchmark, a *phronimos,* an experienced man of practical wisdom. In effect, all the major characters are walking a high wire with lots of normative turbulence but without any safety net, dependent *wholly* on each other and their own talk and negotiations and perceptions for balance. In other words, there is plenty of "high modernism" here, without the usual gods, without even the minor secular divinities of mankind, progress, happiness, custom, or prosperity. Yet there is also no metaphysical boredom, no nihilism, no high-culture nostalgia (with America simplistically demonized as anomic modernity), none of the secularized Christianity of Dickens or George Eliot, not even Conradean stoicism, no *symboliste* new religions. The young (Milly Theale, Ralph Touchett) die innocently, unjustly; but no one shakes any fists at God. Great moral crises are never "resolved," yet no hint of despair or even skepticism sounds in any final tone—however autumnal, even elegiac, those tones can sound in the later works of genius. Some sort of tranquillity is intimated; some moral tone in some way more than resignation, pessimism, or skepticism is struck. Understanding how he accomplishes this tone, and what such a moral mutuality amounts to, depend on understanding the historical and social analysis presupposed in the encounters he presents.

IV

James's treatment of the thick fabric of a whole moral life in this new world, his not treating morality as some distinct, autonomous institution, is also quite important to stress. His interest lies in the relevance of moral considerations within and not as mere judge of a life; he does not treat the moral point of view as a kind of external constraint on permissible living, a mere occasional call of conscience. To be sure, many of the features of morality are recognizable in the situations that James presents, especially implied claims about the reality of painful moral conflict (that there can be a conflict between considerations of one's particular interests and well-being and some moral claim on us). But James has quite a distinctive way of portraying the place of such claims and entitlements within a modern life, distinctive both because of his historical and social sensitivity and because of the way he presents the institution of morality itself. He does not, that is, portray morality as some distinct or separable goal one should formulate and pursue; he does not portray moral heroes and heroines striving *to be good* or dutiful or striving not to allow their venal self-interest to get in the motivational way of their duty. His characters, even and especially the best of them, are striving simply for a life, trying to live. For the most part they are trying to get or stay married or to endure a marriage or to avoid marriage, but all in all the best of them seem to be trying to live, as if figuring out how to lead a life or to have one's own life were a difficult task, not a course one pursued simply by being alive. And it is within arrangements with each other in such a pursuit that the claims of morality are presented as practically unavoidable if one is to lead a life, or avoidable only at very great personal cost. How James does that—portray that claim that way, within the kind of historical world he constructs for his characters—is one of the basic questions in any reading of James. Put negatively: how does James show what is lost, for these sorts of (historically situated) subjects from their point of view, not just as objects of blame, when such considerations are neglected or qualified away in self-deceiving rationalizations (as with Osmond, Densher, Kate Croy, and, I think, Maggie Verver)?

One way he accomplishes this is by stressing one theme especially, in manifold and complex variations: the mutuality of social relations between free subjects, some unavoidable dependence on, and claims to equal acknowledgment by, other subjects. And this is an issue also prominent in the international theme in his treatment of the implications of the deceptive, even disastrous, American aspirations toward a presumed, modern ideal of individual independence, or "self-reliance," and the equally deceptive, destructive European insistence on the centrality of esteem and social dependence, on *the* benchmark of being "appropriately seen" rather than seeing or even enacting. If characters like Isabel Archer and Strether and Maggie, in other words, do manage a kind of morally significant independence, do manage to break free in some sense, it is not a heroic or romantic independence but also involves some sort of concession to the specific requirements of modern sociality and others (often in the problem of marriage, a figure for this whole dance of recognition; sometimes, in Strether's case, enacted in not marrying), a concession, which, while it can appear resigned or fatalistic, seems to me rather evocative of a more complex, Jamesean sense of the sort of mutual independence or freedom possible and valuable in modern societies and his refusal to be tempted by various false alternatives.

The dual insufficiency of any straightforward ideal of dependence or independence also suggests a distinct form of moral mutuality, a way of taking another into proper account, now possible for some, and necessary for any who aspire to live a worthy, free life. A famous exchange in *The Portrait of a Lady* raises the theme directly and begins to suggest and I hope to pull together the many related dimensions, some involving radical suggestions about the nature of consciousness and self-consciousness, thereby implied.

Isabel has just remarked about what had been called someone's supposedly "ugly brick house": "I don't care anything about his house." Madame Merle replies:

"That's very crude of you. When you've lived as long as I you'll see that every human being has his shell and that you must take the shell into account. By the shell I mean the whole envelope of circumstances. There's no such thing as an isolated man or woman; we're each of us made up of some cluster of appurtenances. What shall we call our 'self'? Where does it begin? Where does it end? It overflows into everything that belongs to us—and then it flows back again. I know a large part of myself is in the clothes I choose to wear. I've a great respect for *things*. One's self—for other people—is one's expression of one's self; and one's house, one's furniture, one's garments, the books one reads, the company one keeps—these things are all expressive."

This was very metaphysical; not more so, however, than several observations Madame Merle had already made. Isabel was fond of metaphysics, but was unable to accompany her friend into this bold analysis of human personality. "I don't agree with you. I think just the other way. I don't know whether I succeed in expressing myself but I know that nothing else expresses me; everything's on the contrary a limit, a barrier, and a perfectly arbitrary one. Certainly the clothes which, as you say, I choose to wear don't express me; and heaven forbid they should!"

"You dress very well," Madame Merle lightly interposed.

"Possibly; but I don't care to be judged by that. My clothes may express my dress maker, but they don't express me. To begin with it's not my choice that I wear them; they're imposed upon me by society."

"Should you prefer to go without them?" Madame Merle enquired in a tone which virtually terminated the discussion.[13]

Such passages reveal already how ambitiously, even how metaphysically, James addresses the problems of modern moral life. As the above quotation indicates, what he clearly thinks must be understood, if competing and often opposed claims for certain sorts of treatment and entitlements are to be understood, is nothing less than the nature of conscious subjectivity itself, or at least how discursive intelligences come to settle on, to share, some view of what is happening to them, and how any, especially differing, moral claims based on such views are to be themselves settled, or again to use his familiar word, how one could end up "squared."[14] And many very recent readers of James have begun to appreciate his very unusual and even revolutionary treatment of such issues. Sensitized perhaps by modern literary theory and thus suspicious of the very possibility of "individually owned" intentions and meanings,[15] and thus of the traditionally psychological readings of James, some writers have begun to emphasize what is clearly there in him and so, somewhat ironically, have begun to make a virtue out of what other earlier critics found a vice: first, the great *elusiveness* of psychological meaning, determinate intentions, or even stable identities in his characters and, second, the complex relation between consciousness itself and power, or the thin line, in human life as he presents it, between interpreting and understanding, on the one hand, and manufacturing and imposing, on the other.[16]

The most obvious *dramatic* evocation of this characteristic of Jamesean consciousness is simply failure, the constant failure of characters to understand sufficiently or determinately enough what is going on, what the gestures and words of other characters could mean. Sometimes, of course, this is because the characters are simply dense or, especially, are being deceived, but the former situation is not where the problems arise, and even this latter explanation is rarely a suitable analysis, since the moral meaning of "deceit" is often just as much in question (or so the two deceiving principals in *The Wings of the Dove,* for example, and Madame de Vionnet and Chad at least try to persuade themselves).

What is even more at issue, and what is of greatest relevance for the moral themes, is what appears to be the general instability or unreliability of possible mental content in general in James's characters; James has a general implicit interest in how thoughts could be said to have content, to be fixed in meaning, and presents that phenomenon in a way that defies many standard options in explaining it. Although there is of course no Jamesean position on consciousness itself, no account of sensory perception, mental causes, practical rationality, etc., at least in the domains where he is clearly taking implicit positions (on issues of motivation or the understanding of others' actions, and the like), he does not present us with a receptacle or window view of consciousness, as if a mind just grasps thoughts present for it or uses its words to fix onto meanings, or as if a mind could be said individually, by effort of thinking, to achieve some intention or insight, to seize on a determinate meaning. In contrast to all such images of searching, finding, dis-ambiguating, and grasping in the struggles depicted by James, what one could be said to think seems to depend in some complex way on the possible reactions, dispositions, hesitations, and activities of others, as if just to be aware is to be engaged with others in some normative ways, attuned to various proprieties and improprieties, or not. (I shall present an example of this in a moment.) This is often elliptically expressed by James by highlighting what he calls the "in between" nature of consciousness itself, as if it actually *exists* somewhere between and not in persons. And this also makes for great uncertainty and unclarity, for those characters and for us. Because of this, there does not appear to be any reassuring way, not just for us but *for them,* to identify reliably the content of their own thoughts, *to know what they think.*

V

Several situations in Part 1 of *The Golden Bowl* make the above point about the oddities and radical implications of James's treatment of thinking, understanding, and possible meaning with great compression and complexity. James's treatment of the theme there directly sets up the enormously complex moral issues of that novel and so is worth an extended digression here.

Now, of course, *The Golden Bowl* is not an easy novel to "digress into." In the first place, it defies any sort of economical discussion. It is the James novel where the least happens dramatically but where what does happens means the most. James piles on layer after layer of possible meaning and ambiguity and uncertainty, as if to see just how far he could go, when the "ice" would finally break.

The plot is simple enough. A very, very rich American businessman and widower, Adam Verver, is traveling through Europe with his daughter, Maggie, collecting art for a planned grand museum, apparently a whole town financed by Adam, "America City." Through the matchmaking efforts of an American friend, the most obviously named of all James's characters, Fanny Assingham, Maggie meets and marries an Italian Prince, Amerigo, now reduced to genteel poverty. Prior to his engagement, Amerigo had been the lover of the formidable but poor American Charlotte Stant, who, it turns out, is both an old friend of Fanny and a school friend of Maggie. Neither Amerigo nor Fanny informs Maggie of this prior romantic relationship. After the wedding, Maggie senses that her father might feel like a third wheel in their party and encourages her father to marry. He does; he marries Charlotte Stant. Maggie and her father assume everyone is "squared" and seem then to revert completely to their life before Maggie's marriage, spending almost all their time with each other and Maggie's new baby, thereby throwing Charlotte and the Prince more and more together socially. We are given to believe that there is still considerable electricity between these two. (They had broken off only because neither had money.) At Charlotte's instigation, they finally begin an adulterous affair. Maggie discovers it and does not expose them. Instead she works very hard to keep everything under wraps and in control. She succeeds. Charlotte and Adam end up sailing for America City, a fate, we are led to believe, worse than death, and Maggie and the Prince begin their new life together.

The real difficulty in any economical discussion comes from the great subtlety of the moral tone created by the way the story is narrated and the characters are presented, a subtlety so complex that the novel inspires nothing but controversy in readers. (The key issue has always been one of great relevance here: how to evaluate from a moral perspective Maggie's efforts to hold her marriage together and to remove the offending Charlotte.) I can only give here a few examples of the way I think James links his psychological-historical and moral themes to create this complexity, but these will do very little justice to those controversies.

For one thing, *the meaning* of Charlotte Stant's return to London just before the wedding of the Prince and Maggie is not, we come to see in Fanny's worried speculations, just ambiguous, as if it could be taken in one of two ways and the problem is to figure out which way has more evidence to support it. It, the meaning, is not, oddly and frustratingly, "there" yet at all, even for Charlotte, even if *she* thinks her intentions are clear and could explain everything. Such a possible meaning seems dependent instead on a constellation of reactions, expectations, and intentions and assumed proprieties that no one character can grasp as a thought at a time. And this is often presented by James as radically as it sounds: that the issue is not whether a plausible possible interpretation is correct or confirmable. The very sense of such a possibility is originally in some way a function of a particular social constellation that one does not, as an individual mind, grasp so much as take an ongoing, negotiating, active part in. Persons are locked into such tight relations of dependence and mutual reflection in James's presentations that such persons themselves seem nothing but the tissue of their relations, however uncertain and constantly self-forming.[17] (Part of any such understanding on the part of a putative individual would have to be a kind of correct anticipating of another, something that itself depends on this other person rightly reading or originally anticipating such an engagement, or possible anticipation, on the part of the first subject.)[18]

Since the possible resolution of such a question of meaning is not treated as a hidden thing to be found, James must suggest what he thinks *is* going on when the characters try to resolve their perplexities about it, which they must at least tentatively do if they are to act. The novel, as it introduces us to Charlotte's return, opens with nothing but perplexities like this. Fanny tries to believe that Charlotte has acted "generously" in coming back before the wedding, but she is clearly very deeply disturbed by the act, a reaction quite inconsistent with this ascription of motives; she thinks Charlotte has not calculated the "costs." We have no sense yet of what these may be, and we are confused that Fanny is so worried, if the arrival *is* so innocent and a matter just of possibly indelicate but innocent effects and not of deliberate and perhaps selfish design. Fanny's views on the issue are actually a complex of inconsistencies; she thinks that just as Charlotte voluntarily got out of the way after it was clear she and the Prince could not marry, she has acted now just as "sacrificially," coming back with no thought of herself or of painful memories but to be of "positive" reassuring help to Maggie, as if to show her generosity and no-hard-feelings forgiveness of the Prince. But Fanny has already made clear that the best way to do *that* would have simply been to stay away. Wishful thinking, guilt at her own optimism about Charlotte and the Prince, at *her own silence* about the two of them to Maggie (which she does not mention), all clearly complicate (and make quite wholly unreliable, despite appearances) her point of view, although she continues to seem throughout the novel as some sort of critic, making sense of the plot.

We then learn that Charlotte wants the Prince to help her pick out a wedding gift, a proposal too full of potential sarcasm to be treated lightly by anybody. Fanny, in effect, goes so far as to protest, to offer herself as guide instead. The Prince is also hesitant and, as a clear pretense, protests that Charlotte hasn't the money for a gift, but Charlotte persists and they meet, in strange secrecy, agreeing, as if to preserve the surprise, not to visit any areas that Maggie frequents. (Not a problem; Maggie does not slum in antiquarian shops, looking for values.)

Then the key scene: Charlotte makes a speech to the Prince while they are out—a strange, elusive, allusive speech. She wants, she says, only to "have had" this moment, before what he is "going to do." (She can't apparently say the word "marriage.") She wants only not "to have not had it," this moment alone, when she can "give herself away," willing to "do it for nothing."

But, of course, it is not for nothing. It must be a secret for one thing (the Prince has promised) and it does change a great deal; it compromises the Prince deeply, whatever spin they put on it. (Imagine you are the wife. You find out *from someone else* that your new husband had met the—secret, thus far undisclosed—love of his prior life right before your wedding day, and he kept it from you. Your inference?) And Charlotte precisely does not, by "giving herself away," *give* herself away. She says, finally, nothing determinate, and thereby everything continues to hang fire, even, I am suggesting, for herself. She has gotten the Prince to go with her, under these odd circumstances, and she has said what she wanted to say: that she wanted there *to be* something said between them. But about what; for the sake of what? What does it mean that they went together?

On the one hand, of course, modern readers suspect everything in this scene. We suspect Charlotte of trying to compromise the Prince, to put him in her power in some way (thanks now to the "secret"), to play on his guilt about his love of money, to initiate some renewal between them, to remind him about whom he really loves and always will, to manipulate him. But there is also something courageous and heroic in her act, and she does seem to be saying good-bye: she *will not* let what passed between them go unremarked, swept under the rug of private history. There *must be* some acknowledgment. And we know enough of the Prince already (and we shall learn much more) to suspect his weakness and admire her insistence on a gesture which refuses complete forgetfulness, even while leaving so open the content of the acknowledgment.

And his reaction is just as complex. He is relieved that he has been "let off," that she makes no new demands, asks for no explanation. But, of course, just as she has and has not given herself away, he has and most definitely has *not* been let off. That had been the whole point, not to let him off, something he wants not to see and so does not. Since he has been "let off" from a direct response, he lets *himself* off completely and does not respond to or engage her directly at all, a fatal problem in the possibility of what they are doing *meaning* anything at all, a moral refusal or hesitancy we shall see several times in this novel, especially in its concluding chapters. (The figure for this problem is again a gift, a small gift Charlotte wants to give him, and he refuses.) He does not respond, and his "lips remain closed to the successive vaguenesses of rejoinder, of objection, that rose for him within." [19] (The rejoinders, we note, are still vague *for him,* as if he only feels some "objection." And what would he be objecting *to?*)

All of this builds to the great scene and lines which define the problem of the book. Charlotte wants to buy a lovely antiquity, the golden bowl, as a gift. The Prince sees immediately that it is really crystal, not gold, and that it is flawed, and he walks out of the shop. (Such is his way of dealing with flaws; we see later Maggie's and Fanny's.) Charlotte cannot see a flaw but has deduced from the price that there "must" be one.

Hence the great question from the shopkeeper: "But if it's something you can't find out, *isn't it as good as if it were nothing?*" [20]

Indeed. That summarizes all at once a very typical, prominent Jamesean question. It might be (as good as nothing) but everything then hangs on whether and how and what it would mean to "find out," or to avoid finding out. The Prince has (so he believes) seen immediately that the bowl is flawed and stalked out. But Charlotte goes so far as to lie, directly and finally unambiguously, about the price, making it easier to pretend that she can afford it. (It is fifteen pounds; she tells the Prince it is five pounds.) And the novel is off and running.

Much of this of course could be fit into a conventional framework of intelligibility for actions. We understand what others are doing by understanding their motives and reasons, their desires and beliefs, by understanding what they take themselves to be after and why. This all obviously implies that they can somehow identify what they desire and believe, and either disclose it or not, to others or even to themselves. And, however hard to explain philosophically, it is obvious that in some cases, they might keep their own motives not only from others but from themselves. Fanny, the Prince, and Charlotte might all clearly be trying to avoid admitting to themselves why they act or have acted, even though at some level they know. (They would of course have to know, in order to keep such motives from themselves.) They all certainly seem busily engaged tying large, obscuring bows and ribbons around their own and others' possible motives, keeping the wedding, and their own later deniability, right on track.

Some of this sort of account is doubtless apt. But it fatally misses the pathos and confusion of the scenes, even the desperation of the problem of meaning for each of the characters, their own confusion about what is happening to them. (Certainly, imputing direct motives *to deceive others* and act in a strategically self-interested way would be a gross exaggeration of the tone of the treatment here and would be especially and unfairly harsh on Charlotte.) But the idea of self-deceit here presupposes that something of that basic issue—what is happening, what such a gesture or other would mean (what motives are really behind it)—had been resolved and that they are now keeping secret from themselves some motive in dealing with it or some motive to see it, or to have seen it, in certain lights. They are *much* more at sea than this picture would allow, in large measure because of the kind of world they have to inhabit, a world fully appreciated as such by James. The great density of the opening pages of *The Golden Bowl* is a density of nearly unmanageable possibilities, not of hidden meanings or self-deceived motives, actually there, waiting to be seen or exposed, and the resolution of such possibilities does not require honesty or deeper insight but requires a kind of dependence on and engagement with others, personally and individually, and requires another sort of dependence, on the range of actions and reactions historically available; all as if all and any meaning could be determined only retrospectively, and cooperatively, as if life cannot be lived as life but only as material for remembered life, to allude to Proustean affinities. As with Proust, life seems led in perpetual future perfect tenses and subjunctive moods. One says, not "My motive for S-ing now is A, given my current understanding of situation R"; but "I will have meant to S, because of what I take to be A, should the situation have turned out R." "The merely spontaneous description of the case," as James put it once, would simply be that the agent's motives in such intentional contexts are dependent on certain descriptions. If these descriptions are inaccurate, it may then be true to say, given what they wanted to achieve, that they should have had other motives. But James has introduced such a massive instability into any such possible description, made it so dependent on various possible interpretations of mutual reflections and inferences, and future actions, that this anodyne formulation is of no help.[21]

VI

I close with a final example from this novel, meant now to emphasize how James understands what is lost when this historically necessary mutuality is not acknowledged.[22] It is the most complex example of the way James's apparent presuppositions about consciousness and meaning (what I am suggesting is the social and therewith historical character of intentionality for him) will undergird his account of modern moral meaning (the unavoidable claim of the other to be treated as a distinct and free being). It occurs at the beginning of the second book (chapter 27), after the Prince and Charlotte have begun their affair, and after Maggie has begun to suspect that something is not right in her relations with her husband. Maggie and her father had been planning a private trip together to Spain. Maggie has delayed mentioning it, wanting to keep up her new campaign to win back the Prince (whom at this point she just believes she has neglected) and hoping that her father will catch the hint. He does and volunteers that, since everyone is getting on so famously, they had better not go.

In a carriage together on the way home, after Adam has declined to go to Spain, Maggie and the Prince have an amazingly dense, elusive conversation. Something has gone a bit wrong in Maggie's more intense, new dedication to her husband and her social life. Something seems a bit too "beatific"[23] in the way Charlotte and the Prince refer to a recent time together in the country, and something continues to resist her being a full, adult member of the scene. She begins to sense a hint of pity and condescension in the great interest people take in her as the wife of Amerigo (as in: how *interesting* that someone "like her" should be his wife); she even feels "like a dressed doll" passed back and forth.

What we see in Maggie's and the Prince's conversation is the beginning of a mutual exploration of where Adam's decision and Maggie's new involvement have "left them." What is so striking is that neither of them can be said yet to "have views" about this. What they both have are views about the possible views of the other and, however cumbersome to say, views about what the other's views of their own views are. Again, each will have a motive to respond in a certain way, based on some proper anticipation of the other, but each such possible response by the other is just as conditioned by an expectation of the first.

They cannot find a way to break through this uncertainty, to lay down interpretation as a weapon of protection and advantage. Maggie is expecting the Prince to express great happiness that he will not be away from her and to propose a vacation himself for the two of them. He does not and she is puzzled. But the Prince senses this expectation and does not quite know what to make of it. He must be always vigilant not to assume too robustly the role of paid husband, lest he spoil the illusion of mutuality, so he is clearly always cautious about these things, preferring to follow Maggie's lead. And now for the first time, she will not lead. But what Maggie does not know of course is that the affair between the Prince and Charlotte has begun, and, in the first place, the Prince is not eager to leave Charlotte, or is at least, in his usual way, uneasy about *her* possible response. And he is also mindful of Charlotte's subtle advice about successful lying: don't be too eager to act well and generously (especially untypically) lest you look guilty. But, crucially, James lets us see that Amerigo hesitates too because he expects Maggie to say something like: "Father could see the real reason we shouldn't go. He sees how much in love with you I am, and how much I am enjoying it." Maggie, though, senses that he expects that (and we sense that the Prince needs such an expression, though whether in human or strategic terms is never clear), and perversely or defensively, for some reason, she deliberately withholds any such affirmation, insistently waiting for him to make the first major move. He senses this insistence and doubly hesitates. She senses the hesitation, and so on. . . . They thus end up with what are called "crudities of mutual resistance."[24]

These crudities remain, in my view, throughout the novel, and it ends, I think, in a great moral crash—all precisely because such "resistance" is never overcome, and the kind of "free" mutuality necessary to have even a chance to settle such questions of meaning and so to be able to lead lives together (as they must be led) is experienced only by implication and suggestion and absence. This is not a popular view of the ending or of Maggie. Many readers seem to require a heroine out of all this ambiguity, this "milky fog," "white curtain," or "golden mist," as the Prince sees it. And Maggie is often therefore read as a Milly Theale with a steel will—someone willing to love and forgive, not in the transcendent and otherworldly fashion of Milly, but rather with a resolve and even a somewhat Machiavellian tolerance of the moral compromises necessary to save what is worth saving in her life.

It is true that Maggie loses a good deal of her innocence and seems finally to realize that she must choose between an adult life with her husband and a continuation of her infantilized relation to her father. And she chooses. But to think of her "in intention rather like Beatrice in the *Divine Comedy,* the Lady of Theology," who "suffers the pangs of the highest human love,"[25] is quite a stretch, as much as her own rather self-pitying characterization, willing to suffer everything "for love." What love? There is very little substance or passion in this love, at least that we ever see; it is almost always described in terms of the problem of possession and objects, and Maggie's ardor is usually inflamed most when she sees the Prince desired by another, ultimately by Charlotte. She is her father's daughter and wants mostly to keep what she has; she wants above all not "to have been" a fool and to assert herself as an equal, especially if it means first tormenting, then destroying, Charlotte. She plays at the role of suffering-for-their-sins Christ even as Adam plays the God the Father role (allusions that ought to alert us to the heavy irony involved). But there is precious little "forgiveness" in her treatment of Charlotte, the apparent satisfaction she takes in it, or the self-serving pity and crocodile-tear guilt with which she congratulates herself and enacts her power. She even goes so far as to encourage the Prince and Charlotte, after all they have been through, to get together one last time, alone, before Charlotte leaves Europe. The insensitivity and schadenfreude in such a gesture are so manifest that it takes a great act of will to admire Maggie for it, to see it as she does as truly selfless and beneficent. (It is just as hard to see the Prince somehow redeemed by this purported forgiveness. Charlotte was his great link to the social world he loved. There is very little evidence that Maggie, however hard and willful she has become, will ever be able to fill that role, being the prim "little nun," "Roman matron," "Madonna," and "doll" she has always been. We can only imagine the Prince spending his time as he does when he waits for Charlotte's exile: arranging and rearranging and rearranging his books, voting in his club.)

And Adam remains as always: a fatuous romantic whose interest in beauty is never shown to have any dimension other than possession. America, and the modern moral world it figures, can indeed produce people like Isabel and Milly and Strether and, I would even say, Charlotte, whose willingness to accept the dangers, uncertainties, and possibilities that the new American situation has created is immense and courageous. But it can also produce people like Adam, the aesthetic analogue to New England moralists, resistant to such vast changes, looking for consolation in a presumed past or, in the moral analogue, in some religiously inspired moral code; someone who, like Maggie, believes there must be some "real thing" that the Europeans have in their art and culture, beneath all the surfaces and social light and mirror show. Their simplistic confidence that their great wealth allows them simply to "find" it and "buy" it reflects a parallel moralistic view that evil can be discreetly "located," "named," and then by force of will and effort destroyed (here a great American theme; not for nothing is our national epic *Moby Dick*). Adam's taciturn, reticent ways, his show of generosity but his isolation and aloof bearing, reflect in his almost complete asociality the consequences of such a romantic hope, as does his manipulative, wholly insensitive "wooing" of Charlotte and, in the greatest figure of all for his detachment, his antigenerative, antifuture stance, his unwillingness (or perhaps even incapacity) to have sex with Charlotte.

Said another way, the great final moments of the final great novel are dominated by something extraordinarily rare in a James novel: silence.[26]

352 ROBERT B. PIPPIN

After Maggie's brief confrontation with the Prince when the golden bowl was broken, he tries to "see" what she might have told Adam, or even what she might actually know (and he is obviously not eager to ask); she tries to "see" what he might have told Charlotte, or even something of the nature of their affair, what it was, how far it went (and she is not eager to ask); they both wonder what Adam might "see." He occupies the same position here as he does throughout the novel, accumulating great power by never really "speaking," by being only the silent object of wonder. And hardly anybody says anything to poor Charlotte, who seems the only character in the book capable of generating real human heat.[27]

None of this, though, should suggest that such a judgment about a "moral crash" is to be taken as James's last word on Maggie's fate. Of course she is a victim too, has been treated badly by the Prince and Charlotte, has been protected to the point of controlled and manipulated by her father, and if she remains a defensive, cold, prim little nun, that is certainly not a moral failing, not her (moral) fault. All of this does, and ought to, affect a reader's judgment.

Moreover, as noted at the outset, the relevance of the moral category, or any claims about moral failure, only gets one so far in understanding the end of the novel. It is an indispensable and real category; as enacted by the Prince and Maggie, their "crudities of mutual resistance," their refusal to acknowledge and enact their dependence, are at the heart of a real failure in the story. But all of this also directly introduces different sets of questions not answerable in moral terms. What, for example, is the source of this resistance to mutual engagement, the basis for the silence, the refusal to love? It is a moral issue of some significance that there *is* such silence and evasion at the end of the novel. But that phrase of James about mutual "resistance" clearly invites a psychological question as well. Why the resistance?

Here too a moral category might be partly relevant. Such a refusal of another might be explicable in some sense as motivated simply by morally corrupt motives: self-indulgence, vanity, laziness, venal self-promotion. But it is also true that James does not portray his characters in such a morally final way, as if only individual examples of moral turpitude. We often know so little about many of them, and see them during such a small slice of time, that it would be hasty to see such moral evaluations as final or definitive. So much of the dramatic framework, too, is so clearly typological, even mythical, rather than stories only about individuals with moral or psychological failures. The plot for several novels from *Washington Square* on (the Jamesean triangle: the heiress, the fortune hunter, and the duplicitous accomplice; all often complicated by the tyrannical father) is so frequently and confidently invoked that its presence alone implies some ambition toward a repeated or even archetypal pattern of resistance.[28] Some element of the basic Jamesean human drama (especially in its specifically modern framework) makes self-exposure, the risks of love, or even moral acknowledgment difficult, potentially painful, even frightening. For example, when the tyrannical father is added to the mix (as in *Washington Square* or *The Golden Bowl*), the suggestion of some original trauma or fear as source of future resistance—that frequent hint of incest or "unspeakable" desire as source of repression—is not negligible.

But these are complications for future discussion. However important, such necessary questions do not qualify or reduce away the moral phenomena themselves,[29] which are easy enough to summarize again.

"But if it's something you can't find out, *isn't it as good as if it were nothing?*"

Indeed. I think James rejects the attitude evinced in this question, and that the silence or refusal or mutual resistances that dominate the end of his great novel are meant to show, even so indirectly and elliptically, what is missed by this refusal to see, which is always at the same time a refusal to struggle with others to see. Calling that dimension and that kind of wrong a "moral" one, a refusal to acknowledge a dependence on others without which even an independent life cannot be led, might seem exaggerated, but I hope that these examples begin to provide some evidence that this is the way James understands the problem of modern moral life.

Notes

1. The remarks that follow are more suggestions about a way of reading Henry James than they are well-worked-out, exhaustive arguments. The remarks form part of a book, *Henry James and Modern Moral Life,* to be published this year by Cambridge University Press, and I give there a fuller and more thorough defense of such suggestions.

2. I am particularly uneasy about an essay on this sort of topic appearing in a Festschrift for David Grene. Perhaps the most important of the many things I have learned from David Grene has to do with the unique power and great, even inestimable value of a literary work as such and, correspondingly, the kind of resistance to and even fear of literature itself that can accompany so-called philosophical, social, or historical interpretations (or that can mar a literary work which wears its nonliterary pretensions all over its sleeve). Since I count this an extremely valuable lesson and count David Grene as among the wisest teachers and friends I have known, it would be a painful and embarrassing fault in this context to be guilty of such anachronism and, more simply, such bad taste. My hope to have avoided such a failing rests with a trust in James himself, a trust in his ability to show something quite radical: the great beauty of moral sensibility itself and the moral importance of imagination. If he has succeeded, he will have re-created, in effect, the

notion of moral assessment itself and so have rendered less relevant the usual worries about "nonliterary" themes. Or, if *he* succeeds, and I am right about him, then *I* have succeeded in avoiding these failings.

3. While a necessary condition for any such moral acknowledgment, such an intelligence is clearly not sufficient, or there must be some broader question at stake about the depth and extent of the intelligence required. Mrs. Brook, for example, in *The Awkward Age,* is in some respects as intelligent as they get in James, able to intuit at a glance all the various possible implications of an action or the avoidance of an action. But she is also in some sense a moral monster, coldly indifferent to her own children, supremely selfish. One might say that there is something that she simply does not or cannot "see" but that is not in itself clearly a matter of intelligence. We encounter in her something like a resistance to the kinds of dependencies and contingencies and uncertainties that this "new" society has made necessary—a self-serving insistence that some compromise with the old forms, the old language which she mastered so well, is still possible.

4. It is not "unconditional" or absolute in the Kantian sense either, whatever that might possibly mean in Kant, nor is it a kind of pragmatic presupposition, without which I would be lost in some performative contradiction. The *nature* of my dependence on the freedom of others, its indispensability in *my* leading a free life of my own (or what is lost by my not acknowledging that freedom and enacting such an acknowledgment), is, I think, best described simply in the language in which it is presented by James. I will make use here only of the language developed in *The Golden Bowl,* and it will not issue in anything like a philosophical theory of such a dependence. I'm not sure that there can be any such thing.

5. By "reality" I do not mean that moral predicates refer to metaphysically real moral properties. I mean that within certain historical communities agents find that they cannot engage with or understand each other *or themselves* without taking various actions or policies to count as disloyal, egoistic, cruel, selfish, unfair, etc. All such terms may also count as what they are only within such communities, but all of that is, I think, "reality" enough. But that is also another, much longer story.

6. For example, in Frederick Crews's *The Tragedy of Manners: Moral Drama in the Later Novels of Henry James* (Hamden: Archon, 1971). Crews emphasizes the great difficulties of both individual moral integrity (something, he thinks, that would require far too much separation, even alienation, from society) and any clear moral judgment about others, even though called for (given the great difficulty in assigning personal responsibility and the obvious complexity of meaning and motives). Hyacinth's suicide in *The Princess Cassimassima* and Strether's sacrifice and loneliness in *The Ambassadors* are presented by Crews as "tragic" expressions of such unresolvable Jamesean dilemmas. See p. 83 on "the two parts" of James's "moral awareness" and their irreconcilability, "intuitive inclusiveness," and "social conscience." There is unmistakably a tragic dimension to the later novels, but we also need, I think, to investigate first and in some detail what sorts of moral and ethical issues come to gain some purchase on the lives of individual characters and why, especially given James's awareness of the historical uniqueness of this context. When we do, I think we can begin to see that not every tragic situation implies a claim about fundamentally tragic human alternatives. Said in a simpler way: "tragedy" is not the right *ultimate* category for the later novels. The invocations of melodrama, comedy, and fairy tale and the general tone taken suggest something at once more positive, more tranquil, and deliberately undefined.

7. *The Portrait of a Lady,* ed. Robert D. Bamberg (New York: Norton, 1975), 22.

8. In *The American Scene,* the question is just as explicit, as James surveys modernizing

America: "what turn, on the larger, the general stage, was the game going to take? . . . the great adventure of a society reaching out into the apparent void for the amenities, the consummations, after having earnestly gathered in so many of the preparations and necessities?" (*The American Scene,* ed. John F. Sears [New York: Penguin, 1994], 13).

9. Ibid., 127.

10. The phrase is from the funniest Jamesean account of his own failures as a popular writer and dramatist, "The Next Time," a wonderful story about James's own inability to write for the new reading public, to make a "sow's ear out of a silk purse."

11. *American Scene,* 104. One might also cite Gertrude's complaint about the phoniness of the American/Puritan pretensions to simplicity and naturalness, or the natural grace of the artificial Eugenia in *The Europeans.*

12. I thus disagree with Sallie Spears when she asserts, as the governing framework for her study, that all James's basic results are "negative," a failure and irresolution so great she will not even call them tragic (*The Negative Imagination: Form and Perspective in the Novels of Henry James* [Ithaca: Cornell University Press, 1968]; see, e.g., 38–39). It is true that no writer ever pointed more to the complexities of competing and irreconcilable points of view, and no one relied less on pat syntheses or merely resigned acceptance, than James. But Spears's approach far too narrowly categorizes the moral in James (essentially as moralism) and does not do justice to the sources from which our sense of admiration for some characters, and especially our condemnation of others, stem. It is also just unlikely on the face of it that an imaginative talent like James *could* be so boldly and undialectically categorized as "negative." Reading a James novel is not like watching some psychological or moral train wreck, a great crash of competing points of view. *What Maisie Knew* is *not* all about the "ambiguity of human meaning" (28). Maggie's parents are simply awful, and there is no ambiguity about that at all. The same could be said about Osmond, the moral position of Kate and Merton, the narrow-mindedness of Mrs. Newsome, the views on life and art of Lady Agnes or Julia or Sherrington in *The Tragic Muse,* or Mrs. Brookenham's salon conversation in *The Awkward Age.* (Spears's negative take, though, does free her somewhat from the great attraction which so many readers seem to feel for that "little nun" of the last novel, Maggie Verver. See below.)

13. *Portrait of a Lady,* 173. I do not, of course, mean to suggest that James simply identifies with Madame Merle's views (they already hint at her self-serving cynicism), just that her remarks introduce the framework within which James understands the problem, and especially the problem of Isabel's contrasting innocence and willfulness. Cf. also a similar discussion in *The Awkward Age* (Harmondsworth, England: Penguin, 1975) after Mr. Longdon had asked Nanda, "What you suggest is that the things you speak of depend upon other people?" Her response indicates James's awareness of the historical, as well as the social, character of such dependence and of how deep the dependence goes. The "her" in question in the following is Nanda's grandmother, Lady Julia, an almost mythic figure of nostalgia in the novel for the "lost time" of premodern sensibilities. Nanda says, "If we're both partly the result of other people, her other people were so different" (141). And, in a formulation with a perfect Jamesean grammatical pitch: "Granny wasn't the kind of girl she couldn't be—and so neither am I" (141).

14. One of the most interesting of such contemporary discussions (and a valuable guide through many others) is Sharon Cameron's *Thinking in Henry James* (Chicago: University of Chicago Press, 1989). Cameron is a persuasive critic of the psychologically realist reading of James (even James's own in his prefaces). She makes interesting use throughout of spatial metaphors in analyzing, mainly, *The American Scene, What Maisie Knew, The*

Golden Bowl, and *The Wings of the Dove* to show that James, despite what he says, does not portray consciousness as "stable, subjective, interior" or as "unitary" (77). I think she is quite right to say, and will try also to defend, such things as, "For in the novels conscious-ness is disengaged from the self. It is reconceived as extrinsic, made to take shape—indeed to become social—as an intersubjective phenomenon" (77).

However valuable, however, the spatial framework throughout makes it easier for Cameron to defend claims about where consciousness isn't, about what always "exceeds" any "container" view of awareness, and so forth. We do not, though, get a richer sense of what James is trying to show us—*how* that "in-between" where real consciousness exists gets established and sustained within the mutual reflections and corrections, and the mutual caring and normative constraints, constitutive of modern social life.

I believe Cameron is thus correct, at p. 175, to criticize phenomenological readings of James like Paul Armstrong's but is also right to suspect that "earlier" forms of a phenom-enology, like Hegel's, might provide a model of both a less subject centered and a more morally rich intersubjectivity. That is partly what I am trying to show here.

A consequence of this problem is that when faced herself with the problem of mean-ing and its shareability (given all the many things it *cannot be* in James), Cameron resorts to what is, finally, a familiar formula of untrustworthy speech, impenetrable thought, and "therefore" the "imposition" of meaning (108). This is how, especially, she treats Maggie. In the view I am presenting, by contrast, it is not *because* "we are unable to sustain the idea of meaning as a question" that we "moralize about the novel, see its thematic as one of morality, which is an ultimate act of codifying the arbitrariness of our interpretation by making a special case for its inevitability" (120). It is rather precisely because of our ac-knowledgment, in reading the novel, and the characters' realization in living, of the un-availability of individually owned, discoverable, even hidden or secret "meaning" that morality, a certain sort of absolute acknowledgment of our dependence on others and entitlement from them, arises in the first place.

15. Interestingly, the position James could be said to be opposing is often expressed in William James's individualism and the latter's claim that we speak not of that thought but "my thought, every thought being owned" (Williams James, *The Principles of Psychology* [Cambridge: Harvard University Press, 1983], 221). This and much else are pointed out and developed in persuasive detail in one of the best recent books on James, Ross Posnock's *The Trial of Curiosity: Henry James, William James and the Challenges of Modernity* (Oxford: Oxford University Press, 1991). I am much indebted to this study but I should note a first pass at a statement of disagreement. Posnock, like Cameron in the note above, states James's aesthetic and ethic in terms that seem to me still too Adornoesque, too captivated by the importance of some "negative" moment in James's picture of modern life, as if the irruption of some ineffable, "inevitable deviation," the "illegible" or "unassimilable particularity," shows the eternal impossibility of any "totalized" modern, instrumentalist, commercialized world. I disagree with this picture of Jamesean redemption as, or at least mostly as, some commitment to "nonidentity thinking" or the "mimetic," or as transgres-sion, violation of limits, excess, etc. (This is true even if one concedes Posnock's point that Mead, Dewey, Adorno, and Henry James can be read as attempts "to socialize the James-ean [W.]/Bergsonian abandonment of identity logic"; 136.) For all the greater historical and social sensitivity captured by Posnock's picture, and for all his attempts to differentiate himself from approaches like Trilling's (see 83), such a negative dialectics still shares too much of Trilling's original high-modernist celebration of ambiguity (and finally not much else) as the great ideal of the truly liberal imagination.

16. Leo Bersani, *A Future for Astyanax: Character and Desire in Literature* (Boston: Little, Brown, 1969), 128–55, "The Jamesean Lie." Bersani claims that James is "remarkably resistant to an interest in psychological depth." This forms the basis for one of the most sophisticated, sustained criticisms of the achievements of James's fiction, summarized in the following extreme, idealist reading: "The mind of the Jamesean center of consciousness is free in the sense that it invents and satisfies desires which meet only a minimal resistance from either the external world or internal depths. Language would no longer be principally a reflection or sublimation of given desires; it would promote new versions of being." This he says, "re-enslaves consciousness in James," because "intelligence detached from psychology traces designs that belong to no one" and "the absorption of character into language can also be the dehumanization of desire" (146). This view seems based on a (purportedly Jamesean) view of language itself as a kind of "neutral territory," "always 'outside' any particular self" (146).

I want to show that this is most definitely *not* James's view of language, or intelligence; he sees language much more as a social practice among selves rather than a system outside selves; and the Jamesean "I" is most definitely always and everywhere "limited" and radically dependent—on *other such selves* in a constant enactment of a struggle for mutuality that resonates with moral claims and thereby, most definitely, with a distinctly *human* desire.

17. After Charlotte and the Prince return to London from a time together in the country, during which their affair has begun, Maggie begins to sense that something is not quite right in her relations with her husband. She tells herself that the problem is her own overzealous attention to her father, that she has let the Prince assume that she expects him to play only a marginal role in her life. She resolves to correct this by attending to the Prince much more ardently. What is happening, what her new attention means, could be described in any number of ways. Maggie is already intimidated by and somewhat jealous of Charlotte's clothes and worldliness and must sense the differences in the Prince's reactions to Charlotte and to the "little," "prim," "nunlike" Maggie, but she keeps from herself a full formulation of what she "knows." Or, Maggie only now begins to *want* the Prince when she realizes he is desired by her "rival" and, in some true sense of the word, step-*mother*. (God knows how complicated *this* could be: in pulling the Prince away from Charlotte, she is proving that she is more desirable than the woman who sleeps with her father?) The same problems emerge in explaining her motives in asking everyone who was at Matcham (in the country) for *all* the details. In some sense, although she tells herself that this is part of her new strategy of more intense involvement in the Prince's life, she is also clearly checking the stories against one another, but she also just as clearly doesn't know that, or won't let herself admit it, and so on. But any of these sorts of explanations would, I think, presume something not yet there: something of Maggie's own sense of who she is, where she fits in, what is at stake in her marriage, what she wants. She doesn't have hidden, self-deceived, or unconscious views about any of these. She has no possible views and must enter this intensely sophisticated world of supremely intelligent mirrors and lights and shadows in order to form views. This is particularly manifest in the incredible carriage scene described below.

18. One effect of this sort of ambiguity is that James ends up making far greater and far different sorts of demands on the reader than almost any other novelist. Not only is it hard to figure out what is going on, but James, in effect, keeps hinting that he doesn't know either and rather invites us to enter the novel as characters, often giving us figures for The Reader, like Fanny here or like Maria Gostrey, Henrietta Stackpole, or Susan Shepard Stringham, while showing us through them how easy it is to get things wrong.

(This partly explains the unusual tone—at least, I find it unusual—of so much criticism of James; a kind of foot-stomping American impatience with all the supposed fussiness and folderol.) And this fact—how much trust James asks for, with so little promised—touches again upon the question of moral reality in his books. This is, I think, the hardest issue to state properly but is by far the most important. A simple formulation: *the fact that there can be no final fact of the matter that settles everything (one of the implications of his historical theme) does not mean that the whole question of "getting it right" is hopeless or ends in skepticism.*

19. *The Golden Bowl,* ed. Virginia Llewellyn Smith (Oxford: Oxford University Press, 1983), 102.

20. Ibid., 86.

21. Thus, consider Wayne Booth's remark (about the unreliable narrator in *The Aspern Papers*): "Again and again in the story one is forced to throw up his hands and decide that James has simply provided insufficient clues for the judgments which he still quite clearly expects us to be able to make" (*The Rhetoric of Fiction* [Chicago: University of Chicago Press, 1962], 361). But there are no "clues" and there can't be. *There is no* "figure in the carpet" or "real thing" to be found. This again does not mean there is just moral skepticism everywhere in James. That absence is precisely the *moral* point, precisely what binds us together in a distinctly normative dependence. Or such is my thesis.

22. Although I am making heavy use here of *The Golden Bowl* to make these points about consciousness and motivation, I should also take note of the great interest the book inspires in James's moral or ethical outlook. I am thinking especially of Martha Nussbaum's "Flawed Crystals: James's *The Golden Bowl* and Literature as Moral Philosophy," and "'Finely Aware and Richly Responsible': Literature and the Moral Imagination," in *Love's Knowledge: Essays on Philosophy and Literature* (New York: Oxford University Press, 1990), and Frederick Olafson's essay "Moral Relationships in the Fiction of Henry James," *Ethics* 98, no. 2 (1988): 294–312. Since I find the ending of *The Golden Bowl* a moral, as well as a personal, disaster for all four of the principals, my disagreements with Nussbaum's reading and with the ethical ideal she sees finally evinced in Maggie (see 134) require much more space than a note to do them and especially her position justice. I agree with Olafson that the novel's resolution still rests on a tissue of lies, that this is bad and understood by James to be bad, and that one need not be either soft-hearted about what a successful marriage requires or a narrow moralist to see why such a state is unacceptable (303–12). But, in exploring the question of how James "shows" us just what is wrong in Kate Croy's and Maggie's actions, Olafson relies on Kantian and even Habermasean criteria of publicity and the conditions of communication that do not fit James's use of the international theme (or his historical understanding of modern moral life) or the more radical conceptions of consciousness and meaning that underlie his moral sense. Or so I am trying to show.

23. *Golden Bowl,* 334.

24. Ibid., 342.

25. R. P. Blackmur, *Studies in Henry James* (New York: New Directions, 1983), x.

26. I take seriously here Manfred Mackenzie's point in chapter 4 of *Communities of Love and Honor in Henry James* (Cambridge: Harvard University Press, 1976) that there is a kind of knowledge obtained by James's characters that *cannot* be shared or spoken at all. There is much that is unspoken in Isabel's resolve or Strether's decision, or in "What Maisie Knew," for that matter. But here James seems so intent on treating this sort of silence, not as an acknowledgment of the simply unsayable, as a way of not knowing what one knows, or as a wise way to avoid a scandal and preserve a marriage, but, as noted, as "crudities of mutual resistance." It is true that this reading breaks the string of heroic

Americans like Isabel and Strether and Milly, but I have tried to show how dark are the shadows around Adam's collecting and pretensions and Maggie's egoism as these are painted by James.

27. As in 1878 with *Daisy Miller* or in 1880 with *Confidence,* the problem remains the possibility of trust, confidence, a fundamental acknowledgment and acceptance of the other, all in ways consistent with the ideal of a free life. One sometimes hears that James simply did not believe such trust was possible, that all love was a zero-sum game: someone gaining, someone losing. What is more interesting, I think, is that James treats the aspiration to such mutuality, however difficult, unlikely, or risky, as unavoidable in any attempt at a free or independent life, and that he does not treat the failure of such hopes as due to the nature of things, as if human love is subject to some cruel cosmic fate. It is essential to note that the questions of equality and mutuality are also treated as reflections of the *modern* problem of money and power, and that these issues are treated historically and so contingently, not essentially or as if products of some psychological necessity.

28. In a paper on *Washington Square* recently published in *Raritan,* Bette Howland has shown in detail how important this basic triangle is in the most important of James's novels and how variations on it work ("*Washington Square:* The Family Plot," *Raritan* 15, no. 4 [spring 1996]: 88–110). I am much indebted to this fine article and to several conversations with Bette during a co-taught seminar on James for the Committee on Social Thought at the University of Chicago.

29. Here again, I would note a common confusion about what is involved in the moral point of view, a confusion similar to the "trumping" expectation mentioned earlier. Moral categories need not be ultimate or exclusive to be real or to have an indispensable purchase on the intelligibility of an event. An action can be wrong and motivated by objectionable motives; and a successful attempt to understand such motives in nonmoral terms is possible without being necessarily exculpatory. The latter is simply a different question, and the relation between the two categories is a different question still.

Edmund Burke and Thomas Jefferson: Mutually Antipathetic Minds

CONOR CRUISE O'BRIEN

The mutual antipathy between Edmund Burke and Thomas Jefferson is mostly a matter of inference rather than direct evidence. As far as I know, the two men never met, nor did they correspond, nor did Burke ever refer to Jefferson. The only reference to Jefferson in Burke's *Correspondence* is in a letter from Thomas Paine to Burke on 17 January 1790. The reference there is substantial, and I shall come to it later. Except for that letter of Paine's there is no direct evidence that Burke was even aware of Jefferson's existence. We can safely infer, however, that he was well aware of it. Even before Burke entered Parliament, at the beginning of 1766, he had been a keen student of American affairs and remained so until the conclusion of the American War of Independence, seventeen years later. It was impossible, therefore, that he could have failed to be

I am proud and happy to be asked to contribute to David Grene's Festschrift. I have known him now for more than fifty years and have learned much from him. We first met when I was a pupil at Sandford Park School and he—then a young graduate from Trinity College—came there to teach Latin. His classes were a delight. He taught with immense zest and humor working on deep familiarity with the text. I remember his enactment of a line of Horace describing the peace that followed the decisive victory of Emperor Augustus in the Roman civil war. The line was *Tutus Bos Etenim Rura Perambulat:* "The ox in safety perambulates the field." David—who is a natural actor as well as a great teacher—mimicked the action of the perambulating ox, stamping vigorously up and down the classroom, and almost seeming to have four legs. That was the beginning of a lifelong friendship even though, during most of it, we have been physically separated by the Atlantic Ocean. I owe him an immense amount, both intellectually and morally, and I am deeply grateful.

aware of the activity of Thomas Jefferson from 1769 on, when Jefferson played a leading part in the Virginia resolution on nonimportation of British goods. Burke must have known quite a lot about Jefferson but never found occasion to refer to him.

Jefferson's awareness of Burke, however, has left a number of traces and goes back quite a long way. Jefferson was fourteen years younger than Burke and, as a young man, read Burke's earliest work: *A Philosophical Enquiry into the Origins of Our Ideas of the Sublime and Beautiful* (1756). Jefferson's comments are noncommittal, as are his few and brief other remarks about Burke in the period before the French Revolution.

There is a general impression—fostered principally by Thomas Paine, who knew both men—that Jefferson and Burke were on the same side over the American Revolution but on opposite sides over the French Revolution. That they were on opposite sides over the French Revolution admits of no doubt whatever. But it is simply not true to say that Burke and Jefferson were on the same side over the American Revolution. Burke and his friends had striven to *avert* the American Revolution—by timely concessions from Britain—and that was still their position even after the Declaration of Independence, of which Jefferson regarded himself, and has come to be regarded, as the author. A little more than a month after the Declaration, Burke wrote to his oldest friend, Richard Shackleton,[1] that he could not wish for a complete success for either side in the American Revolution: "I do not know how to wish success to those whose Victory is to seperate [*sic*] from us a large and noble part of our Empire. Still less do I wish success to injustice, oppression and absurdity"—the last words referring to British policy over the previous ten years. Throughout 1777, Burke maintained that position, still hoping for a compromise, under which Britain would renounce her attempts to tax the colonists and would rescind the Penal Acts, and the colonists would resume their allegiance. It was only after the news of Burgoyne's defeat at Saratoga had reached England early in December 1777 that Burke and his friends reluctantly decided that compromise was now impossible and American independence would have to be conceded. Burke did not acknowledge that decision until a year later. In the same speech in which he declared that Britain must now recognize American independence, he recorded the abhorrence with which he had heard the news of the Declaration of Independence two and a half years before:

It was [now] incumbent on Great Britain to acknowledge it [independence] directly. Yet on the day that he first heard of the American states having claimed

independence,—it made him sick at heart; it struck him to the soul; because he
saw it was a claim essentially injurious to this country, and a claim which Great
Britain could never get rid of: never! never! never![2]

It is clear from this passage that Edmund Burke and Thomas Jefferson
were already thinking on very different lines as early as July 1776.

Burke has been rightly regarded, both in his own time and since, as
a consistent friend of the American colonists. He had been instrumental
in securing the repeal of the Stamp Act in 1766. He had opposed the
Townshend Act; later he had opposed the Penal Acts (known to Americans as "the Intolerable Acts") in two great speeches. In the last phase of
the war, Lord Rockingham, by then completely under Burke's influence,
had refused to accept office unless the king was prepared to accept the
independence of America. That precondition brought the king to the
verge of abdication but it also—directly contrary to the king's wishes and
original intentions—brought an end to the American war.

This series of positions has led to the widespread modern perception
that Burke was "on the side of the American Revolution" and that the
American revolutionaries—including Jefferson himself—generally assumed that he was on their side.

Yet it is clear that Burke regarded the American Revolution and
American independence as great misfortunes, brought about by the follies
and obstinacy of George III and his Parliaments. Burke came down in
favor of independence, at the end of 1778, only because he regarded the
prolongation of the war as an even greater misfortune, which could not
in any case even avert independence.

The basic divergence between Burke's thinking and Jefferson's—a divergence which was to culminate in blazing antipathy (explicit on Jefferson's side, implicit on Burke's)—in the period of the French Revolution
is already evident during the American Revolution. It is manifested in the
approach of the two to the idea of liberty. For Jefferson, liberty does not
require to be defined; it is absolute, self-evident, and sacred: a value that
mere human beings have no authority to tie down and limit. Burke's
concept of liberty is very different. It is best set out, for the period of the
American Revolution, in the *Letter to the Sheriffs of Bristol* (1778):

Civil freedom, Gentlemen, is not, as many have endeavoured to persuade you, a
thing that lies hid in the depth of abstruse science. It is a blessing and a benefit,
not an abstract speculation; and all the just reasoning that can be upon it is of so
coarse a texture as perfectly to suit the ordinary capacities of those who are to
enjoy, and of those who are to defend it. Far from any resemblance to those

propositions in geometry and metaphysics which admit no medium, but must be true or false in all their latitude, social and civil freedom, like all other things in common life, are variously mixed and modified, enjoyed in very different degrees, and shaped into an infinite diversity of forms, according to the temper and circumstances of every community. The extreme of liberty (which is its abstract perfection, but its real fault) obtains nowhere, nor ought to obtain anywhere; because extremes, as we all know, in every point which relates either to our duties or satisfactions in life, are destructive both to virtue and enjoyment. Liberty, too, must be limited in order to be possessed.

This is exactly the same concept of liberty which Burke was to assert, twelve years later, in *Reflections on the Revolution in France* (1790). In fact, the positions of Burke and Jefferson in relation to the American and French Revolutions were both *internally* consistent, though in opposition to one another. On the one hand, Burke was committed to an ordered, limited liberty; on the other, Jefferson was committed to liberty as a sacred absolute, manifest in both revolutions, the latter of which was destined to fulfill and rejuvenate the former.

Over the American Revolution, the mutual antipathy of the two minds never became overt. The victory of what was to Jefferson a sacred cause was, for Burke, something to be accepted as a regrettable necessity. Philosophically, there is a gulf between the two positions, but in terms of practical politics the gulf was not visible. For all American revolutionaries, including Jefferson, the important thing was that the British opposition— whose intellectual leader was Edmund Burke—was urging, from 1778 on, the recognition of the independence of America. They *urged* it from 1778 to 1782, and in 1782–83, after Yorktown, they were in a position to insist on it. So Jefferson and Burke ended up as allies over the American Revolution, despite the gulf between their thinking—and feelings—both on the Declaration of Independence and on the general question of the nature of the American Revolution.

Over the French Revolution, on the other hand, the differences between Burke's thinking and Jefferson's erupted into conflict, conducted through intermediaries. For Jefferson, the American and French Revolutions were continuous and similar phenomena. For Burke, they were not. The American Revolution was something limited and local. That it had happened at all was a regrettable consequence of British folly. But because it *had* happened, Britain could cut its losses there, without risk to its liberties. This was not the case with the revolution in France, a cosmic phenomenon. The French revolutionaries—as Burke saw it—were trying to impose their own "extreme of liberty" on all other countries, with ruinous consequences. Burke, therefore, thought and preached from 1790 on that the French Revolution should be resisted, in words with regard to its intellectual expansion, and in arms against its military expansion, which began in the spring of 1792. Jefferson, on the other hand, thought that the French Revolution should be aided in its holy task of liberating the world. The intellectual hostility between the two men was irrepressible from 1791, the year Americans learned of Burke's *Reflections on the Revolution in France* (1790), a work of which Thomas Jefferson was one of the first, and the most vehemently hostile, of American readers.

The basic incompatibility between the minds of Burke and Jefferson is best demonstrated on a theoretical level by contrasting a letter written from Paris by Jefferson to Madison in September 1789 with a famous passage in Burke's *Reflections* published more than a year after Jefferson's unpublished letter. Jefferson had been minister plenipotentiary of the United States in Paris since 1785, and at the time he wrote this letter he was preparing to return to the United States. Jefferson wrote:

The question Whether one generation of men has a right to bind another, seems never to have been started either on this or our side of the water. Yet it is a question of such consequence as not only to merit decision, but place also, among the fundamental principles of every government. The course of reflection in which we are immersed here [Jefferson is referring to the French Revolution] on the elementary principles of society has presented this question to my mind; and that no such obligation can be so transmitted I think very capable of proof.— I set out on this ground, which I suppose to be self evident: "*that the earth belongs in the usufruct to the living*": that the dead have neither powers nor rights over it.

On similar grounds it may be proved that no society can make a perpetual constitution, or even a perpetual law. The earth belongs always to the living generation. They may manage it then, and what proceeds from it, as they please, during their usufruct. They are masters too of their own persons, and consequently may govern them as they please. But persons and property make the sum of the objects of government. The constitution and the laws of their predecessors extinguished them in their natural course with those who gave them being. This could preserve that being till it ceased to be itself, and no longer.[3]

The "natural course," according to Jefferson, has a precise duration: seventeen years.

Perhaps the most extraordinary thing about this extraordinary letter is that it was addressed to James Madison, who had done so much, two years before, to shape the American Constitution. If the Jeffersonian doctrine promulgated in this letter had prevailed, the American Constitution would have become obsolete in 1806—which, as it happened, was to be halfway through Thomas Jefferson's second term as president of the United States.

Compare Jefferson's "the earth belongs . . . to the living" with the following passage in Burke's *Reflections,* published a little more than a year after Jefferson's letter to Madison:

Society is indeed a contract. Subordinate contracts for objects of mere occasional interest may be dissolved at pleasure—but the state ought not to be considered as nothing better than a partnership agreement in a trade of pepper and coffee, calico or tobacco, or some other such low concern, to be taken up for a little temporary interest, and to be dissolved by the fancy of the parties. It is to be looked on with other reverence; because it is not a partnership in things subservient only to the gross animal existence of a temporary and perishable nature. It is a partnership in all science; a partnership in all art; a partnership in every virtue, and in all perfection. As the ends of such a partnership cannot be obtained in many generations it becomes a partnership not only between those who are living, but between those who are living, those who are dead, and those who are to be born.[4]

Between Burke and Jefferson this is not a meeting of minds; it is a *collision* of minds. Burke is committed to societal continuity over time; Jefferson, to societal *dis*continuity. This theoretical difference—which is also a temperamental difference—underlies the difference between the attitudes of the two men toward the two great revolutions of their time. Jefferson was unreservedly *for* the French Revolution as well as the American one. He rejoiced in the shattering of continuity in both cases: the rejection of the dominion of the dead. Burke deplored both revolutions as breaches of the Burkean partnership between those who are living, those who are dead, and those who are to be born. In the American case, Burke put the blame for the breach mainly on the British side and came reluctantly to accept the American Revolution as a regrettable fait accompli, limited to a particular region of the globe. He saw the French Revolution, on the other hand, as an attempt to enforce what he feared most: liberty without limit, an attempt to destroy the Burkean partnership, universally and for all time. Between that enterprise and Edmund Burke, there could never be peace.

The theoretical and temperamental differences between Burke and Jefferson inevitably affected their ideas of where the French Revolution was going. On 11 July 1789, Jefferson wrote a glowing account of the triumph of the French Revolution to Thomas Paine:

The *National Assembly* then (for that is the name they take) having shewn thro' every stage of these transactions a coolness, wisdom, and resolution to set fire to the four corners of the kingdom and to perish with it themselves rather than to relinquish an iota from their plan of a total change of government, are now in complete and undisputed possession of the sovereignty. The executive and the aristocracy are now at their feet: the mass of the nation, the mass of the clergy, and the army are with them. They have prostrated the old government, and are now beginning to build one from the foundation.

Tom Paine liked the bit about setting "fire to the four corners of the kingdom," etc. so much that he quoted it at length, naming Jefferson as his source, in a letter which he wrote to Edmund Burke (of all people) on 17 January 1790. Paine assumed that Burke, since he liked the American Revolution, must love the French one (a proposition that seemed self-evident to Paine and Jefferson and many others). Actually, when he received Paine's letter, Burke was already at work on *Reflections on the Revolution in France* (published 1 November 1790). A distinguished French historian of the eighteenth century, Patrick Thierry, believes that Paine's letter (with the quotation from Jefferson) "made no small contribution to the fury" with which Burke reacted against the French Revolution.[5] This is the only example of a Jeffersonian influence—or, rather, impact—on Edmund Burke that I am aware of. The case is of considerable interest in view of Jefferson's later reactions to Burke's *Reflections,* on whose composition Jefferson had unwittingly impinged. The idea that it is admirable on the part of a representative assembly to resolve "to set fire to the four corners of the kingdom and to perish with it themselves rather than to relinquish an iota from their plan" is a product of the wilder shores of Thomas Jefferson and therefore peculiarly repugnant to the mind of Edmund Burke.

Throughout the great international controversy over the French Revolution, Burke was indirectly at grips with Jefferson. Jefferson's friends in Britain were British radicals, enthusiasts for the French Revolution. The most important of these correspondents of Jefferson were Richard Price and Tom Paine. Richard Price was the radical divine whose sermon of 4 November 1789, linking the French Revolution to the Glorious Revolution of 1688, was part of the flame that set off the explosion of *Reflections on the Revolution in France*. Another part of the flame appears to have been Paine's letter of 17 January 1790, which included that incendiary quotation from Thomas Jefferson.

In August and September 1789, Jefferson was busy preparing for his return to the United States with his daughters and house slaves. On 13

September he wrote his last letter from Paris to Paine. In this letter Jefferson is just as confident as he was immediately before the fall of the Bastille that the French Revolution is over and that nothing remains but to embody it in constitutional form:

Tranquility is well established in Paris, and tolerably so thro' the whole kingdom, and I think there is no possibility now of any thing's hindering their final establishment of a good constitution, which will in its principles and merit be about a middle term between that of England and the United States.

It is instructive to compare this letter, of 13 September 1789, with one written by Edmund Burke later in the same month. Burke was replying to a letter from his friend William Windham that was written two days later than Jefferson's to Paine, and in exactly the same mood of confident optimism. Windham had written:

What is said of the disorder and irregularity of the national assembly has, I think, a great deal of exaggeration: at least, if a due consideration be had of all the circumstances. My prediction was, (and accounts which I heard since my being there, have contributed to confirm it) that they would very soon become perfectly orderly.

Burke replied, on 27 September:

That they should settle their constitution, without much struggle, on paper, I can easily believe, because at present the Interests of the Crown have no party, certainly no armed party, to support them; but I have great doubts whether any form of Government which they can establish will procure obedience, especially obedience in the article of Taxations. In the destruction of the old Revenue constitution they find no difficulties—but with what to supply them is the Opus. You are undoubtedly better able to judge, but it does not appear to me, that the National assembly have one Jot more power than the King; whilst they lead or follow the popular voice, in the subversion of all orders, distinctions, privileges, impositions, Tythes, and rents, they appear omnipotent! but I very much question, whether they are in a condition to exercise any function of decided authority—or even whether they are possessed of any real deliberate capacity, or the exercise of free Judgement in any point whatsoever, as there is a Mob of their constituents ready to Hang them if They should deviate into moderation, or in the least depart from the Spirit of those they represent.

Eight days later, events occurred in Paris which demonstrated—as later events were also to demonstrate—that Burke, not Windham or Jefferson, had got it right. According to a French historian:

On 5 and 6 October a crowd of 30,000 Parisians, men and women, marched to Versailles and forced their way into the palace shouting "A Paris! A Paris!" Louis XVI, promoted by Lafayette, gave way, with the words: My friends, I shall go to Paris, with my wife and my children: it is to the love of my good and faithful subjects that I entrust my most precious possessions. The royal family then made their way from Versailles to the Tuileries, in the midst of the crowd, which included women carrying pikes. . . . The sun had ceased to set at Versailles in the splendid isolation determined by Louis XIV. The October rain brought back the King to the Tuileries, which he was not to leave, except for prison, and then the scaffold.[6]

Edmund Burke's *Reflections on the Revolution in France* had been published in London on 1 November 1790. On 22 February 1791 Paine's reply, *Rights of Man,* was published in London, dedicated to the president of the United States (whose permission for the dedication had not been asked). About four weeks later, the first copies of *Rights of Man* arrived in Philadelphia. After (apparently) having read both *Reflections* and *Rights,* Jefferson wrote to a sympathetic English correspondent, Benjamin Vaughan:

The Revolution of France does not astonish me as much as the Revolution of Mr. Burke. I wish I could believe the latter proceeded from as pure motives as the former. But what demonstration could scarcely have established before, less than the hints of Dr. Priestley and Mr. Paine establish firmly now [*sic*].

Jefferson's sentence breaks off there, possibly through effects of adrenaline. The letter goes on:

How mortifying that this evidence of the rottenness of his mind must oblige us now to ascribe to wicked motives those actions of his life which wore the mask of virtue and patriotism.

The mode of reasoning here is curious. The "rottenness" of Burke's mind is deemed to be "firmly established," beyond the need for argument, by the "evidence" of his book in its totality (combined with unspecified "hints" by Priestley and Paine). Then this imputation of "rottenness," now claimed to be an established fact, must "oblige us" to ascribe everything in Burke's whole life to wicked motives. This is a clear case of the old *Odium theologicum* transferred to a new and nominally secular sphere. The heretic and blasphemer who opposes the French Revolution represents the forces of evil in the universe and is himself totally evil and all the worse for having formerly worn the mask of virtue and patriotism (over the American Revolution). Fortunately, *Rights of Man* is there as a heavenly antidote. Jefferson goes on:

We have some names of note here who have apostatized from the true faith. [By the "true faith," which elsewhere he calls "the true God," Jefferson means the common cause of the American and French Revolutions.] . . . but they [the apostates] are few indeed, and the body of our citizens are pure and unsusceptible of taint in their republicanism. Mr. Paine's answer to Burke will be a refreshing shower to their minds.

The manner in which the "refreshing shower" should first fall on American soil was a matter of considerable concern to Jefferson and his friends. Merrill D. Peterson, one of Jefferson's biographers, writes:

In the spring [Jefferson] was unwillingly thrust on the stage as a political gladiator against his old friend John Adams. The controversy between Edmund Burke and Thomas Paine on the French Revolution supplied the background. American opinion of the Revolution, favorable at the outset, had already begun to divide when the English polemics reverberated across the Atlantic in the early months of 1791. Burke's *Reflections on the Revolution in France* captured conservative feelings for the cause of order, tradition, church, privilege, and royalty in France. No sooner was Paine's vigorous democratic reply, the first part of the *Rights of Man,* received on this side of the water than arrangements were made to publish it. John Beckley, Clerk of the House of Representatives and political accomplice of his fellow Virginians, had this purpose in hand, but before sending the pamphlet to the printer, he lent it to Madison, who then passed it on to Jefferson with instructions to return it to Beckley. But that gentleman called before Jefferson had finished. [Jefferson] promised to hurry Burke to his grave and then sent the murderous tract to Jonathan B. Smith, whose brother was to print it. Jefferson sent the book to S. H. Smith's father, Jonathan Bayard Smith, with the following note:

Apr. 26, 1791.

Th: Jefferson presents his compliments to Mr. Jonathan B. Smith, and in consequence of the inclosed note and of Mr. Beckley's desire he sends him Mr. Paine's pamphlet. He is extremely pleased to find it will be re-printed here, and that something is at length to be publicly said against the political heresies which have sprung up among us. He has no doubt our citizens will rally a second time round the standard of common sense.[7]

Jefferson's endorsement of Paine's attack on Burke was universally regarded as itself an attack on Jefferson's great rival, John Adams, whose position with regard to the French Revolution was almost identical to that of Burke. Jefferson told Washington that he had not intended his letter to the publisher to be published. Washington did not believe him. Jefferson also told Adams that he had not had Adams in mind when he wrote the endorsement of Paine. Adams did not believe him either. But Jefferson's putatively unintentional public endorsement of Paine as against Burke was hugely beneficial to Jefferson politically. The cause of the French Revolution was extremely popular with most Americans at this time, and Jefferson was now the only member of Washington's first administration who was known to support that cause. As James Monroe put it in a letter to Jefferson:

The contest of Burke and Paine, as revived in America with the different publications on either side is much the subject of discussion in all parts of this state [Virginia]. Adams is universally believ'd to be the author of Publicola [an attack on Paine's book] and the principles he avows, as well as those of Mr. Burke as universally reprobated.

Thus, Jefferson's antipathetic relationship to Edmund Burke became a major help to Jefferson along his tortuous but well-charted course toward becoming, nine years later, the third president of the United States.

By that time, fortunately for Jefferson, the French Revolution was over. Its demise was proclaimed by Bonaparte a year before Jefferson's election to the presidency. On 15 December 1799 the first consul made his historic announcement: "Citizens, the Revolution is established upon the principles which began it: it is ended."

The way in which the French Revolution would end had been predicted by Burke, nine years before the event. In *Reflections on the Revolution in France,* Burke had written:

In the weakness of one kind of authority, and in the fluctuation of all, the officers of an army will remain for some time mutinous and full of faction until some popular general, who understands the art of conciliating the soldiers and who possesses the true spirit of command, shall draw the eyes of all men upon himself. Armies will obey him on his personal account. . . . But the moment in which that event shall happen, the person who really commands the army is your master, the master of your whole republic.

Burke's capacity to predict how the French Revolution would end was the result of his profound understanding of the phenomenon itself. *As a political thinker,* Burke was vastly superior to Jefferson. Jefferson's superiority was in the domain of practical politics and in the art of rallying mass support. The difference of roles and functions was related to the mutual antipathy of the two minds, but the antipathy went much deeper. Basically it was the gulf between the view that "the earth belongs to the living" and the belief in a partnership between the dead, the living, and those not yet born.

Notes

1. TORS 11 August 1776, *The Correspondence of Edmund Burke,* ed. Thomas Copeland (Cambridge: Cambridge University Press; Chicago: University of Chicago Press), III, 286–87.

2. Speech on the Army Estimates, December 1778.

3. *Papers of Thomas Jefferson,* ed. J. P. Boyd (Princeton: Princeton University Press, 1958), 15:392–97.

4. *Reflections on the Revolution in France,* ed. Conor Cruise O'Brien (London and New York: Penguin Books, 1968; reprint, London and New York: Penguin Classics, 1986), 194–95.

5. Patrick Thierry, *De la Révolution américaine à la Révolution française* (Paris, 1986), 483.

6. Denis Richet, "Journées révolutionnaires," in *Dictionnaire critique de la Révolution française,* ed. François Furet and Mona Ozouf (Paris: Flammarion, 1988), 116.

7. Merrill D. Peterson, *Thomas Jefferson and the New Nation: A Biography* (New York: Oxford University Press, 1970), 103.

Postlude

Problems in American Literature

S A U L   B E L L O W

I came back to Chicago to give this talk and I give it in a hall that I have known for more than sixty years. I sat here in the early thirties listening to lectures in the humanities survey course by Professors Schevill, Scott, Norman MacLean, and others less memorable. Professor Scott when he proctored the final exam wore a tailcoat, making fun of the old-fashioned academic formality of his own youth. I didn't do too badly in this course. I should have been happy to do half so well at the pool tables upstairs. I longed to be a pool shark but I simply didn't have what it took, and I spent more hours than I could afford in Mandel Hall, trying to master reverse-English while my conscience grew more swollen and painful with every failure.

I was seventeen years old, theoretically capable of going it alone. My father resented signing tuition checks for me. The university's quarterly fee was then one hundred dollars—no trivial amount in the days of the Depression. I was mentally not steady enough to qualify for a scholarship. On Saturdays I was gainfully employed; I worked in the window-shade section of Goldblatt's department store at Forty-seventh and Ashland. The three dollars I earned were not quite enough to cover El fares and lunches at the Commons. I was not doing a pre-med course, like so many of my high school classmates. Nor did I study chemistry. Nor law. Nor economics. My father couldn't readily explain to his friends just what I was doing at the university, and perhaps he resented the embarrassment I caused him.

Most affectionately dedicated to my old and dear friend and colleague D. G.

Most of my classmates knew exactly what they were here for; they plugged away at their biochemistry. Even the mathematicians thoroughly understood that it was wrong to dream away three hundred dollars in tuition at a time when the banks were tottering. Serious energetic students understood what sacrifices their families were making. Their outlook was practical.

I shared a room on Ellis Avenue at Fifty-sixth Street in the spring of 1934 during exam week with one of my high-school friends. This man confessed one evening after swearing me to secrecy that he was the nephew of Dora Kaplan, the woman who early in the twenties had shot Lenin—giving him wounds from which he never recovered. I suspect that my roommate, knowing me to be something of a Marxist, was warning me to sober up and stick to my books. Our room looked down into the garden of what was then the Home for Incurables across the way, and I was fascinated by the arm- or foot-propelled chairs, whose high wheels were driven by intricate gears and long chains. I was absorbed by these contraptions more than by the texts I should have been studying.

I *did* stick to books, but those were not books connected with the courses I was taking. Early in my freshman year at the University of Chicago I drifted into a group that met in the Wiebolt Lounge to talk about literature. In my high-school days I had already read the leading novelists of the time: Sherwood Anderson, Sinclair Lewis, John Dos Passos, Theodore Dreiser. I became an enthusiastic Shavian, and Shaw had put me on to Ibsen. From Ibsen I passed to Strindberg, and from Strindberg I got into Nietzsche. The leaders of the Chicago group in the Modern Languages lounge—Eduard Roditi, Paul Goodman, William Barrett—were discussing T. S. Eliot, André Gide, Proust and Joyce, Hemingway and Gertrude Stein. We had all of course read Edmund Wilson. His *Axel's Castle* introduced us to the Symbolist movement. The shelves of the reading room were filled with contemporary literary magazines. It's not too much, I think, to say that these modern books and authors were certified or accredited *physically* by the Quadrangles themselves, by the gothic gables and ornaments of the campus. True, the Stockyards were not far away, and we had all read Upton Sinclair. *The Jungle* was not one of the books discussed by Roditi and company. We were concerned with modern civilization in its entirety as seen by Freud, as described by Marx, Lenin, and Sorel, as presented by Cocteau, or sent up by the Surrealists and the postwar Dadaists.

We seemed to take it for granted that books would continue forever to be written and read and discussed enthusiastically. It was here to stay and we took it to be the common and abiding interest of a considerable number of devoted people who would always be there, publishing articles, stunning us with poems, bowling us over with novels.

We were to learn better. But during the Great Depression the appreciative public increased greatly. The city libraries were crowded—perhaps because the reading rooms were comfortably heated but also, it must be admitted, because of the development of serious interests among the unemployed. To hear books discussed in the Thompson's cafeterias or at Raklios and other one-arm joints in the Loop was not unusual. The government itself recognized the importance of intellectuals and artists and the WPA provided for painters, dramatists, actors, novelists, and even poets.

I have made all this seem sophomoric, and in its early stages it can fairly be seen as an enthusiasm of the immature. But it is, and remains, a serious enterprise. The writer describes the inner life of humankind. The supremacy of the poetic drama is not challenged by the prose novel. Defoe or Dickens could not do what Shakespeare did. But prose fiction is the best we can offer in these times. We, the likes of us, are its material, and we are no Caesars and Antonys, no Lears and Hamlets. We are not even the Bolkonskys of *War and Peace.* When he was asked to compare Anna Karenina with Emma Bovary, Henry James pointed out, in his intricate manner of pointing, that Anna was, after all, an aristocrat, poor Emma a bourgeois, a commoner. Flaubert himself was distressed by her commonness and provinciality. He did not deny that her passions were great. He took them seriously, but in her provincial world she could find no man capable of satisfying her craving for love.

Ours is after all a democratic age—and ours is a mass democracy at that. Beyond all things else our politics, our economy, our mental life are democratically organized. Or disorganized. When we hear or think in such terms we are impelled to take hold of them analytically. A writer may understand that he can't allow himself to be fully circumscribed by analytical terms. These will lead him from externals to externals and finally push him away from imagination. A novelist can't be too careful about ideas and cognitions. He is apt to see thought as a pitfall. It's not only that democracies in modern times are organized on intellectual principles but that what people think or say to one another comes from widely held opinions, ideologies, or the prevailing ideas of the age. The novelist and critic Albert Murray was right on the button when he wrote that few American writers have gone beyond the social science outlook they absorbed as undergraduates. Add to social science Marxism, Freud's psychoanalytic theories, French and German existentialism, books like Weber's *Religion and the Rise of Capitalism,* and a multitude of phrases such as "the Protestant work ethic." And there are also powerful Nietzschean books whose radical ideas about history, religion, and art are the source of so much that people say (or think they are saying), and you begin to understand why novelists are compelled to deal with key concepts which are after all the concepts that fill the heads of the fictional characters they describe, and of their readers as well.

I will avoid going into historical detail, because I am after all an amateur in these matters, but the theorizing geniuses of the seventeenth and eighteenth centuries made our mental life for us. For many generations the West has taken counsel from them. If they have not taken it, they have nonetheless been involved with these Bacons, Spinozas, Lockes, and Rousseaus. The aim of these philosophers was to guide us toward order, law, and liberty. They saw our human instability and our ignorance and they tried to tell mankind what was what in the present age, to protect our liberties and provide for our needs.

You will think that in speaking of these matters I am giving in to the weakness for intellectuality often attributed to me. A recent essayist, Robert Boyers, wrote wonderfully well about this tendency of mine on the occasion of my eightieth birthday. He said it was hard not to think of me as an intellectual force "in a culture little accustomed to regarding its writers in this way." I don't think I am anything remotely like an intellectual force. And he was kind enough to say that there were pleasures in reading me that had nothing to do with ideas. Those are the pleasures that concern me. But he does refer to me as a Captain of Intellect. I coined this expression myself, I think. It was applied to a character named Victor Wulpy, an abrasive New York intellectual who figures in a story called "What Kind of Day Did You Have?" Boyers describes this Wulpy as "a turbulent force of nature, a compulsive anecdotalist, cultural analyst and spokesman for the free imagination." He may well also seem—this is not invariably the case—an incorrigible son of a bitch. Wulpy figures in my story as a New York intellectual, a midcentury Greenwich Village type. I did not mean to examine or challenge his ideas. My interest was in the man himself.

To Boyers's credit he does not accuse me of posing as a thinker. What he sees is that I take a special interest in people standing or claiming to stand higher than most on the mental scale. He says that I have helped to make readers feel that "there is a strange dignity in those who are mad for transcendence or for some impossible idea of nobility." I am grateful to him for helping to set the record straight.

The fact is that about fifty years ago I came across a short essay by Paul Valéry in which the great French poet and critic called for the writing of a vast modern comedy based on the intellectual life of the present century—something like a *Comédie humaine* of ideas. I was not qualified to write anything of the sort but I didn't mind trying my hand occasionally at an anticipatory sketch—a suggestion to others better qualified than I was, and with a better grasp of intellectual history.

As a matter of fact I have often thought of intellectuals as would-be princes or kings who suggest to us for our good how to organize a society based on political systems that would in all respects make us better, wiser, more intelligent, more kind—would-be kings or heroes or founders. In *Crime and Punishment,* Dostoyevsky's Raskolnikov, who compares himself to Napoleon, is clearly aware of this. He mentions Mohammed and other founders as well. Like any lawgiver he is prepared to kill. It's not the old usurer whose murder he regrets but that of the woman's sister, a devout simple creature, a *yurodivy,* or naive mystic and believer, a reader of the Gospel according to John.

One more comment on Raskolnikov before I leave him. Raskolnikov is fighting the impotency of thought. As he lies in his attic revolving entire universes in his mind, he is incapable of extricating his sister from her humiliations or of raising a few rubles for his rent. His crime is committed in order to save his intellectual honor. He is challenged to go beyond speculation and to act.

He passionately resists the disgrace of pointless thinking.

We today are much less aware than intellectuals were in the nineteenth century that we are saturated by thinking and that we feel the disgrace of a pointless intellectual life.

Since I am not professionally a thinker I hesitate to make a formal argument on these lines, but as writers, if they are any good at all, are apt to be good observers it may not be a waste of time to consider what they have to say. My notion is that there is a greater volume of consciousness today than there ever was in the history of mankind. That this consciousness swells and aches at times intolerably—for some people it is a calvary. That this consciousness is related somehow to our freedom and the increasing mass of essential rational decisions to be made. That around us ideas proliferate madly; concepts are elaborated but intelligent effective direction is lacking. Is our modern mass democracy with its endlessly proliferating technologies to blame for this? My brief account of what seems to be happening is the predictable result of a trade devoted to the description of the inner life of humankind—the sphinxlike work of artists in every age.

In my generation, when we were young, we believed that novels and paintings would always be read, seen, and taken into the soul. It never crossed our minds that it was the Great Depression that made the country so rich in readers.

Our naivest error was the confidence that books could turn American society around and change Nebraska farmers into lovers of art. This, literally, was the hope of Vachel Lindsay when he wrote his *Gospel of Beauty* and went out to distribute it to field hands at harvest time. (I recommend his "Adventures while Preaching the Gospel of Beauty" and also his "Handy Guide for Beggars.") This declamatory poet was something like a hobo. He was a pious Christian, praying in his yard in Springfield while the neighbors' kids crowding up to his fence jeered at him. His great heroes were Lincoln, Governor Altgeld, and William Jennings Bryan. Lindsay was not a Captain of Intellect. As I describe him here, I recall what Rebecca West wrote of Othello as Shakespeare created him— Othello, she wrote, spoke "a special kind of music, rolling and splendid and unintellectual as thunder."

I think it safe to assume that Vachel Lindsay knew nothing at all about Tocqueville and his *Democracy in America*. I bring these two together because Tocqueville had so much to say about the future of the arts in the USA.

He warned us not to expect too much in this line. He wrote: "In democratic communities where men are all insignificant and very much alike, each man instantly sees all his fellows when he surveys himself." Let me remind you here, lest these words about insignificance put your backs up, that Tocqueville was fair and thorough about American democracy and admired many of its institutions.

"I am persuaded," he went on, "that in the end democracy diverts the imagination from all that is external and fixes it on man alone. Democratic nations may amuse themselves for awhile with considering the productions of nature, but they are only excited in reality by a survey of themselves. Here, and here alone, the true sources of poetry among such nations are to be found." Evidently Tocqueville assumes that men in democratic communities, basically insignificant, can be interesting only in numbers, and collectively. He makes this quite explicit. "Nothing conceivable is so petty, so insipid, so crowded with paltry interests, in one word, so anti-poetic as the life of a man in the United States. But among the thoughts which it suggests there is always one which is full of poetry, and that is the hidden nerve which gives vigor to the frame." This hidden nerve, the epic theme for Americans, probably has to do with the conquest of the continent, of nature itself, by pioneers and settlers, while following the political plan laid down by the founders. The influence of those founders is contemporary in character, for democratic nations care little for the past but are haunted by visions of what will be.

In the chapter on democracy and philosophical method Tocqueville finds in Americans a hint of or natural gift for Cartesianism. Americans, according to Tocqueville, follow the maxims of Descartes because their "social conditions dispose their understanding to accept them. Everyone shuts himself up in his own breast and affects from that point to judge the world. . . ." And further, "as it is on their own testimony that they are accustomed to rely, they like to discern the object which engages their attention with extreme clearness: they therefore strip off as much as possible all that covers it, they rid themselves of whatever conceals it from sight, in order to view it more clearly and in the broad light of day."

To be shut up in one's own breast applies as well to the bourgeois in all modern countries as to the nineteenth-century American. It suggests also a reason for the powerful effects of majorities in the formation of public opinion and public taste.

Tocqueville was a younger contemporary of Wordsworth, and like Tocqueville, Wordsworth in his lyrical ballads wrote of simple people. But his leech-gatherer was certainly no Cartesian. In low, rustic life Wordsworth looked for "the essential passions of the heart," a Rousseauian project if ever there was one, aiming at a poetry purged of civilized prejudices.

It was actually very generous of Tocqueville to tell us (no kidding) that the Americans were Cartesian by nature. By now the moisture of the green continent Tocqueville saw has dried out on city sidewalks and endless interstates.

The first postulate of Tocqueville's book is that aristocratic Europe is done for. A new democratic age is upon us, with unprecedented opportunities for free development and personal expansion but bringing forward as well unique opportunities for corruption and decadence. Nineteenth-century America often gave Europeans the willies. See, for example, the American chapters of Dickens's *Martin Chuzzlewit* or the pages in which he describes, in his *American Notes,* flatboat men on the Ohio spitting tobacco juice into the water while disputing fine points of theology. Henry James in his essay on Hawthorne made a formidable list of what this raw country lacked, its cultural barrenness—its destitution.

Tocqueville, while he sees political advances and possibilities here, is hard on the mental life of the Americans: "a motley multitude whose intellectual wants are to be described. These new votaries of the pleasures of the mind have not all received the same education: they do not possess

the same degree of culture as their fathers, nor any resemblance to them—
nay, they perpetually differ from themselves, for they live in a state of
incessant change of place, feeling and fortunes." He then says, for he is
writing about the curious anticipated barrenness of democratic literature,
"it is however from the bosom of this heterogeneous and agitated mass
that authors spring," and in the same paragraph he asserts that "among
democratic nations each generation is a new people."

This is a statement to be taken seriously. It means that every generation is forced to look anew for guarantees of stability that it is not likely
to find. It hints also that the speed of social change may be too great for
adaptation. Tocqueville has already observed that we democrats have not
all received the same education. In the judgment of a European, this is a
most serious hindrance to mutual understanding and cultural continuity.
Of course, insofar as nations also produce secular and characteristic varie-
ties of collective wickedness or perversity, the standardization of education
is not always and altogether a desirable thing.

I have said that I am, as we all should be, grateful to Tocqueville. The
extent of the gratitude is another matter. We can see for ourselves that up
to a point his descriptions of democratic man are accurate enough. And
although he describes the American (of his day) faithfully, he makes no
claim to prophetic powers. Still, *Democracy in America* was published in
1835. Melville's *Moby Dick* appeared in 1851. Here the same thought will
have occurred to everyone: What about Emerson, Whitman, Henry Adams, Abraham Lincoln (a greatly gifted writer who regrettably did not
read novels); what about E. A. Poe, Emily Dickinson, Mark Twain, the
James brothers, etcetera?

This question is meant to suggest that the ways of imagination are
different from those of cognition. Of course it might be argued that the
great fertility of the European arts in the nineteenth century was bound
to overflow into the United States. An international culture was available
to gifted readers in all countries. Melville read Shakespeare and Milton.
Baudelaire read Edgar Allan Poe. Flaubert saw in the basic Frenchman of
his day just about what Tocqueville saw in the representative American of
paltry interests.

For the imagination piercing everyday appearances, following the inner life is the primary impulse. The imagination of course may be and in
some cases is familiar with the prevailing cognitive readings or interpretations of reality. The great modern philosophers and political thinkers are
often very hard on us, indeed merciless. It is they that made our mental
life for us.

A century and a half after Tocqueville, intellectual dislike of the human product of mass democracy has been sharpened by the wars and the revolutions and dictatorships put upon us by demonic leaders far worse than the moronic Last Man, who, for Nietzsche, epitomized modern decadence.

Our own country has long been identified as the worst case—as a warning to the rest of the civilized world. The USA is known for its material achievements but it has not matched these achievements with a high culture. Freud called America a *misgeburt*. A German general remarked to André Malraux during the last days of the Occupation that surely used-car salesmen from the United States could not be expected to fight a war. I suspect that in de Gaulle's view the USA had been a dumping ground for all the refuse of Europe. The Hegelian scholar Alexandre Kojève, famous for having introduced the concept of the end of history to American thinkers, wrote in a lengthy footnote in his *Introduction to the Reading of Hegel* that "the United States has already attained the final stage of Marxist communism, seeing that practically all the members of a classless society can, from now on, appropriate everything that seems good to them without working any more than their heart dictates." This is as much as to say that the goals of the Russian Revolution were realized only in the USA. If only Lenin had understood this! He might have built an American Jerusalem in Russia's green and pleasant land.

But Kojève has still more to tell us. He says that when History ends, Man also disappears: "if one asserts that Man remains alive as an animal . . . all the rest can be preserved indefinitely: art, war, play, etcetera."

To elaborate this just a bit, in Kojève's own words: "If Man becomes an animal again, his arts, his love and his play must also become purely 'natural' again. Hence it would have to be admitted that after the end of History, men would construct their edifices and works of art as birds build their nests and spiders spin their webs, would perform musical concerts after the fashion of frogs and cicadas, would play like young animals and would indulge in love like adult beasts. But one cannot then say that all this 'makes Man *happy*.' One would have to say that post-historical animals of the species Homo Sapiens (which will live amidst abundance and complete security) will be *content* as a result of their artistic, erotic and playful behavior."

Since we as a species have the peculiarity of being ready to entertain any and all possibilities, with a consciousness open to all suggestions, we can accept this as a fantasy. But it is worth noting that the worst thing Kojève can say about the Communist revolution that disappointed him so severely is that its objectives were realized in America. The Russians and the Chinese, he remarks, "are only Americans who are still poor."

Kojève is obviously a man of genius, a great philosopher who is also as playful as Aristophanes. In this lengthy footnote on the future—nothing less than an essay packed with bitter fantasy and humor—he stands between the no-longer and the not-yet. He makes us remember that democracy in the modern world is marked by an unparalleled acceptance of libels against itself, and by a strange sort of guilt, or openness to all charges. It may be relevant here to remember what Tocqueville said about the weakness of a democratic public for lurid entertainments. That we should get a kick out of Kojève's posthistorical interpretation of our regression to an animal state (plus high-tech barbarism) ought not to surprise us too much. Kojève may well believe what he is saying about posthistorical man, but he has the air also of a super comedian.

It's very hard for writers to deal with the great cognitive chieftains of modern times, but there's no avoiding the difficulty, because these chieftains have powerfully dominated us for centuries now. The choice of terms has been theirs throughout, and twentieth-century writers frequently find that they have been held captive by Freud or by Marx, just as their predecessors' minds were dominated by Rousseau. In modern France Proust evidently felt that he had to cope with Bergson. But, as I have recently learned, so did General de Gaulle. Better Bergson than Norman Vincent Peale, I concede, or Shirley MacLaine, but the truth is that I do not like being forced onto any sort of cognitive turf. Infinitely better, from my point of view, is the language of Othello described above by Rebecca West as a special sort of music "rolling and splendid and unintellectual as thunder." It is the unintellectual part of this that appeals strongly to me. I see many contemporary writers functioning as mere illustrators for the century's most influential—not necessarily its best—thinkers. With a little practice you can easily see where these writers are coming from, philosophically. I feel one is better off without the middle man, going directly to one's nihilistic source. Stand before the bartender and order your Heidegger straight.

You will fail to understand the inner lives of your contemporaries, and in particular those who are subtler and better developed, if you have no idea how their minds were formed. You are sure to be depressed often by what you discover about this process—and, for that matter, about yourself. You can't always feel secure in numbering yourself among the happy few, nor can you be certain that the multitude was accurately and truly judged by a Stendhal, a Kojève, or a Tocqueville. There are hundreds of millions of people in the civilized and partially civilized countries of the world, and among them you will find all the viciousness of mankind but, inevitably, all the potentialities of genius as well. If you won't take my word for it, I refer you to Nietzsche's *Beyond Good and Evil*. He writes (aph. 224) that "the historical sense, which we Europeans claim as our special distinction, has come to us via the bewitching and insane half-barbarism into which Europe was plunged by the democratic upheaval of the castes and races. It is only the Nineteenth century that knows this sense—as its sixth sense. The past of every form and every mode of life, of creatures that formerly clashed—horizontally or vertically—is flowing into our 'modern souls' thanks to that upheaval. Our instincts can now run back in all kinds of directions; we ourselves are a kind of chaos. But ultimately the mind seizes on its advantage." It's the advantage that is the important word here.

It is not difficult to project the limitless and possibly frightening consequences of such an idea. There is, for instance, an observable and universal tendency to realize or to make actual notions which invade our minds. You think of something? You try to give it material form. This may result in crank experiments, it may take the form of eccentric or marginal business enterprises, or express itself in plans for bacterial warfare or for the elimination of entire classes of the population, the bombing of a federal building in Oklahoma City. It may limit itself to theme parks; on the other hand, it may go as far as genocide. I have occasionally diverted myself by thinking that the idea of history, if you suppose it to be grasped by everyone today, shows us everything under the sun as the work of our species—a sense that all that has been achieved on the face of the earth is a result of human action. Our species has done it all. *We* have done it. Once we had heroic ages, we created epics and great systems of philosophy—the world religions, too, were our own human products. But now everything that has been done, the noble things and also the enormities, are our work. Perhaps the idea has taken hold that in the present age we must complete the work of history and that today belongs to the low as the past belonged to the high. In art, if you start with the caves of Altamira today's counterpart are subway graffiti. The past gave us Athens and Jerusalem, the present gives us the trial of O. J. Simpson.

Now this is all well and good as a joke. We all recognize that it is irresponsible to overdo the joking. A joke is good only insofar as it contains the germ of a true insight. The insight here is that the serious ideas of leading intellectuals are bound to reach the masses and be taken up by them and enter into our half-conscious motives. Vast numbers of people today are open to millenarian ideas. If history should indeed be closing down, no one is barred from making a contribution to the process along the lines I have suggested. If under the influence of Rousseau people were for roughly two centuries sincere, they can be authentic today under a changed intellectual standard.

Suppose that we turn back here to Tocqueville's statement that "Nothing conceivable is so petty, so insipid, so crowded with paltry interests, in one word, so anti-poetic, as the life of a man in the United States." If this accurately describes the prevailing condition, what is there to write about?

Those who feel responsible for the maintenance of civilized stability, who try to think more calmly than people generally do, tell their fellow Americans how well the economy of this superpower is doing. Their aim perhaps is to compensate for their cultural miseries.

It seems to me that Americans have by now found all this out for themselves. When I said a moment ago that they were open to millenarian and apocalyptic ideas, I had in mind also the revolutionary transformation of the material world by a technology that is streaking ahead too rapidly to be intelligible to our ill-prepared minds. All that needs to be said here is that the inventory of technological miracles goes far beyond anything in the Arabian Nights.

The modern psyche, in ways peculiar to it, does try to meet the challenge of "the end of scarcity." I am no Sovietologist, but I'd be much surprised if the boredom which was the singular creative specialty of the Soviet regime, and its obvious inability to keep up with the West in the manufacture of consumer commodities, hadn't contributed greatly to its downfall.

Americans discovered long ago how crowded with paltry interests their lives were, and they tried to find remedies in sports and entertainments, in sex, in drink, in drugs, in world travel, in organized social movements aiming at emancipation, in politics, in animal rights, in environmentalism, etcetera.

My own mind with its more or less fixed interests and questions goes about shopping for answers or even hints of answers. In a typical moment about a week ago I looked into Samuel Butler's prose translation of the *Iliad* and read in Butler's preface, "A translation should depart hardly at all from the modes of speech current in the translator's own times inasmuch as nothing is readable, for long, which affects any other diction than that of the age in which it is written." He therefore puts his Homer into Victorian English. Victorian English is readily accessible to us in America today. Butler says that it takes two people to say anything—"a sayee as well as a sayer. . . . Poem and audience are as ego and non-ego"—adding that the two audiences, Homer's and his own English one, did not differ so widely as we might have expected after an interval of some three thousand years.

What this comes to then is that there exists somewhere in each of us a reader of Homer. The thing Butler argues can be done. The connection is not ideal, we are better off reading Homer in the Greek; but there is nevertheless a connection.

We can understand Alexandre Kojève, too, when he informs us that Man dies when History ends, and when he explains further that now that history is over, we shall surely turn into animals again, playful brutes whose wants are supplied by miraculous technology. Nor will there be any need to forage for edible seeds, roots, berries, or mushrooms. Posthistorical Man will be surrounded by abundance.

To whom are all these arguments addressed? Why, to us, of course— to human beings, beings on whose comprehension all expositions depend, to anyone who has learned to read.

Sometimes, when I revolve these problems in my mind and consider the mystery of our frail existence, I very often recall a paragraph from the Russian writer V. V. Rozanov, who died just after the 1917 Revolution— a near-contemporary. In a book called *Solitaria* Rozanov reflects, "A million years passed before my soul was let out into the world to enjoy it."

It does seem weirdly mysterious, our appearance in a world of which we knew nothing beforehand, and from which we quickly learn that we are destined quite soon to disappear.

It is presumptuous to speak with too much confidence about so strange an occurrence.

Rozanov, well aware of this, says to his soul, "Have a good time my lovely, my precious one, enjoy yourself. Toward evening you will go to God."

"For my life is my day," Rozanov concludes, "and it is my day and not Socrates' or Spinoza's."

No disrespect to Socrates or Spinoza is intended here. But your life *is* your day. And it *does* often feel that a million years had passed while we waited for our souls to be let out into the world to enjoy it. This sense of existence is recognized in the inner life as something which stands opposed to the paltriness of our daily doings, the events we read about in the papers and watch on the television. But after a million years of darkness, one has a perfect right to object to the disappointments that history has prepared for us. To accept these disappointments is to renounce our freedom.

When our night falls, Rozanov tells us, our souls return to God. Enlightened modern people will not agree with him. But the novelists and poets these enlightened people turn to for their description of contemporary life are restlessly and continually questioning and probing the ordinariness of the ordinary lives represented in their books. Consciously or not, they feel called upon to reopen and reconsider the inner life of humankind. They hint, and sometimes they openly declare, that the "ordinary" is quite simply a convention—a cover thrown over a multitude of mysterious qualities and powers.

This is one of the forms in which the inner life, intimidated and frightened, nevertheless persists.

Select Bibliography: Works by David Grene

BOOKS

Man in His Pride: A Study in the Political Philosophy of Thucydides and Plato. Chicago: University of Chicago Press, 1950. Reprinted as *Greek Political Theory: The Image of Man in Thucydides and Plato*. Chicago: University of Chicago Press, 1965.
Reality and the Heroic Pattern: Last Plays of Ibsen, Shakespeare, and Sophocles. Chicago: University of Chicago Press, 1967.
The Actor in History: Studies in Shakespearean Stage Poetry. University Park: Pennsylvania State University Press, 1988.

TRANSLATIONS

Three Greek Tragedies in Translation. Chicago: University of Chicago Press, 1942.
The Complete Greek Tragedies. Edited with Richmond Lattimore. Chicago: University of Chicago Press, 1952–64.

Aeschylus:	*Seven against Thebes*	(1956)
	Prometheus Bound	(1942)
Sophocles:	*Oedipus Rex*	(1942)
	Electra	(1957)
	Philoctetes	(1957)
	Antigone	(1991)
	Oedipus at Colonus	(1991)
Euripides:	*Hippolytus*	(1955)

Herodotus, *The History*. Chicago: University of Chicago Press, 1988.
Aeschylus, *The Oresteia*. Translated with Wendy Doniger O'Flaherty. Chicago: University of Chicago Press, 1989.

Hesiod, *Works and Days*. In *God and the Land: The Metaphysics of Farming in Hesiod and Vergil with a Translation of Hesiod's* Works and Days *by David Grene,* by Stephanie A. Nelson. New York: Oxford University Press, 1998.

EDITED WORKS

The Authoress of the Odyssey, by Samuel Butler, with an introduction by David Grene. Chicago: University of Chicago Press, 1967.

The Peloponnesian War, translated by Thomas Hobbes. Ann Arbor: University of Michigan Press, 1959. Reprint, Chicago: University of Chicago Press, 1989, with introduction by David Grene.

ARTICLES

"*Calidus iuventa* (The Nurse's Speech, *Romeo and Juliet*)." *Hermathena* 47 (1932): 281.

"The Comic Technique of Aristophanes." *Hermathena* 50 (1937): 87–125.

"The Interpretation of the *Hippolytus* of Euripides." *Classical Philology* 34 (1939): 45–58.

"Method and Doctrine in Plato and Aristotle." *Transactions of the American Philological Association* 71 (1940): xxxvi–xxxvii.

"Prometheus Bound." *Classical Philology* 35 (1940): 22–38.

"Herodotus: The Historian as Dramatist." *Journal of Philosophy* 58.18 (1961): 477–88.

Introduction to *Most Ancient Verse.* Edited by Thorkild Jakobsen and John A. Wilson. Chicago: University of Chicago Press, 1963.

"Chance and Pity." *Midway,* no. 27 (1966): 79–91.

"The Strangest Work of Classical Scholarship: Samuel Butler's *The Authoress of the Odyssey*." *Midway,* no. 8 (1967): 69–79.

"The *Odyssey:* An Approach." *Midway,* no. 9 (1969): 47–68.

"Aeschylus: Myth, Religion, and Poetry." *History of Religions* 23 (1983): 1–17.

"On the Rarity Value of Translations from the Greek." *Journal of General Education* 39, no. 2 (1987): 69–76.

"Hesiod: Religion and Poetry in the *Works and Days.*" In *Radical Pluralism and Truth: David Tracy and the Hermeneutics of Religion,* edited by Werner G. Jeanrond and Jennifer L. Rilke, 142–58. New York: Crossroad, 1991.

"Response" to Stephanie Nelson's "Justice and Farming in the *Works and Days*." In *The Greeks and Us: Essays in Honor of Arthur W. H. Adkins,* edited by R. Louden and P. Schollmeier, 36–42. Chicago: University of Chicago Press, 1996.

Contributors

SAUL BELLOW is University Professor, Boston University. His most recent novel is *The Actual* (1997).

SETH BENARDETE is Professor of Classics, New York University. His most recent work includes *On Plato's Symposium* (1994) and *The Bow and the Lyre: A Platonic Reading of the Odyssey* (1997).

TODD BREYFOGLE is a doctoral candidate at the Committee on Social Thought, University of Chicago, and a Fellow at Liberty Fund. His articles on ancient history and theology include contributions to *The Oxford Classical Dictionary* (1996) and *St. Augustine through the Ages: An Encyclopedia* (1999).

AMIRTHANAYAGAM P. DAVID is Tutor at St. John's College, Annapolis. He is currently finishing a book entitled *Dance of the Muses: Choral Theory and Greek Poetics,* a treatment of Homeric verse.

WENDY DONIGER is Mircea Eliade Distinguished Service Professor of the History of Religions, University of Chicago. Her most recent books are *Splitting the Difference: Gender and Myth in Ancient Greece and India* (1999) and *The Bedtrick: Telling the Difference* (forthcoming).

MARY DOUGLAS, C.B.E., is Professor of Social Anthropology, Retired, University College, London. Her most recent book is *Leviticus as Literature* (1999).

JOSEPH N. FRANK is Emeritus Professor of Slavic Languages and Literatures and of Comparative Literature, Stanford University; and Emeritus Professor of Comparative Literature, Princeton University. He is presently finishing the fifth volume of a series of books on Dostoyevsky's life and works.

VICTOR GOUREVITCH is William Griffin Professor of Philosophy (Emeritus), Wesleyan University. His editions, with introductions and notes, of Rousseau's *Discourses, The Social Contract,* and other political writings were published in two volumes in 1997.

NICHOLAS GRENE is Associate Professor in the School of English, Trinity College, Dublin. He has written books on Synge, Shaw, and Shakespeare, including *Shakespeare's Tragic Imagination* (1992). His most recent book (forthcoming) is *The Politics of Irish Drama*.

W. R. JOHNSON is Emeritus Professor of Classical Languages and Literatures and of Comparative Literature, University of Chicago. His books include *Horace and the Dialectic of Freedom* (1993) and *Momentary Monsters: Lucan and his Heroes* (1987).

BRENDAN KENNELLY is Professor in the School of English, Trinity College, Dublin. His most recent book is *The Man Made of Rain* (1997).

EDWIN MCCLELLAN is Sumitomo Professor of Japanese Studies, Yale University. He is the author of *Woman in the Crested Kimono* (1985). His translation of Soseki's novel *Kokoro* was republished with some of Soseki's essays in 1992.

FRANÇOISE MELTZER is Professor and Chair of the Department of Comparative Literature and Professor of Divinity and of Romance Languages and Literatures, University of Chicago. She is coeditor of *Critical Inquiry*. Her most recent book is *Hot Property: The Stakes and Claims of Literary Originality* (1994). She is currently writing a book on Joan of Arc and feminine subjectivity.

STEPHANIE NELSON teaches at Boston University. Her book *God and the Land: The Metaphysics of Farming in Hesiod and Vergil* (1998) also contains a translation of Hesiod's *Works and Days* by David Grene.

CONOR CRUISE O'BRIEN is a historian and writer on public affairs. His most recent books include *The Long Affair: Thomas Jefferson and the French Revolution, 1785–1800* (1996) and *The Great Melody: A Thematic Biography of Edmund Burke* (1992).

MARTIN OSTWALD is Emeritus Professor of Classics, Swarthmore College and University of Pennsylvania. His works include a translation of Aristotle's *Nicomachean Ethics* (1980), as well as *From Popular Sovereignty to Sovereignty of Law* (1986).

ROBERT B. PIPPIN is Raymond W. and Martha Hilpert Gruner Distinguished Service Professor of the Committee on Social Thought, of Philosophy, and in the College, University of Chicago. Among his publications are *Idealism as Modernism: Hegelian Variations* (1997) and *Henry James and Modern Moral Life* (1999). He is currently working on a book about Hegel's theory of freedom.

JAMES REDFIELD is Professor of Classical Languages and Literatures and of the Committee on Social Thought, University of Chicago. He is the author of *Nature and Culture in the "Iliad": The Tragedy of Hector*

(1975) and is presently finishing a book entitled *The Locrian Maidens: Love and Death in Greek Italy.*

SANDRA F. SIEGEL is Professor of English, Cornell University. She has edited the manuscripts of W. B. Yeats's *Purgatory* (1986) and has written and lectured widely on Irish and English literary culture.

NORMA THOMPSON is Associate Professor of Political Science and of Special Programs in the Humanities, Yale University. She is the author of *Herodotus and the Origins of the Political Community* (1996) and editor of the forthcoming *Instilling Ethics.* She is currently at work on a book entitled *Democratic Statecraft: Reclaiming the Past.*

DAVID TRACY is Andrew Thomas Greeley and Grace McNichols Greeley Distinguished Service Professor of Divinity and of the Committee on Social Thought, University of Chicago. His most recent book is *On Naming the Present* (1994). He is currently working on a book entitled *On Naming God.*

Index